Home Theater For Dumm
3rd Edition

D0473046

Surround Format	Number of Channels	Type of Channels	Compatible Media
Dolby® Pro Logic® **DOLBY SURROUND™ PRO · LOGIC**	4	• 2 discrete, full-bandwidth channels (front left and right) • 1 matrixed, full-bandwidth channel (center) • 1 matrixed, limited-bandwidth surround channel (sent to left and right surround speakers)	• VHS movies • Broadcast TV • Dolby Digital sources downscaled to analog stereo (DVDs, DTV, DBS, digital cable)
Dolby® Pro Logic II™ **DOLBY SURROUND PRO LOGIC II**	5.1	• 2 discrete, full-bandwidth channels (front left and right) • 3 matrixed, full-bandwidth channels (center, surround left and right) • 1 subwoofer channel via Pro Logic II's bass management	• All the same Dolby Surround sources as Pro Logic (VHS movies, broadcast TV) • All stereo sources, including music CDs and MP3s
Dolby® Pro Logic IIx™ **DOLBY PRO LOGIC IIx**	6.1 or 7.1	• 2 discrete, full-bandwidth channels (front left and right) • Adds 4 or 5 matrixed, full-bandwidth channels to stereo sound, or 1 or 2 matrixed rear channels to Dolby Digital 5.1-channel sound • 1 subwoofer channel via Pro Logic IIx's bass management (or via Dolby Digital, if the source is a Dolby Digital 5.1 source)	• All the same Dolby Surround Sources as Pro Logic and Pro Logic II • All 5.1-channel Dolby Digital inputs in a 6.1- or 7.1-channel home theater system
Dolby® Digital™ **DOLBY DIGITAL**	Up to 5.1	• 5 discrete, full-bandwidth channels (front left and right, center, surround left and right) • 1 discrete LFE channel (subwoofer)	• All DVDs, HD-DVDs, and Blu-ray discs • Some broadcast DTV
Dolby® Digital EX™ **DOLBY DIGITAL SURROUND·EX**	6.1	• 5 discrete, full-bandwidth channels (front left and right, center, surround left and right) • 1 matrixed, full-bandwidth channel (back surround) • 1 discrete LFE channel (subwoofer)	• Some DVDs are Dolby Digital EX – encoded • Regular Dolby Digital 5.1 DVDs can also be played with a Dolby Digital EX decoder

WOO Discard

For Dummies: Bestselling Book Series for Beginners

Home Theater For Dummies,®
3rd Edition

Cheat Sheet

Surround Format	Number of Channels	Type of Channels	Compatible Media
THX Surround EX™ **THX**®	6.1	• 5 discrete, full-bandwidth channels (front left and right, center, surround left and right) • 1 matrixed, full-bandwidth channel (back surround) • 1 discrete LFE channel (subwoofer)	• Dolby Digital EX – encoded DVDs • Regular Dolby Digital 5.1 DVDs can also be played with a THX Surround EX decoder
Dolby® Digital Plus™ **DOLBY DIGITAL · PLUS**	Up to 7.1	• 7 discrete full-bandwidth channels • 1 discrete LFE channel (subwoofer)	• All HD-DVD discs • Some Blu-ray discs • Some HDTV broadcasts
Dolby® TrueHD™ **DOLBY TRUEHD**	Up to 7.1	• 7 discrete full-bandwidth channels • 1 discrete LFE channel (subwoofer) • Lossless encoding for exact duplication of the original recorded sound	• All HD-DVD discs • Some Blu-ray discs
DTS® **DIGITAL dts SURROUND**	5.1	• 5 discrete, full-bandwidth channels (front left and right, center, surround left and right) • 1 discrete LFE channel (subwoofer)	• Some DVDs are DTS-encoded • Some CDs are DTS-encoded
DTS-ES™ **dts ES**	6.1	• 6 discrete, full-bandwidth channels (front left and right, center, surround left and right, and back surround) • 1 discrete LFE channel (subwoofer)	• Some DVDs are DTS-ES-encoded • Regular DTS 5.1 DVDs can also be used with a DTS-ES decoder
DTS-HD™ **dts HD**	7.1	• 7 discrete, full-bandwidth channels • 1 discrete LFE channel (subwoofer) • Lossless encoding for exact duplication of the original recorded sound	• Some HD DVDs • Some Blu-ray discs

Logos courtesy of Dolby, THX, and Digital Theater Systems. (Dolby, Pro Logic, and the double-D symbol are registered trademarks of Dolby Laboratories. Surround EX is a trademark of Dolby Laboratories.)

For Dummies: Bestselling Book Series for Beginners

Home Theater

FOR

DUMMIES®

3RD EDITION

Home Theater

FOR

DUMMIES®

3RD EDITION

by Danny Briere and Pat Hurley

WILEY

Wiley Publishing, Inc.

Home Theater For Dummies®, 3rd Edition

Published by
Wiley Publishing, Inc.
111 River Street
Hoboken, NJ 07030-5774

www.wiley.com

Copyright © 2009 by Wiley Publishing, Inc., Indianapolis, Indiana

Published by Wiley Publishing, Inc., Indianapolis, Indiana

Published simultaneously in Canada

For general information on our other products and services, please contact our Customer Care Department within the U.S. at 800-762-2974, outside the U.S. at 317-572-3993, or fax 317-572-4002.

For technical support, please visit www.wiley.com/techsupport.

Wiley also publishes its books in a variety of electronic formats. Some content that appears in print may not be available in electronic books.

Library of Congress Control Number: 2008939212

ISBN: 978-0-470-41189-6

Manufactured in the United States of America

10 9 8 7 6 5 4 3 2 1

WILEY

About the Authors

Danny Briere founded TeleChoice, Inc., a telecommunications consulting company, in 1985 and now serves as CEO of the company. Widely known throughout the telecommunications and networking industry, Danny has written more than 1,000 articles about telecommunications topics and has authored or edited eight books, including *Wireless Home Networking For Dummies,* 3rd Edition, and *Smart Homes For Dummies,* 3rd Edition. He is frequently quoted by leading publications on telecommunications and technology topics and can often be seen on major TV networks providing analysis on the latest communications news and breakthroughs. Danny lives in Mansfield Center, Connecticut with his wife and four children.

Pat Hurley is Director of Research for TeleChoice, Inc. specializing in emerging telecommunications and digital home technologies, particularly all the latest consumer electronics and access gear, including wireless LANs, DSL, cable modems, satellite services, and home-networking services. Pat frequently consults with the leading telecommunications carriers, equipment vendors, consumer goods manufacturers, and other players in the telecommunications and consumer electronics industries. Pat is the coauthor of *Smart Homes For Dummies,* 3rd Edition, *Wireless Home Networking For Dummies,* 3rd Edition, *Wireless Network Hacks and Mods For Dummies,* and *Windows XP Media Center Edition 2004 PC For Dummies*. He lives in San Diego, California with his wife, a fiery red headed preschooler named Annabel, and two smelly dogs.

Dedication

Danny wants to thank his wife, Holly, and kids, who have endured their home theater being the test bed for just about every new technology known to mankind. They've had to learn the intricacies of beta testing everything from remarkably exciting motion-controlled TV to sadly disappointing Apple TV test gear. When their friends ask how to turn things on, the response is usually prefaced by, "Well, this week . . ." However, they also get to appreciate true breakthroughs, such as when they moved to RF control and no longer had to point in a certain direction to get something to happen. Ah, the good life! To all of them, thanks for their perseverance.

Pat, as always, thanks his wife, Christine, for her infinite patience. (Is it patience when one refrains from bonking his or her spouse over the head with a cast iron skillet?) He also thanks her for gamely smiling and nodding when he introduced, over and over, pictures of the newest future member of the Hurley family home theater, only to change his mind when he discovered the next silicon (not silicone!) laden object of his desire. Pat's daughter Annabel (hi princess — or is it mermaid princess today?) gets a special thanks as the primary consumer of home theater time in the Hurley household and as a four-year-old expert in using Harmony remotes, working through scratched DVDs, and participating in big-screen Wii marathons.

Authors' Acknowledgments

Many folks provided us with their time, knowledge, and expertise as we researched and wrote this edition, including Jessica Loebig and Krista Weirzbiki at TiVo, Kate Brinks and Lloyd Klarke at Logitech Harmony, Steve Venuti at HDMI Licensing, Keith Claytor at Klipsch, Chris Fawcett at Sony, and Andy Parsons from Pioneer and the Blu-ray Disc Association. Special thanks go to Craig Eggers at Dolby, who's been our go-to resource (along with Roger Dressler and Jeanne Alford) for all things surround sound for the past five years.

The following folks helped with previous editions of this book and provides the knowledge base upon which we built this edition: Joel Silver at Imaging Science Foundation, Jeff Denenholz at X10 Ltd., Larry Becker at Crutchfield, Nick Carter and the rest of the crew at AudioRequest, Kaleo Willess and Roger Dressler at Dolby Laboratories, Shawn Gusz at G-NET Canada, John Dahl and Amy Brighouse from THX, Ltd., and all the people manning the booths at the past seven or eight CES shows in Las Vegas who let us stare and gape at their rear-projection, plasma, and LCD screens for hours on end. We'd thank them personally, but none of them gave us one.

Thanks also to our acquisition editors, Steve Hayes and Amy Fandrei (congrats on the baby Amy!), and especially to our project editor, Susan Pink. Susan, you do know we always ask for you, don't you? So you'd better tell us now if you've had enough of Pat and Danny. Seriously though, thanks for making our writing clearer, easier to read, and just plain better!

Publisher's Acknowledgments

We're proud of this book; please send us your comments through our online registration form located at www.dummies.com/register/.

Some of the people who helped bring this book to market include the following:

Acquisitions and Editorial

Project Editor: Susan Pink
   (*Previous Edition: Kala Schrager*)

Acquisitions Editor: Steve Hayes

Copy Editor: Susan Pink

Technical Editor: Dale Cripps

Editorial Manager: Jodi Jensen

Editorial Assistant: Amanda Foxworth

Sr. Editorial Assistant: Cherie Case

Cartoons: Rich Tennant
   (www.the5thwave.com)

Composition Services

Project Coordinator: Katherine Key

Layout and Graphics: Reuben W. Davis, Melissa K. Jester, Christin Swinford, Christine Williams

Proofreaders: Toni Settle, Amanda Steiner

Indexer: Steve Rath

Publishing and Editorial for Technology Dummies

   Richard Swadley, Vice President and Executive Group Publisher

   Andy Cummings, Vice President and Publisher

   Mary Bednarek, Executive Acquisitions Director

   Mary C. Corder, Editorial Director

Publishing for Consumer Dummies

   Diane Graves Steele, Vice President and Publisher

Composition Services

   Gerry Fahey, Vice President of Production Services

   Debbie Stailey, Director of Composition Services

Contents at a Glance

Table of Contents

Introduction

●　●

*T*he onscreen image looks crisp and sharp, like a huge moving photo-
graph. You feel entranced. More to the point, you feel the immediate
urge to own this video projector, provided it works with the DVD player and
the rest of your fledgling home theater gear.

An enthusiastic salesperson sees your look and enters the demonstration
room. "It's really beautiful," the salesperson proclaims. "That's the 50-inch
plasma unit that works in true 1080p at 16:9. Yup, she's a dream."

Moments like that make you wish that people came with a pause button — or
at least an instant replay and color commentary.

For all the fun they bring and the good times they facilitate, home theaters
(and their sundry technologies) come with a bewildering blizzard of terms
and acronyms. Worse yet, it seems like everybody involved with the industry either knows what the terms mean but can't explain them or has no clue
about the true meanings but spouts the terms anyway. And neither of those
cases helps *you* make any sense of the whole thing.

That's where the new and greatly improved third edition of *Home Theater
For Dummies* makes its heroic entrance. (We'd cue up a low fog, some dramatic lighting, and that mysterious "something cool might happen anytime
now" music to enhance the moment, but there's only so much you can do in
a book.) Even without the special effects, this book still rescues you from all
kinds of home theater perils. Read on to find out how.

About This Book

The book takes you through the world of home theater from the bottom to
the top. Starting with a broad look at the basics of home theater concepts
and technology, *Home Theater For Dummies* presses onward with more
detailed information about source devices, surround-sound gear, video display equipment, and PCs. The book even advises you about the theater room
itself, giving guidance about everything from furniture to popcorn machines.

Best of all, this book delivers the information in the friendly, patient, and
easy-to-understand manner that you know and expect from a title in the *For
Dummies* line.

Get ready for one of the most enjoyable trips of your life. With this book at your side, you're ready for anything and everything that the industry (and those questionable salespeople at the local equipment store) can throw at you.

Conventions Used in This Book

Unlike its famous and prolific computer-oriented brethren, *Home Theater For Dummies* keeps things pretty simple in the conventions department. We use just a single bit of textual oddness that relates to Web sites. Any time we talk about a Web address, you see the site address formatted in a special font, like this: `www.dummies.com`.

Why? For one thing, the font makes the text stand out so that you know exactly what to type into your browser. (Besides, we think the production department got a special deal on that font, so they just like seeing it in the books as much as possible.)

Just the (Techie) Facts, Ma'am

Although everything in the book meets rigorous standards for comprehension, usability, and lack of pointless geekiness, a few technical tidbits slipped in accidentally. Well, they didn't slip in accidentally; we wrote them that way.

At some point in the home theater process, you come face to face with technical tripe whether you want to or not. It's better that you hear this stuff from us than from some name-tagged know-it-all on a sales floor.

Foolish Assumptions

To write this book, we had to spend a lot of time in malls, video stores, and movie theaters (that's the hard part) doing "research." While doing so, we pondered all kinds of questions concerning you, the reader. Who are you? Where are you? What did you eat for lunch? Which movies pique your interest? How do your home theater desires line up with your budget? Queries like that fill our minds constantly, much to the consternation of our spouses, who prefer more useful thoughts like, "Shouldn't you take out the trash?"

Because we never get to meet you in person, we end up making a few assumptions about you and what you want from this book. Here's a peek at our thoughts about you:

✔ You love movies, television shows, or video games — or perhaps all three.

✔ You've experienced wide screens and surround sound at the theater, and you liked it.

✔ For one reason or another, a 19-inch TV set with a single built-in speaker doesn't adequately meet your audio or video entertainment desires.

✔ You probably own a computer or will soon.

✔ You don't shy away from high-tech products, but you also aren't the first person on the block with the latest electronic goodie.

✔ You've heard a lot about digital TV (and the impending *digital TV transition*), and though it gives you a vaguely uneasy feeling, you know that you need to know more about it.

✔ The weird technicalities of home theater circle around you like planes buzzing King Kong.

✔ You know something about the Internet and the Web and probably have high-speed access to the Internet or will soon.

✔ You (or someone in your family) enjoy watching movies, listening to MP3 audio, playing games, and possibly making movies on your computer.

If that describes you in detail or at least catches some of your shadow in passing, this book is for you.

How This Book Is Organized

Rather than haphazardly fling information at you and hope that some of it sticks, we clump related topics together into six parts. Here's a peek at what they cover.

Part I: Welcome to the World of Home Theater

With home theater, the trek begins here, in Part I, which covers the basics of the basics, starting with a look at what home theater really means, includes, requires, and offers. From there, it looks at what it takes to get into a home theater, in terms of space, timing, budget, and equipment. In Chapter 4, we get a little techie, but necessarily so, by giving you some solid insight into the terms and technologies that you will encounter. More and more, terms such as DLP, 3LCD, and HDMI are on the shelf description tags when you go to Best Buy. You need this baseline knowledge for the rest of the book, so read Chapter 4 closely. In fact, read it twice. (It's even better the second time around.)

Part II: Getting Video and Music into Your Theater: Source Devices

Home theater installations really contain two parts: source and presentation. Part II covers all kinds of sources, ranging from the prerecorded offerings of DVD players and VCRs to the over-the-air-and-through-the-sky action of broadcast TV and satellite dishes. As a bonus, this part even takes you on a tour of the personal video recorder (PVR), possibly the most groundbreaking entertainment device since the VCR itself, as well as state-of-the-art gaming platforms. (Pat performed that excruciating gaming research.) We also talk about your PC and the growing role it plays in sourcing audio, video, gaming, and other content for your system. To top that, we then tell you all you need to know about accessing the Internet for cool things like finding that episode of *Lost* that you missed.

Part III: Watching and Listening: Display and Control Devices

Part III focuses on the control and presentation aspects of your system, with in-depth looks at your receivers, controllers, speakers, and video displays. We look at all-in-one receivers and separates, such as controllers and power amps. On the video side, this part explores the strange world of television sets (which looked pretty simple until a few years ago when HDTV arrived on the scene) and video projection systems, which are home theater's answer to the movie house's silver screen and are becoming so affordable we think you'll get one just so you can watch the Super Bowl on a 12-foot screen! Then, all eyes — er, ears — turn to audio for details about surround-sound systems, speakers, and more. Finally, we talk about remote controls — an often overlooked area that deserves more attention. A remote control is your single biggest interface to the system, so we give you some options here.

Part IV: Putting It All Together

With your location selected, your gear picked out, and your walls trembling in fear, it's time to install your theater, and Part IV guides you through the process. In fact, hooking up your home theater is one of the harder parts of the experience. We start with the basics — the different types of cabling — and work our way up to connecting all the components into a working system. Toward the end of Part IV, we give you advice on how to link your home entertainment system to other TVs and systems in the house. After all, you paid a lot of money for your theater — why not get the most use from it that you can?

Part V: Letting Your Home Theater Be All It Can Be

You might think that your home theater equipment is out-of-the-box ready to be plugged together and to start playing movies, but it's not that simple. Almost every part of your system needs to be tuned like a nice grand piano. Although we use big words and phrases such as *calibration* and *bass management* in this part, these merely relate to fine-tuning your system to itself and its environs. We also give you ideas for sprucing up your home theater with fancy lights and soundproofing (the latter of which is great for those late-night sleepovers the kids have). We tell you how to access your home theater content from your car as well as from your cell phone (very cool) and laptop when out and about. We end the part with a cool look at the higher end of home theater — the things you can dream about during those long trips to Grandma's.

Part VI: The Part of Tens

Like all other *For Dummies* books, *Home Theater For Dummies* closes with a look at life from the humorous side with perky Part VI, the Part of Tens. Each chapter counts off a bunch of goodies that help you show off, troubleshoot, and generally accessorize your theater.

Icons Used in This Book

A lot of stuff is in here, and amidst all that material, the important details can sometimes be overlooked. To point out the important stuff (and highlight the technicalities you might want to avoid), the book relies on several helpful icons. Each icon identifies a particular type of information. Here's a quick field guide to what each of these little billboards means.

Whenever you see the Remember icon, grab a handy mental highlighter (and maybe a real one, too) and mark the section because this information might come in handy at any moment, either now or in the future.

Everybody looks for tips (particularly in the stock market, the race track, and at your favorite restaurant). When a Tip icon shows up in *Home Theater For Dummies,* it points out information destined to simplify your life. You can't go wrong with a Tip!

When a topic includes technology, technical tripe always finds its way into the book. At some point or another in the home theater experience, you need to know the geek-speak. Don't fear paragraphs with these icons, but don't rush to them, either. Just brace yourself for the technical onslaught, secure in the knowledge that this book protects you from the worst of the techno-drivel.

Nothing in your home theater really threatens personal peril — at least no more peril than you get from plugging in a toaster or accidentally watching a bad movie at your local theater. In those rare moments when inserting the right plug in the wrong socket could spell doom for your gear, the Warning icon hops into action. When you see one of these, stop for a moment, read the text, and double-check your progress before continuing.

Where to Go from Here

Apart from the pleasing shade of yellow on the cover, the best part of a *For Dummies* book is its open and available layout — you can start anywhere you want. If you already know the stuff in Chapter 1, dive in somewhere else instead. Where you start and what you read depends entirely on what you need to know right now.

Read over the Table of Contents to see whether any topics jump out at you. If nothing does, try finding a starting point in one of these:

- ✐ If you're a newcomer to home theaters, start in Chapter 1. It gives you a good overview of how a home theater works, what it takes to put one together, and what your next steps are if you want to build one.

- ✐ Curious about the content — the movies and shows — appearing in your theater? Part II delves into DVD and VHS, plus satellite, broadcast, and cable TV. It even peers into the promising realm of personal video recorders (the TiVo is a good example) and PC-driven content.

- ✐ For an in-depth look at the sound and video presentation side of your entertainment empire, visit the chapters of Part III.

- ✐ For help getting your system connected and tweaked for the finest audio and video quality, skip on over to Part IV.

With that, leap into the world of home theater. Lights, camera, action — welcome to your adventure!

Part I

Welcome to the World of Home Theater

The 5th Wave   By Rich Tennant

"I don't care how good it will look on the 60" plasma display."

In this part . . .

1t's important to start your adventure with some solid basics — what's a home theater, why do you want one, and what do all the various terms mean?

Part I lays a foundation for talking about home theater. An understanding of all your options helps you not only on the showroom floor, but also when the time comes to install your gear and tune it so that it does what it was intended to do. Indeed, a lot of home theater setup is about making sure that your system is configured correctly for your environment, and to do that, you need to know what the system is supposed to be doing in the first place. (We're sure there's some pithy phrase, like "the cart before the horse," to throw in, but we never use those correctly. So insert a phrase of your choice here.)

We follow up with some high-level basics about your home theater and its environment. We discuss where to put a home theater in your house and how to control it. We also delve into that hot topic — price. Then we walk you through all the things that make up the home theater at a high level — sources, outputs, PCs, cables, broadband, and so on.

And finally, we go a little deeper into the key terms, standards, and technologies that we use throughout the book. Here's where we talk about a lot of the things that probably got you to buy this book in the first place — the alphabet soup of home theater.

After you finish this part, you'll know enough to be dangerous in your local electronics store. (So be sure to read the rest of the book, too, so that you know how to control your now dangerous mind.)

Chapter 1

The Zen of Home Theater

*W*hen you hear the term *home theater,* you probably think of big screens, cool sound, DVDs, CDs, and lots of remote controls sitting around your living room. We're sure that football games, beer, and other fun images sneak into that image as well.

Home theater is truly for everyone — regardless of the size of your house or apartment, your economic wealth, or your taste in movies. And home theater is bound to mean something different to everyone. It's not just about the gear — boxes, cables, remotes, DVDs, CDs, iPods, whatever. It's really about embarking on what can be a great adventure.

Appreciating the Art of the Home Theater

Before you start on your home theater adventure, it's critical to understand what the makers of the equipment, movies, standards, audio CDs, and so on mean when they say that they support home theater.

To the companies that produce the equipment and media, home theater is all about trying to recreate — in your home — the experience of watching a film in a movie theater, hearing the cheers of the crowd in a football stadium, or feeling the reverberations of music at an open-air concert. Many of the people who devote themselves to creating atmosphere and mood using this medium consider what they do to be an art form. These are usually the people who are listed in the credits at the end of a movie.

When you take all the sensations of a movie theater and insert them in your living room, you're on your way to successfully recreating that immersive feeling you get at the movies. All the improvements in sound compression, surround sound, digital screen imaging, and more have been done not to sell more equipment at Circuit City or Wal-Mart but to try to perfect the ability to draw you into another world where you can experience a truly creative piece of work.

So a lot of this book is about explaining the technologies and ideas behind the home theater that you are going to put together, because it's not just about seven speakers hooked into your stereo or a big honking TV screen. It's about how to make sure everything is put in its proper place to maximize your home theater out-of-body experience — the way the media creators intended.

Fitting Home Theater's Many Faces into All Kinds of Spaces

You've probably watched enough TV shows and movies about Hollywood and the rich and famous to know that, for some people, home theaters are as common as a kitchen or a bedroom. Indeed, home theaters were spawned from the necessity of filmmakers to preview footage, screen tests, and full movies. They gradually grew to be a status symbol among actors, too, and spread out from there.

In those early days, a home theater was pretty much literally that: a small theater with Peerless Magnarc carbon-arc lamphouses and theater seating. They were often extensive and elaborate affairs — to match the surrounding house.

Today, you too can get into the act, and you're lucky enough to have a broad range of projectors, screens, displays, seating, and equipment — heck, even popcorn machines — available to create your own home theater.

Probably the first big decision you have to make is where you want to put your home theater. It's one thing to figure out where to put your 19-inch TV set; it's another thing to think about where to put a big-screen TV with six (or more) speakers and associated A/V gear. Few people are prepared for how overpowering a full home theater setup can be in a small home, so it's especially important to plan if you have limited space.

Defining your home theater space is a necessary first step. If the only place to put a TV is on the mantle above the fireplace, you're looking at a flat-panel (plasma or LCD) TV and not much else. If you have to fit the whole system into the corner of the living room, that narrows the search as well. Remember, you don't want to buy a home theater that just won't fit into your home and your lifestyle. A home theater is all about creating a theatrical atmosphere, so choose your spaces and work from there.

You can most certainly put a home theater in your present living room, your bedroom, or a room devoted to your theater. In the end, what matters is not so much the size but the way you establish the room's ability to coax you into its sound field and video experience.

Budgeting for Home Theater

We believe in setting expectations. We don't want to get you salivating over a 52-inch LCD and a nice Harman Kardon system and then smack you over the head with an unrealistic price. Unfortunately, a quick stroll through any consumer electronics store could lead you to believe that you can get all you need in an entry-level home-theater-in-a-box (without the video display) for just $199. However, that $199 system will be right for some people and not for others.

Exploring equipment and prices

So what does it cost to get into a home theater system? Table 1-1 gives you an idea of what you can spend. We've broken this table down by the roles that each group of audio/video (A/V) components plays in your home theater. (*Audio* sources are devices that provide audio-only playback in your system, whereas *video* sources provide movies or TV content.) The A/V system provides the control for your home theater (meaning it lets you select what you want to watch or listen to) and does all the heavy lifting in terms of sending surround-sound signals to your speaker system. The video display, of course, is what you watch (think TV). We've also included some optional components — gaming systems and home theater PCs (which let you use a PC as a high-quality audio source device, or video source device, or both).

Table 1-1	Home Theater Budget Guide	
Role	*Device*	*Price Expectations*
Audio sources	Audio cassette player*	$50 to $250
	CD player/recorder*	$50 to $600+
	Turntable*	$100 to $5,000+ (really!)
	AM/FM tuner*	$200 to $1,000
	Satellite radio tuner	$75 to $300

(continued)

Table 1-1 *(continued)*

Role	Device	Price Expectations
Video sources	DVD player	$50 to $1,200+
	Blu-ray disc player	$300+
	VCR*	$50 to $300
	Personal video recorder*	$0 to $700 ($0 "payment" when leased as part of a service)
	Satellite TV receiver*	$0 to $500
Computer/gaming	Gaming console*	$100 to $400
	Home theater PC*	$800+
A/V system**	All-in-one systems	$200 to $3,000+
	A/V receiver	$200 to $4,000
	Controller/decoder	$800 to $5,000+
	Power amplifier	$500+
Speakers	Center, left, right, and surround speakers	$150 to $10,000+
	Additional surround-sound speakers*	$100 to $5,000+
	Subwoofer speakers	$150 to $5,000+
Video display***	Up to 73-inch rear-projection TV	$1,000 to $4,000
	Up to 120-inch front-projection TV	$1,000 to $15,000+
	32- to 60-inch plasma or LCD flat-panel TV	$500 to $10,000+
Portables	Portable MP3 player*	$50 to $350
	Portable video player*	$100 to $500
Car system	Car PC*	$800 to $2,000
Accessories	Speaker and A/V interconnection cables	$50 to $1,000+
	Surge suppressor/ power conditioner	$20 to $1,500
	Home media server*	$1,000+
	Internet media access devices*	$100+

* Optional.
** You don't need all of these parts, just an all-in-one system, an A/V receiver, or a controller/decoder and power amplifier combo.
*** You only need one of these displays.

Over time, components have been doing the integrating thing better and better. You can find really good DVD/VCR combos, for instance. Receivers can now control your video signals as well as audio ones. Personal video recorders are now a part of many digital cable and satellite set-top boxes. We talk about the advantages of individual components versus more integrated units in Chapter 11.

Also note that these prices are a snapshot in time — they are continually dropping, so don't be surprised to find everything on this list available for even less money when you go shopping.

Certainly, you don't need all the gear In Table 1-1. You can buy a nicc all-in-one home theater system and a smaller (but high-quality) flat-panel TV for not much more than $700. Of course, you can spend a lot more money, too. One thing is for sure: Pricing is competitive and is changing all the time. Two years ago, a lot of the gear listed in Table 1-1 cost twice as much as it does now. As we go to print, the first 50-inch plasma screen TVs for under $1,000 are hitting the market.

To get a quick grasp on pricing, go to a few Web sites, such as `www.circuit city.com`, `www.plasmatvbuyingguide.com`, and `Pricegrabber.com` to get a sense of the going rate for different items. Compare that with Table 1-1 to get a sense of how much pricing has dropped just in the time it took for this book to hit the shelves.

Buying on a budget

Given that you are probably working within a budget, here are some ideas about what you can expect to buy and install for different total budget ranges:

- **$0 to $500:** Definitely the entry-level package for home theater, a system in the under-$500 range basically uses your existing TV (or includes an inexpensive flat-panel TV in the 27-inch range) and an entry-level all-in-one home theater system package (which comes with all the speakers you need for surround sound and a receiver/DVD player combo). You can probably throw in a $50 VCR if you don't already have one, but even the lowest level all-in-one home theater sets include DVD players. (Gotta have DVD!)

- **$500 to $2,000:** By spending a little more, you can go up a range in a number of the components and get HDTV into your home theater, which we highly recommend — especially because all TVs convert to digital in 2009! You can spend some of this money on a midsized flat-panel TV (perhaps in the 37- to 42-inch range), though with the way flat-panel prices are dropping, you may be able to get a 50-inch or larger flat-panel TV, while leaving money in your budget for audio equipment. Or if you need a bigger screen, consider a rear-projection TV; the 50-inch screens start at around $1,000. This price range has a range of options for better surround-sound systems, with packaged options available for your five surround-sound speakers plus your subwoofer. And you can buy a fairly good A/V receiver to drive the system. Top this all off with a portable MP3 player and a DVD player for the car, and your kids will love you (more).

✔ **$2,000 to $5,000:** At this level, you start to create serious options for a very decent home theater system. You should be able to get a high-quality 50-inch or bigger 1080p (this term refers to the resolution of the screen — 1080p displays are the highest available) flat-panel TV or an even larger LCD or DLP (digital light processor — a special micro-mirror–based chip system) rear-projection unit with a great high-def picture (starting at around $1,500). You might make the move from DVD to Blu-ray at this budget level. (Entry-level Blu-ray disc players are hitting around $300 as we write.) On the audio side, you can spend $1,000 or so on a relatively fancy all-in-one system, but at this price level you can also start to get serious with separate components, getting a very good A/V receiver, DVD/CD player/recorder, personal video recorder, gaming system, surround-sound speakers, and potentially even more. At this price range, the average person can get a mighty fine system.

✔ **$5,000 to $10,000:** When you top $5,000 as your budget, you can start expanding in some wonderful ways by adding more throughout the house through multizone capabilities, whole-home audio, and universal remote-control capability, or you can continue to go up the ladder in terms of higher-quality separates. We swear by audio servers that store all your music in one box. Get one for the car, too, and have them sync up when you drive in the driveway. Front-projection TVs become a viable option in this price range; good projectors start around $2,000. No matter what you choose — flat-panel, rear-projection, or front-projection — in this price range, you should expect a big (50-inch or more) high-definition display. Or you can get fancy with furniture. Good home theater seats start around $350 each. A high-quality universal remote control costs about $500.

✔ **$10,000+:** Above $10,000, the sky is truly the limit. For $10,000 to $20,000, you get to enjoy a lot of the next generation of home theater. At this point you'll be buying the top-of-the-line 56-inch or larger plasma or LCD flat-panel TVs, or a very high-end projection system. Your DVD player should be the best available and should play not only DVD but also Blu-ray discs. You probably want some extra amplifier equipment in the system, and you may also want to boost your controls, perhaps with a nice Control4 wireless touch-screen control. If you get above $20,000, you are into high-end audiophile-type stuff all the way. Whole-home audio and video, integration with home automation systems, consultants — the works. Believe it or not, it's not unusual for people to spend $1 million or more on a home theater. At that point, we think a lot of money is being paid for custom interior design, high-end projectors, and so on. Nothing is held back. To us, given more modest expectations, a $25,000 system is stunning in almost all senses of the word.

Getting Your Money's Worth

In deciding how much to spend overall, we can give you only this advice: Your home entertainment system is probably one of the most-used parts of your home. It helps define your family, social life, business relationships, and so on. It's important, but spend within your means. You also want to save something for the future. Building and later adding onto a home theater is fun, too.

One of the great things about home theater is that it's modular, so you don't have to buy the whole thing all at once. If you really want a great TV display, get it, and go cheaper on the other components. And when you're ready to trade up, figure out what you want next. The better stereo stores have a trade-up policy that gives you credit toward getting something better. And then there's always eBay (www.ebay.com) or similar auction sites, where you can get all sorts of gear in great condition — everyone is always trading in stuff to move to higher levels, so don't feel pressured to do it all at once.

Realize that, even if you are installing home theater wiring and speakers into the walls and such, you're not likely to 'get that money back' when you sell the house. People are leery of other people's homegrown solutions — even the professional ones — and equipment becomes outdated quickly in this industry. So if you're going to do some remodeling and spend some money, recognize that you are doing it for yourself first, everyone else second, and by all means not for the money.

Indeed, a lot of this book is about getting your money's worth out of whatever you buy. If you get an all-in-one home theater system for $199 from Radio Shack or a high-end system with, say, a $37,000 Faroudja projector, $18,000 worth of MartinLogan Prodigy speakers, a $4,000 B&K receiver, and other similarly priced components, you're still going to need to figure out how to get the most out of the system. So stay tuned to find out how to get more per kHz, or disc, or channel, or whatever you track your home theater fun by.

Chapter 2

Defining Your Home-Theatered Home

• •

In This Chapter

▶ Checking out basic and elaborate home theaters

▶ Choosing the right space for your home theater

▶ Configuring your gear for your room or for the whole home

▶ Installing your theater yourself versus hiring a pro

• •

Consumer electronics have played a major role throughout the years in defining not just how we live in our own homes but also how we live as a society. The radio, then black-and-white TV, then color TV, and then all the various adjuncts to the TV and radio — VCRs, gaming consoles, tape decks, and so on — have all helped define who we are and how we interact with each other. The edgier radio and TV shows over the years have had a profound social impact by acting out for us the crossing of various social barriers — for instance, the first on-screen interracial kiss, the first portrayal of a woman president, and the first portrayal of a black president.

The home has grown around these devices, so when it comes time to put these together on a pedestal and proclaim them a "home theater," this act seems to acknowledge the role that home electronics have come to play in our lifestyles.

The Basic Home Theater

So, what's in a home theater then? Well, a home theater is largely what you make of it, but we think that at least three major elements constitute the core of a home theater:

✓ **A large-screen display:** Note that we do not say *television*. More and more, the receiver aspect of a television is divorced from the display aspect, in the form of set-top boxes, external TV tuners, computers, and other source devices. Appropriately, the display is being optimized for its main purpose — displaying the wide range of video output from a home theater system. These displays can be huge. We're talking greater than 120 inches diagonally, which is 10 feet for those of you who didn't do the math!

✔ **A digital video source:** At a minimum, this means a DVD player; and for most folks, it will also mean a TV source (such as digital cable or a digital satellite TV service). We think DVD is a bottom-line must-have when you're building a home theater because that's the way most of us access the movies we want to watch.

For most people, the digital video source includes a source (or sources) of *high-definition* video, from TV broadcasts or the high-definition-capable Blu-ray disc player we talk about in Chapter 4.

✔ **A surround-sound capability:** You find out about the details of surround sound in a few pages, but you need to have surround sound to take full advantage of all the audio power stored in your DVD content. With surround sound, you truly start mimicking the theater experience.

If you're lacking any of these, you really don't have a home theater. Without the display and surround sound, you lose the effect of the visual and audio experience, and without a digital video source, you just have a loud and big TV system. You really need all three.

But you need not stop there. You can get digital video up on your big screen display in all sorts of other great ways — besides a DVD player — and you can add great devices to enhance your overall experience. The rest of this chapter is devoted to exploring the boundaries of your home theater realm.

The Complete Home Theater

In our discussion of budgets in Chapter 1, we give you a peek at what a really fleshed-out home theater might contain. Here's a fairly comprehensive list of what you typically put in your home theater (we leave out the all-in-one units because they merely integrate various combinations of these devices into one unit):

✔ **Sources:** These provide the content you watch or listen to.

- Audio cassette player/recorder
- CD player/recorder/MP3 player
- Turntable
- AM/FM tuner
- DVD player/recorder

- Blu-ray disc player

- VCR

- Personal video recorder (PVR, also called a digital video recorder [DVR] by some folks)

- Camcorder

- Satellite or cable set-top box

- Video/audio server

- Gaming console

- Home theater PC or Windows XP Media Center PC (a specific Microsoft software product; see Chapter 8)

✔ **Receivers/controllers:** The heart of the system, these feed content to your displays and speakers.

- A/V receiver

- Controller/decoder

- Power amplifier

✔ **Displays:** This is what you watch.

- Direct-view, rear-projection, or flat-panel TV display

- Front-projection system with separate display screen

✔ **Speakers:** These are what you listen to.

- Two front speakers

- One front center speaker

- Two side speakers

- Two or four rear speakers

- Subwoofer

✔ **Connections:** These are connections to content inside and outside your home.

- Over-the-air antenna

- Satellite or cable video feed

- Internet connectivity — preferably broadband, such as DSL or cable modem

- Home network — preferably both wired and wireless to make the connection between your Internet service and your home theater and your home theater and your PC (with Media Center Edition) or Mac (with Apple's Front Row)

✔ **Accessories:** These are devices that make your home-stored content accessible from elsewhere.

- Universal remote controls and touchpads

- Internet access devices

- Home media servers and digital media adapters

Naturally, as you extend your home theater to other points in your home, you can add to the quantities mentioned here, but most of the components are the same. You also might choose different qualities and (in the case of displays) sizes of these things, but the basic formula remains the same.

Using Your Existing Gear

A question that comes across most people's minds when they look to upgrade to a home theater is whether any of their existing A/V gear can be used in their new home theater.

The answer usually is, "Well you probably can, but you lose a lot by doing so (unless the gear is less than two years old, and in some cases, even that is old)." If you are thinking about using existing equipment, consider the following:

✔ **TVs:** If it's smaller than a 27-inch display, why bother? Home theater needs a big-screen display for maximum effect. More importantly, ask yourself this: Can my existing TV display HD (high-definition) pictures? If not, you'll probably want to consider an upgrade. Particularly if that TV is also not capable of picking up the digital TV signals that will be broadcast by all TV stations starting in February 2009. Also check for features such as picture-in-picture, and make sure your TV has the right kinds of inputs to accept the latest and greatest source devices (look for HDMI or DVI, discussed in Chapter 13).

TV size requirements are actually a mix of three things: the size of the display, the display's *resolution* (or number of individual picture elements that make up the picture on your screen), and your viewing distance from the screen. In Chapter 13 we provide some concrete guidance about the best size display for your particular home theater. For most home theaters, a bigger display *is* better, but if you're planning on viewing from a relatively short distance (a few feet, for example), you might be better off with a relatively small screen.

✔ **Receivers:** Chances are that your receiver is an audio (stereo) receiver, which probably doesn't have surround-sound processing capability, inputs for video gear, or built-in amplifiers for your surround-sound speakers. You can use an audio-only receiver as an amplifier to drive some speakers, but if you want to listen to the latest surround-sound capabilities, which are encoded on most DVDs and Blu-ray discs (and on many TV broadcasts), you're going to need a new audio/video receiver, period. What's more, if you have a lot of video sources, you're going to want to switch among them — and for that you'll need a receiver with sophisticated video switching.

✔ **VCRs:** As long as your VCR is a VHS hi-fi VCR, it's just fine. But it won't replace a DVD player, which has about four times the picture resolution of a VCR (meaning the picture is about twice as sharp and detailed). We feel that VCRs are something you keep in your home theater if you have a lot of old tapes that you still want to watch (probably homemade and full of priceless memories). You might consider finding a service or buying a device to convert these to digital formats that you can burn onto your own DVDs!

✔ **CD players:** Your CD player will probably work fine. Depending on your space constraints, however, you might just use your DVD player to play your CDs because the two are compatible. Over time, CD players will disappear from your system in favor of a combined disc playing/recording unit.

✔ **DVD players:** Your DVD player will probably play fine, but if it can't record, you'll miss out. With the latest personal video recorders, you'll want to archive and offload all sorts of content to DVDs, and for that, you'll want a DVD player/recorder to burn the DVDs. Keep in mind that you can often use a PC (with the right software onboard) for the DVD recording functionality — we talk about PCs in the home theater in Chapter 8.

✔ **Speakers:** Chances are these are not going to be useful because you really want a *set* of speakers, not ones that are pieced together. Speakers work in tandem and therefore should have a similar foundation of performance. If you have a pair of stereo speakers that you can match into a complete set of surround-sound speakers from the same manufacturer, you might be able to use what you have (we recommend that you choose additional speakers that are *timbre matched* with your existing speakers).

✔ **Other stuff:** Most other stuff can work with your system. Turntables, cassette decks, laser disc players, and so on can plug in and play their part without any problems.

✔ **Internet connection:** Okay, your connection isn't gear in the traditional sense, but still, if you're using a dial-up connection, you should seriously consider upgrading to broadband if you want your home theater to take advantage of the Internet. As present and future consumer devices become increasingly reliant on the Internet for accessing information and content, you'll need a broadband connection to download this content.

Choosing a Room

As you build your home theater, all roads lead back to optimizing that illusion of participation, and where you put your system plays a big part. Here's a list of things to think about when determining the right place for your home theater — and there are definitely *wrong* places to put your home theater:

- ✔ **Think about lighting:** The amount of ambient light in a room, day or night, can substantially affect the experience. A nice, dark room makes the room itself disappear when watching a film, enabling that suspension of disbelief we keep aspiring to. Think about how lights from other rooms or street lighting might affect the experience.

- ✔ **Think about dimensions:** You tend to get more awkward sound patterns in perfectly square rooms. The best place to put the centerpiece of your system — the TV display — is along the short wall of a rectangular room, preferably a wall without windows or doors on it. Fully enclosed rooms are best for sound. You can pull heavy curtains across an open wall when you are watching films in your home theater.

- ✔ **Think about sound:** Although people typically place a couch up against a wall, with a home theater you want enough space behind you so that the sound can get in back of you and truly surround you. So the ideal position for the seating is more central to the room.

- ✔ **Think about the picture:** Sit close enough to your display to maximize the perceived size of the picture, but not so close that you see a somewhat grainy picture because you can see the lines on the TV set. The bigger your display, the farther back you need to be to not see the lines. Also think about angle of viewing — all displays have a preferred angle of viewing.

- ✔ **Think about walls:** A muted color or wall covering — bookcases are ideal — absorbs stray light. A dark gray or black room is best, or one with heavy, colored drapes. (Now you know why you see all those drapes and carpeted walls in theaters!) The *last* thing you want is a brightly colored high-gloss paint that reflects light, creating light ghosts to the sides of the screen! Think also about removing or covering mirrors and picture frames; they do the same thing.

    Take note of the front and rear wall surfaces because, in general, you want to control the way your sound reflects off these surfaces. Typically, you want the back wall to be a little reflective to help build a more general sound field behind your seating area.

- ✔ **Think about floors:** Yup, the floors, too. Bare tile or wood causes acoustical reflections that mess up your sound field. A good rug can absorb stray sounds that can affect the audio crispness.

> ✔ **Think about stray noise:** Listen closely to your room for regular interfering sounds, such as a clock ticking or a fish tank pump. Consider moving these devices if you can. And if the sound is coming externally, such as from the dryer or washer, consider some cheap absorptive wall coverings to muffle it.

We talk about creating a home theater environment in more detail in Chapter 20.

Organizing Your Gear

The most obvious and easy place for all your home theater gear is where you historically have placed it — right next to the TV. And indeed, nothing is inherently wrong with this approach. However, we ask you to look ahead for a moment and think about the investment you'll make in your home theater and how you'd like to take advantage of that throughout your home. To do this, you need to think of ways your home theater's components can be used in a whole-home network. This whole-home planning can make your home theater itself better, too, because it facilitates connections between the home theater and other networks that might feed in to it, such as your cable connection or your Internet connection.

Setting up a central wiring panel

Think about designating a space in your house as a *central wiring panel* where you can centrally house a lot of your whole-home infrastructure equipment (devices that let you connect the home theater to the rest of the house).

Remember that most of your commonly used, ultrasensitive electronics gear will probably go right next to your home theater. You are better off relegating the gear that you just "plug and forget" (such as video distribution panels that send your cable TV throughout the home) to a panel in an out-of-the-way place. Some of the devices that you might connect on a wiring panel include the following:

> ✔ Home cable interconnections with your cable company
>
> ✔ Home phone interconnections with your telephone company
>
> ✔ A centralized distribution point for satellite dish wiring, if you have one
>
> ✔ Cable, DSL, satellite, or ISDN modems and routers, if you have them
>
> ✔ Ethernet hubs or switches for your Internet connection

You can also put items such as home servers and some of your central media equipment on the wiring panel if you don't need to get to it regularly and you need the extra space. Multizone amplifiers or MP3 servers are examples of such equipment.

Appreciating the advantages of a central wiring panel

By designating a central wiring panel, you gain some huge benefits:

- **Hiding wires:** Your home theater gear has a lot of cables and can have a lot of gear you rarely touch. A well-integrated home theater setup has a lot of cables hidden in the walls or running out of sight. We're talking not just component wiring (such as the wires between your DVD player and your A/V receiver) but also connections to your phone network (required by a satellite dish), to your Internet connection (could be wireless, but wireline is better long term), to your IR (infrared) remote-control network (more on this in Chapter 15), and other connections. Think of your wiring panel as a place where everything can connect to everything else in the easiest fashion.

- **Hiding hardware:** Much of the hardware that facilitates home theater and whole-home networking (things such as power amps, video modulators, distribution panels, and punchdown blocks) is designed with function rather than form in mind. A central wiring panel can put this hardware out of view. And that means less clutter where you have the stuff that you get at the most, such as your VCR or your DVD player.

- **Connecting at a single point:** Having a central connection point makes it easier to get networks such as cable or your Internet-connected computer LAN (Local Area Network) into the home theater. It also makes it easier for you to get movies and music *out* of your home theater and share them throughout the home or access them when traveling.

- **Providing easy access:** When you want to change the capabilities of your networks or troubleshoot a problem, having everything neatly arranged and easily accessible can eliminate a source of frustration.

The wiring panel should be in a place that is out of sight but easily accessible. It needs to have plenty of space and adequate power to run a great deal of equipment. Then you can bring it up to the media hub in the home theater whatever you need, through a range of easily connected wiring plates that make your otherwise unsightly mess of wires look both neat and more accessible.

Locating your wiring panel's home

In the best-case scenario (like when you've struck it rich and are building a custom-designed home), you can create a dedicated room for your home theater and associated equipment — a central wiring panel just like modern offices and other commercial buildings have.

If we were starting a home from scratch this way, we'd try to design the wiring panel

- ✔ On the main floor of the house
- ✔ Near an outside wall for easy interconnection to incoming service feeds
- ✔ Above an accessible part of the basement (if you have a basement)
- ✔ With adequate lighting, ventilation, and climate protection (not in the garage, in other words)
- ✔ With adequate AC power line receptacles to power devices, such as video amplifiers, Ethernet hubs, and phone systems

Such a panel needn't be too large. Most home theater equipment takes up one rack at the most.

Of course, the vast majority of homeowners or remodelers simply don't have the luxury of adding a dedicated space for a wiring panel. In these cases, you have to try to make some part of the house do double duty as your wiring panel. A first stop is the place where your cable, telephone, and electrical connections currently come into the house. You can mount some plywood on the wall on which to mount your gear. Here are some other places to consider locating your wiring panel:

- ✔ **The utility or laundry room:** The biggest disadvantage of this location is the potential for high humidity, so make sure your clothes dryer is well ventilated to the outdoors. Good ventilation also keeps all the dust and lint from your dryer out of your sensitive electronics.

- ✔ **A protected garage:** The potential for dust and extreme temperatures may make this location less than optimal for some homes, but the garage can be a useful location.

- ✔ **The basement:** Many people choose the basement for a central wiring node because it's easy to run wires through a drop ceiling. The basement can be a very good location, but keep in mind that basements can be both dusty and damp.

- ✔ **A weather-protected outdoor panel:** We recommend this location only as a last resort, but it could be acceptable in a place with a mild climate. We wouldn't recommend putting any active electronics, such as Ethernet hubs or phone systems, out here.

An important thing to keep in mind is that the natural enemies of electrical and electronic equipment are moisture, dust, and temperature extremes. So locations that may work for someone in Florida or California may not make as much sense for your house in Maine.

Setting up a hub

Your home's wiring panel provides a centralized place for all sorts of whole-home networks that connect into your home theater (and elsewhere). Within your home theater, wherever you happen to locate it, you also need a similar centralized connection point for all that A/V gear we discuss in Chapter 1.

For most people, central to this area is the A/V receiver. An important thing to consider up front is the capability of this receiver to act as the hub of your home theater. An A/V receiver should be capable of accepting the connections from just about every single piece of A/V gear in your home theater (with the exception, perhaps, of an HDTV tuner/set-top box) and providing a central connection and control point.

With the right pieces and parts and the right approach to making connections, your A/V receiver (or surround-sound decoder/controller, if you go with separate components) should be the primary connection point in a home theater. With a small number of exceptions (mainly related to HDTV), you shouldn't connect components directly to the TV or display unit. All your audio and video should be routed through the A/V receiver, which then *switches* — or distributes — these signals to your speakers and display. We discuss receivers in more detail in Chapter 11.

Switching is a cool concept that we want to make sure you understand. If you think of your receiver as a generic box with lots of cables coming into and going out of it, the switching capability of the device merely cross connects these lines. So let's say you have a Sony PlayStation 3, an AudioReQuest audio CD server (with video output to the TV screen to select your CDs), a DVD player, a VCR, and a TiVo personal video recorder all connected to your A/V receiver, which in turn is connected to your display. In the past, you would have to link these in a daisy chain and press TV/video buttons and L1/L2 channel selectors and the link to see what you want on the TV. With an A/V receiver with video switching onboard, you can switch among these video sources by merely turning a knob on the receiver or pressing a button on the remote. Simple as that. No more fudging, cursing, and screaming by your spouse that *Desperate Housewives* has already started and you'd better get the TV working *now!* (Not that that ever happened to Pat.)

Some folks feel that sending *any* video through the receiver's video-switching circuitry slightly degrades the quality of this video. We think that, unless you're talking about a really high-end HDTV system, you probably won't see the difference. If you're worried about your receiver degrading your video quality, try it both ways (with the source device connected through the receiver and connected directly to your display) and see which looks better to your eyes.

Discreetly installing all this whole-home wiring (and "local" cables within your home theater) for your home theater can be problematic and messy. Your home theater room, unlike your wiring panel, is meant to be a public space in your house, not a place where you can hide away unsightly bundles of wire and racks of equipment. So your aesthetic requirements will be higher.

The best solution to this problem is to design the room so that you have an enclosed equipment and connection area where you can put the equipment that you don't need to physically access to watch a program or listen to something — such as special equipment needed for whole-home audio and video systems. Your equipment and connection area could be a well-ventilated closet, if one is available. We've even seen sophisticated setups with a false wall behind the TV and equipment racks to allow access to the backs of all the gear (or pull-out shelves that give you easy access to the back, as well). If you have space for a rack, you can probably store a lot of your active components there, too.

If you can't find a separate space for your gear, you can at least make your environment neater and more professional looking by hiding some of the wiring in the walls or in fake molding and by making the local connections available through wall outlets. You can use short cables to connect these outlets to the equipment itself. In this fashion, you don't have lumpy wires traveling under the rugs and cables that little children (or the dog) can easily grab.

Zoning inside your home

When most people think about a home theater, they think within a pretty confined box — the place where the home theater is going to be. And certainly, that's the predominant focus of this book.

However, a major theme that we'll hammer at (until you agree with us) is that you should spend a little extra money and be a little smarter in your planning so that you can access this great asset elsewhere around the house and from the Internet as well.

Creating *zones* around your house is a great way to extend your audio asset. When you buy your receiver or amplifier, the concept of *multizone* is going to come up. A multizone system allows you to access different sources and send them to independent outputs simultaneously. For example, your kids could be watching *Rugrats* in the living room, and you could be listening to Dunne Roman (www.dunneroman.com) in the kitchen. How cool is that!

We don't go into a lot of detail on multizone audio systems here; we cover them extensively in Chapter 18. But we want to mention it up front for the following reasons:

- ✔ Planning for whole-home audio is a good reason why you are going to need to think outside just your home theater (and another reason why a wiring panel is a good idea).

- ✔ Multizone means extra wiring and cables, extra speakers, possibly an extra amplifier, possibly extra controls, and some extra cost, so you need to plan and budget for it. (But it's well worth it.)

Doing It Yourself versus Hiring the Pros

A lot of home theater setup you can do yourself. However, if you want it done right, you may want to bring in experts to complement your work. If you don't have the right electrical outlets at your desired electronics station, for instance, you might call in an electrical contractor to put in dedicated home-run electrical cables (so you're not on the same circuit as the dishwasher and don't have electrical current spikes hitting your system all the time). Also, setting up front projection is an art and better left to professionals. And there's nothing like having your system fine-tuned by a professional who can tell if your video and sound are just right. Still, you can do all this yourself, with some patience — and respect for the live conductors in your electrical system.

If you want a professional to set up your entire system, you probably need to shop in the high-end price range. We rarely see anyone brought in to help on systems less than $10,000, and it almost always takes a $25,000+ system to get most contractors excited. So if you are on the low end of the equation, you'll probably do a lot yourself or rely heavily on the local installation services of the store where you buy your equipment. Even if your dealer doesn't want to do the entire installation for you, we suggest you see whether he or she can do a system calibration for you. If you buy online, expect to do most of the work yourself.

Home Theater For Dummies does not presume that you are going to hire anyone. You should be able to plan, design, and install a professional sounding (and looking) home theater system after reading this book. We just want you to know your alternatives in case you get halfway through and need some help. Check out the sidebar, "Who can help if you need it?" for some ideas.

Who can help if you need it?

All sorts of people can help you if you need advice:

✔ **Architect:** If you're building or renovating, an architect is probably involved. Home theater design usually isn't an architect's strong suit, but he or she can help you lay out the initial plans for your home and coordinate with other designers to get their respective visions on paper.

✔ **Audio/video consultant:** Your audio/video (A/V) consultant helps you select the right mix of components for your sight and sound systems and then integrates all those components. Your A/V consultant makes sure that the appropriate wiring is run to support your installations and then installs the gear when you're ready. If you're installing a dedicated home theater, expect your A/V consultant to get involved with the architect early on, too, making recommendations for room sizes, building materials, and so on. The A/V consultant may also hand you off to a specialized home theater consultant if the job is too complex for his or her comfort. (Home theater consultants get into additional details, such as soundproofing, seating, lighting, and the room's shape and construction.)

✔ **Contractor/builder:** The general contractor/builder's role is to direct the other specialty contractors and make sure that they carry out the intent of the designers. Passing correct information from one contractor (such as the home theater consultant) to the people doing the work (such as the cabinet-maker who builds the home theater cabinetry) is crucial. The details are what count here, such as cutting out the right size cubbyhole for the kitchen media center.

✔ **Computer systems contractor:** If you work at home or have complex computer-networking needs, bringing in a computer systems contractor to network your computer hardware and interface it to the appropriate systems can be a great timesaver.

✔ **Electrical contractor:** Your home theater may require additional or different electrical wiring (for example, running dedicated electrical wiring to your media center).

✔ **Home networking consultant:** Your home networking consultant will help you create a wired computer network, or wireless computer network, or both that can carry voice, data, and video all over your home. Many alarm companies, electricians, and others are expanding their services to include home networking. We're big believers in home networking and think it should be a core part of your home theater, too. These folks can also help with a whole-home automation system that can control your home theater and automate things such as lighting, drapes, and even movie screens.

✔ **Interior designer:** This person is responsible for making sure that your home theater technology doesn't stick out like a sore thumb. Installing a state-of-the-art home entertainment center in the living room is one thing; making it fit with the overall scheme of your home is another.

✔ **Lighting consultant:** Often an overlooked task on a to-do list, lighting design has an important effect on the ambiance of your home theater, so consider specialized lighting in key accent areas.

Whew! Did we leave anyone out? Depending on the amount of money you want to spend, you may indeed have this many people making your home theater a reality. A more modest project has fewer people stomping around your house. Also, many of the previously mentioned professionals — A/V designers, for example — include their services when you purchase their equipment.

Which people get involved in your project depends on the size of your project and whether you are building a new home, renovating an old one, or simply making do with that spare room in the basement. In the end, it will vary according to what you're trying to accomplish. If you plan to put a major home theater in your home — complete with theater seats, a popcorn and candy stand, and screen curtains — you may want to bring a home theater consultant into the process. However, we've seen some imaginative do-it-yourself (DIY) home theaters that traded love and patience for consultants and big bills, and the results were amazing.

Want some confidence that you can do this (and get some neat ideas for your own installation)? Check out the DIY home theater projects at www.home theatertalk.com and www.hometheaterforum.com.

If you do bring in some help, make sure you choose advisors who share your vision of an ideal home theater. The people you choose should have experience with a broad range of home theaters, not just expensive or cheap ones. Find your home theater personality and match it with your contractor's, and you'll have a winning combination.

You might have a hard time finding some of these contractors. For the more traditional groups of professionals (such as architects), we tend to rely on word of mouth, recommendations from in-the-know friends, and a thorough review of the contractor's references. For contractors who will be installing your home's electronics and wiring infrastructure, we do these same things, as well as check their credentials. The Custom Electronics Design & Installation Association, or CEDIA, has a rigorous training and qualification program for people who do nothing but build and install home theater systems for a living. There is a CEDIA Finder Service at www.cedia.net/ homeowners/finder.php. Many home theater magazine Web sites also have directories of contractors — for instance, you can find a listing of installers at *Electronic House*'s Installers Guide: www.electronichouse. com/installer.

Chapter 3

The ABCs of Home Theater Audio

*I*n the early days of corporate video conferencing, system designers struggled to balance the audio and video needs for a video conference with the cost for the transmission to carry the signals (which was really expensive). Necessity being the mother of invention, a lot of the focus was on compressing the audio and video to low data sizes and figuring out the right mix between the two.

One trend became clear rather quickly: When test subjects were presented with all the different variants and permutations possible for different transmission speeds, they always preferred to have better audio at the price of video rather than the opposite. In other words, they preferred to accept crappy video rather than deal with bad audio.

Although you'd like to have the best of all possible worlds in all aspects of your home theater, we think you'll probably focus on audio first (at least we'd recommend it) for three reasons:

- ✔ The video conferencing effect we just noted.

- ✔ The fact that your home theater also doubles as a home concert hall, so you want your audio CDs, MP3s, and other audio sources to sound perfect, too.

- ✔ Video display prices are dropping faster than any other device in home theater, so if you are going to put off one purchase, putting off the video display makes a lot of sense.

For these reasons, we start our discussion of home theater technologies with audio first.

Surrounding Yourself with Sound

Unless you plan on installing a 360-degree Cinema-in-the-Round screen in your home, just like you'd see at Disney World, video plays a confined (but still big) role in creating the home theater illusion of being "in the movie." The real job of surrounding yourself in the scene falls to your multichannel surround-sound audio system.

Imagine that you see on the screen in front of you the soon-to-be victims of a firing squad, and that — from behind you — you hear the clicks of the rifles as they chamber a round. That sensation is brought to you by your rear-channel-driven surround-sound system. Now, if you had heard that sound coming from in front of you — the traditional TV experience — it simply would not have the same impact because, in the "real" world, that click of the rifle would *have* to come from behind you. Which all goes to show that if you really want the dickens scared out of you, you need surround sound.

Two-channel sound versus multichannel surround sound

Most of us are used to age-old *two-channel* sound — that is, the stereo sound that gives us a left and a right speaker effect. *Multichannel surround sound* adds a front center speaker between the front left and right speakers and adding two surround speakers. More recent versions of surround sound add even more rear speakers and side surround speakers to enhance your surround-sound field (the latest version of Dolby Lab's surround sound — Dolby TrueHD — can support up to 14 channels!). A subwoofer is part of almost all home theater setups, but as we discuss later in this chapter, a subwoofer is more a part of the bass management of the collective speakers than part of the surround-sound system itself. Nonetheless, something needs to shake the room when the dinosaur's feet stomp the jeep in *Jurassic Park!*

To understand the impact of the concept of surround sound on your home theater, you need to understand a bit about *encoding* and *decoding* sound. When the master mixers at the movie studios create the audio track to go with the movie, they encode the music in very specific ways. They designate which *channel* (you can read *speaker* into that if you like) the specific sound goes through. In addition, each different channel is designed to provide *spatial* sound effects — meaning that the channels can work together to make sounds come from different locations relative to you, the listener. The goal is to decode those signals onto the correct channels to replicate the studio's intent.

So, let's say that a squadron of jets in a scene from *Top Gun* is doing a fly-by of the carrier command bridge. If we were in the command bridge, we would hear the jets come in from the left, sweep across in front of us, and then disappear to the right and the rear as they turn off to the starboard side of the ship. If you are sitting in a well-tuned home theater, you should hear no differently. And as the bridge shakes, your subwoofers (and bass shakers, which we talk about in Chapter 22) provide you with the vibrations to make you feel like you're actually there. Now we're talking surround sound!

To get you to this point, the encoders have to designate on the movie or TV program soundtrack the specific sounds that, at specific times, are to be sent to specific channels in your system. The speakers connected to those channels are given those signals by your surround-sound–equipped A/V receiver (see Chapter 11), which properly decodes those tracks from the DVD or other video source. A home theater audio system needs to have it all correct from beginning to end.

In a two-channel system, you might hear some of that effect, in that it might get the left and right parts right. A two-channel system can't help with the front to back movement, however, and that's the critical part of a surround-sound system — it surrounds you!

Understanding surround-sound lingo

For the most part, the entertainment industry boils down a lot of the surround-sound terminology into numbers such as 2.0, 5.1, and 7.1. Sometimes these numbers refer to the playback system's speaker configuration, and sometimes they refer to the audio signal format being delivered. The lingo can be confusing, especially when the number of speakers in your particular system doesn't match the number of channels in your source — like when you play back a 5.1 channel recording on your 7.1 channel system — but it's all perfectly normal for that to occur.

The first number represents the number of speakers or main audio channels involved, and the 1 or 0 after the decimal point indicates whether the system has a subwoofer or supports a low-frequency effects channel. Systems that end in 1 have a subwoofer or an effects channel. Here's a rundown of the different numbers you'll probably encounter and what they mean:

- ✔ **2.0:** Normal stereo — the kind with a left and a right channel — is 2.0 in surround-sound speak.

- ✔ **5.1:** This is the primary format for creating and delivering surround sound. It is in wide use in movie theaters, digital television, DVD-video and audio, and even the latest game consoles. Source signals have the five main channels and one LFE (low-frequency effects) bass channel. Playback systems usually have five main speakers and one subwoofer.

✔ **5.1-channel-ready:** Such an audio system has six discrete inputs to accept a 5.1 signal from a signal source such as a 5.1-channel DVD player. It does not necessarily mean that these products can decode signals to a 5.1-channel output. The best way to ferret out true 5.1 systems is by reading reviews of the devices before you buy. (We recommend many places to find these reviews in Chapter 23.)

✔ **6.1:** 6.1-channel systems have an additional surround channel called the *back surround channel*. This drives a speaker (or preferably two) situated right behind the viewers, in essence providing the same smooth flow in the back sound field that the center speaker enables in the front speaker group. Dozens of DVDs are encoded with extra back surround information for this back surround speaker, and these DVDs also play perfectly well on regular 5.1 systems.

✔ **7.1:** Not to be outdone, some have taken the 5.1 or 6.1 channel encoding on a DVD and used some computer horsepower to create two independent back surround speakers for even more surround sound, making it 7.1. Note that 7.1 is not a true discrete surround-sound format (no DVDs on the market have 7.1 channels of sound); instead, it refers to the manufacturers' own systems used to derive two back surround channels from existing stereo (2.0), 5.1-, or even the 6.1-channel sources just mentioned.

✔ **8.1 and beyond:** You'll probably hear about even higher designations — 8.1, 9.1, 10.2, and so on. These are in the realm of the home theaterphile, and if you're evaluating such gear, a home theater consultant is probably standing next to you, so just follow his or her recommendations. The newest systems (such as Dolby Digital Plus, discussed later in the chapter) can theoretically support systems up to 13.1. Wow!

Bass management

Bass management is how your home theater manages low-frequency sounds. Better A/V receivers and other controller devices have several options for handling the bass sounds in your system. If you have nice, big main speakers that have an effective bass range of their own (often called *full-range speakers*), you might pass all bass frequencies to them. If you want smaller speakers that can sit on a shelf or hang on the wall alongside your plasma TV, the bass frequencies might fall to the subwoofer, which is a speaker designed to play low-frequency sounds.

One area that causes a lot of confusion is the difference between the *Low Frequency Effect channel* (LFE), which is part of your movie/game/TV show soundtrack and the physical subwoofer channel on your receiver or amplifier. The LFE channel is encoded in the soundtrack of a DVD or other surround-sound source; the subwoofer channel is the connection on the back of your A/V receiver that provides amplified low-frequency sound signals to your subwoofer. The LFE channel is encoded in surround-sound material — it's the *.1* in 5.1 and other surround-sound formats. This low frequency sound, along with the bass from any channels that cannot be reproduced by the small main speakers, is often sent to the subwoofer channel in your surround-sound system, but it doesn't necessarily have to be sent exclusively to your subwoofer. For example, some people send these low-frequency sounds to both the subwoofer and to the front left and right speakers if said speakers are large. The bass management system in your A/V receiver (or A/V controller) lets you customize these settings to best fit your A/V system. (We discuss how to set this all up in Chapters 19 and 20.)

You don't have to have a subwoofer to take advantage of the LFE channel because many normal left/right speakers can take these cues from your receiver and play the sound accordingly. But having a subwoofer gives you that stomach-rattling, vibrating-room effect at just the right times — an effect we're sure you'll want to take advantage of.

Dolby Galore

As we begin discussing surround-sound formats, things can get a bit complicated, unfortunately. A host of different terms and brand names are applied to everything we just described, and these terms can get downright confusing.

When you start to optimize your home theater, however, you need to understand these terms. Because you probably have some older gear in your home audio and video system already, and because some older movies use older encoding schemes, we mention older terms, too, so that you can have the big picture.

We start with Dolby Laboratories (www.dolby.com). You've probably seen Dolby on your cassette tape deck for years and seen advertisements for Dolby Digital at the beginning of movies. But you've probably never known exactly what Dolby does. Well, stand by, because we're going to make you look smart on your next date at the movies.

Dolby surround sound

You have to go back a few years to get to where we are today. Although Dolby has been enhancing sound for decades, the true mother of all surround-sound encoding schemes is Dolby Surround (introduced in 1982), which encodes four analog audio channels into two channels for storage and transmission or both. If you play Dolby Surround on a normal stereo, you get two channels. If you play it on a Dolby Surround–enabled decoder device, the device separates the full four channels for playback. Many tens of millions of consumer products have been shipped with Dolby Surround Pro Logic (the current version of this system) decoding onboard. That's a lot.

With Dolby Surround, the four channels encode front left, front center, front right, and monophonic surround as their channels. The left, center, and right channels are *full-range* channels, meaning that they carry the full range (20 Hz to 20 kHz) of audio frequencies. The fourth (rear) surround-sound channel is a *limited bandwidth channel,* meaning it carries only a subset of the frequency range (not the real low-frequency or high-frequency stuff).

At first, consumer audio/video receivers with Dolby Surround decoders could separate only the left, right, and monophonic surround speaker channels. However, with the advent of Dolby Pro Logic in 1987, receivers could decode the center channel as well. The consumer devices just took awhile to develop the same processing power that the more expensive movie theaters had onboard.

Dolby Pro Logic is what's called a *matrixed* multichannel system, meaning that output channels are electronically derived from input channels. None of the four outputs are identical to the two inputs used to transport the encoded signals, but all the signals being output from the decoder are indeed present in the two-channel source — nothing new, such as reverb, is being added.

So with Dolby Pro Logic, you have four channels and five speakers, with the two surround speakers playing essentially the same monophonic sound. You often see a subwoofer channel on Pro Logic receivers as well; note that this is not a separate channel but is derived from the low-frequency information from the front channels.

One problem with the dual monophonic surround-sound channels is that, in some ways, they defeat the purpose of having surround sound. You can't send information specifically to one speaker, as is done with a left or right front speaker. And because they have the same signal, they tend to create a localized sound field between the speakers — and that goes against surround sound's goal of creating a large, diffuse background sound field. Proper placement of the surround speakers on the side walls aiming across the listening area helps achieve the optimal results. (In Chapter 12, we discuss dipole speakers and how they can help with this.)

A newer version of Dolby Pro Logic, Dolby Pro Logic II, came out in 2001. The biggest new feature that Pro Logic II offers is a fuller sound experience for two-channel stereo or Dolby Surround–encoded sources that were being played over 5.1-channel systems. Pro Logic II does extra processing and extends the Pro Logic work substantially. Importantly, Pro Logic II decodes the surround-sound speakers in full-bandwidth stereo and therefore provides a more complete rear sound field.

Just about all surround-sound decoders sold since 2002 or so support Dolby Pro Logic II. Most now support an even newer and more advanced version of Pro Logic — Pro Logic IIx, discussed next.

Dolby Pro Logic turns 7 (point 1!)

As more and more folks build 7.1-channel home theaters to support Dolby Digital EX (discussed in the next section), they find that they have two channels that aren't being used when they view material that's not multichannel encoded (for example, many DVDs of older material have a simple 2.0-channel Dolby Digital soundtrack) or even when playing regular stereo content.

To fill all seven speakers with sound, Dolby's engineers came to the rescue with a new version of Dolby Pro Logic II called *Pro Logic IIx.* This system provides a full 6.1- or 7.1-channel output — meaning you can take any incoming stereo (2.0) or 5.1-channel signal and turn it into a 6.1- or 7.1-channel output that uses *all* the speakers in your home theater system. So don't be afraid to go 7.1! Pro Logic IIx has come to your rescue!

Dolby Digital arrives on the scene

The advent of Dolby Digital in 1997 really started to make things interesting. As you would surmise, Dolby Digital is an all-digital surround format that handles audio compression, so it's available only for digital content. DVDs and HDTV use Dolby Digital (DVDs may also contain some other system, such as DTS, or Digital Theater Systems). To give you an idea of Dolby Digital's reach in the market, by the beginning of 2006, more than 1 billion consumer devices had shipped with Dolby Digital onboard, and more than 7,600 films had been encoded in Dolby Digital. It should come as no surprise, then, that it's the scheme we think your equipment should support.

Dolby Digital 5.1 represents the current minimum level of performance that you should require from your system. Also keep in mind that any receiver with Dolby Digital decoding can also decode Dolby Surround Pro Logic.

Although Dolby Digital is the more widely known consumer moniker, it also goes by the more techie name of AC-3, which is actually the name used in the official part of the DVD video standard (for "regular" non-HD-DVDs), as well as the ATSC (Advanced Television Standards Committee) standard for DTV and HDTV. (See Chapter 4 for more on this.) AC-3 is also part of the standards for HD-DVD and Blu-ray discs. As you can see, Dolby Digital is *everywhere,* and you definitely want your home theater gear to support it. Luckily, just about every home theater receiver built since the late '90s supports Dolby Digital.

What's so great about Dolby Digital is that it encodes six discrete audio channels. (*Discrete* means that the sound signal contained in each of the six available channels is distinct and independent from each of the others.) Remember that the older Dolby Surround encoded four channels onto two-channel soundtracks, which often resulted in all sorts of bleed-overs between channels and less-than-clear demarcations in the sound details.

Because Dolby Digital has six clean channels, your receivers and controllers can precisely control the different elements of your sound mix. More importantly, the rear surround speakers are each fed by their own independent channels, enabling true spatial separation for that rear sound field. With this setup, when you hear that bullet whiz by or that starship warp overhead, the sound moving across your entire speaker system is smooth and controlled — and digital. This is the home theater your momma always warned you about!

Dolby's ability to encode and decode information is only as strong as its source data. If it's working with a two-channel stereo movie, you may see something like "Dolby Digital 2.0" on the package, designating that it is a stereo signal being encoded and decoded using Dolby Digital. All fine and dandy, but it's still a stereo signal. However, if your receiver includes Dolby Pro Logic, Dolby Pro Logic II, or even Dolby Pro Logic IIx, the stereo signal on the disc can still be listened to as a multichannel surround signal, thereby allowing you to achieve full playback on your system.

We talk more about how your DVD, HDTV, and other gear supports Dolby Digital, and how to make sure it's all set correctly, in later chapters, notably Chapter 6. For now, know that this is the baseline upon which you grow.

Dolby Digital Surround EX

Rear surround speakers are a relatively new development made possible by an additional surround channel that drives the center rear surround speaker. This is 6.1 in industry parlance. Dolby avoids 6.1 and calls it Dolby Digital Surround EX.

The rear Surround EX channel does not have its own discrete channel. Instead, its signal is *matrixed* (intermixed) with the left and right surround channels, just like Dolby Pro Logic has the center speaker information encoded in the left and right front channels. When a Dolby Digital EX program is decoded, the three surround outputs are all derived from a 3-channel Pro Logic process — none of them are strictly discrete anymore. It is also the case that many conventional 5.1 movies decode nicely with Dolby Digital EX processing, thus keeping the added back speakers active. Newer processors offer Pro Logic IIx technology, thereby deriving four separate surround outputs instead of three, making much more effective use of 7.1-speaker systems for all movie and music programs, whether Surround EX encoded or not.

The first consumer devices with Surround EX were based on licenses from Lucasfilm THX (www.thx.com), so you'll also see it called THX Surround EX in stores and online when you're shopping.

THX isn't a surround-sound format itself but rather a *certification and testing* program for home (and movie) theater equipment and movies. So equipment such as A/V receivers and speakers may be THX certified, as may DVDs themselves. THX's main mission is to create a set of standards for surround-sound playback and then certify the equipment or DVDs that meet those standards. A big part of these standards revolves around THX's criteria for the levels and equalization of the sound sent to the surround speakers.

Many newer DVDs are encoded for Dolby Digital EX and have that extra channel of surround information onboard. Also, if you're playing a regular Dolby Digital 5.1-channel DVD, a THX Ultra 2 decoder can simulate 6.1- or 7.1-channel surround by processing the audio information in the regular surround channels and sending the information to your rear surround speaker.

If you're playing a movie (say on a DVD) that has been encoded using Dolby Digital EX, and you have only a regular Dolby Digital decoder in your A/V receiver, you won't have any problems. You still get the full 5.1 surround sound you expect, with nothing missing. You just won't get certain sounds re-routed to the extra surround speakers behind you.

DTS: Bring It On!

Dolby is not the only game in town, although it clearly has the lead in the marketplace. Digital Theater Systems (DTS) has invented a competing lineup of surround-sound encoding schemes. The first movie to use DTS was *Jurassic Park*.

As with Dolby Digital, DTS Digital Surround provides 5.1 channels of digital audio. However, DTS uses less compression (higher data rate) than Dolby Digital. Where Dolby Digital encodes six channels with 384,000 or 448,000 bits per second, DTS, in its higher-quality mode, encodes 1,536,000 bits per second, which many audiophiles believe delivers a better sound quality. Of course, that means that the DTS encoding takes up more space on a DVD, so the DVD doesn't have as much room for extra features, such as foreign languages, commentaries, and multiple versions of the movie.

It's an open question among experts as to which technology (Dolby Digital or DTS) sounds better or is a better choice. On the one hand, people point to DTS's higher bit rate and say, "Aha! Better sound!" Others say, "Well, Dolby is just more efficient at encoding sound, so it can have just as good a sound quality with fewer bits." You know what? Both can sound good. You'll most likely use whatever's encoded on the DVD or other programming you watch. Dolby is the most prevalent system, but DTS is also widespread. We suggest you choose receivers and other equipment that support both standards.

The DVD powers-that-be require all NTSC (the North American standard) DVDs to carry either a Dolby Digital or a PCM (Pulse Code Modulation) — a common digital audio format — soundtrack to ensure compatibility with all DVD players. Because DTS is an optional feature of DVDs, DTS has an uphill battle getting studios onboard because the space on DVDs is limited. (For these space reasons, most DVDs containing a DTS soundtrack are encoded at half the 1.536 Mbps rate mentioned to retain a sufficient bit rate for high-quality video and other content.) Today, a few hundred DVDs are issued with the higher-quality (1.536 Mbps rate) DTS Digital Surround.

You might hear of some other DTS innovations:

- **DTS-ES:** DTS-ES Discrete uses existing digital multichannel technology to deliver the 5.1 channels of regular DTS. It also adds a *discrete* full-bandwidth back surround channel — meaning that each channel is individually encoded rather than being matrix decoded from the others. That additional channel may be played through one or two speakers, allowing for the ES — Extended Surround — that gives DTS-ES its name. More prevalent is the DTS-ES Matrix system, which is electrically identical to Dolby Digital EX but uses Neo:6 matrix decoding to derive the three surround outputs.

- **DTS Neo:6:** DTS Neo:6 Music and Neo:6 Cinema are decoding techniques for stereo or Dolby Surround–encoded two-channel sources. Neo:6 Music keeps the front left and right channels intact while synthesizing the center and surround channels from the 2-channel source. Neo:6 Cinema can create a 6.1-channel signal from 2-channel movie sources.

The bottom line on DTS is that the DTS folks have some innovative algorithms, but the sheer prevalence of the Dolby solutions clearly makes Dolby Digital the most common choice for studios and home theater enthusiasts. Most A/V receivers offer both DTS and Dolby Digital options, so you can try them both and set your receiver (or choose your DVDs) according to your preference.

Understanding the Next Generation of Surround Sound

The Dolby Digital EX and DTS-ES surround-sound formats that bring 6.1- or 7.1-channel sound to your home theater are great. But time marches on, technology improves, and surround sound keeps getting better. So it should come as no surprise that both companies have something new up their sleeves.

The advent of improved digital connections between disc players or set-top boxes and the receiver (connections such as HDMI, or High-Definition Multimedia) and the enhanced data capacities of entirely new formats of recorded high-definition content (HD-DVD and Blu-ray) have made it possible for Dolby and DTS to launch new and improved surround-sound formats that promise more channels, purer sound, and an improved surround-sound experience.

The new surround-sound formats we discuss in the coming sections are not widely available. The only place you're likely to find them for the time being is on Blu-ray discs (or on an HD-DVD disc — but this format has already been discontinued, so unless you already bought one, you can safely ignore it). Eventually you may see these new surround-sound formats on TV broadcasts, in games, or on content downloaded from the Internet, but for now they're only on Blu-ray discs.

Dolby Digital Plus

The folks at Dolby Laboratories have improved their super-popular Dolby Digital/ Dolby Digital EX system and have created *Dolby Digital Plus.* Dolby Digital Plus improves on Dolby Digital and EX by

 ✔ **Increasing the *bit rate:*** Dolby Digital Plus can be encoded with up to 6144 Kbps (kilobits per second) of data, where Dolby Digital tops out at 640 Kbps. (448 Kbps is the maximum from current formats, however.) In Chapter 5, we point out that all else being equal, higher bit rates mean better sound quality because the audio signals need to be *compressed* less.

✔ **Improving the *encoding:*** Not only does Dolby Digital Plus provide a much higher bit rate, it also does a better job of encoding (or digitizing and compressing) sound. Therefore, at a given bit rate, you get better sound quality. Combine this with the vastly increased bit rate of Dolby Digital Plus, and you get great sound!

✔ **Adding more channels:** Dolby Digital Plus can provide up to 13.1 discrete channels of sound (14 total speakers, including the subwoofer). You can really envelop yourself in the action with 14 speakers!

✔ **Providing backward compatibility:** Dolby Digital Plus decoders can automatically *downconvert* your sound to the older Dolby Digital formats. So you can play Dolby Digital Plus programs on your older system without having to buy new hardware. And when you do upgrade, you gain all the advantages just mentioned. Because the conversion process from Dolby Digital Plus to Dolby Digital outputs a 640 Kbps Dolby Digital stream, your existing system, which normally tops out at 448 Kbps, can actually sound better than ever before.

One drawback of Dolby Digital Plus is that the very high bit rates it supports overwhelm the digital audio connections that are traditionally used to connect DVD players or set-top boxes to your receiver. If all you have on your receiver is coaxial or optical digital connections, you'll still be able to listen to Dolby Digital Plus, but you'll have to get by with using analog audio connections or by letting your DVD player downconvert to 640 Kbps Dolby Digital. If you have a newer receiver with an HDMI 1.3 connection, you won't have this restriction and will get the full Dolby Digital Plus experience because the decoded signals can be carried as multichannel PCM over these high-bandwidth interfaces without sonic compromise.

Some receivers have HDMI connections but still can't handle Dolby Digital Plus — you'll need a receiver with HDMI 1.3 capabilities *and* an internal Dolby Digital Plus decoding capability. If your receiver doesn't have these capabilities, it won't keep you from enjoying the benefits of Dolby Digital Plus, but you'll need to use a set of analog connections or configure your receiver to send the Dolby Digital Plus signal as *linear PCM* instead of as a *bitstream.* We discuss this in further detail in Chapter 19.

Dolby Digital Plus is an *optional* format for Blu-ray discs, so any Blu-ray disc player should support Dolby Digital Plus, though not all discs will use the format. Dolby Digital Plus may also be used for other HDTV content — and may end up being encoded in a lot of the HDTV shows you get from your cable, satellite, or other TV service provider.

Dolby TrueHD

Dolby's other new format — one that gets us excited! — is *Dolby TrueHD*. Like Dolby Digital Plus, this format can support up to 13.1 channels of surround-sound goodness.

The big difference is that Dolby TrueHD is a *lossless* format. That means that the sound being encoded into the Dolby TrueHD data stream will come out the far end (at the decoder in your home theater) *exactly the same as it went in*. For the first time ever, the home consumer will be able to experience multichannel movie soundtracks exactly as they were heard in the mixing studio during content production. All other surround-sound formats we've discussed are *lossy* — some data is discarded in the compression/decompression process. (DTS-HD Master Audio, which we discuss in the next section, is also a lossless format.) With Dolby TrueHD, the audio track is bit-for-bit identical to the studio master.

Dolby TrueHD uses the same MLP (Meridian Lossless Packing) encoding as DVD-Audio (which we discuss in Chapter 5), but with an even higher bit rate, which allows for more channels of high-resolution audio.

A lossy encoding system throws away bits of the audio (using sophisticated acoustic modeling that determines what your ears actually do and don't hear) to achieve greater compression of the audio. Greater compression is a good thing if you have a limited amount of storage space on a disc or a limited amount of *bandwidth* (or data throughput) on your video transmission system (like cable or satellite). But if you have the space (or the bandwidth) — like Blu-ray does — you can compress your audio less and get better sound quality.

You probably won't hear Dolby TrueHD on broadcast HDTV programming any time soon because of the bandwidth issues we just mentioned, but Dolby TrueHD support is included in Blu-ray disc players and many Blu-ray discs. So you'll be able to enjoy some awesome lossless surround sound when you watch a movie in this new format.

Like Dolby Digital Plus, to listen to Dolby TrueHD, you need a receiver capable of decoding Dolby Digital Plus with an HDMI 1.3 connection (these are still pretty rare as we write, but gradually becoming more common). If you don't have Dolby TrueHD decoding and HDMI 1.3 in your receiver, you use the Dolby TrueHD decoder in your DVD player and connect it to your receiver using either an HDMI 1.1 connection or a set of analog audio cables.

DTS-HD

The folks at DTS have developed their own lossless surround-sound format known as *DTS-HD Master Audio*. DTS-HD is available on Blu-ray discs and players, and can provide (to begin with) up to 7.1 channels of lossless surround sound when it's used with one of these discs. There are two variants of DTS-HD:

- ✔ DTS-HD High-Resolution Audio: This format is roughly equivalent to Dolby Digital Plus, providing a compressed but higher-resolution surround-sound format with up to 7.1 channels of 96 KHz, 24-bit surround sound. It's used on Blu-ray discs when there isn't enough space on the disc for the uncompressed Master Audio format, discussed next.

- ✔ DTS-HD Master Audio: This is the top dog of DTS audio formats, and can be thought of as DTS's equivalent to Dolby's TrueHD. Master Audio provides up to 7.1 channels of uncompressed surround-sound audio.

DTS-HD has the great feature of being backward compatible with older variants of DTS. So although you need a DTS-HD decoder to gain the full benefits of the lossless encoding that DTS-HD provides, you can still get great sound with your existing gear.

In fact, a DTS-HD-encoded Blu-ray disc — when connected to an existing DTS-capable receiver — will be able to send a relatively high bit rate (1536 Kbps) surround signal to *any* existing DTS receiver. And although this same bit rate has been used on hundreds of conventional DVDs, this is about twice the bit rate of the average DVD using DTS encoding, providing a good boost in sound quality.

Of course, when you have a DTS-HD decoder in the loop, you'll get that great lossless decoding and superb sound quality.

Just as with Dolby's two new formats, both variants of DTS-HD require an HDMI 1.3 connection and a receiver with a built-in DTS-HD decoder if you want to decode the high-resolution surround sound inside your receiver. Without those two features in your receiver, you'll need to use the DTS-HD decoder inside your Blu-ray disc player, along with either an HDMI 1.1 connection (for linear PCM) or a set of analog audio connections.

Other Key Audio Standards

In the realm of "music only" (and yes, we play a lot of music in our systems, in addition to movies and college basketball games and other video content), you might hear about a few other audio standards. We don't spend a ton of time beating these into your head, mainly because you don't need to do a lot to your system to accommodate them. With the exception of MP3s (which might take some special gear), these are things that you just plug in, and they work.

1 want my MP3

MP3 is great for online music trading and downloading because it uses a compression scheme to make the files small enough to be easily downloaded. You don't find any MP3 music encoded in movies on DVD, nor will you (typically) find MP3-encoded music in stores. MP3 comes into play when you start getting involved in online music downloading or when you want to move your CD collection to a computer hard drive. We talk about these activities in more detail in Chapter 5.

MP3 is designed to be an efficient encoding system for taking big fat PCM music files and moving them to download-friendly computer files. MP3 trades a little sound quality for a lot of room. (It's another of those *lossy* compression systems, which means that the system removes some information.) So MP3 files are typically ten times smaller than the corresponding PCM files on a compact disc.

In Chapter 5, we discuss computer audio files in greater detail, including an in-depth discussion of the MP3 system and other encoding systems used for these types of music files — such as the AAC files used by Apple's iTunes and the WMA files used by Windows Media Player.

PCM is perfect

PCM (or Pulse Code Modulation) is not really perfect — nothing is. But it's pretty darn close. PCM is an older but still vital system for encoding analog music into a digital format that can be saved on a computer or burned onto a CD.

We say that PCM is nearly perfect because it's a *lossless* coding system, which means that what goes in comes out exactly the same, bit for bit. In a PCM world, none of the sound is thrown away. The only limitations to PCM are the accuracy, sample rate, and word length (the number of bits used to digitally capture a sound) of the analog-to-digital conversion process, all of which define the quality of the signal carried in the PCM format. If you have sharp ears and a good system, PCM-based files sound better than MP3s, for example. Traditional CDs are based on PCM, as are the sound files on many computers, such as .wav files on a Windows computer.

PCM isn't the only lossless system out there. Another one is MLP, or Meridian Lossless Packing, which is used by the new DVD-Audio format we discuss in Chapter 5. Another new audio format is SACD, which we also discuss in Chapter 5. It uses its own coding format called DSD (or Direct Stream Digital).

You can also find some lossless codecs in the digital music file realm — Apple's Apple Lossless compression system and Microsoft's Windows Media Audio Lossless compression system, for example, are both lossless formats.

The bottom line here is that for the utmost in digital audio reproduction, lossless is the way to go.

Chapter 4

Getting the Big (Video) Picture

. . . .

. . . .

We call the video portion of a home theater a *display.* Your display can be a direct-view television, a rear-projected television, a front-projected screen, a plasma or LCD screen, or even a properly painted wall (as long as you combine it with a projector).

Whatever its form factor, the video aspect of your home theater tends to be the main focus for many people. Let's face it — a big-screen display simply overpowers mere A/V source equipment and controllers. Big screens are just plain cool!

There's a lot to know about video formats, though, and in this chapter, we lay the groundwork for a more detailed discussion of specific video options in Part III.

Learning to Talk Videoese

Before we talk about the different kinds of analog and digital video, it's worthwhile to find out how to talk about video. Like any other technology, video has its own set of arcane terms and other jargon that makes casual listeners just want to give up. We promise not to lay too much on you here, but a few key concepts are essential:

> ✔ **Resolution:** Speaking in very general terms, resolution is basically the level of detail that your eyes (or a good pair of eyes, if yours have gotten a little blurry from too much time in front of the computer like ours have) can *resolve,* or see, on the screen. In the PC world, this is measured according to the number of *pixels* (the individual points of light and color) on your monitor. For example, older home-PC displays are set

to show 800 x 600 pixels. The resolution of video systems are typically described by the vertical number (the smaller of the two) — usually by measuring the *scan lines* that move across your screen (from left to right) and by adding the number of these lines stacked on top of each other. Video systems typically display 480, 720, or 1080 of these lines (though some displays — many plasma TVs, for example — have a non-standard number of lines such as 768).

When you look at specs for a particular display, you might see resolution discussed in two related but different ways:

- **Display resolution:** Also called a display's *native resolution,* this is simply the number of pixels or lines of resolution that the display has on its screen. Most digital TVs (with the exception of the nearly no longer available, traditional CRT tube TVs, discussed in Chapter 13) have a *fixed* display resolution — meaning that they are physically built with a certain number of pixels and anything they display on the screen will consist of that number of pixels, regardless of the resolution of the video signal going into the display. Display resolution is what it says it is — the measure of your display's resolution.

- **Input resolutions:** Different video sources, such as analog TV, DVDs, and high-definition TV (HDTV) signals, have their own resolution. For example, HDTV signals have 720 or 1080 lines of resolution, and analog TV signals have 480 lines. A display's input resolutions are simply the resolutions of the video signals that the TV can accept and display. As an example, a specific high-definition display may have a display resolution of 720 lines and be able to accept inputs of 480, 720, and 1,080 lines of resolution — but will display the 1080 signal at the lower 720 resolution. We talk more about display and input resolutions in Chapters 13 and 14.

✔ **Fields and frames:** Frames are a holdover from the film world, where each individual picture on a reel of film is called a *frame* (and 24 of them flash by the projector bulb each second). When TV was developed, the technology of the day wouldn't allow full frames to be displayed at the rate at which TV signals worked, so each frame was divided into two *fields,* each of which contained half the scan lines we discuss in the preceding bullet (all the odd lines in one field, and all the evens in the other). Traditional TV systems display 60 fields every second — 30 frames per second — but the newest systems, discussed in the next bullet, can be capable of up to 60 *frames* per second.

✔ **Scanning method:** Up until very recently, just about all common video systems used *interlaced* scanning, which we describe in the preceding bullet. In an interlaced system, half the lines are drawn on the screen in one cycle of the video system, and the other half are drawn in the next cycle. (The lines are drawn not top to bottom but by weaving — or interlacing — every other line.) Because this happens really fast (each set of lines is drawn 30 times per second), your eye can't really tell that things are being drawn this way — unless you stop to think about the flickering you see and the way some vertical and diagonal lines on your TV screen appear jagged. *Progressive scan* systems (see Figure 4-1) draw all the lines (a whole frame) at the same time and can help reduce these characteristics. The effect is a picture that is more like film, which is what we're shooting for in a home theater.

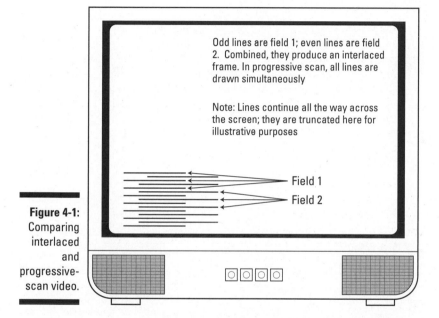

Odd lines are field 1; even lines are field 2. Combined, they produce an interlaced frame. In progressive scan, all lines are drawn simultaneously

Note: Lines continue all the way across the screen; they are truncated here for illustrative purposes

Field 1

Field 2

Figure 4-1:
Comparing
interlaced
and
progressive-
scan video.

Switching from Analog to Digital

Television is undergoing some radical changes — and we're not talking about programming. Like most other devices before it, the television is beginning to make the leap from the analog to the digital world. Unlike many of those devices, however, TV has been making the leap in a series of agonizingly slow steps. In this section, we discuss how this transition might affect your choices in the video world. We talk also about the various kinds of TVs you can buy.

The conversion from analog to digital and old-style TV to next-generation TV comes into play in many places:

✔ The encoding of the programming signal itself, whether it goes onto a DVD or over a cable to get to your home theater

    ✔ The transmission (or production) path that the signal takes in getting to your house

    ✔ The receiver — internal or external — that receives and decodes the signal for display

In the progression of standards and technical development, change is taking place along all three of these paths.

Understanding the old standard: The analog signal

The majority of television signals coming into homes are still analog. Analog TV signals reach homes through over-the-air broadcast TV, by traditional cable TV systems, and by satellite.

Making film into video

As if resolution and scan methods were not complex enough, you may run into something called *3:2 pulldown removal or correction,* or simply *3:2 pulldown.* This is a process that deals with the fact that an extra field (screen) image appears when the 24-frames-per-second films are transferred to 30 frames (or 60 fields) per second for TV. See, when you take 24 frames and make them fill a 60-field space, your system copies each field two or three times, in alternating sequence, to fill the 60 fields required. This creates *motion artifacts* that appear like jerky movements on the screen when you look closely.

What 3:2 pulldown does is remove that extra third field, so the original balance between frames is restored. You want a progressive-scan DVD player with great 3:2 pulldown removal. You can tell how good it is by looking at sharp lines on the screen, such as telephone wires or

porch railings. Many high-definition TVs have built-in 3:2 pulldown systems as well, in case your DVD player can't do this for you.

With the advent of the Blu-ray disc player and the latest generations of high-definition TVs, you can now play movies in your home theater at their native 24 fps rate. That's because Blu-ray isn't tied to the legacy 30 frames per second rate of TV. The system includes a special 24 frames per second film mode, and many newer 1080p HDTVs can support this mode, which is called *1080p24.* If your TV and Blu-ray disc player support this mode (and the film you're watching was thus recorded and encoded onto disc), you'll be set for a great movie-watching experience without any of the film-to-video issues that the rest of us have been dealing with for decades! Lucky you!

In North America, an analog system known as NTSC (National Television Standards Committee) has been in place for decades. (The standard is more than 60 years old, having been developed in the 1940s!) In fact, it hasn't been changed or updated since the advent of color television in the 1960s. Although this system is capable of producing a surprisingly good picture under ideal circumstances, its analog nature makes it susceptible to various kinds of interference and signal degradation. Consequently, the picture can be downright awful by the time it gets to your television, which is why the TV world is slowly turning digital.

Analog television displays a maximum of 480 scan lines (525 total, but you can't see them all because some are used for things such as closed captioning), displays 30 frames (60 fields) per second, and is an interlaced system. See "Learning to Talk Videoese," earlier in this chapter, for explanations of these specs.

Just as the NTSC standard is common in North America (and Japan), a couple of other standards — known as PAL and SECAM — are common in other parts of the world. Unless you have a special TV designed for the purpose, you can't tune in to PAL broadcasts with an NTSC TV or NTSC with a PAL TV. This is one reason why you can't buy videotapes in many parts of the world and use them in the United States.

Anticipating the rise of digital TV

The move from analog to digital is well afoot. Millions of homes have some form of digital TV, but the conversion from analog to digital is still an evolving process. The key concept behind any kind of digital TV is that the audio and video programming is converted from an analog signal into a series of digital bits (a whole lot of ones and zeros). The primary technology behind any kind of digital TV (at least in the United States and Canada — other countries have their own variant of digital TV) is something called *MPEG* (Motion Picture Experts Group).

Several video and audio compression and digitization standards are based on MPEG. Most are named by adding a number to the end of *MPEG*. The MPEG-2 standard is by far the most common in the video world, with MPEG-4 coming on strong. (Another, older standard, MPEG-1, is also supported by DVDs and is used for VideoCD, which is more common outside the United States.)

The digital television (cable or satellite) signal and DVDs that most people receive today use MPEG-2 as their encoding to digitally transport or store standard analog NTSC signals. This is an important fact to repeat: Often, when you use a digital TV system (such as a DSS satellite service like DIRECTV) or a prerecorded digital source (such as a DVD), you get an analog signal that has been transmitted or stored digitally. The signal itself — the program that goes into your TV — is often still analog. Digital over digital is our nirvana, and it will soon be the law of the land as analog TV gets turned off in 2009, as we discuss shortly.

As you might have suspected, high-definition TV — which is becoming much more widely available, but which still makes up only a portion of the total TV landscape — is digital all the way.

Even though the video signal coming out of a DVD player is NTSC (an interlaced format, as we mentioned previously), some DVD players can convert this into a progressive-scan version of NTSC, which you can use if you have a progressive-scan TV.

When this digitized signal gets to your house (over a digital cable system, a Direct Broadcast Satellite system, or on a DVD), a set-top box, satellite receiver, or DVD player converts the signal back to analog NTSC TV, which your TV understands and can display. This digital transmission signal coming into your house usually looks and sounds better than an analog one because the digital transmission path is cleaner and isn't susceptible to the interference that usually messes up analog signals. The same is true of DVD versus analog sources, such as laser discs and VCR tapes. When it comes to TV, digital is just about always better.

You can get better-quality analog content on DVD, and higher-quality DVDs are available. For instance, you might run across Superbit DVD, which is a Sony system for superencoding (using more digital bits and bytes to store) DVD content. Superbit DVD follows the existing DVD format, so you don't need a special player to play a Superbit DVD. These discs simply use storage space that's normally taken up by fancy on-screen menus and extra features (such as movie trailers and outtakes) to store more encoding (about double the bits) for the movie signal itself. The result is a more stunning picture.

Now that Blu-ray disc players are on the market, you can get disc-based digital high-definition sources for your home theater. We talk about these new disc formats in Chapter 6.

The real takeaway we want you to understand here is that many things that are called "digital" — like most (but not all) digital cable, digital satellite TV services, and regular DVDs (that is, DVDs that aren't using the new Blu-ray or HD-DVD formats) — provide you with a nice digital picture that *is not high-definition TV.* These digital video signals are usually just the same resolution as the older analog TV signal — they're simply stored and/or transmitted by digital systems. There's nothing wrong with these digital systems (they're great, in fact!), but we mention this because we have run into many people who think that digital cable or digital satellite or DVD is the same thing as HDTV, and that's just not true.

Looking toward the next generation of digital TV

Most of today's digital television isn't all it can be. Several years ago, the FCC (Federal Communications Commission, the controlling regulatory authority for broadcasters, cable companies, and telephone companies in the United States) brought together a big bunch of television industry folks. After a long, painful, and contentious process, the group came up with a new generation of digital TV. This new system goes by the catchy name ATSC (Advanced Television Standards Committee) and follows a bunch of new, higher-definition television standards.

On February 19, 2009, the FCC and the U.S. Congress have mandated that all broadcast (that is to say, over-the-air) television stations turn off their old analog broadcasting equipment and begin broadcasting only in digital ATSC format. This doesn't mean that *standard definition* television is going away — it simply means that all broadcasts will be digital, even if the original source material was analog, standard definition NTSC. This *DTV transition* also means that anyone who uses an antenna to pick up their TV signals will need to have a digital ATSC receiver (either built into their TV or in a separate, standalone device). We talk about the DTV transition and its impact on your TV buying and using needs in Chapter 13.

Introducing ATSC

ATSC uses digital video signals (not analog ones) transmitted using digital technologies and played on TVs set up to display these digital signals. Even the connection to the TV itself is digital. "It's digital all the way, baby," as sportscaster Dick Vitale would say. (Did we mention we're Duke Blue Devils fans, too? Nothing better than watching Duke basketball in high definition on the big screen!)

Many people call ATSC *digital TV* or *DTV*. We do, too, sometimes, but we're going to stick with the name ATSC in this discussion to help keep the difference between ATSC and other digital television services (such as digital cable or digital satellite TV) distinct. Aren't we user-friendly?

Even though ATSC is all digital, all the time, TVs designed for ATSC can also connect to good old analog NTSC systems. And some of the stuff coming in over an ATSC system *is* NTSC. For example, most commercials will probably continue to be taped using NTSC systems for quite some time, and the vast majority of reruns will be NTSC as well (although these NTSC signals will be carried digitally over the ATSC system).

ATSC television standards are different from the digital cable or satellite TV we discuss in the preceding section. To view them in all their glory (and we've seen enough of high-definition television to tell you that it is indeed glorious), you need to buy a newer, fancier, better, more expensive TV — an HDTV.

Exploring HDTV

When we talk about new ATSC-capable televisions, we're talking a whole new ballgame (or at least a whole new way to watch a ballgame). It takes only a glance to see the striking difference between older NTSC displays and the new ATSC ones.

ATSC signals can be divided into different groups, depending on the signal's resolution and the scanning method (which we discuss in the beginning of this chapter). They are further divided into

- **SDTV (standard-definition television):** These signals are about the same or a little better than NTSC. *Note:* A related category here is *EDTV,* or enhanced-definition television, which is essentially a widescreen version of NTSC.

- **HDTV (high-definition television):** HDTV has truly spectacular — dare we say filmlike? — picture quality.

Within the ATSC standard are eighteen SDTV, EDTV, and HDTV variations, but you're most likely to see just six, as shown in Table 4-1.

Table 4-1		Common Digital-TV Variants	
Name	*Resolution*	*Scanning Method*	*Quality*
480i	640 x 480	Interlaced	Standard definition (SDTV); same as NTSC
480p	640 x 480 (normal)	Progressive	Standard definition (SDTV)
480p	720 x 480 (wide-screen)	Progressive	Enhanced definition (EDTV)
720p	1280 x 720	Progressive	High definition (HDTV)
1080i	1920 x 1080	Interlaced	High definition (HDTV)
1080p	1920 x 1080	Progressive	High definition (HDTV)

You sharp readers will probably note that we threw in an extra format that's not currently available in any digital TV broadcast (or cable system or satellite system) but which may become available some day in the future. That's the final one — 1080p — which has become something of a holy grail amongst TV manufacturers even though no 1080p signals are available to display on such a set. 1080p is simply a progressive-scan variant of 1080i. The only movie/video programming source of 1080p today is the Blu-ray disc. Certain video games on the new Microsoft Xbox 360 and Sony PlayStation 3 may support it as well, but there are no, we repeat, *no* TV signals today or in the near future that will be 1080p. We mention it for the sake of completeness and because you'll hear it all the time when you go shopping. We get into 1080p in more detail in the chapters in which we talk about TVs and displays (Chapters 13 and 14, to be precise).

From the breaking news department: Both major satellite TV providers (DIRECTV and DISH Network) announced in August 2008 (as we were going to print) that they will indeed begin broadcasting *some* of their HDTV programming in 1080p. Specifically, both networks will be broadcasting pay-per-view (PPV) movies in 1080p; neither will broadcast their normal HDTV channels in the format yet. We haven't seen this new programming yet, but we are very much looking forward to checking it out.

To take advantage of *all* the benefits of digital TV, you need a high-definition-capable television and a TV *tuner* that can decode the ATSC signal. That tuner can be inside the display (just as most TVs have analog NTSC tuners), it can be in a separate tuner component, or it can even come inside a satellite TV receiver or cable set-top box.

Traditional televisions don't have the internal circuitry to decode digital TV signals, and they generally don't have screens that can display high-definition ATSC pictures in all their glory. (And HDTV is the big deal in this story — we focus our discussion on HDTV rather than SDTV.)

Traditional TVs aren't even the right shape. The *aspect ratio* (the ratio of screen width to height) of HDTV signals is wider than that of NTSC signals. NTSC is 4:3; HDTV is 16:9. Figure 4-2 shows the difference in aspect ratios. The HDTV screen has an aspect ratio like the elongated screens in movie theaters. (You may have already been exposed to this aspect ratio because many movie DVDs today allow for this sort of viewing as an option. See the sidebar, "Wide, wider, widest: Aspect ratios," later in this chapter.)

A lot of people see 4:3 and 16:9, do the math quickly in their heads, and think they are the same thing. It's confusing because 4 and 3 are the square roots of 16 and 9. The actual math used to determine the ratio of screen width to screen height is 16 *divided* by 9 (which rounds out to 1.78) and 4 *divided* by 3 (which is 1.33). So for a given display height, a 16:9 screen is about 34 percent wider than a 4:3 screen.

Figure 4-2:
An HDTV
screen is
much wider
than today's
NTSC
screen.

| 4:3 / 1.33:1
Standard TV and
older movies | 16:9 / 1.78:1
US digital TV
(HDTV) | 1.85:1
Standard widescreen | 2.35:1
Anamorphic widescreen
(Panavision or Cinemascope) |

HDTV-capable TV sets, which became available at the end of 1998, are more expensive than traditional sets. However, prices have come down significantly. Just three or four years ago, HDTVs often cost more than $2,000, but now you can get one for $500 or less — you can even get a good-sized (32-inch) flat-panel LCD HDTV for about $500.

We talk a lot more about HDTVs in Chapters 13 and 14.

After the switch to digital TV is complete, you don't have to pitch your old TVs. Special, separate digital TV tuners (much like set-top boxes used for older TVs on cable networks) enable you to watch DTV programming on older TVs. Of course, the picture quality and resolution won't be as high as it would be with a new digital set, and you might not have a widescreen (16:9) aspect ratio, but you'll see (at today's resolutions and quality) the programming coming in over tomorrow's digital networks. Again, we talk about these converters in more detail in Chapter 13.

Wide, wider, widest: Aspect ratios

Aspect ratios are one of the more confusing parts of video, although they used to be simple. That's because television and movie content was all about the same size, 4:3 (also known as 1.33:1, meaning that the picture is 1.33 times as long as it is high). The Academy (as in, "I'd like to thank the Academy") Standard before 1952 was 1.37:1, so there was virtually no problem showing movies on TV.

However, as TV began to cut into Hollywood's take at the theater, the quest was on to

differentiate theater offerings in ways that could not be seen on TV. Thus, innovations such as widescreen film, Technicolor, and even 3-D were born.

Widescreen film was one of the innovations that survived and has since dominated the cinema. Today, you tend to find films in one of two widescreen aspect ratios:

✔ Academy Standard (or Flat), which has an aspect ratio of 1.85:1.

✔ Anamorphic Scope (or Scope), which has an aspect ratio of 2.35:1. Scope is also called Panavision or CinemaScope.

HDTV is specified at a 16:9, or 1.78:1, aspect ratio.

If your television isn't widescreen and you want to watch a widescreen film, you have a problem. And the industry powers that be have come up with two solutions (other than "go out and buy a widescreen display").

The most common approach in the past has been what's called *Pan and Scan.* For each frame of a film, a decision is made as to what constitutes the action area. That part of the film frame is retained, and the rest is lost. What's left is usually a fraction of the main frame, sometimes as little as 65 percent of it, and this can often leave out the best parts of a picture. Imagine some of the scenes from *Gunfight at OK Corral* with the two gunslingers at each end of the picture. One of the gunfighters would have to go off the screen in Pan and Scan.

The second (and growing more popular) approach is to display the original full image on the TV set without filling the whole screen. When watching content formatted for a wide-screen TV (1.85:1, 2.35:1, and so on), you see black bars at the top and bottom of the image. This technique is known as *letterboxing* (after the effect of seeing an image through an open mail slot in a door). Conversely, when watching content formatted for TV (4:3) on a widescreen TV, you see black bars on the left and right of the images. This is known as *windowboxing.*

An obvious problem with viewing widescreen images on a normal 4:3 TV is that the image does not use all 480 scanning lines of the screen. Some of those 480 lines get used just to draw black bars instead of drawing video you actually watch. (Some 4:3 TVs use a technique called *anamorphic squeeze* to eliminate this issue.) This yields lower resolution, something that anamorphic formats attempt to resolve. Also known as *16:9 Enhanced, Widescreen Enhanced,* or *Enhanced for 16:9 Televisions,* anamorphic presentation squeezes the image horizontally until the full 4:3 frame is filled. If you look at an anamorphic picture on a 4:3 screen, the picture appears somewhat distorted because everything is compressed, but the full 480 lines of content are retained. Luckily, when you tell your DVD player you have a 4:3 screen, it puts the anamorphic image back into a let-terbox. When played through a 16:9 player, the original width is presented, while maintaining the full 480 vertical lines of resolution.

Most DVDs have both a Pan and Scan and a widescreen format (either letterboxed or ana-morphic) on a DVD. Because including both versions creates an added expense to the studios, some DVDs ship with just one format onboard, and some titles actually have different formats on different discs. Be sure to check before you buy a disc if this is important to you.

As an interesting note, there are a few examples (Pixar's *Finding Nemo* being the most famous) where movie producers have specially modified their content to have different widescreen and 4:3 versions — so the folks with 4:3 displays aren't robbed of part of the image while still filling their screens.

Part II

Getting Video and Music into Your Theater: Source Devices

The 5th Wave   By Rich Tennant

You kidding!!! True home theater experience?! Me can't wait, pull lever, open screen!

In this part . . .

Part II builds on the basics with more detailed coverage of all the things that you might want to drive your home theater — the *source devices* that feed audio and video into your system.

We start at the, er, source of 21st-century entertainment — audio sources. These range from the venerable AM/FM tuners up to the fanciest MP3 players. After that, it's on to the video realm, where we talk about DVDs, VCRs, and PVRs (personal video recorders), and even how you can bore your neighbors with home movies. Yawn!

Then we discuss sources from outside your home — cable, broadcast TV, satellite, and even new services that offer you video on demand and other network-based content.

Then comes the fun stuff — the gaming systems. Whether your heart is in Xbox 360, Nintendo Wii, or Sony Playstation 3, you'll want to know how to set these up — even if you don't have kids. PCs are on tap next, and we help you understand how to take advantage of all the audio and video sources that the Internet has to offer and how to get them into your home theater system. We help you understand how to download movies (legally) off the Internet to watch whenever you want to and how to record those episodes of *The Office* that you keep missing.

We close this part with the cool component in your home theater — content accessed over the Internet. Whether it's watching YouTube videos or TV shows you downloaded — either via iTunes or with the help of some more specialized device such as Vudu — we'll help you make your home theater Internet savvy.

Chapter 5

Treating Your Ears to Music

. . . .

. . . .

A home theater is about more than just movies and TV. Most people spend as much money on the audio side of their home theaters as they do on their video equipment.

In this chapter, we discuss the components you might add to a home theater system for listening to prerecorded music and audio broadcasts (what we used to call *radio* back in the old days — but it's more than just AM/FM now).

Checking Out Your CD Player Options

Since the CD format debuted in the 1980s, tens of billions of CDs have been pressed. So it goes without saying that you need a CD player in your home theater, right? Well, actually, that was a trick question.

Although you *definitely* want your home theater to have a device that can play CDs, you may not need (or want) a traditional CD player in your system. Your DVD player, which we think you absolutely must have in your home theater, can do double duty as your system's CD player. You can also play CDs on the game consoles we talk about in Chapter 8, or you can use a home theater–ready PC, which we discuss in Chapter 9.

Despite this, you might want a standalone CD player (instead of using another device to play your CDs) for the following reasons:

- ✔ **You are shooting for the highest-quality CD reproduction:** If you're an audiophile, you might want to spend a considerable chunk of cash on a fancy, no-holds-barred, top-of-the-line CD player that can eke that last bit of musical fidelity out of a disc. If so, check out companies such as Arcam, Naim, and Rega, which make fancy and expensive ($1,000 and up) CD players.

- ✔ **You want special CD features:** Some people buy jukebox CD players that can hold hundreds of CDs (so they never need to load a new disc after the hours-long initial setup). Others want a CD player that can also burn (create) CDs. Keep in mind that these features are percolating over into the DVD world as well, but for now, the CD versions of these devices are much cheaper.

- ✔ **You are creating a multizone system:** In a multizone system (which we discuss in Chapter 10), you can listen to different source components in different rooms. For example, you can watch a movie on the DVD player in the home theater while the kids listen to a CD in the kitchen. You can't do that if the DVD player is your only CD player.

These three reasons are all perfectly valid — for some people. Don't let them scare you into buying a CD player. Today's DVD players do a great job of playing back CDs, so skipping over the standalone CD player is a good way to save a few bucks.

All Blu-ray disc players currently on the market are capable of playing back CDs (although the first few models on the market back in 2006 couldn't). So if you have (or are considering purchasing) a Blu-ray player, you probably don't need a CD player.

Choosing a CD Player

So you know you want a standalone CD player, but which one? If you already have a CD player, go ahead and use it. The following list highlights some things you might want to look for if you choose to buy a CD player (or aren't sure about the one you have):

- ✔ **Digital outputs:** You can often get better sound out of a CD player if you connect it to your receiver via a digital connection instead of an analog one. On the back of most CD players, you can find one (or both) of two kinds of digital outputs — optical and coaxial — which are equal in quality. (We discuss these in Chapter 16.) The key thing to consider, however, is finding out what kind of inputs you have on your receiver and buying your CD player accordingly.

✔ **The ability to play CD-Rs, CD-RWs, WMAs, and MP3s:** If you're into burning your own CDs or like to listen to others' homemade CDs, make sure the player you buy has these buzzwords on the box. Otherwise, you won't be able to listen to those homemade discs.

✔ **Multidisc capability:** If you like to load up the CD player with a bunch of CDs, consider a CD changer, which usually holds five to ten discs, or a CD jukebox that can hold hundreds.

✔ **Remote control:** Many manufacturers have special connectors that can go between their components (such as a CD player and a receiver) to facilitate controlling everything from a single remote control. For example, with Sony's BRAVIA-Link, a Sony receiver and remote can control a whole bunch of different Sony devices. As you shop for a CD player, keep your receiver in mind, but if you're set on, say, a Sony CD player and a Pioneer receiver, don't let the remote options hold you back. It's very easy to get a universal remote control that can operate gear from different vendors.

In addition, always look for some basic quality measures when you're choosing gear. For example, does the CD tray open and close smoothly? Can you read the display from across the room? Before you buy, always try to test drive gear in the showroom or your home (if you're shopping at the high end).

The New Kids on the Block —
SACD and DVD-A

The CD is overwhelmingly the most common source of prerecorded music in a disc format, but around the turn of the millennium, two new formats hit the streets — SACD (Super Audio Compact Disc) and the DVD-Audio disc.

Both formats are designed to sound better than a CD while maintaining that familiar, 12cm (quick — grab that metric converter) disc format. Although you may remember the marketing tag line, "Perfect sound, forever," from when CDs debuted, SACD and DVD-A have managed to improve upon the now old-fashioned CD:

✔ **Sampling:** SACD uses very small sample sizes but records them 64 times more often than regular CDs. The DVD-Audio system uses a lower sampling rate (still two or more times faster than CD) but a much larger sample (20 bits or more, compared with 16 for CDs). Either way, you get higher audio frequencies with less noise and thus greater *dynamic range* (the difference between the quietest and loudest musical passages on the disc).

✔ **Multichannel format:** Because the discs can hold more data than the older CD format, record companies can release DVD-Audio and SACD discs in both traditional 2-channel (stereo) and home theater–friendly 5.1-channel formats (with five channels of surround sound and a subwoofer channel). Some folks don't particularly like the surround sound for music; they say it makes sense only for movies, where things are happening all around you. But lots of others, us included, like surround sound for at least some of the music we listen to.

Some of the early SACD players didn't support the multichannel format, though all the current models we know of do. Also, not all SACD or DVD-Audio discs are recorded in surround-sound format.

Both the SACD and the DVD-A have been tested by the experts, measured by the measurers, and reviewed by the reviewers, and the consensus is that both sound better than CD. How much better is a matter of great debate, but in a high-quality system, with a good recording, you'll probably be happy to have one of these systems. Before you buy, though, keep three things in mind:

✔ **You can't find much material in either of these formats . . . and you may never be able to.** Chances are, you can't buy all your favorites in these formats. A lot of classic recordings have been reissued in one or the other format, but the number is still small compared to all the music out there. For the most part, these formats have become niche players, and small record labels focused on audio enthusiasts are the primary folks still putting out discs in these formats.

✔ **Not all players can play both formats.** Unless you are committed to only one or the other format (SACD or DVD-A), make sure you choose a "universal" player that can play CD, DVD, SACD, and DVD-A. Pay attention because some manufacturers (notably Sony, who was the primary technical supporter of SACD) don't make many (or even any) universal players.

Most SACD players and DVD-Audio players *do* play regular CDs and regular DVDs, which is nice. Look for ones that can play MP3s, CD-Rs, and CD-RWs as well, so that you can play homemade CDs, too.

✔ **Because of copy-protection concerns, you might not be able to connect your DVD-Audio or SACD player to your receiver *digitally*.** This means that all that high-resolution audio must travel to your receiver in the analog domain, making the audio more susceptible to picking up noises or generally degrading during its trip to your ears. To make matters worse, multichannel systems require six of these analog cables. Ugh. Some manufacturers of disc players and receivers have implemented a version of the HDMI cabling system (see Chapter 16 for more on HDMI) that *will* let you make a digital connection — you'll need to carefully check the documentation of both your disc player and your receiver to see if this will work for you.

Many home theater receivers have only a single set of multichannel audio inputs. So if you use them to connect an SACD/DVD-A player, they won't be available for other multichannel audio inputs (such as an external surround-sound decoder or a DVD or Blu-ray player with a built-in surround-sound decoder). Keep that in mind as you're shopping around.

Neither SACD nor DVD-Audio have taken off in the marketplace. Both formats sound great, but many folks have begun to move toward online music (such as Apple's iTunes Music Store) and computer-based audio and away from these higher-quality, disc-based audio formats. We think that you can't go wrong with a nice universal disc player that handles both formats, but unless you're really an audiophile and have (or plan to buy) a bunch of discs in these formats, you don't have to spend too much time worrying about SACD or DVD-Audio. The bottom line: Get a universal player if the DVD player you're shopping for includes this functionality, but don't go out of your way for one of these formats unless you're sure you're going to be using it.

Many SACD discs, like ABKO Records's remastered editions of the classic 1960s Rolling Stones CDs, are *dual layer.* This means there is a layer of CD data *and* a layer of SACD data on the same disc, so you can play the same disc in your car and in your home theater SACD player. You can't do that with a DVD-Audio disc today — at least not until someone comes up with dual-layer DVD-A discs. However, discs known as *DualDiscs* (www. dualdisc.com) include a CD on one side and a DVD on the other. Note that this isn't DVD-Audio but rather a regular DVD that can include video and even a surround-sound mix of the record but isn't in the higher-resolution DVD-Audio format.

Moving Computer Audio into Your Home Theater

The really big trend in audio these days (for the past several years, in fact) is computer-based audio files. At the simplest level, these files are just like any other file on your computer, except they contain digitally encoded music files that you can play back on your computer, on a portable device, or in your home theater.

MP3 is the most common format for digitally storing music and other audio files on a computer or computer-like device, but it's not the only format out there. A few others, such as Microsoft's Windows Media (WMA) and Advanced Audio Codec (or AAC, used by Apple's iTunes Music Store), are also incredibly common — as are the formats most often used for music *purchased* on the Internet.

We use the term *MP3* to refer to online music because it's still the most common music format, but online music files may be encoded using other file formats (as we discuss throughout the chapter).

MP3 mania has exploded worldwide over the past few years, initially because online services such as Napster (now dead as a file-sharing program but reborn as an online music store — www.napster.com) and KaZaa (www.kazaa.com) have enabled people to share and download songs converted from CDs to the MP3 format. MP3 has retained its popularity because its small file size has made it an attractive system for carrying music around on computer-like portable audio players, such as our (and everybody's!) current favorite, Apple's iPod (www.apple.com/ipod), or Microsoft's Zune (www.zune.com).

Lots of people are moving their MP3 files beyond the PC and the portable player and are beginning to find ways to incorporate MP3 music into the home theater. This makes a lot of sense to us — why not listen to all your MP3s on the highest-quality audio system in the house?

Learning about digital audio file types

As we mention in the preceding section, MP3 is not the only game in town when it comes to digital audio file formats — other formats, such as AAC and WMA, are becoming increasingly popular due to their use in online music stores.

These audio formats have two main categories (often called *codecs* — from their function, which is to *c*ompress and *dec*ompress music into digital files). The first category is *lossless* codecs. This means that all the musical information that forms the basis of the audio file is preserved when the file is compressed and stored on the computer. Lossless codecs provide the highest audio fidelity, but the files they create are relatively large, which means that you can fit fewer songs on a computer hard drive or music server.

On the other hand, the second category, *lossy* codecs, discard some part of the musical information to make the files smaller — for faster downloads on the Internet or to cram more music on a given size of computer storage device. These lossy codecs use sophisticated models of the human ear (and how it hears sounds) to throw away bits of musical information that are *less important* when you are listening to the music. You probably won't notice the difference when listening casually, but many people (especially folks with good hearing!) can hear a difference when a lossy and lossless version of the same music are played back over a high-quality home theater audio system.

The most common lossless codecs you'll run across are as follows:

✓ **Windows Media Lossless:** Part of Microsoft Windows Media Player 9 and 10, this codec is built into the Windows Media Player software and is supported by some of the media adapter systems we discuss in Chapter 10.

✓ **Apple Lossless:** Included with iTunes software, Apple's Lossless Encoder is Apple's competitor to Windows Media Lossless.

✓ **Free Lossless Audio Codec (FLAC):** Free Lossless Audio Codec is, as its name implies, a lossless codec that's free. It's part of an open-source initiative; you can find out more at `http://flac.sourceforge.net`. A few of the audio players we discuss in Chapter 10 are beginning to support the FLAC codec, including the Sonos Digital Music System and the Slim Devices Squeezebox.

Among the most popular lossy codecs are the following:

✓ **MP3:** MPEG-1 (Motion Picture Experts Group 1) Audio Layer 3 is the full name of the most common digital music format. MP3 audio files are the ones commonly traded (usually illegally) on the Net, and they are the most common digital music codec used on PCs and digital music systems in a wireless network.

A limited number of systems and software applications also support the more advanced *mp3PRO* codec, which adds a technology called *SBR* (Spectral Band Replication) to improve the sound quality over standard MP3-encoded music files.

✓ **WMA:** Windows Media Audio is the standard audio format used by Windows Media Player and compatible hardware. A lossless version of WMA (discussed previously) does exist, but most WMA files use a lossy compression system.

✓ **AAC:** Advanced Audio Codec is the format used by Apple Computer's popular iTunes Music Store and is the default codec for music encoded using the iTunes application. Like WMA, AAC files are lossy (though within Apple's iTunes system there is a lossless codec as well, called Apple Lossless).

✓ **Ogg Vorbis:** Another free codec is Ogg Vorbis (`www.vorbis.com`). Ogg Vorbis is designed to be free from the licensing fees that software and hardware companies must pay for other codecs such as MP3, and also provides improved sound quality compared to other lossy codecs.

Your choice of codec will depend on several things:

✔ **Where you get your music:** If you buy digital music at an online music store, you're stuck with the codec it uses. Most stores use WMA or AAC and not MP3 because these formats allow the record companies to stick *DRM* (digital rights management) software into the music files, which keeps buyers from sharing this music on the Internet. If you create your own music from CDs at home, your choice will be influenced by the software you use.

✔ **The devices you use to play your music in your home theater:** As we discuss in Chapter 10, you can use a large number of devices (usually called *media players* or *adapters*) to get music from a computer into your home theater. Most of these devices support only a limited number of codecs, so you have to match the codec you use to create and store digital music with those supported by your media player.

✔ **Personal preference:** Many folks simply find that they prefer a lossless codec or a codec such as AAC (which is newer and takes advantage of advances in codec technology) to MP3. We recommend that you figure out the first two criteria, and then try out a few different codecs and see whether you can tell a difference.

We talk in great detail about the sources for digital music and also about the devices that you can use to integrate this music into your home theater in Chapter 10. The Media Center PCs we discuss in Chapter 9 are also a great way to get digital audio into your home theater.

Getting your hands on MP3s

We bet you've heard a lot about MP3 music, but where do all these MP3s come from, anyway? Is there an MP3 fairy out there who magically dumps them on the hard drives of good girls and boys?

Well, in fact, there used to be something pretty similar. Napster (which is now gone, due to legal actions) and other file-sharing services allowed people to put their music collections online and share them with the world. Of course, record companies weren't all that supportive of this grassroots music revolution, so most of these services soon got sued out of existence.

Today, you can get your own MP3 files (and notice we call them *files,* because they're just that — computer data files on a hard drive) in two legal ways:

- **Rip your own:** You can convert your CDs to MP3s on your computer (this process is called *ripping*). To do this, you need a PC with a CD or DVD drive (which we bet you already have) and an MP3 program. Our favorite programs are MUSICMATCH Jukebox for Windows (`www.musicmatch.com`) and iTunes for the Mac and Windows (`www.apple.com/itunes`).

- **Download legally:** These days, it's really easy to find legal places to download the most popular music on MP3 (or in AAC or WMA formats). Some of our favorite online music stores include Apple's iTunes Music Store (available within Apple's iTunes software or at `www.apple.com/itunes/`) and Rhapsody (`www.rhapsody.com`). We talk about a bunch of these stores in Chapter 10.

Old-School Jams — Turntables

For most of the world, the LP has unfortunately gone the way of the dodo. But although LPs are far from the public eye, they've never really gone away. Many artists still release LP versions of their new records, and a handful of small manufacturers (and a few big ones) continue to crank out turntables.

In fact, the turntable has become hip again in some circles. And many audiophiles have long felt that LPs (at least when played on super-high-quality turntables) sound better than CDs.

Buying a turntable isn't as simple as buying a CD, a DVD-A, or an SACD player. It's a much more subjective process. In the digital world, it's easy to keep a checklist of features in mind, such as digital output or MP3 CD support. But when you start shopping for turntables, you're getting into a whole different world. Some esoteric stuff is out there, such as vacuum hold-down systems (which suck the record flat on the platter to alleviate warps), as well as what we call "religious wars" between proponents of different turntable design philosophies. Having said that, here are a few things to consider when buying a turntable:

- **Belt drive or direct drive:** The platter (the thing that the record sits and spins around on) can be spun in two ways. There are pros and cons for each.

  - **Belt drive:** In this setup, the motor is separated from the platter and spindle and turned by a rubber belt that runs around the outside of the platter. A belt drive tends to isolate the rest of the turntable from any vibrations coming from the motor (vibrations that the stylus or needle could pick up and transmit to the receiver and to your ears). On the downside, a belt drive tends to be less accurate than a direct drive in its playback speed, which can lead to changes in the pitch of your music.

- **Direct drive:** An electric motor is directly attached to the spindle (the small cylinder that the platter rests upon). Direct drive turntables tend to be a bit more constant in their speed, so the turntable is more likely to turn $33\frac{1}{3}$ times per minute without any speed variations (such variations tend to make your music sound warbly). Some folks, however, feel that direct drive turntables are more susceptible to vibrations (both external, such as footsteps, and internal, such as the vibrations of the motor itself).

✔ **Suspended or unsuspended:** Vibrations are a big deal with a turntable because the stylus dragging through the grooves of the LP can pick up extraneous vibrations (such as those caused by your four-year-old daughter doing a particularly bouncy dance while listening to music) and transmit them along with your music. Some turntables have elaborate suspension systems designed to isolate the platter (and therefore the record) from these vibrations, whereas others rely on the user to isolate the *entire* turntable (by placing the whole thing on a very sturdy rack, for example).

✔ **Automatic, semiautomatic, or manual:** An automatic turntable lets you put a record on the platter, push a button, and listen. The turntable itself moves the tone arm over the record, drops it down before the first song, and then lifts it up and returns it to the resting position when the side of the record is finished. High-end audiophiles *hate* these because they — well, we don't know why they hate them so much, though we guess they just love to drop that needle down. Manual turntables require you to manually move the tone arm over the record and then lower it onto and off the record. Semiautomatics do half your work for you — you lower the stylus onto the record, but when the record side is finished playing, the turntable lifts the tone arm and stylus up off the record automatically so you don't have to hear that repeating *fpppt fpppt fpppt* sound as the stylus does an endless loop at the end of the record.

In our opinion, good turntables can have any of the attributes we just mentioned. We've heard good automatic turntables and good manuals, good belt drives and good direct drives, and so on. If you're buying a turntable, think about your needs. Do you have a lot of records that you're going to play all the time? If so, invest $500 to $1,000 dollars in a nice turntable from a company such as Rega (www.rega.co.uk) or Pro-Ject (www.project-audio.com). Have just a couple of old favorites you can't get on CD? Check out some of the $150 to $200 models from Sony or Denon. Want to be a DJ (and do some scratching like the late, great Jam Master Jay)? Check out Panasonic's Technics brand of DJ turntables.

Whatever you do, don't leave a turntable out of the equation if you have a few boxes of records in the closet.

Catching up with cassettes

If you need a cassette deck because you have a ton of tapes filling shoeboxes in your closet, or because you want to make tapes for playing back in the car or in a portable headset, here are a few things you should look for:

✔ **Single or dual well:** If you think you might end up dubbing (or making copies of) a lot of cassettes, you need a *dual-well* tape deck that has this capability. If you plan to record only the radio or your own CDs, you can save money by getting yourself a single-well deck.

✔ **Noise reduction:** Before Dolby Labs became famous for its surround-sound standards (such as Dolby Digital), millions of audiophiles knew the company for its Cassette Noise Reduction standards. These standards (which go by the names Dolby B, C, and S) are electronic processes designed to increase the sound quality of cassettes by decreasing noise (such as tape hiss — the sound you can hear when quiet passages are playing). The general rule for these systems is that the higher the name of the system, alphabetically, the better (so S is best, then C, then B). The key thing to keep in mind is that, for the best sound quality, you need to play tapes back on a deck that supports the system with which the tape was recorded. If you record with Dolby C, you need to play your tape on a Dolby C deck. Dolby S is a slight exception to this

rule; tapes recorded with this system can be played back on Dolby B decks with some of the benefits of S intact.

✔ **Number of heads:** Most tape decks have two heads (the heads are the electromagnetic devices that read and write audio signals onto the tape itself). The two-head design uses the same head for both playing back recorded music and for recording music on the tape (the other head is used for erasing the tape when you are recording). Fancier tape decks have a three-head design, which has separate playback and record heads. Because each head is used for only one function, each head can be designed for optimal functionality for its purpose.

✔ **Number of motors:** A tape is moved over the heads by means of a pair of spindles (which fit in the little wheels on the cassette) and — more importantly — by a pair of devices called a *capstan* and a *pinch roller*. The capstan and pinch roller are the essential devices that keep the tape moving over the heads at the correct speed, without any speed fluctuations. Inexpensive tape decks use a single electric motor and a belt (like a radiator fan belt in a car) for this function, while higher-quality decks have a motor for each of the spindles and a third for the capstan/pinch roller combo.

Because LPs are much less popular than they used to be, many new A/V receivers don't have the proper inputs to connect a turntable. So before you plunk down some cash on a new turntable, check to see whether your receiver even has a turntable connection (usually labeled "phono"). If it doesn't, you can use an external *phono preamp*, which connects between the turntable and the receiver. You simply plug the cables from the turntable in to the phono preamp and then use a standard audio cable to connect the preamp to any open audio inputs on the receiver (most people use the ones labeled "aux"). Recoton (`www.recoton.com`) makes an inexpensive phono preamp for about $50, but you can buy more expensive (and better) preamps from some of the turntable manufacturers that we mention in this section. You can also build your own phono preamp from kits available online at places like `www.bottlehead.com`.

Tuning In to Radio

Sometimes, you just can't be bothered to put in a CD or an SACD or cue up an MP3 (not to mention pull out, clean off, and play a record). You know that couch potato lethargy we're talking about? If you're a music lover (and we bet you are), nothing allows you to enjoy music with absolutely no involvement like turning on your favorite radio station and vegging out.

Local radio

When putting together a home theater, you don't usually have to think about much when it comes to radio. Unless you're buying separate components, a radio tuner is built into your A/V receiver.

If you *do* buy separate components instead of an A/V receiver (sneak over to Chapter 10 if you don't know what we're talking about), you probably will have to buy a radio tuner and plug it in to your system as an audio source device, just as you plug a CD or DVD-audio player in to your system. AM/FM radio tuners usually cost about $150 to $500 (though, like any A/V component, you can buy high-end versions that cost ten times the average). Things to look for include the following:

- ✔ **AM and FM sensitivity:** Measured in the oh-so-familiar decibel femto-watt (dBf), this is a measurement of how well the tuner can pick up signals. The lower this number (it's usually in the range of 9 to 11 dBf), the better.

- ✔ **Adjustable selectivity:** Some tuners come with a switch on the front (or on the remote control) that lets you choose between wide and narrow selectivity. The wide mode gives you better reception and sound quality on powerful stations, whereas the narrow mode can tune in weak signals from distant stations while avoiding interference from stations on adjacent frequencies.

✔ **Antenna diversity:** Not a necessity, but some fancier tuners have *two* antenna inputs. You can manually or automatically have the tuner choose between the inputs when you're trying to pull in a radio station.

If you're lucky enough to live in an area with some good radio stations, you might want to invest in a high-quality tuner near the top of your price range.

Satellite radio

If you're like us, you live where there isn't a whole lot of programming you want to listen to. In that case, you might check out satellite radio, which offers a huge number of stations (each of the two satellite radio providers offer more than 100 channels) beamed to your house or car from a handful of geostationary satellites hovering above the equator. We find there's a ton more diversity and just plain interesting stuff coming across these space-based airwaves than we find on our local radio. Satellite radio services from XM Radio and Sirius require you to — gasp — *pay* for your radio (both start at $12.95 a month).

If you want to get into satellite radio, you need to first check out the Web sites of the two providers, www.xmradio.com and www.sirius.com, to see which one has the programming that you prefer. Then you need to get your hands on a satellite radio tuner (you can find a bunch of models listed on each company's Web page). The majority of these satellite tuners are designed for in-car use (because people tend to listen to the radio most often while they're driving), but you can find radios suitable for in-home (and home theater!) use from both providers.

If you want to put satellite radio into your home theater, you have a few choices:

✔ You can get a dockable tuner. You can put these tuners in your car and, when you get home, pull them out and plug them in to your A/V receiver via a simple docking station that provides power, an antenna connection, and the proper connectors to hook in to your receiver. This is usually the cheapest and most convenient approach if you're going to be in the car a lot but still want satellite radio in the house.

✔ You can buy a dedicated in-home satellite tuner that looks like any other piece of A/V gear and sits on your equipment rack along with your receiver and DVD player. These models (such as Polk Audio's XRt12 Reference Tuner — $299.99 list price, www.polkaudio.com) have bigger displays and higher-quality internal components for the best sound quality, but they aren't portable like dockable radios.

✔ You can buy an A/V receiver with a built-in or add-on satellite receiver. A growing number of A/V receivers (see Chapter 11 for the lowdown on these devices) have a built-in satellite receiver. Just add an antenna kit and a subscription and you're off to the races (or listening to Howard Stern if it's a Sirius radio!). A good example here is Denon's AVR-1708 (www.denon.com, $499.99), which includes a built-in XM radio receiver. You just need to add an inexpensive antenna kit. (This receiver even has an option for an iPod dock — it does it all!)

If you're using a dedicated indoor satellite tuner (or one inside your receiver) *and* you also want to listen to satellite radio in your car, you'll end up needing more than one subscription. Each tuner requires its own subscription. Luckily, the second subscription can be part of a package deal and will run you $6.99 per additional radio on either service.

These satellites are down by the equator, so no matter where you live in the United States, you need to be able to put the antenna in a south-facing window to pick up a good signal in your home.

A digital alternative to satellite: HD radio

Although satellite radio has a lot of fans, many folks have shied away from paying $13 a month just to listen to the radio. The traditional radio broadcasters have begun broadcasting with their own digital system, called *HD Radio* (www.hdradio.com), which is designed to offer similar "digital quality" advantages as satellite but without the monthly fee.

HD Radio doesn't have a fee, but it also doesn't have the continent-wide coverage of satellite radio. So if you're a road warrior who travels long distances by car, you might prefer satellite's ability to stay tuned in to a station no matter where you go.

HD Radio is, essentially, a second broadcast signal that a radio station can use to send digital broadcasts alongside their existing analog ones. HD Radio can be used by both AM and FM stations — the FM variant, like FM analog radio, is the higher quality one, with sound that is claimed to approach that of CDs.

Because of its digital nature, HD Radio is capable of sending a lot of additional data alongside the audio signal that's going out over the airwaves — so you can see more programming data (such as the name of the song and the artist) along with data streams such as traffic info and stock prices.

To get HD Radio into your home theater, you simply need to choose a home theater receiver capable of receiving HD Radio, such as Yamaha's RX-V863 (www.yamaha.com) or use a separate HD Radio receiver as an audio component connected to your existing home theater receiver. The HD Radio Web site has a listing of HD Radio-capable devices, as well as a station listing, so you can find out what HD Radio offers in your area.

We think that the coolest feature of HD Radio is the iTunes Tagging feature (http://www.hdradio.com/iTunes_Tagging/). If you hear a song that you like on HD Radio, some HD Radio receivers (those with iPod docks included) let you press a button (labeled — no surprise — "tag"). When you do this, the song title, the artist, and other information are saved to a playlist that is transferred to your iPod the next time you dock it. When you then connect your iPod to your computer for synchronization, those tagged songs appear with links to the iTunes Store for purchase. Pretty neat.

Internet radio

If you set up a home theater PC in your A/V system, you can get lots of great radio programming from Internet radio broadcasts. Using an MP3 player, such as Musicmatch Jukebox or iTunes, or a streaming media player, such as Windows Media Player or Real Player (www.real.com), you can tune in to literally thousands of radio stations from around the world. With a broadband DSL or cable modem Internet connection, the quality is pretty decent, too.

So if you're like Pat, and you find that San Diego is just out of range of the great PBS station in Santa Monica (www.kcrw.org), you can just tune in on the Net. Pretty cool, and it doesn't cost you an extra penny. This is also a great way to get the radio broadcasts of your favorite college sports teams. Neither of us ever misses a Duke basketball game, even if we're on the road, because we can tune in on our laptops. Go Blue Devils!

In Chapter 10, we tell you about media players and adapters that can support Internet radio. You can also use a Media Center PC, as described in Chapter 9.

Chapter 6

Feeding Video into Your Theater

*I*f you're like us, watching movies is the main reason you decided to get a home theater in the first place. High-quality music reproduction and high-impact video gaming are just (awesome) side benefits. You can get movies (and TV shows and other video content) into your home theater system in many ways — such as plugging in to a cable or satellite TV system or even hooking up an antenna for broadcast TV. (We talk about all of these TV systems in Chapter 7.) For most folks, however, watching a movie means watching a *prerecorded* movie (typically a movie on DVD that you've bought or you've rented from the local video store or online through a service such as Netflix).

In this chapter, we talk about the key sources of prerecorded video in your home theater. We spend most of our time discussing the source that's most important to us and likely to you as well — the digital video disc, better known as the DVD. (They're also sometimes called *Digital Versatile Discs* because they don't just carry video.) But DVDs are not a high-definition format. So, now that we're well into the age of the HDTV, we're going to talk a fair amount about a disc format that many folks in the industry hope will replace the DVD: the high-definition Blu-ray disc. We finish the chapter with that old standby, the VCR, its replacement, the personal video recorder (or PVR), and some other nonbroadcast sources of video.

In Chapter 9, we talk about how PCs and Macs can take over the role of a DVD or Blu-ray disc player in your home theater, and in Chapter 10, we describe specialized, Internet-connected devices that can do the same thing. These days it's all about the convergence between consumer electronics and PCs and the Internet. We tell you how to make these previously separate realms come together (and why you'd want to do so) in Chapters 9 and 10.

DVD (Still) Rules the Roost

The DVD is a high-quality centerpiece to a home theater. Keep in mind the cardinal rule of any A/V system: Garbage in equals garbage out. The corollary states that no matter how good your video display and audio system are, if you put a junky, low-fidelity signal into them, you're going to see and hear junky, low-fidelity home theater. That's why DVD is so important — it's an inexpensive, easy-to-use, high-quality system for movies and movie sound-tracks. And the better your display (such as an HDTV), the more you'll appreciate a high-quality signal being fed to your display.

In this section, we spend a little time talking about the DVDs themselves and what they can do. Chances are good that you are already familiar with the DVD (after all, DVD has been one of the most — if not *the* most — rapidly adopted new technologies of all time). But DVD is a moving target — manufacturers of DVD players have continually improved their gear and added new features that both improve picture quality and make your DVD viewing more convenient. So read on and be prepared to discover something new!

Getting to know DVDs

The DVD is a 12cm optical disc (by the way, *optical* means that the data on the disc is read by a laser). From a distance, a DVD looks just like a CD. The big difference between the DVD and the CD is the format that each uses for burning those little digital pits into the disc (pits that turn into digital 1s and 0s when the laser reads them). Because the DVD uses a more complex for-matting scheme, it has the capacity to store a lot more data than a CD. A DVD can hold a minimum of 4.7GB of data (dual-layer DVDs, discussed later, can hold more), whereas a CD's limit is about 700MB. So a DVD can hold more than six times as much data as a CD.

A DVD's extra capacity is crucial to home theater because it lets the DVD store about two hours of high-quality digital video *and* digital audio signals using Dolby Digital or DTS (see Chapter 3 if you don't know what these are) *and* an analog two-channel stereo signal as well. A CD, well, it can't hold more than a few dozen minutes of this kind of home theater data.

You'll also hear, as you begin getting deeper into the home theater world, about *dual-layer* and *double-sided* DVDs. These discs (which work just fine in any DVD player) hold even more data for long movies and cool extras, such as deleted scenes or director commentary. The additional space is made possi-ble by putting the extra data on — no surprise here — a different layer of the DVD or on the other side (so you just have to flip the disc, like an LP).

Like a CD, the DVD stores its information in a digital format (you probably guessed that from the name) and, for video, uses the MPEG format that we discuss in Chapter 4. The DVD can also hold the audio soundtracks that correspond to this video in a variety of Dolby and DTS formats, as well as store cool extra features, such as additional foreign language soundtracks, subtitles, and scene indexes (which let you skip to different scenes in a movie, just like you can skip to different songs on a CD).

The DVD can also do something that most other home theater source devices (we talk about a few others later in this chapter) can't do. It can display *true* widescreen video.

Not all DVDs (the discs themselves, not the DVD player) give you a true wide-screen anamorphic picture. Many DVDs have been formatted in the standard 4:3 aspect ratio instead. If you want widescreen, you need to choose DVDs with labels that say "anamorphic," "widescreen," "16:9," or something similar. Many movie companies put both versions on a single disc (using the dual-layer technology we just mentioned) or release both widescreen and Pan and Scan (frames cropped to fit a traditional television screen) DVD versions of an individual movie. See Chapter 4 for all the details about widescreen viewing, including a handy explanation of the term *anamorphic*.

Choosing a DVD player

Well, we've talked a lot about why we think DVD players are so important in a home theater. Now comes the fun part — choosing one. There's some really good news here, especially if your budget is like ours (and most people's), which is to say, limited.

DVD technology has advanced incredibly in the few years that DVD players have been on the market, and the price drops have been stupendous. For example, Pat's then-not-quite two-year-old somehow laid an impressive beating on his old DVD player. No worries though! He was able to buy a sweet new *upconverting* (we'll explain this in a moment) HDMI-equipped player for about half of what he had paid for the previous DVD player. (So thanks, Annabel, for letting Daddy get a new DVD player! Now go beat up the new one so he can upgrade to Blu-ray.) Bottom line is this: If you're still sitting on the DVD fence, get off it!

Like every single piece of A/V gear we discuss in this book, you can spend a fortune on a DVD player if you want to. And you may want to if you're building a really fancy, no-holds-barred, high-end home theater. Although you can get a great picture from that $59 model, if you have a high-end video projector and a top-of-the-line surround-sound audio system, you might want to buy a fancier model. Such a system yearns for higher-quality electronic components and more powerful chips to convert the digital data on the DVD into video and sound. Just to give you an idea of the range of prices, as we write, the current prices of a single company (Denon) range from $150 to $3,500.

So what should you look for in a DVD player? We think the following items are the key things to put on your mental checklist as you start shopping:

- ✔ **Connections on the back:** We talk in detail about the hierarchy of connections in Chapter 16. At a minimum, you'll want a DVD player featuring a component video connection, and just about all DVD players these days have this (as do almost all displays these days — and all HDTV-capable TVs will). If you have a TV that can accept these connections, make sure you get a DVD player that can also use them. On the audio side of things, you'll find two kinds of digital connectors (for Dolby Digital and DTS digital surround sound) — the coaxial and optical (or Toslink) connections. The key thing here is to make sure that the connectors on your DVD player match up with those on your A/V receiver.

  Most new DVD players have moved on to digital video outputs. If your display supports an HDMI connection, consider a DVD player that has one of these outputs — read the section titled "Playing DVDs on an HDTV" for more details.

- ✔ **Single or multidisc capability:** DVD players come in single-disc and multidisc models. For just watching movies, a single-disc player is fine, but if you plan to use your DVD player as your only CD player, you might want to pay a bit more for a multidisc player that lets you provide hours of background music during, for example, a party.

- ✔ **Progressive or interlaced:** Progressive scan is becoming a big deal because the video industry is gradually moving from interlaced video toward a progressive video future. We discuss progressive and interlaced scans in more detail in Chapter 4, so we don't bother you with that here. Bottom line: If you have an HDTV or other progressive-scan monitor, you want a DVD player that offers progressive-scan capabilities. Although most progressive-scan TVs have a built-in deinterlacer for playing interlaced material (DVDs are still interlaced), the deinterlacers in many progressive-scan DVD players are better. Even if you don't have a progressive-scan display but might someday, consider a progressive-scan DVD player as well, especially considering that prices on these DVD players have dropped so much that they're hardly more expensive than a regular DVD player — in fact, all but the cheapest DVD players these days have progressive-scan functionality.

✔ **Upconversion:** The latest and greatest feature found in many new DVD players is the ability to *upconvert* a DVD to a higher resolution for play-back on your HDTV display. An upconverting DVD player has an internal *scaler* (see Chapter 13 for more on this device's functionality) that allows it to take the 480i resolution stored on DVDs and convert it to 480p (progressive scan) or, more significantly, to a 720p, 1080i, or even 1080p signal. Essentially, an upconverting DVD player gives you a simulated high-definition version of the video on your DVD. Just as important, an upconverting DVD player uses the HDMI outputs we discussed previously to send this picture to your HDTV display — so you get all the benefits of a digital connection *and* a picture that's designed for a high-definition display.

✔ **Support for other formats:** Many DVD players now support online video file formats such as DivX or xvid. This can come in handy if you are downloading HDTV video clips from the Internet using these formats — you can burn DVDs on your computer and play them back on your DVD player.

✔ **Adjustability:** To get the best out of a home theater, you need to do more than just plug everything in properly. You also need to spend some time tweaking the audio and video settings to get the best picture in your room. Most of these adjustments are done on the TV or projec-tor itself, not on the DVD player. But some DVD players allow you to adjust things such as brightness (or black level) in the DVD player.

✔ **Surround-sound decoder:** If you're starting your home theater from scratch, we recommend that you buy a home theater receiver (or separate components decoder) that is capable of decoding (at a mini-mum) Dolby Digital 5.1 and DTS Digital surround-sound signals. If, however, you are adding a DVD player to an existing home theater with an older receiver that doesn't support digital surround sound, you can buy a DVD player with a built-in surround-sound decoder. The downside of this is that you need to use *six* analog audio cables to connect the DVD player to your receiver, instead of a single digital interconnect. Some of the older receivers were marketed as "Digital ready" with six preamp jacks on the back for just this purpose; if your receiver doesn't have a built-in Dolby Digital decoder and it doesn't have these six inputs (or its own Dolby Digital decoder), you can't play back digital 5.1-channel surround sound with it!

✔ **Audio disc support:** All DVD players can play back store-bought, prerecorded CDs. Not all, however, can play back homemade CD-R or CD-RW discs, nor can many DVD players play back CDs containing MP3 music files. If these features are important to you (and you don't have a CD player that can handle this for you), make sure your DVD player can handle all these formats before you buy.

✔ **Recording capability:** Just as the CD has moved from a factory-produced, read-only CD to a "make your own" medium (such as CD-Rs and CD-RWs), so has DVD recording started to become a truly consumer-friendly technology.

✔ **Remote control:** Most people have too many remote controls when they get into home theater. To avoid remote overload, look at how other systems in your home theater can control your DVD player. For example, many A/V equipment vendors have special system link cables that let the receiver control the DVD player and other components. The downside of such systems is that you must buy all your equipment from the same vendor to take advantage of them. The alternative (which we discuss in Chapter 15) is to use a *universal remote control* to control everything. If you're going down this route, ask your dealer if you need to consider special codes or other things before buying a specific DVD player.

The folks behind the HDMI audio/video connection system have developed a standardized multicomponent control system, called *CEC* (Consumer Electronics Control) that will eventually work like the manufacturer-specific system link control systems — but across all manufacturers. As we write today, CEC is not yet widely adopted, but it is on the product development roadmap of many manufacturers and we expect to see it soon. If you see this feature, it's worth considering.

✔ **DVD extras:** Many DVDs include extra features that you'd never get on a VHS tape, laserdisc, or other (older) video source. For example, some DVDs have alternate camera angles — so you can click a button on the remote control and see the film from a different character's perspective. Most DVD players support this feature. You can also find DVD players that have special features, such as a digital zoom that lets you enlarge part of the picture on your screen, or a frame-by-frame fast forward, so that you can watch that starship explode in excruciating detail. You can even buy DVD players that can display standard PC or Mac JPEG picture files from Kodak's PictureCDs or from your own homemade CD-R.

✔ **All-in-one functionality:** The DVD players with built-in surround-sound decoding are a first step in this direction, but if space is limited in your home theater, you may want to take the full leap — DVD players and A/V receivers in an all-in-one slim chassis. Lots of these models are part of lower-priced home-theater-in-a-box systems, but you can also find high quality (and expensive) all-in-ones. For example, the Scottish high-end A/V manufacturer Linn (www.linn.co.uk) has a cool all-in-one system called the Classik Movie System.

If you're buying an inexpensive DVD player, it's probably okay to choose one based on features and reviews (we list a bunch of places to find these reviews in Chapter 23). But if you plan to spend $400 or more on a DVD player and are lucky enough to have a good home theater shop or dealer nearby, take the time to get a good audition of the DVD player. Do this in the showroom of the dealer, at a minimum, and at home with a demo model, if possible. You're the one who's going to be watching movies on this machine, so make sure your eyes like what they see.

What's the region thing all about?

Region codes, which you may see in catalogs or on DVDs themselves, enable movie studios to control who can watch DVDs (the studios are like that about a lot of things). The codes are embedded in the DVD itself and also coded into the circuitry of the DVD player primarily so that movie studios can release movies and DVDs at different times in different places. So a movie may be released theatrically in the United States first, and then, several months later, it is released theatrically in Europe and also released on DVD in North America. The region code prevents North American retailers from selling the DVD to European customers while the movie is still in theaters there.

If you dig around on the Internet, you can find region-free programs for the PC or modified, universal, region-free DVD players. We're generally supportive of this concept (especially when we find that some foreign movie we *really* want on DVD isn't available in our North American region code), but we're going to leave you to your own devices when it comes to region-free players. The movie studios are

really down on this concept, and often aggressively pursue legal actions (including jail time) against people who try to crack the region codes. In fact, we're not going to say any more on the subject — jailhouse uniforms don't fit our sense of fashion and style.

By the way, here are the regions:

✔ **Region 1:** North America

✔ **Region 2:** Western Europe, Middle East, Japan, and South Africa

✔ **Region 3:** South Korea, Taiwan, Hong Kong, and Southeast Asia

✔ **Region 4:** Australia, New Zealand, and Latin America

✔ **Region 5:** Eastern Europe, Africa, and India

✔ **Region 6:** China

✔ **Region 7:** Reserved (For the moon maybe? We're not too sure.)

✔ **Region 8:** Special international venues (such as cruise ships and airplanes)

Playing DVDs on an HDTV

Many folks hear "widescreen" and "digital" and think "HDTV." Well, DVD is not HDTV. DVD is digital. It provides a great picture, but it isn't a true high-definition video source. Although DVD looks better than ever before when you play it back on an HDTV (using a progressive-scan DVD player we mention earlier in this chapter), DVD doesn't give you the same quality of picture that a full-on HDTV signal (coming in over a broadcast TV signal or from your cable or satellite provider) can give.

Why don't traditional DVDs "do" HDTV? Well, for one reason, HDTV wasn't fully finalized and on the market when the DVD was developed, so DVD was designed to work with the TVs of the time (which are still the majority of TVs today). More importantly, HDTV requires a ton (literally, we measured) of digital data. Using the traditional NTSC signal, you can fit a two-hour movie comfortably onto a DVD, but you wouldn't be able to fit more than a fraction of that movie onto a DVD if it was encoded as an HDTV signal.

Upconverting DVD players give you something approaching HDTV, but the video being fed from these players into your display is *not* true HDTV. To get true HDTV, manufacturers have to go beyond the traditional DVD — and the next section spells out the path that movie studios and the consumer electronics industry are taking to bring disc-based HDTV movies to the masses.

Until you're ready to invest in a Blu-ray disc player (as we write, the cheapest players are around $300 — about four times as expensive as a good upconverting DVD player), you can get a good, widescreen experience with an upconverting DVD player using an HDMI connection to your HDTV. But to get the most out of your HDTV, we highly recommend that you consider Blu-ray.

Bringing High-Def to Discs: The Blu-ray Disc

The consumer electronics industry has been through a wrenching *standards war* over the past few years as it tried to come up with a *high-definition* replacement for the DVD. Disc player manufacturers and movie studios took sides by joining one or another of two groups with competing standards for the DVD replacement:

- **Blu-ray:** Sony led this group of studios and manufacturers — and forced the issue by making Blu-ray the standard in the PlayStation 3 game console.
- **HD-DVD:** This competing format was championed by Toshiba, and supported by a number of other studios and manufacturers.

For about two years these two formats fought it out in the marketplace, with each claiming technical superiority, lower prices, and greater movie studio support at various times. Finally, in January 2008, a major movie studio (Time Warner) announced that it would move its new HD movie titles from HD-DVD to Blu-ray. That was the straw that broke the camel's back, and only a few weeks later Toshiba pulled the plug on HD-DVD, leaving Blu-ray disc as the sole high-def disc format.

That makes it easy for us to recommend that you consider purchasing a Blu-ray disc player for your high-definition home theater. (And you have no idea how happy it makes us to be able to finally make a recommendation — after two years of being asked and having to recommend that people wait for one format or another to win out!)

Go ahead — let the kids play with the disc

If you have younger kids (like Pat does), or even if your kids are old enough to know better (like Danny's), you've probably experienced the infamous scratched-DVD phenomenon. Kids love to play with shiny things, and their favorite DVD is usually high up on the "ooh, shiny" list. In Pat's house, the *Finding Nemo* DVD has taken the worst of this abuse.

Well Blu-ray has a solution for you. Because the physical structure of a Blu-ray disc is even more susceptible to scratching than DVD, the Blu-ray folks decided up front to include a hard coating on each Blu-ray disc. Advanced polymers cover the surface of a Blu-ray disc, so go ahead and let the two-year-old carry the disc to and from the player — she won't make her favorite scene unwatchable due to scratches. Go science!

Understanding Blu-ray

The Blu-ray disc, as mentioned, was developed by Sony. Blu-ray disc players are now manufactured by almost all major consumer electronics companies. Blu-ray is a very capable disc format — by which we mean that there will be *lots* of storage space on a Blu-ray disc. Storage space is the key for high-definition disc formats simply because HDTV takes up as much as nine or ten times the storage space (for any given length of video) than does a standard-definition DVD-quality video. So you really need to be able to cram a lot of bits on the disc to make high definition work.

The good news here is that Blu-ray can hold a *lot* of bits and bytes — up to 50GB of data (more than five or six times what a standard DVD can hold). That 50GB capacity is for a dual-layer disc; a single-layer disc can hold 25GB of data — enough space for at least two hours of high-definition programming. Blu-ray discs can hold even more data if the disc is encoded using a more efficient *codec* (such as MPEG-4 instead of MPEG-2), which means you can potentially fit *four hours* of high def on a single-layer disc.

Blu-ray discs support the same audio formats that a regular DVD supports but also include the latest and greatest from Dolby — Dolby Digital Plus and Dolby TrueHD. (See Chapter 5 for more on these formats.) Because very few A/V receivers include decoders for these new formats today, Blu-ray disc players have a built-in surround-sound decoder that lets you use these higher-resolution audio formats.

Combating Blu-ray FUD

Many new technologies face FUD (*fear, uncertainty, and doubt*). So-called experts of all sorts crawl up out of the woodwork and raise objections to the new technology, making potential customers unsure about whether they should become adopters of that technology. Sometimes these objections are true (or based in truth but exaggerated); sometimes they're not even close to being true. Regardless, they make it difficult for regular people to feel comfortable about buying a new system.

Well in the Blu-ray world, the protracted standards war led to a lot of FUD on both sides of the aisle. A few of the most common misconceptions about Blu-ray discs and players follow:

✔ Blu-ray disc players won't play CDs: This one is based on a bit of truth. The first few models of Blu-ray disc players didn't have the right lasers and related mechanisms to play audio CDs. That's a thing of the past, though, and all Blu-ray disc players we know of on the market today play audio CDs and regular DVDs, as well as (of course) Blu-ray discs.

✔ Blu-ray discs are too susceptible to damage: Another one based on an older truth. As we

discuss in the sidebar titled "Go ahead — let the kids play with the disc," the Blu-ray disc is more susceptible to damage than a standard DVD, because the data stored in the disc is physically closer to the surface of the disc (and therefore, more likely to be destroyed by a scratch). In response to this, you'll find that all Blu-ray discs on the market today have a special hard coating that makes them *more durable* than regular DVDs.

✔ Your Blu-ray disc player will be obsolete soon: This one is based on the fact that new features are being added to Blu-ray over time — features that allow more extras on the disc and allow the Blu-ray disc player to connect to the Internet for more content. It *is true* that not all Blu-ray disc players on the market support (or will ever support) these features. But neither will these players be obsolete anytime soon — their primary job is to play high-definition movies, and nothing in current or future Blu-ray disc plans will keep a player you buy today from doing this.

You can use a standard digital audio cable, however, for regular Dolby Digital or DTS, if your receiver doesn't have an HDMI or a multichannel analog input.

Blu-ray gets its name from the *color* of the laser that reads the discs inside a Blu-ray player. Instead of the traditional red laser used by CDs and regular DVDs, Blu-ray uses a blue laser. (We bet you knew what we were going to say there, huh?) The blue laser has a smaller wavelength and is more suited to reading the physically smaller *spots* on the disc itself. This ability to focus in on smaller spots allows the disc to have more spots — and more spots means more data.

Choosing a Blu-ray disc player

Choosing a Blu-ray disc player is just like choosing any component (see our advice on buying a DVD player, in the previous section titled "Choosing a DVD player"). Because Blu-ray is the newest technology around, most of the advanced features you'd look for on a DVD player (such as HDMI outputs and upconversion for regular DVDs) will be available on every model, so you're more likely to be shopping based upon more generic characteristics such as price, brand name, and aesthetics.

Having said that, there are a few things you can look for when you compare Blu-ray disc players:

✔ **Video output formats:** In Chapter 5 we talk about the various video formats in home theater (the main ones are 480i/p, 720p, and 1080i/p). The Blu-ray disc is the only disc-based source of the highest-resolution video format (1080p), and all Blu-ray disc players can send a 1080p signal to your HDTV via an HDMI cable. Many Blu-ray disc players are also capable (and this is the thing you should look for) of sending a specific kind of 1080p signal — 1080p24 — to HDTVs that can display this format. The *24* here refers to the frame rate of the video; most movies are filmed at 24 frames per second. If your TV and Blu-ray disc player both support 1080p24, you can get the best playback of movies using this format. Support for 1080p24 is worth seeking out when you shop for Blu-ray disc players even if your HDTV doesn't support it — after all, you may upgrade HDTVs before you upgrade your Blu-ray disc player!

To get a 1080p24 signal out of your Blu-ray disc player and in to your HDTV, the disc itself must be recorded with a 1080p24 signal — most movies are indeed encoded this way on Blu-ray discs.

✔ **Surround-sound formats:** In Chapter 3 we talk about Dolby TrueHD and DTS-HD Master Audio, the newest surround-sound formats that provide a superior surround-sound experience by offering *higher-resolution* audio (higher resolution, in this case, means that more digital data is used to store the recorded audio, so it sounds truer to life). We think it's worth looking for players that can handle both formats (most can). Blu-ray disc players can deal with TrueHD and DTS-HD Master Audio in two ways:

• **Internal decoding:** With an internal decoder, a chip *inside* the Blu-ray player decodes the surround sound from TrueHD or Master Audio (as opposed to a chip inside your receiver doing the decoding, which is typical for regular DTS or Dolby Digital). The internally decoded surround sound is then sent to your receiver over analog audio cables or over HDMI in a *PCM* format.

- **Bitstream output:** A few Blu-ray disc players can send the TrueHD or Master Audio *bitstream* — the undecoded audio bits as recorded on the Blu-ray disc — to your receiver over an HDMI connection. This approach allows your receiver to decode TrueHD or Master Audio internally, yielding the highest possible sound quality.

  For the bitstream output to work, you'll need an HDMI-equipped receiver with its own built-in TrueHD or Master Audio decoder, which is rare (as we write in mid 2008). But if you're looking to future proof your Blu-ray disc player choice, you might want to choose a player that can support this bitstream output, even if your current receiver doesn't support it.

- **Player profiles:** All Blu-ray disc players can play high-definition 1080p movies with great surround-sound performance. Some, however, can do additional stuff that has nothing to do with picture or sound quality. These additional features were, until recently, described as Blu-ray *profiles* (Profile 1, 1.1, 1.2, and so on). Luckily the folks in the Blu-ray industry have dispensed with those ungainly names and call the features by regular English names. Specifically, some Blu-ray disc players support two feature sets:

  - **BonusView:** BonusView is an enhanced menu and extras system for Blu-ray. BonusView includes secondary audio and video circuitry that lets you do things such as view a secondary video source in a picture-in-picture window, or hear a secondary audio source (such as a director's voiceover) while you listen to the primary soundtrack. All players introduced after November 2007 should have this feature — older models may not.

  - **BD-Live:** BD-Live brings the Internet to your Blu-ray disc player. With BD-Live your Blu-ray disc player can access Internet sites related to the movie or video you're watching. For example, BD-Live can be used to provide up-to-date supplementary content to a movie (such as previews and trailers, commentary, and other bonus content). BD-Live can even be used for truly interactive features such as online chat or content relevant to you directly (for example, a forthcoming Blu-ray disc of *Sleeping Beauty* will allow kids to superimpose their local weather conditions on the screen — so if it's raining where they live, it's raining at the castle).

- **Startup times:** A seemingly trivial characteristic that can end up driving you crazy is startup time — the amount of time between pressing the On button on your Blu-ray disc player and the movie starting to play on your HDTV screen. Keep in mind that Blu-ray disc players are complicated bits of machinery (like a PC in many ways) and early models often took a minute or more to start playing a movie. Newer players can start in a matter of seconds — which saves your sanity. If a Blu-ray disc player has a good startup time, the manufacturer will probably advertise that fact, and reviews will mention it.

Gaming your way into Blu-ray

Many (perhaps even most) Blu-ray disc players in homes around the world today are not dedicated, standalone disc players. Instead, they're found inside one of the most popular video game consoles out there — Sony's PlayStation 3. The PlayStation 3 (PS3) is Sony's latest console with killer 3D graphics for games, a built-in Web browser, and support for playing music and photos on your HDTV screen. The PS3 also has a built-in, fully functional Blu-ray disc player. (Sony chose Blu-ray as the format for storing games in the PS3.)

The great thing about using the PS3 as your Blu-ray disc player is that it doesn't cost any more than a standalone Blu-ray disc player. (You can pick up a new PS3 starting at about $399, which is a typical price for a Blu-ray disc player.) So for the same price you get a great disc player and a fully functioning game console. We talk about the PS3 in depth in Chapter 8.

VCRs Ain't (Quite) Dead Yet

We spend a lot of time talking about DVD players because we love them so much. But we realize that some movies just aren't available on DVD yet (or ever, in some cases). And you probably want to record TV shows or watch home movies you've recorded with your camcorder. Or, like Danny, you have a zillion VHS tapes that you're stuck with in a DVD age. These are all areas in which a videocassette recorder (VCR) comes in super handy.

You can buy three kinds of VCRs today:

- ✔ **VHS VCRs:** These are your standard, garden-variety VCRs that have been around for 40 years or so. They use VHS videocassettes and record a low-resolution TV signal (only about 240 lines of resolution). Most of these VHS VCRs are cheap (less than $100), and most include stereo audio capabilities (if so, they're labeled HiFi) and analog Dolby surround-sound capabilities.

- ✔ **S-VHS VCRs:** The S-VHS (or Super VHS) VCR uses a special S-VHS tape to provide a higher-quality, higher-resolution (400 lines, instead of 240) picture. Regular VHS tapes work on these decks, but S-VHS videocassettes don't work on most regular VHS decks. (If you plan on trading tapes with someone or using a regular VHS VCR you have elsewhere, keep that in mind.) S-VHS VCRs start at around $90.

- ✔ **D-VHS VCRs:** The latest and greatest in the VCR world, these are high-definition VCRs. D-VHS VCRs can play and record standard VHS and S-VHS videotapes. More importantly, D-VHS VCRs can also record all HDTV formats (discussed in Chapter 5). You can get a limited number of movies on prerecorded D-VHS videocassettes, but it's a small number compared to what you can get on DVD. You can buy a D-VHS VCR for about $500 — if you can find one.

The D-VHS system has been out for more than seven years and has essentially been a major flop. These recorders work pretty well, with great picture quality, but folks are accustomed to the wonders of DVDs, with their almost instant access to any spot on the disc, their durability, and just the plain fact that you never need to rewind a tape (nothing worse than forgetting to rewind!). And PVRs (personal video recorders, discussed in the next section) have pretty much taken over the TV show "time shifting" role in most homes. So although one or two manufacturers still make D-VHS recorders, they're all but gone from the market. We suspect that Blu-ray will kill them off for good. We can't recommend that you buy a D-VHS deck, but we won't try to stop you — just be aware that there's probably not a lot of future in these devices.

When buying a VCR of any kind, look for the following:

- **Hi-Fi capability:** All D-VHS and S-VHS VCRs and most regular VHS decks have this feature. If you buy a model without it, you won't even get stereo sound — just crummy mono (one-channel) sound.

- **VCR Plus+:** This system enables the average human being to record a certain show at a certain time more easily. You simply punch in a special code listed in your paper's TV listings (or in *TV Guide*) next to the show you want to record. More advanced versions of VCR Plus+ (called Silver and Gold) allow you to localize your VCR Plus+ settings for your area.

- **All-in-one units:** Some VCRs are incorporated into a single chassis with a DVD player or with a MiniDV or other camcorder tape player. These all-in-one units take up less room on your equipment rack. And the VCR/camcorder tape combo units make it easy to make VCR copies of your home movies.

Even if your VCR is in the same chassis as a DVD player, you can't make tapes of your favorite DVD movies. A copy protection system called Macrovision keeps you from doing this, and it's built in to all DVD players, all VCRs, and most commercial DVD discs. Even if you want to copy your favorite movie from DVD to VHS to play back on a VCR in your vacation home or somewhere else, you're out of luck.

We're not all that enthusiastic about the VCR these days (although we think the D-VHS would be pretty cool if many people weren't restricted from using it for its intended purpose — recording HDTV shows for later playback). All big movie rental places such as Blockbuster have phased out VHS tapes in favor of DVDs and Blu-ray. But we do think it's worthwhile to have an inexpensive VCR in your home theater, just to have the capability of playing older movies that you can't find on DVD. We recommend you get an inexpensive S-VHS model — and don't spend too much money on it.

Chapter 7

Feeding Your Home Theater from Outside Your Home

*I*n the previous two chapters, we talk about a bunch of different audio and video sources that let you enjoy prerecorded content (such as movies on DVD or music on CD) or content that you've created yourself (such as home movies and recordings you've made of broadcast TV). For most people, this kind of content is just part of the overall home theater experience. You may also want to use your cool A/V equipment to do standard couch potato stuff — watching the big game or sitcoms on TV. In this chapter, we discuss the different ways you can bring these "outside the house" sources into your home theater.

We talk about three primary ways you can get television into your home — satellite, cable, and over-the-air broadcasts. We don't think these three things need to be mutually exclusive. You might, for example, get a satellite TV system but also have an antenna to pick up local stations. Or you might get digital cable to pick up those mythical 500 stations but still hook up an antenna to pick up the local HDTV broadcasts. So keep an open mind as you plan your theater.

Many local phone companies are beginning to offer TV services, often using fiber-optic cables, which are replacing regular copper phone lines. In most cases these services don't (currently) differ all that much from the services offered by cable TV providers — they connect to your TV the same way, use similar set-top boxes, and offer similar feature sets. In the future, however, these IPTV (Internet Protocol TV) services may offer a richer mix of channels — on demand — and more cool features than either satellite or cable. The biggest telephone company provider of TV services today is Verizon (with its FiOS fiber-optic deployments), and AT&T (formerly SBC) is right behind them with something called *uVerse*. Keep an eye out for your own phone company — pretty soon, we expect it'll be competing directly with your cable and satellite TV services.

Digital Satellite Does It All

For many home theater enthusiasts, TV means one thing: satellite TV. DSS (Digital Satellite Service) is the way people do satellite today (many people also call it DBS, Direct Broadcast Satellite). If you wanted satellite TV twenty or so years ago, you were stuck with something called C-Band (named after the radio frequency on which these satellites operated), which required that you to put a *huge* (9-foot or so) satellite dish in your backyard.

DSS is a much more user- and landscape-friendly version of satellite TV. DSS dishes can be as small as 18 inches across and are much easier to integrate into the average backyard. Despite this more compact size, DSS has all the advantages that drew people to those big dishes back in the '80s — tons of channels and interesting programming you can't get from your local broadcast channels.

If your cable company offers a digital cable service (which we discuss in an upcoming section), you can probably get just as many channels on that service as you can on a satellite service.

Signing up for digital satellite

In the United States, the two main providers of DSS services are DIRECTV and EchoStar (EchoStar's service is called DISH Network), and they are pretty similar. Both services offer digital transmission of their video content using MPEG-2 (discussed in Chapter 4) — with an increasing amount of their programming being moved to the even more efficient (more video in less bandwidth) MPEG-4 system. This digital transmission has advantages for both the satellite companies (because it lets them fit more TV channels into the radio waves over which their satellites broadcast) and the customer (because it eliminates the distortions that often occur in nondigital transmissions).

Both of the major satellite TV providers, DIRECTV and DISH Network, have announced (just as we are going to print) that they will begin offering some of their HDTV (pay-per-view movie) programming in the Full HD 1080p format. This is big news, and we'll be keeping our eyes on this as it happens. Check out www.directv.com and www.dishnetwork.com for more info, and we'll give you our take on this service at www.digitaldummies.com as soon as we have a chance to test it out.

Both DSS service providers are furiously launching new satellites into orbit, outfitted with systems that support the newer MPEG-4 system, which provides greater compression (using about 40 percent fewer bits for the same quality of video). These new satellites are being used to offer more high-definition (HDTV) channels — both more nationwide channels (that everyone can get) and more local HDTV broadcasts.

To pick up stations coming from these new MPEG-4 satellites, you need a new satellite receiver that can decode MPEG-4. All current high-definition receivers available from DISH and DIRECTV are capable of this, but if you have a receiver that was made before 2005, you may need to replace your receiver with a newer model.

We like both services. To decide between the two, shop for pricing and the channels that are best for you. You can look at channel lineups and prices online at www.directv.com and www.dishnetwork.com.

As mentioned, the beauty of MPEG-4 is that it's more efficient and can carry more channels of HDTV over the airwaves. This feature, along with the extra satellites launched over the past few years, means that DSS providers offer arguably the largest number of HDTV channels of any TV service provider.

Some of the key features of both DSS systems include

✔ Hundreds of channels, including movie, sports, and sometimes even local broadcast channels

✔ On-screen program guides that include all current and upcoming (for a week or so) programming scheduled on the system

✔ Dozens of digital audio channels

✔ High-definition TV

Understanding the drawbacks

DSS services are pretty awesome, we think, but they *do* have a few drawbacks. If you decide to go the DSS route, keep a few things in mind:

✔ **You might not get local stations.** In some parts of the country, you can get a local package that includes most if not all local broadcast stations. In some smaller cities and more rural areas, you still need to get cable or set up a broadcast antenna to pick up local stations.

You won't get local stations in HDTV unless you're lucky enough to be in one of the cities receiving the new MPEG-4 broadcasts discussed earlier in this section. Most HD-capable DSS satellite receivers have built-in, over-the-air, broadcast TV tuners that can pick up the HDTV signals being sent out by the TV stations in your town.

✔ **You need a special satellite receiver.** You can't just plug the cable from your satellite dish in to a TV; you need a special satellite receiver. You can share this receiver with other TVs in your house, but if you want to watch different programs on different TVs, you need a receiver for each TV.

✔ **You need to hook into a phone line.** Your satellite receiver has to "talk" back to the service provider to maintain your pay-per-view account and to check for software upgrades. The receivers usually do this in the middle of the night so they don't interfere with phone calls. If you never use pay-per-view or some of the premium sports channels, you may be able to skip the phone line entirely. Check with the provider before you buy in on this if getting a phone line in your home theater is an issue.

✔ **Your satellite dish antenna must be able to "see" the satellites.** It must have a clear line of sight to the satellites, which hover over the equator. Some folks in northern areas (or in Hawaii) might not be able to pick up all the satellites, so they get only some of the channels. Even if you're in the right spot, geographically speaking, you still need to have a clear view to the south, without hills and trees (or even tall buildings) in the way.

✔ **You have to install the system.** This isn't a really big deal for most folks, particularly when free installation deals are constantly being advertised. If you don't own your home, however, installation could be a deal breaker, so check with your landlord first.

One more thing: You may run into some resistance from a homeowner's association, neighborhood covenants, and the like. Don't take this lying down. The FCC ruled in 2001 that these "local" regulations can't be used to prevent you from installing a DSS dish. The only big exceptions are for safety (for example, you can't be too close to a power line) and for homes in historic districts. You may also be restricted from attaching your dish to "common" areas such as shared exterior walls in condos. Otherwise, no one can keep you from using a dish if you want to. Know your rights! Check out www.fcc.gov/mb/facts/otard.html for the long-winded text of this ruling.

Getting the dish on the dish

On your roof (or on the side of your house or on top of a big rock in your backyard or just about anywhere) goes an 18- to 30-inch round or oval satellite dish. This dish is your main link to those satellites floating around in space, so it has to be aimed properly to pick up the signals. (By the way, this aiming is the hardest part of the installation — despite the existence of self-install kits, we think aiming is sufficiently difficult that it warrants a professional installation.)

When you're buying a DSS system for high-definition TV, make sure that you buy the corresponding HD-capable dish. These dishes are typically a bit bigger (about 24 inches) and are often oval. The HD dishes are capable of picking up more satellites (including the ones that carry local HD channels).

Within this dish assembly is a device called an LNB, or Low Noise Blocker — the horn-shaped dingus that sits in front of the parabola of the dish. This device sifts the high-frequency satellite signals out from other radio signals and blocks extraneous signals. Dishes can have one or more LNBs, depending on what you want to do with them. (Dishes with more than one LNB are referred to as *dual-*, *triple-*, or *quadruple-*LNB dishes — the newest DIRECTV dish, the AT9, has *five* LNBs.)

Deciding how many LNBs and antenna shape you want can be confusing. It depends on where you live, what service you are subscribing to, and how many TVs you want your satellite to feed into. There's no simple formula because there are multiple variables (and we really hated that multiple variable stuff back when we were in school).

One key factor to remember is that single-LNB dishes can feed only a single DSS receiver. If you want to watch different programs on different TVs simultaneously, you need at least a dual-LNB dish. We recommend that you get at least a dual-LNB dish; it's a false economy to get the marginally cheaper single-LNB dish.

If you subscribe to DIRECTV, you should consider the five-LNB dish if you want HDTV (or local channels in some parts of the country). DISH Network uses a second dish for HDTV, so you won't ever run into a triple-LNB dish for that service.

Choosing a receiver

The television signals feeding in from a dish (or dishes) and through an LNB (or LNBs) are in a format that basically no TV can decode and display. So between the dish/LNB and your TV, you need to install a DSS receiver.

Regardless of which service you choose, you have a few decisions to make before you buy. Right at the top of the list, you're going to need to work out whether or not you want a receiver that's

> ✔ **HDTV-capable:** If you have an HDTV or an HDTV-ready monitor, you can get awesome high-definition programming through your DSS system. If you don't have one of these HDTV-capable TVs, you gain nothing from an HDTV-capable DSS receiver. You may still want to buy one if a TV upgrade is in your near future, but if you don't plan to upgrade for several years, we suggest you wait. Receiver prices are always dropping, and you'll probably get a much better deal in two years, even if you have to get rid of your existing receiver.

✔ **Home theater–capable:** Any DSS receiver can be used in a home theater, but some of the cheaper receivers don't have the proper chips inside or connectors on the back to provide the highest quality home theater experience that DSS can offer. We highly recommend that you make sure your DSS receiver has at least a component video connection on the back (we talk about video connectors in Chapter 16), as well as a digital audio connector (coaxial or optical) for Dolby Digital surround sound (which some, but not all, DSS programs include).

✔ **PVR-equipped:** Some DSS receivers now come with a built-in hard drive–based PVR (personal video recorder). Although you can certainly add your own PVR to a DSS-fed home theater, the integration of these units is kind of nice because the program guide that lets you select what show you want to watch live is well-integrated into the PVR's recording scheduling system. See Chapter 6 for a discussion of PVRs.

You might also want to keep an eye out for more prosaic features when choosing a DSS receiver. For example, some receivers have better (and easier to use) parental lockout controls that keep the kids from watching stuff you don't want them to watch. Others have remote controls based on RF (radio frequencies) instead of IR (infrared), so you can control them without a direct line of sight to the receiver. It always pays to check out the little details when you're making these investments. (By the way, the investment isn't too steep. You can find complete dish and two-receiver packages for free, but the price can rise to $200 or more for each HDTV-capable receiver, though you're likely to get a rebate on the receiver price if you sign a long-term contract.)

Cable Cornucopia

The biggest competitor to the DSS companies comes from local cable companies, such as Time Warner, Comcast, and Cox Communications. Until recently, most home theater buffs didn't consider cable TV much of a competitor to DSS — old-fashioned *analog* cable systems didn't offer nearly as many channels (particularly when it came to movie channels) as the satellites did. That fact has changed, however, with the advent of *digital* cable systems. These systems use MPEG-2 compression technology to carry analog (NTSC) programming into your house, and many provide you with Dolby Digital signals for at least some of the programming.

Lots of people confuse digital cable with HDTV, but for the *majority* of channels, digital cable is not HDTV. Most cable companies offer a dozen or so channels of HDTV over their digital cable systems (for example, Pat's cable company offers him about 35 HDTV channels, out of about 500 total channels). But the rest is just digitally compressed and transmitted analog NTSC TV.

Can I see your CableCARD please?

Most new HDTVs are DCR, or digital cable–ready. When you buy one of these TVs, you can plug the coaxial cable right from your wall into the TV, skipping the set-top box, at least for nonscrambled (encrypted) channels. A smaller number of HDTVs let you dispense with the set-top box for even those premium scrambled channels. To get these premium channels (such as HBO), you need to rent a device from your cable company known as a *CableCARD,* which plugs in to a CableCARD slot on your TV.

The CableCARD is a smartcard with an embedded chip that can decrypt, or descramble, premium channels. Essentially, your cable company uses the CableCARD as a mini set-top box, built right into your TV.

As we write in 2008, only the 1.0 version of CableCARD is available. It's limited in its capabilities because it's a *one-way* system. That means it can only descramble systems coming *into* your TV; it can't communicate back with the cable company, in other words. So you lose the onscreen program guide, video-on-demand

(VoD), and other features that a true set-top box gives you.

A 2.0 version of CableCARD has long been promised but never delivered by the cable industry. 2.0 was supposed to offer two-way communications, providing all the fun program guide and VoD that 1.0 lacks. Unfortunately, CableCARD 2.0 never appeared.

There's good news to report, however. In early 2008, a number of cable companies and consumer electronics manufacturers (meaning, most importantly, TV manufacturers) announced support for a new system called Tru2way (www.tru2way.com). When cable companies implement Tru2way (which they claim they'll do by the end of 2008 or so) *and* when Tru2way is built in to TVs, the TVs will have the ability to finally dispense with the set-top box once and for all. Tru2way-enabled televisions (or other devices, such as PVRs) will be capable of downloading applications from the cable network and running them just like a set-top box can. We absolutely cannot wait for Tru2way to hit the market!

Functionally, DSS and digital cable are very similar. Both offer hundreds of channels, including tons of movie channels, pay-per-view movies, and every iteration of the Discovery channel you can imagine (Discovery Brain Surgery Channel, anyone?). Like DSS, digital cable includes a pretty onscreen interface that lets you browse through TV listings, set reminder timers, and more.

The way that digital cable connects to your A/V system is even very similar to DSS. Digital cable requires a set-top box (equivalent to the DSS receiver) that converts these digitally compressed MPEG-2 channels into analog NTSC signals for your TV. And like DSS, if you want to get HDTV signals over digital cable (if your cable company offers them), you need a special set-top box with HDTV capabilities and HDTV connectors on the back, such as HDMI or wideband component video.

What about analog cable?

Most cable companies now offer digital cable service. They have to if they want to compete with the DSS guys, and they can do so if they've also upgraded their cable plants to two-way in order to offer cable modem Internet access (which most cable companies have done). In a few areas, however, you're still stuck with analog cable. There's nothing inherently wrong with analog cable. It was good enough for the cable TV industry to convince about 70 percent of Americans to buy their service in the first place, but it's not a particularly sexy service. If you need or want to get analog cable into your home theater, there's not a lot that needs to be done.

Any TV purchased in the past five to ten years (and certainly any TV you may shop for when building a home theater) is cable ready, with one big exception: Some high-end TVs (such as plasmas and front-projection models) ship as monitors without a built-in TV tuner. Besides this small group, any modern TV should be able to plug directly in to an analog cable system and work without any extra pieces or parts. In a few cable systems, you need a set-top converter box (the analog equivalent to a digital set-top box) to get pay-per-view or certain movie channels, often called *premium channels.*

Although most home theater builders will move up to digital cable or DSS, there's still a place for analog cable. For example, a basic analog cable package (which might cost less than $20 a month) is a good way to add local channels to your DSS-based home theater system, particularly if you live in an area where over-the-air broadcast is spotty and you can't get local channels via DSS. If Pat ever switches to DSS, he's going to keep his basic analog cable service for two reasons: He has a cable modem that he can't live without, and he gets all the Padres games on cable and can't get them anywhere else.

A number of HDTVs are available with the equivalent of a built-in cable set-top box. These DCR (or digital cable–ready) TVs use a small *smartcard* known as the *CableCARD,* which you rent from your cable TV provider. With a CableCARD, you can skip the set-top box, but you lose some of its features, such as video-on-demand (VoD) and an onscreen cable guide. See the sidebar titled "Can I see your CableCARD please?" for more information.

The big difference between DSS and digital cable, in our minds, is the fact that DSS gives you a choice of receivers (that you have to pay for), whereas digital cable gives you no choice. You rent the digital cable set-top box as part of your monthly service fee, and you get what the cable company gives you. The advantage of this approach is that the cable company has to fix or replace your set-top box if it stops working, but the disadvantage is that you can't choose a set-top box that has the features you want. Like Model Ts, they come in any color you want, as long as it's black.

The other big difference between DSS and digital cable is one that we can't measure ourselves (we'd need to invest much of our book royalties on the test gear) but which we've heard many industry experts tell us: Many cable companies *compress* the analog NTSC signals carried over digital cable more than the DSS providers do. Because MPEG-2 is a *lossy* compression technology (when MPEG-2 files are uncompressed for viewing, some of the original data is lost), this extra compression means your picture is less sharp and detailed than it would be at a lower compression level.

It's not all bad news, however. Going with digital cable over DSS has two big advantages:

- ✔ **Digital cable systems always carry all your local channels (they're required to by law).** You might even get local cable-only channels that you might never get over DSS (if you live in a rural area) or with a broadcast TV antenna.

- ✔ **Digital cable systems are two-way systems, communicating back to the cable company over the same line that carries your cable TV to you.** So you don't need a phone line (like you do with DSS), and you can do neat interactive TV stuff with digital cable. In many areas, you can do video-on-demand (or VoD) over a digital cable system. (We talk about VoD in more detail at the end of this chapter.)

Another great feature of cable is that it is generally immune to weather phenomena that can cause DSS services to freeze up or blur. Obviously, a big storm could blow over the poles that carry your cable signal into your home, but you won't have to worry about heavy winds or rain affecting your signal as you do with satellite.

Making a decision between DSS and digital cable is tough. In some parts of the country, however, the decision won't be difficult at all. Digital cable may not be available, or it may be in a primitive state (for example, no HDTV channels, no VoD, and fewer channels than DSS). In these cases, it helps to have either a good dealer or a lot of friends with home theaters so that you can judge different systems with your own eyes.

Antennas Make a Comeback

Remember the good old days? Yeah, neither do we, but we can remember a day (not so long ago) when all the homes in our neighborhood sported rooftop TV antennas, sort of like how many homes in our neighborhood now sport rooftop DSS dishes. For most of us, the rooftop TV antenna (and its close ally, the back-of-the-set rabbit ears) went the way of black-and-white TVs and dodos a long time ago. Tuning in to broadcast TV was just too much of a pain in the butt compared to the plug-and-play of cable (or the "have a professional aim it and then play" of DSS).

But a funny thing happened on the way to obsolescence. Antennas became hip again. HDTV is the reason. (It's always the reason for us, but we're like that.)

Moving everyone to ATSC and HDTV

HDTV is the reason because our good buddies at the FCC (the Federal Communications Commission) came up with a ruling a few years back that made a huge deal with every single TV broadcaster in the nation. The deal was this: We'll give you an extra chunk of the airwaves for a second TV channel absolutely free, but you have to use it to broadcast digital TV (and eventually you have to give us back your old channel so we can use it for other purposes, like wireless Internet connections).

Now this deal was supposed to be totally complete by 2006. And when we say *totally,* we mean that by 2006, every single station in America was supposed to be broadcasting all its programming digitally, using one of the many different digital TV (ATSC) formats. Well, as we write, that has not happened, but almost all stations across the U.S. are now broadcasting both digital and analog signals.

The next step in the digital TV transition is for the few remaining analog-only holdouts to begin transmitting digital TV and then — the big step — for all stations to turn off their analog broadcasts. The *new* deadline for this step is February 17, 2009. By that date, all older analog TVs will need an inexpensive digital TV tuner that will pick up the over-the-air digital signals and convert them to an analog signal that older TVs can pick up. In Chapter 13 we talk about TVs with built-in ATSC (digital TV) tuners — most new TVs these days have this feature, and before 2009, all TVs with any kind of tuner built-in will as well.

The government is helping the transition along. In the summer of 2002, the FCC made a ruling that, by 2007, every TV sold in America must have a receiver that can get ATSC broadcasts. Keep in mind, this doesn't mean that these TVs will be able to display HDTV (for example, they might not have a high enough resolution, or they may not be able to display widescreen content properly), but they will be able to receive it and display it at lower resolutions and at a 4:3 aspect ratio. Eventually, when enough of these TVs are in people's homes, analog TV as we know it will go away, replaced by ATSC and HDTV. The government is also helping by offering a rebate check to anyone who purchases one or two *DTV tuners* for their older analog TVs. We suspect that you will have a digital TV in your home theater, but this rebate could come in handy for that spare TV in the guest room or garage that only picks up over-the-air channels. Check out www.dtv.gov for all the details.

This transition has caused a revitalization of the TV antenna industry. DSS and some digital cable systems carry a few HDTV stations, but they each have severe limitations to how many they can fit on their systems because HDTV is a bandwidth hog. It uses a lot more bandwidth than NTSC programming does — especially when the NTSC has been compressed using MPEG-2 — and bandwidth is a limited commodity on cable and DSS systems. To give more to HDTV means taking some away from something else. It's a zero sum game.

Sorry for the long background discussion, but we really felt it was important to understand what's happening before we discuss what you can do today.

Picking up ATSC with an antenna

Today, if you live in or around a large city, you can pick up ATSC programming by hooking up an antenna and tuning it into your local broadcasters. If you live in a smaller town, you may have to wait it out for a while. The costs of putting in the new transmission and other broadcast station equipment to do ATSC are high, and small are having a hard time affording the job and also of finding the resources to do it — so some will be broadcasting analog right up to the cut-off time in 2009.

Some low-power stations are typically found in rural areas or in geographically odd regions where the main tower can't reach — in Pat's home in San Diego a low-power station is in the toney La Jolla neighborhood because the public broadcasting station's tower doesn't reach into the ocean cliff-side $30 million homes very well. These low-power and *booster* stations will be allowed to continue broadcasting in analog for the foreseeable future.

Before you start investing in an antenna, check with your local broadcasters and see who has ATSC channels up and running. You can also look online at www.hdtvpub.com. Just type in your zip code and find out who's broadcasting in your area.

The law requires these TV stations to broadcast in ATSC, not HDTV. HDTV is a subset of ATSC (check back in Chapter 4 if you missed this distinction). In general, of the 18 formats allowed under ATSC, we consider only 2 of them, 720p and 1080i, to be HDTV.

We focus on ATSC antennas here, and not older NTSC antennas, but the same general characteristics apply to each.

You can choose from both indoor and outdoor antennas. Indoor antennas work just fine if you are lucky enough to live in an area with great signals coming over the air, but most people get better results with outdoor antennas. Outdoor antennas are further categorized by three features:

- **Size:** We won't spend too much time explaining the concept of size to you, but ATSC antennas fit into small, medium, and large groups.

- **Directionality:** Some antennas (multidirectional) can pick up signals coming from any point of the compass, whereas others (directional) need to be aimed toward the incoming signal.

- **Amplification:** Most antennas are unamplified (meaning they don't have an electronic signal booster), but for weak signals, some antennas use a small *preamplifier* to boost the signals and help your TV tuner decode them.

Tuning in over-the-air HDTV can be tricky. The good news is that digital broadcasts are free of the snow, fade, and other things that made broadcast analog TV so frustrating. The bad news is that instead of these distortions, digital broadcasts tend to be, well, digital. In other words, they're either on (working) or off (nothing, nada, zip). It's not even a matter of being too far from the broadcast tower either. We've heard of people being too close or being in the right range but behind a hill.

The Consumer Electronics Association (CEA) has developed a great system to help you figure out which kind of antenna you need to get ATSC signals in your home. Go to its Web site at www.antennaweb.org, type some basic address information, and its database spits out an antenna recommendation for you. The CEA even has a color-coding system that participating antenna manufacturers put on the outside of their boxes so you can choose the right one at the store. Very handy.

Neat Network-based Services

As service providers (such as cable companies) have spent their billions of dollars building broadband networks for Internet access and digital cable, they've come across one big issue: They need to make money to pay back this investment. So they are constantly looking for new services that take advantage of these high-speed networks — services they can charge users for.

Well, we're often leery when service providers try to charge us more (well, not really; our day job is helping them figure out what these services might be!), but we definitely think that these new services are a case in which the customer also wins. These companies are looking at offering lots of different entertainment services (including neat stuff such as video games on demand), but the two most interesting (in our minds) are the following:

- **Video-on-demand (VoD):** Like to watch movies but hate to go to the video store? One alternative is to join a service that does movie rentals online (and via the U.S. mail), such as Netflix (www.netflix.com). Another cool way to watch movies is to use a VoD service (now being offered by many cable companies as a part of digital cable services). VoD is kinda like pay-per-view (PPV). You pay for individual movies and shows, and you watch them on your cable-connected TV. But the similarities end there because VoD movies aren't run as scheduled broadcasts (like every hour on the hour). Instead, VoD movies are stored on big computers (video servers) as MPEG-2 files. When you want to watch one, you simply select it on your onscreen guide and press Play on your remote. The movie gets streamed to your set-top box (just like movies you watch on the Internet, but at a much higher quality) and played back on your TV. You have complete control of the stream, so just like using a VCR or DVD player, you can start, stop, pause, fast forward, and rewind — the works — all for the same cost as regular PPV. One other neat VoD service is called SVoD (subscription VoD), which allows you to subscribe to a certain channel or show, such as HBO, and get VoD access to all the episodes of a favorite show (such as *The Sopranos*).

✔ **Networked PVRs:** This is a more futuristic service, but it's on the verge of appearing on the market. Networked PVR is a cross between regular personal video recorders (PVRs), such as ReplayTVs, and VoD. Like a PVR, a networked PVR records the shows you want to save on a big computer hard drive. But like VoD, this big computer hard drive is located in the service provider's office, not in your home theater. So you tell the system what you want to save, and it saves it in a centralized location. When you want to watch, you just click a button on your remote, and the programming is streamed to your TV over the cable company's broadband network. You can still do all the fast forward and pause stuff you do on a regular PVR, but you have no extra boxes in your home theater and nothing to buy, except for a monthly fee.

Getting TV from Ma Bell

Many folks now have a *fourth* choice when it comes to getting TV broadcasts. That's because the phone companies (believe it or not!) are getting into these services. Phone companies are installing new high-speed technologies (such as faster versions of the DSL Internet service they offer now, and even faster fiber optic–based services) that allow them to compete with the cable companies. It seems fair enough, considering that cable companies are now starting to offer Internet access and long distance services.

A phone company can offer television services in two ways:

✔ **By providing cable-like services over their phone networks:** This is what Verizon is doing with its FiOS service — using a separate *wavelength* (or color of light) on its newly installed fiber optic to carry what is essentially a standard digital cable TV signal to the home. In this case, the cable signal is carried over fiber right up to the side of the house, and then converted to a traditional coaxial cable network inside the home. This isn't all that different than what the cable companies do — they've got a lot of fiber in their networks too, but the "last mile" of cable connecting to the sides of customers homes is copper coaxial cable.

✔ **By providing IPTV services:** IPTV (Internet Protocol TV) is an entirely different way of offering TV services, using the same standard Internet systems used for carrying Web pages, e-mail (and yes, even Web video) to your TV over a broadband Internet connection. This is what AT&T is doing with its uVerse system and what many smaller TV providers are doing throughout the United States, Canada, and the rest of the world.

The biggest difference between IPTV and more traditional TV services (whether they're carried over the phone network or a cable company's network) is what is being carried over those wires at any given time. In a traditional system, *all* channels being broadcast are sent to everyone's home all at once (we're ignoring VoD here, which is a special case). So that wire running through your walls has all 500 (or more!) channels on it at once, and your TV or set-top box simply tunes in to the channel you want when you want it. IPTV is a radical shift because the wires running into your home and TVs carry *only* the channels you have selected to watch *right now*. When you change channels, a signal is sent back to the network, and a video server device in the network selects that different channel and begins to stream it to your TV.

Note: This is a vast oversimplification, but it covers about 95 percent of the truth of the situation. In fact, VoD selections in a traditional system work pretty much like IPTV (but they're only a small part of what comes over the wire), and IPTV systems often will send you several channels at once in anticipation that you'll be wanting to change channels.

So what's the difference from a user perspective? Well if everything worked ideally, you really wouldn't see one. But in the real world, there are a few things to keep in mind:

- ✔ **IPTV can potentially offer you more channels.** Any cable or cable-like system (even Verizon's FiOS system with its fiber-optic connection) has a limited amount of bandwidth. At some point, that big fire hose of 500 channels that you're drinking from will be full, and there won't be room for any additional channels. So if you really (really!) want the *Tibetan Yak Milking Channel* and your provider is out of capacity in the network, you're out of luck. In an IPTV network, there's essentially an unlimited capacity for new channels (even HDTV channels), as long as the TV provider can make a business justification to offer it to you. Because IPTV doesn't need to fit all those channels onto the cables running into everyone's home all at once, it can offer a wider range of channels.

- ✔ **Conversely, IPTV can't offer *you* as many channels at *once*.** IPTV is limited by the bandwidth of the broadband (DSL or fiber-optic) connection running into your home. If you have a fast DSL connection, you might be getting 20 or 30 Mbps of bandwidth. Each TV channel (standard definition) can take up 2 to 4 Mbps of that bandwidth, while each HDTV channel you want to watch can take between 10 and 20. Do the math — two HDTV channels can use up *all* the bandwidth on your broadband connection. As an example here, Pat tried the AT&T service when it came out in San Diego in 2007 — and promptly dropped it because, at the time, it allowed only *one* HDTV channel at a time in the *entire house* (they're up to two now). Imagine a scenario like this: Pat's watching *House* on the HDTV downstairs when his wife decides to tune in to a rerun of *Grey's Anatomy* (ahh . . . McDreamy) upstairs on the bedroom HDTV. Poof — one of the screens goes blank (literally). Not a recipe for domestic bliss and tranquility.

Even if you have only one HDTV, this can still be problem. If you have a PVR, you may want to record one program while you watch another. Some IPTV systems won't let you do this (at least in the realm of HDTV). Also, keep in mind that the broadband connection you're using for IPTV is the same one you're using for Internet and potentially phone calling (if you have a VoIP service such as Vonage). The more you use it for TV, the less you have left for downloading gigantic files or watching YouTube on your laptop while your wife is watching *Grey's Anatomy* on the big-screen downstairs (hey, some of us like to multitask!).

We don't mean to scare you off of IPTV here. Pat's experience was in the early days of IPTV — if you have only one HDTV in the house, you'll probably never notice the issue, even with a DVR. But it's something to keep in mind in an era when HDTVs start at around $500 and you can have one in every room in the house without breaking your budget.

In the final analysis, which technology a phone company uses isn't a huge deal. The technologies have a good deal of overlap (as we mentioned, VoD services are essentially IPTV offered as part of a "traditional" cable-style TV service). And over time, as the technology improves, even cable companies are considering a move to IPTV. What you should keep in mind are the attributes of the services you have available:

✔ What do they cost?

✔ How many channels do they offer?

✔ Which channels do they offer?

✔ What are the hidden costs (monthly rentals for set-top boxes, for example)?

✔ How many channels can you receive at one time (for IPTV)?

✔ How many HDTV channels can you receive at one time (again, for IPTV)?

✔ What other features are offered (VoD, audio/radio channels, and so on)?

What we want to let you know here is that your telephone company may very well be a viable competitor to your cable company (and to satellite TV). And more choices typically means better service!

DVRs Rock!

One of the biggest advances in TV watching over the past decade or so has been the advent of the *DVR,* or digital video recorder (often also called *PVR* with *personal* replacing *digital*). DVRs are basically purpose-built computers that record video onto a standard computer hard drive. Think of it as a computer-based VCR. There are no tapes to wear out, break, or jam — just a fast, reliable computer hard drive.

Actually, the metaphor of a DVR being like a computer-based VCR sells the DVR short. Using a DVR is *soooo* much better than using a VCR that it's hard to begin to describe the benefits of the DVR. Don't just take our word for it, look at these things you can do with a DVR but not with a VCR:

- ✔ Play back one recorded show while simultaneously recording another.
- ✔ Pause live TV (if you're recording it on your DVR).
- ✔ Skip the commercials with the click of a button if you are recording the show and have started watching a few minutes past the start time. (Broadcasters *hate* this feature and are suing some DVR vendors.)
- ✔ Let the DVR automatically record your favorite show every time it's on. (All DVRs connect to a program service, usually via a telephone line, that has a complete program guide for weeks at a time, customized for your area.)
- ✔ Use the program service to help you find shows.
- ✔ Connect some DVRs to a computer network (some models even have built-in wireless network connections) and the Internet so you can share recordings with your friends or send copies of shows you've recorded to your DVR at your vacation home (if you have one).

The major manufacturer of DVRs is TiVo (www.tivo.com). The company pioneered the technology and remains the only large manufacturer of *standalone* DVRs (meaning an independent device that functions solely as a DVR — as you'll see next, DVRs are also integrated into set-top boxes and satellite receivers).

TiVo has two models of DVRs: the Series 2 ($149.99), which is a standard definition model, and the $299.99 TiVo HD DVR, which (as the name implies) records high-definition content. Both models can record up to two shows at a time and include a number of cool features, such as the ability to bring Internet content (for example, YouTube) to your TV and the ability to connect over your home network to your PCs and portable devices using TiVo's Desktop Software. A TiVo DVR requires a monthly service plan that starts at $12.95 a month, but you can pay less if you buy a long-term plan (if you want, you can spend $400 on a lifetime plan).

Beyond TiVo, the real action in the DVR world these days comes in the form of PVRs that are *integrated* into other devices. The most common place you'll see this is within a cable or satellite set-top box (and for those of you who can get TV services from the phone company, in their set-top boxes as well).

Integrating the DVR into the set-top box has several huge advantages:

✔ **It makes setup and operation easier.** With the DVR hardware and software as part of the set-top box itself, you have nothing to hook up and nothing to configure; it's just there. (Getting a standalone DVR configured to control your set-top box or satellite receiver is a major pain in the rear end.)

✔ **The whole experience is more integrated.** As we discuss in Chapter 7, most TV providers include onscreen programming guides, video on demand, and more. DVR becomes just another one of these functions and is tightly integrated into the experience — so setting up a recording is typically the work of one or two button pushes while you're looking at your onscreen guide.

✔ **They can support HDTV.** This is the biggest deal for us. Both satellite and cable providers are offering HDTV DVRs that can record and play back high-definition TV broadcasts, to which we can only say, "Thank you!"

✔ **They can support two-tuner operation.** Standalone DVRs can typically record only one show at a time, so you can watch a show while recording it, or watch a recording while recording another show, but that's it. Most cable or satellite DVRs are *two-tuner* models that allow you to view and record *two* shows at a time. This gives you the ability to watch one show while recording a different show or even record two shows at a time while watching a recording of a *third* show. You'd have to be a real TV junkie to miss anything with this capability.

✔ **They might not cost anything up-front.** While standalone DVRs require cash out of your pocket to buy the unit, most cable and many satellite DVRs don't cost you anything up-front. You simply pay a monthly service fee (which you also would pay for standalone DVRs), and you don't need to buy any equipment.

Most people tend to choose the DVRs provided by their TV service provider — it's easier and cheaper to do so. TiVo shouldn't be ruled out, though — TiVo's user interface is unmatched, and the additional feature set is top notch. Remember, though, that TiVo will cost a bit more over time, and it is *not* compatible with satellite (or telephone company-provided) TV services.

All we know for sure is that we gotta have our DVRs (no matter who makes them). It's simply a *must* for our home theaters, and if you ever use a DVR, we're sure it will become a must for your home theater, too.

You can also use a PC as a DVR. We talk about this more in Chapter 9.

Chapter 8

Gaming Galore

Today's video gaming systems are crammed full of high-powered audio and graphics chips that can put your home theater through its paces. With DVD-based games, you get audio that can use all the speakers in your surround-sound system and video that can fill up your screen. Video games aren't just kids' toys anymore; they can be an integral part of your home theater experience!

In this chapter, we talk about how video consoles can fit into your home theater system. (Okay, we realize some folks think they shouldn't play any role whatsoever, but we disagree — and you'll soon discover why.) We talk about the leading console systems as well as how you might bring PC gaming systems into your home theater. By the way, we think game consoles are the best way to bring gaming to the big screen, but if you're handy with your PC, you can get a great gaming experience with a gaming PC as well.

Integrating Cool Consoles into Your Home Theater

If you have (or are considering buying) a modern gaming console, such as an Xbox 360 or PlayStation 3, you need to be thinking about how you plan to integrate it as a source device (in other words, a device that provides audio and video) into your home theater. Yeah, we know — some "high end" home theater folks might be cringing right now. Let 'em. We think video games fit into even top-of-the-line home theaters.

Game consoles are, of course, built for video games, but if you're not deep of pocket, you might even think about letting your game console do double duty as your DVD player (yep, they can do that) or even as a high-definition Blu-ray disc player (as discussed in Chapter 6). Most of the consoles we discuss here can replace a DVD player or a CD player or both in your home theater, and more importantly, all of them can be a heck of a lot of fun. In the following sections, we give you an overview of the different consoles and how you can integrate them into your home theater.

When we say a game console is fast, we're not talking about how many MHz the processor operates at or other computer-centric measures of speed (though these are important). Rather, we're talking about how much information the console can push up onto the TV screen when it's playing a game. (Okay — when *you're* playing a game and the console is *processing* the game.) Most experts use the number of polygons per second as a measurement for speed, and that's a pretty good measure, although some gaming experts use other graphics measurements.

Playing with Sony's PlayStations

Sony has been leading the way in the game console world for years now, first with its popular PlayStation, then with the PlayStation 2, and now with the PlayStation 3. (The names don't get any more original as time goes by, but the performance remains truly exceptional!)

In with the new: PlayStation 3

Sony's top-of-the-line gaming console is the PlayStation 3 (or PS3). The PS3 was designed specifically for high-performance gaming in a home theater with an HDTV display. (Say *that* three times fast.) The PS3 is built around an entirely new kind of CPU called the *Cell* processor, designed by IBM with a little help from Sony and Toshiba. The Cell processor has multiple independent processing sections (called *Synergistic Processing Elements*, if you want to get technical) that give the PS3 the ability to render video at rates previously unheard of for consumer-grade computing devices. You've probably heard various PC and gaming manufacturers describe their systems as "supercomputer-like" over the years — this one truly is.

Because the PS3 includes a built-in Blu-ray disc player (see Chapter 6), it can support high-definition optical discs for playing movies, and the capacity of Blu-ray (well over 20GB of data per disc) lets game makers cram a ton of detail into their game software. Just as importantly, the PS3 makes a great choice for your home theater's Blu-ray disc player. The PS supports all the video formats of Blu-ray (including 1080p24) over its HDMI output, and because it's essentially a computer at heart, is easily upgradeable to support new Blu-ray features such as BonusView and BD-Live (check out Chapter 6 if you're not sure what these features do). All for a price that's little more than most single-purpose, Blu-ray disc players on the market.

Other features of the PS3 include

- ✔ **Built-in wireless networking:** You can easily connect to Internet online gaming services through your Wi-Fi network, as well as an Ethernet connection for wired networks.

- ✔ **A powerful graphics chip:** The chip, developed by NVIDIA, processes the gaming graphics and displays them on your screen at the highest possible resolution.

- ✔ **Connections galore:** Connections include HDMI outputs for connecting to your high-definition display (component video is also available) and optical and coaxial digital audio outputs for connecting to your A/V receiver for Dolby Digital or DTS 5.1-channel surround sound.

- ✔ **Wireless (Bluetooth) controllers for cord-free game play:** You can connect up to seven of these wireless controllers (called *Sixaxis* controllers). They even include a less sophisticated version of the motion control found in the Wii gaming console.

- ✔ **A hard disc drive (most versions):** Store gaming data as well as your own pictures, music, and video. The PS3 can send this content to your home theater's display and audio system.

- ✔ **Two USB 2.0 (high-speed) ports:** Connect peripheral devices such as digital cameras. The PS3 also includes a built-in card reader for Sony's Memory Stick format as well as the SD and Compact Flash formats used by other camera manufacturers.

- ✔ **A Web browser:** Surf the Web or check your e-mail, all from the comfort of your favorite sofa!

Prices for the Playstation 3 range from about $400 to $600, depending on which bundle you choose. The bundles vary in terms of hard drive size, the number of controllers, and the included games.

But not out with the old: PlayStation 2

The best-selling gaming console of all time is Sony's PlayStation 2 (known among the in crowd as *PS2*). This cool black slimline box (now also available in silver!) has a 300 MHz processor under the hood, which might not sound like much in PC terms, but this processor is especially designed for gaming and can really crank out the video. The processor includes secondary processors, called *floating-point* processors, that help the PS2 do the math on a game's polygons (remember polygons from geometry?) at supercomputer speeds.

Besides this high-powered processor, the PS2 includes a bunch of additional features:

✔ **A powerful graphics chip:** The *Graphics Synthesizer* chip does the work of creating all the pixels (or colored dots) that show up on your TV screen as the game video. For you tech types out there, this is a 256-bit graphics chip.

✔ **32MB of RAMBUS:** RAMBUS is a high-speed type of RAM or computer memory, and it holds all the computer instructions and codes that make up the game.

✔ **A DVD-ROM drive:** This drive plays the optical discs containing the PS2 games and can also play PlayStation 1 games, movie DVDs, and CDs.

✔ **Lots of ports and connections:** You get the following:

- Two gaming controller ports. (The controllers are the physical interface between you and the game.)

- Two USB ports. USB stands for *Universal Serial Bus* — like on a PC.

- Two memory card slots (to store game data, such as your current level in a game), as well as an expansion bay that lets you install a computer hard drive for even more storage.

- An Ethernet port that lets you connect your PS2 to your home network for networked and online gaming (this is standard only on PS2s built since 2004, but folks with older PS2s can buy an expansion kit that includes Ethernet).

- A single i.LINK port (Sony's name for IEEE 1394 or FireWire — a super-high-speed connection used for all sorts of computer-related devices, such as hard drives and digital video cameras) that lets you connect multiple PS2s for head-to-head gaming.

  We talk about these fancy connections in Chapter 16.

You can find out more about the PS2 (and the hundreds of games available for it) online at www.playstation.com.

Xbox marks the spot

Microsoft hasn't just let Sony own the gaming console business. In fact, it's quickly established itself as the number-two console maker and may move ahead of Sony with its latest console, the Xbox 360 — which beat the PS3 to market by at least six months.

Get your HDTV gaming on with the Xbox 360

Microsoft didn't just rest on its laurels with the Xbox; it went back to the drawing boards and came out with an entirely new, better, and faster console at the end of 2005: the Xbox 360.

The Xbox 360 uses a custom version of the IBM PowerPC chip, with three *cores* (or independent processing units) providing a huge speed boost over the older Intel chips in the original Xbox. The 360 also includes a much faster graphics processing unit from ATI that can support high-definition (1080i) video on your HDTV.

Other features of the Xbox 360 include

- ✔ **512MB RAM:** Eight times the memory in the original Xbox for faster access to gaming software. (You always get better response times when you access your game in RAM rather than from the DVD or other optical drive.)

- ✔ **A 32-bit audio processor:** This supports 5.1-channel Dolby Digital surround sound.

- ✔ **A wireless controller system:** No need to worry about tripping over the cords; the Xbox 360 offers wireless controllers that operate in the 2.4 GHz frequency band (the same frequencies used by Wi-Fi). Note that this is an optional component — not all Xbox 360s include these controllers in the package. You can "connect" up to four controllers at once using the wireless system.

- ✔ **An optional hard drive:** Two of the three Xbox 360 models include hard drives for storing your photos, music, and video for playback in your home theater.

- ✔ **Network capabilities:** The Xbox 360 includes an Ethernet networking port that lets you connect your console to a home network for online gaming and for media purposes (such as playing video and audio files on your PC). Microsoft also sells an 802.11 (Wi-Fi) wireless networking adapter that lets you connect to a wireless network (802.11a or 802.11g).

    When you read that the Xbox 360 has "built-in wireless" capabilities, remember that this is for the controllers. If you want to use the wireless networking capability to connect your Xbox 360 to a home network and the Internet, you need this optional 802.11 networking adapter.

- ✔ **Front USB ports:** The Xbox 360 has two USB ports hidden under a port on the front of the unit (and a third USB port on the back) that let you connect devices such as an iPod, a Sony PSP (handheld gaming machine), or even a digital camera.

- ✔ **Media Center capabilities:** This is one of our favorite features of the Xbox 360 — if you have a Windows XP Media Center Edition PC, you can use your Xbox 360 as a *Media Center extender* that will allow you to access the TV, music, photos, and video functionality of your Media Center PC over your home's wired or wireless network. So you can have your media stored on the Media Center PC in your home office and use the Xbox 360 to access and enjoy the media in your home theater. Pretty darned cool if you ask us.

The Xbox 360 comes in three versions. Xbox 360 Elite is the fancier package, with a 120GB hard drive and an HDMI cable. Xbox 360 comes with a smaller 20GB hard drive and no HDMI cable. Finally, Xbox 360 Arcade has no hard drive and no high-definition cables (neither component video nor HDMI are included — you'll have to spring for the optional cables), but it is the cheapest way to get into the world of Xbox 360.

If you want to get a lot of detail about the Xbox 360, check out *Xbox 360 For Dummies,* by Brian Johnson and Duncan Mackenzie. Those guys have the insider scoop and can give you levels of detail that we simply don't have room to include.

Unlike the PS3, the Xbox 360 does *not* have a built-in optical drive that can play high-definition movies (the PS3 has a Blu-ray disc drive built-in). You can play DVDs using the Xbox 360's built-in DVD player, but there's no support yet announced for Blu-ray discs. Microsoft *did* offer an accessory external HD-DVD player for the 360, but that was discontinued in 2008 when the HD-DVD format was killed off by Toshiba (see Chapter 6 for more on this event).

Still worth eBaying: the original Xbox

Way back when, in November 2001, Microsoft launched its first competing game console — the Xbox (www.xbox.com). If you've ever picked one up and tried to move it around, you probably already know that this is a serious chunk of hardware. And even though it's old (and discontinued now), it's still a seriously fast gaming console with high-definition capabilities and many hundreds of games available.

Not surprisingly, because Microsoft is primarily a PC software company, the Xbox has a lot in common with a Windows PC. However, everything has been altered, modified, and tweaked for gaming, and you can't use an Xbox to write a book in Microsoft Word. Intel built the main processor, which is a 733 MHz variant of the Pentium III PC processor. More PC hardware can be found in the Xbox in the form of the graphics processor, dubbed the *X Chip,* which NVIDIA built and which is a variant of the company's GeForce 3 PC video cards.

Other cool features of the Xbox include

- **A built-in 8GB hard drive (like a PC hard drive):** You can use the drive to save game data or to store audio tracks ripped from your own CDs so that you can customize your game soundtracks with your favorite music. (*Ripping* is the process of converting CD audio to files on the hard drive, like the creation of MP3 music files.)

- **64MB of high-speed RAM:** This is good for holding the game data that the Pentium processor and NVIDIA chip are processing.

✓ **A built-in Ethernet port:** Ethernet is the high-speed (10 Mbps) networking system that most computer networks use. Ethernet is also the connection found on the majority of DSL and cable modems for high-speed Internet, and this port lets you connect your Xbox to the Internet for online gaming — as we discuss in the section, "Playing games online."

✓ **A DVD optical drive for games, CDs, and video DVDs:** You'll need to make sure that any Xbox you choose has the optional remote control, which plugs in to one of the USB game controller ports and is needed for DVD playback.

✓ **Ports and slots:** You get four USB-type game controller ports (two more than the PS2) for multiplayer games, as well as a slot for an 8MB memory card.

What's cool about the Xbox from a home theater perspective is that the Xbox was the first console that could display its games on 1080i high-definition TV. (It has been joined in this capability by the Xbox 360 and the Playstation 3.) This means you can have some awesome high-resolution gaming going on in your theater. However, as of this writing, few games have been specially designed (as they must be) to take advantage of HDTV. But even if games aren't 1080i games, they still work well with (and look good on) HDTVs.

Giving your thumbs a break: Nintendo's Wii

Not to be outdone by Sony and Microsoft, the granddaddy of game consoles, Nintendo, has its own new, high-powered home theater–ready gaming console called the Wii.

By the way, Wii is pronounced "we" or "wheeee!," which is what you'll say when you're playing it.

We need to get one thing (the only real disappointment, in our minds) about the Wii out of the way up front. It's not a *high-definition* video console. Unlike the current generations of Xbox and Playstation, the Wii doesn't support a 720p or 1080i/p video output. You're limited to standard-definition 480p — though you can at least select a widescreen output (16:9) to fill your HDTV's screen. Check out Chapter 3 if any of these terms we just threw at you aren't familiar.

Now let's talk about the good things about the Wii (and there are a lot of them!). First (and foremost, in our minds) is the Wii's *motion-sensing* control system. The Wii comes with a matched pair of wireless (Bluetooth) controllers known as the *Wii Remote* (all the cool kids call it the *Wiimote*) and the *Nunchuck*. These controllers include special sensors (both optical, using infrared signals, and mechanical, using special miniature sensor chips called accelerometers).

These sensors can tell where your controllers are pointing and which way they are moving (and even how fast they are moving). So instead of getting a sore thumb trying to hit all the little buttons on a traditional gaming controller, you just move the controller through the air to control the action on the screen. Yes, there are still some buttons, but for most games you'll need to use only a few of them. If you're new to gaming or haven't done it since you owned a pong-playing Atari console in grade school, the Wii is your friend. The youngest and oldest gamers can keep up when using the Wii — in fact, it's a huge hit in senior centers.

Some other features of the Wii include the following:

- **Built-in Wi-Fi networking:** You can easily connect to your home network and broadband connection for online gaming.

- **Built-in solid state (flash) memory:** Store game information, photos, and more.

- **A memory card slot that accepts SD cards:** Use this for adding additional memory to the console and for displaying photos on the screen.

- **Two USB ports:** Use these ports to connect devices or for additional memory.

- **Some serious horsepower under the hood:** The Wii has an IBM Power PC CPU and an ATI "Hollywood" graphics chip.

Beyond the lack of HDTV support mentioned earlier, the Wii doesn't have a few other things that the bigger, badder Sony and Microsoft consoles offer:

- The Wii doesn't play DVDs. The Wii uses optical discs for games, but they're a special proprietary type. You can't play DVDs on a Wii (though this feature will eventually be available in future models).

- The Wii doesn't support Dolby Digital or DTS like the other consoles do. You have to make do with Dolby Pro Logic II surround sound. See Chapter 3 for more on this topic.

- The Wii doesn't come with the higher-quality component video cables that give you the highest quality video possible. You need to buy a component video cable set as an option.

Despite these shortcomings, we love our Wiis (so do our kids!). We wouldn't recommend that you try to use a Wii as the basis for a home theater (something you could arguably do with a Blu-ray–disc playing PS3 or even with an Xbox 360). But the Wii is (relatively) cheap, at $299, and lots of folks have one, sitting right alongside their Xbox 360 or PS3, just for the fun of motion-sensing games. And it's not only cheapish but also tiny, about the same size as three stacked DVD cases, so it will fit into your home theater room without taking up a whole shelf on your rack by itself.

Playing games online

Playing a video game by yourself can be a lot of fun, but some games are just meant to be played head-to-head against a human opponent. It's a lot more fun to blow up your friends than it is to bomb an artificial computer opponent. Unfortunately, your friends can't always come over to play — especially if, like Pat, you've bumped into the big "FOUR OH" and find yourself trying to convince your friends to come over to play games. ("Uh, no, you can't bring your baby.")

Luckily, the broadband revolution that's given so many of us high-speed Internet access at home (using cable modems or DSL) has come to the video game world. All three of the gaming consoles we discuss in this chapter now have optional online gaming kits that enable you to connect your console not only to the home theater but also to the Internet.

This connection opens up a world of new opportunities in game play. Play head-to-head against your buddy across town — or across the country. Join online games with complete strangers. Whatever floats your boat.

The Xbox 360 comes with online gaming capabilities as well — a Silver level is free and lets you join online gaming communities, download (or purchase) games online, set up a profile for yourself, and even communicate with others via voice (using the Xbox 360's headset). If you want to get involved in playing head-to-head against other gamers online, you need to upgrade to the Gold level. Everyone gets a free month of Gold with their Xbox 360 — if you like it and want to keep your Gold status, you must pay. There are several subscription levels, depending on whether you buy in a store or online, and for how long. The one-year subscription purchased online is $49.99. Check out www.xboxlive.com for more info.

Playstation 3 users can take advantage of the Playstation Network (http://www.us.playstation.com/PS3/Network). This is a free network that allows game downloads, chat, and online head-to-head networked game play. To use Playstation Network, just sign up from your console (its one of the settings options on the PS3's onscreen display), and you're ready to go. Certain games may require a paid subscription, and you'll have to pay to download some games as well, but the underlying service itself is best described by our four favorite letters: *F R E E*.

The Wii also includes networking capabilities and online game play through *Nintendo Wi-Fi Connection* (http://www.nintendowifi.com/). As with the other consoles, you can play networked games against others (for free), and you can also download and purchase content of all types from Nintendo and other providers. Nintendo uses a system called *Channels* to display various types of content on your TV screen — particularly cool, in our minds, are the news and weather channels that let you use the Wii Remote to navigate around a virtual globe, finding current news and weather predictions around the world just by pointing. The Wii also includes an *avatar* (an online graphical representation of yourself) called *Mii,* which is your face when you go online on the Wi-Fi Connection network.

Consoles aren't just for games

A game console isn't just fun — it can also be a multipurpose device that does more than just games. In fact, all manufacturers of game consoles have scores of engineers in white lab coats squirreled away at their headquarters, developing new ways that game consoles can be the centerpiece of a home's media room. So, although we're about to mention a few of the things that game consoles can do in the here and now, there's more to come.

Let's stay in the present for a moment, however, and look at what game consoles can do today:

- **Play DVD movies:** The Xbox, Xbox 360, and PS2 can all do this, although neither the Xbox nor the PS2 has progressive-scan DVD functionality. (See Chapter 6 if you're not sure what that means.) The PS3, with its built-in Blu-ray disc drive, is capable of playing high-definition movies as well as standard DVDs.

- **Play audio CDs:** Again, both the Xbox and the PS2 can play any audio CDs when connected to your home theater. The Xbox 360 goes further by letting you integrate a USB-equipped portable music player such as an iPod into the system. And if you have a Media Center Edition PC or Windows XP PC, your Xbox 360 can access all the music you've stored on that device.

- **Surf the Web:** The PS3 includes a cool Web browser (developed in-house at Sony) that lets you surf the Web right out of the box. The Wii has an optional Web browser called the *Internet Channel* that you can download from the online Wii store for about $5. The Internet Channel is actually a special version of the Opera browser (www.opera.com), and it works really well — a number of Web sites (such as Google's Google Reader RSS reader program) have been optimized for the Wii Internet Channel and the Wii Remote (which acts just like a computer mouse when you're surfing the Web). Unfortunately, the Xbox 360 doesn't have a Web browser — c'mon Microsoft, we're waiting!

This last item isn't exactly a typical use of gaming consoles, but it gives you a good idea of where consoles are heading — right into the PC mainstream.

Because video game consoles tend to display parts of their images in a *static* fashion — in other words, part of the picture never, or rarely, changes — you need to be careful when choosing a television for your video game–enhanced home theater. Some projection televisions (mainly those that use CRT picture tubes) and some flat-panel TVs (plasma screen TVs) can experience "burn in" when you use video games on them a lot. This means that the thin phosphor layers that light up to show your picture on these TVs become permanently etched with the images from your video game. Check the TV manufacturer's instructions before you use a video game console with one of these TVs.

Integrating PC-based Gaming into Your Home Theater

Although most people think of console gaming as something you do in the living room (or home theater room) and PC gaming as something you do in the home office or at a desk somewhere, PC-based games do have a role in the home theater. Speaking even more generally, we think PCs have a place in — or connected to — your home theater for a lot of functions. (Read Chapter 9 for more on this.)

Gaming on the PC has evolved over the years to be as sophisticated, fast, and graphics-rich as console gaming. In fact, if you want the ultimate in gaming machines — the no-holds-barred, polygon-generating king of the hill — you need to look at a PC, not at a console. And PCs are inherently more networkable than a console; these days, you have to try hard to find a PC that doesn't have a modem, an Ethernet port, and a dozen other ways to connect to other devices and networks. So PC-based gaming can be a great alternative to the consoles we discuss earlier in this chapter. You're no longer limited to that Minesweeper game that comes loaded on all PCs.

 We should mention right up front in this section that purpose-built gaming consoles make the most sense for most people in a home theater. They're ready to go out of the box; with Plug-and-Play, they're simple to connect, set up, and play. Most PCs, on the other hand, need some serious tweaking to do gaming in a home theater environment (and by that, we mean using the surround-sound system and television or monitor of your home theater). So keep that in mind.

Upgrading to Vista Home Premium

The easiest way to get your PC involved in your home theater is to go out and buy an entirely new PC — one that uses the Media Center Edition software included in certain versions of the Vista operating system (the Vista Home

Premium and Vista Ultimate versions include Media Center). You can find out a ton about this new evolution of Windows at Microsoft's "test drive" site at http://www.microsoft.com/windows/products/winfamily/media center/default.mspx.

Media Center is all about the convergence of the PC and the TV (and other home theater components). It was designed from the ground up as an operating system *and* a set of PC hardware that lets you easily connect the PC to your home entertainment gear. To get the most out of Media Center Edition, you need to buy (or build) a PC that includes some hardware that is designed around the new operating system and that will facilitate this new PC-to-TV connection.

Media Center Edition PCs usually include the following extra (or enhanced) components, compared to a regular PC:

✔ A graphics card (or controller) with a TV Out connection that uses component video, S-video, or composite video (RCA) cables to connect to your TV or home theater receiver. (Check out Chapter 16 for more details on these connections.)

✔ A sound board that can output surround sound using Dolby Digital 5.1. (See Chapter 5 for details on Dolby.)

✔ A remote control so you can sit on the couch and click away at your PC.

The only things you need to transform a Media Center PC into a full-fledged member of your home theater are the cables to plug things together and, of course, the games and controllers that you want to play with.

 Media Center Edition plays *very nicely* with the Xbox 360. If you have a Media Center Edition–equipped PC *anywhere* on your home network, you can access the content on that PC via your Xbox 360. This won't necessarily help you do PC gaming on your TV, but it's a nice feature. We talk about this *Media Center extender* technology in Chapter 10.

Building your own gaming PC

You don't *need* to get a Media Center PC to get your PC games hooked in to your home theater. Creating your own home theater PC is a valid approach — as long as you keep in mind that it might take a bit more PC expertise than just buying a new PC designed for such use. We talk at length in Chapter 9 about how to choose PCs and PC components and accessories as source devices and video recorders for your home theater, and the same rules that apply there apply to using your PC as a gaming machine in your home theater.

You need just a couple of things:

✔ A graphics card that can connect to a television and display properly on the television (meaning it can output the right resolution for your particular TV)

✔ A sound card that can connect to your home theater receiver using analog (RCA) jacks or a digital connection and that can provide the receiver with analog Dolby Pro Logic or (preferably) Dolby Digital signals

That's basically it. In Chapter 18, we talk more about setting up your PC and home Internet connection with your home theater.

Adding Extra Game Controllers

Whatever game system you choose — console or PC, Xbox or PS2 (or Xbox 360 or PS3) — you need to interface with it. That is the whole point of games: interactivity. Of course, by connecting your game system to your home theater, you've covered how your eyes and ears (and rear end, if you've got a big enough subwoofer) interface with the system. The other key interface is, of course, your hands (and sometimes feet), which connect to your games with a controller.

All game consoles come with one or two basic multipurpose controllers that usually have enough buttons and joysticks and four-way pointers to drive us adults crazy (though the kids seem to catch on to them right away). These controllers (sometimes called *gamepads*) allow you to play just about any game if you can twist your thumbs in the right direction and have the appropriate level of dexterity and coordination. You might, however, want to consider some specialized controllers if you have certain games that you simply love to play again and again. (You might save yourself from repetitive stress injuries this way — and increase your score!)

Some of the controllers you can buy are

✔ **Wireless controllers:** These are usually just like general-purpose controllers, but they connect by using radio waves, not wires. If you have dogs, small kids, or are simply sick of tripping over wires, pick up a pair of these wireless wonders.

✔ **Wheel controllers:** The kids like *Mario,* but we like *Grand Turismo 3* (at least Pat does). In other words, we want to pretend that we're not stuck in traffic, that we're Colin McRae zipping through the World Rally Championship in our WRX. Thumb buttons don't cut it for this activity. Get a wheel controller that includes brake and accelerator pedals, a big fat racing wheel, and a nice short-throw shift knob. Racers, start your engines! Check out `www.madcatz.com` for our favorite wheels.

✔ **Joysticks:** Want to pretend you're "Cool Hand" Grafton's wing man in *Flight of the Intruder?* Well, need a joystick controller with enough buttons to "pickle" your bombs on target. Check out `www.thrustmaster.com` for some cool joysticks.

You can buy a ton of controllers (really, we bought one of each and weighed them! — okay, that's a lie), including some funky ones. There are skateboard-shaped controllers that you stand on for skating, surfing, or boarding games, and even one that consists of a mat for replicating dance moves you see onscreen. You can find something for everyone, and groovy controllers are truly a way to maximize your home theater fun.

Chapter 9

Introducing the Home Theater PC

・・

In This Chapter

▶ Saying hello to the home theater PC

▶ Going with Windows

▶ PVRing away on your PC

▶ Getting music, movies, and more from the Internet

・・

*F*or years now, a huge digital divide has existed between the PC world and the consumer electronics world. You have no doubt been exposed to the concept of multimedia in a PC in the form of animations, video games, MP3 audio, and maybe even short movie clips. Indeed, the ability to play these forms of media is a basic requirement of a multimedia PC.

Similarly, consumer electronics devices have been enabling much of the same entertainment content (video games, audio, video, and so on), but within its domain — the home entertainment center or home theater.

What most people have been waiting for is a sensible, economical, standardized, and indeed mass-market way to link the two. Well, wait no more — the era of the home theater PC is here and now.

In this chapter, we talk about what a home theater PC is, what kinds of pieces and parts you need to create a home theater PC out of your present PC, and also how you can buy a home theater PC right off the shelf (or off a Web page). We also talk a little about the kinds of *content* (audio and video) that your home theater PC can feed into the rest of your A/V gear in your home theater (and vice versa).

You don't need to put a PC physically in your home theater to gain access to the audio and video content that you might store on the PC. You can also look at the various media players and media center extender devices discussed in Chapter 10. These devices connect to your home network (and all the PCs on it) and also to the Internet, and adapt the audio and video on those networks to a form that can be displayed in your home theater.

If you use digital cable as your primary source of broadcast TV, turning a PC into a full-fledged personal video recorder (PRV) can be a bit problematic. Most of the systems we discuss in this chapter do include hardware and software to enable TV viewing and recording, but only a handful of Windows Vista systems (with a CableCARD-enabled tuner system) can support *encrypted* digital cable (those scrambled premium channels that require a set-top box to descramble and view). When it comes to satellite TV, you're pretty much out of luck when it comes to using the PC's TV tuner for watching or recording TV. In both cases you can use an external set-top box or satellite receiver and connect its outputs to the video *inputs* of the PC. In our opinion, however, this is a lot of work (particularly with regards to handling program guides and programming recording) that doesn't offer much benefit when cable and satellite PVRs are so inexpensive and capable. However, you may still find that a PC is worth incorporating in your home theater for its ability to play DVDs or Blu-ray discs, serve up digital music files and photos, and access Internet-based video. All we're getting at here is that the PVR functionality we talk about in this chapter is most useful if you get your TV over the air or using unencrypted cable/digital cable systems.

Meet the Home Theater PC

You should think of a home theater PC (or *HTPC,* as all the cool kids refer to them) as a high-quality source device attached to your A/V system, just as you think of a DVD player as a high-quality source device. In fact, if you go relatively high end, you can create an HTPC that funnels audio and video into your system at a higher quality level than many moderately priced, stand-alone components. HTPC can be that good.

Building an HTPC is not something you can expect to do without a fair amount of knowledge about PCs, including some skill at opening up a PC and installing new cards and drives and being able to install and troubleshoot *drivers* (the software that integrates hardware devices with the operating system of a PC) and other software. We simply don't have room in this book to give you all the nitty-gritty details, but we will give you a good grounding in the essential pieces and parts you need to build your own HTPC. If you don't want to build your own, you *can* buy a ready-to-go version of the HTPC (and we explain how later in this chapter).

Sizing up a home theater PC

Depending on your needs, a home theater PC should be able to do some or all of the following:

- **Store audio (music) files:** No matter the file type, HTPCs need hard drive space and software for audio files.

- **Store video clips:** Homemade camcorder movies, downloaded movie trailers, or even downloaded full movies and TV shows belong on the HTPC. You need (again) hard drive space and software to make this happen.

- **Play CDs and DVDs:** This is an easy requirement because most PCs can at least play back CDs, but playing DVDs is also essential in a home theater environment.

- **Act as a DVR (digital video recorder):** This is an optional (but almost essential, we think) function that uses the HTPC's hard drive to record television shows — essentially making it act like a TiVo or your cable or satellite provider's DVR.

- **Let you play video games on the big screen:** With the right hardware, PCs are sometimes even better than gaming consoles (which we cover in Chapter 8) in terms of game-type stuff, such as frames per second (or things blown to bits per millisecond).

- **Tune in to online music and video content:** You can grab a lot of awesome content on the Internet these days. If you pay for this content (and you do have to pay for the good stuff, legally speaking), why not enjoy it on the big screen and with the good audio equipment?

- **Provide a high-quality, progressive video signal to your display:** All PCs have a built-in video system that's designed to display on a PC monitor (which, by the way, is inherently progressive — check out Chapter 4 if you don't remember what this is). Most PCs, however, can't display on a TV, at least not at a high quality. An HTPC needs special hardware — which doesn't cost too much money — to make this happen. (This investment also gives you better performance on your PC's monitor, which is never bad.)

- **Decode and send to your display HDTV content:** This is another optional function but a cool one. With the right hardware inside (an HDTV-capable video card and a TV tuner card), HTPCs can provide a cheap way to decode over-the-air HDTV signals and send them to your home theater display.

Building an HTPC

If the idea of putting together your own HTPC puts a twinkle in your eye, this section is for you (and the HTPC we describe here involves a building process — although an increasing number of small, specialty PC builders, such as the folks at www.digitalconnection.com, will put one together for you). So what do you need besides steady hands, nerves of steel, and a handy-dandy TORX screwdriver or two? Well, let us tell you. The key pieces and parts to any HTPC are the following:

- **Fast processor:** Generally, you need a fast Core II Duo processor (preferably 2.0 GHz or faster) or an equivalent AMD processor. You can get away with less, but you might have performance issues (such as DVDs having *artifacts,* or leftover or poorly presented pixels, on the screen because the PC can't keep up the decoding of the DVD's MPEG content).

- **Sufficient RAM:** For an HTPC, you need at least 2GB of RAM, and 4GB or more is a good idea.

- **A big hard drive:** If you're not planning on saving a lot of video on your HTPC (meaning you won't be using it as a PVR — personal video recorder), you can probably get by with a 200GB hard drive. If you are going to start doing the PVR thing (or if you're going to put a lot of MP3 files on the HTPC), we recommend a much bigger hard drive (think terabytes!). You can buy a 750GB drive for about $125, or a terabyte (1000GB) drive for about $200, and most nonlaptop HTPCs have room for several drives inside.

  You should also consider some additional storage for your media on the network in the form of a *network attached storage* (or *NAS*) system. Big PC manufacturers, such as HP, are also selling network storage solutions designed to hold media using the Windows Home Server software system.

- **A powerful, high-quality video card with an appropriate TV interface:** This is perhaps the most important feature. You need a graphics card that has TV outputs (at least component video outputs, preferably HDMI). If you're using a front-projection TV system (see Chapter 13), you might be able to use a different interface (such as a VGA or DVI cable) that is more common to PC applications than home video (because many projectors can also be used as PC projectors — in meeting rooms, for example). We like the graphics cards available from ATI (www.ati.com) and NVIDIA (www.nvidia.com). Some specific things to look for in a video card are the following:

  - *Look for a card with a built-in video processing engine (or VPE).* These are designed for video.

  - *Don't look for a gaming card.* Super-high-end graphics cards designed for the ultimate in PC gaming are typically not optimized for video display. They work, but you can probably do better with a (cheaper) card designed for video.

- *Look for a card with a built-in TV tuner.* Some products, such as ATI's "All-in-Wonder" series of cards, have a built-in, cable-ready TV tuner, so you can plug your cable TV or broadcast antenna directly in to the card for TV viewing. Many cards have built-in ATSC tuners (see Chapter 7 for more on this topic) so you can tune in high-definition TV channels. There are also some systems that can handle digital cable TV, but these are typically external boxes that plug in to your HTPC's USB ports.

- *Remember HDTV.* If you're using your HTPC to record and display television signals, you'll want an HDTV tuner. You can find both internal (PCI) cards and external HDTV tuners that plug in to your USB ports. So if you want to feed HDTV into your HTPC (wow, acronyms galore — sorry!), you need to add an HDTV tuner card (such as the ones made by Pinnacle, www.pinnaclesys.com).

- *Check the supported output resolutions of the card.* If you have a non-HDTV-ready display unit (such as a regular NTSC direct-view TV), you need only a 480-line output (with progressive scan, if your TV can handle it). If you have a projection TV or a plasma flat-panel TV, it may have a *native* resolution (which we discuss in Chapters 13 and 14). Make sure your card can display video at this resolution (you normally set the resolution of the card by using software bundled with your video card).

✔ **A high-end audio card:** Because you'll probably be playing surround-sound formats on your HTPC, you'll want an audio card that can support this. Audio cards may have either a coaxial or an optical output. (Make sure you get one that has the same kind as what you have on the back of your receiver.) Many sound card manufacturers call this an *S/PDIF* (Sony/Philips Digital Interface) interface.

✔ **A CD/DVD-ROM drive:** This one is kind of a no-brainer — you're going to want to listen to CDs and watch DVDs. You might, however, also want to create your own CDs and DVDs, so consider a DVD-RW/DVD+RW drive (that can record DVDs). If you have a slower PC, you might consider adding a hardware device called a *DVD decoder* — this device performs hardware-based decoding of the MPEG video on DVDs, leaving your computer's main processor free to do its thing (like running the operating system). You can get DVD decoders from companies such as Creative Labs and Sigma Designs (www.sigmadesigns.com).

You should at least consider installing a Blu-ray disc drive in your home theater PC. Dozens of them are available, and Blu-ray discs are not only the only prerecorded high-definition format on the market, they're also the best in terms of picture quality — even HD content you download from online services will be more compressed (and have a worse picture) than Blu-ray, not to mention the fact that most online content is *not* yet HD. Blu-ray discs can also be used for backup and can hold as much as 50GB of data.

✔ **An appropriate operating system:** We recommend that you use a modern operating system, such as Windows XP/Vista (with the corresponding Media Center or Macintosh OS X. (If you use Linux, you're on your own — though we give a few tips in the "Got Linux?" section.)

✔ **Software for playing or recording content:** At a minimum, you need some MP3 jukebox software to take care of your CD/MP3 playing, storage, and organization needs, and a similar DVD player program. For music, we like Musicmatch Jukebox (www.musicmatch.com) or iTunes (www.apple.com), and for video, we like InterVideo WinDVD (www.intervideo.com) — and don't forget that Microsoft's built-in-to-the-system Windows Media Player does a great job with both audio and video. A great free option is the VLC Media Player (VideoLAN Client, www.videolan.org/vlc), available for Mac, Windows, and Linux! If you want to use your HTPC as a PVR, you need some software (and perhaps hardware) to make that work, which we talk about in the following section.

✔ **A remote control:** Now, very few PCs come out-of-the-box with a remote control, but many of the HTPC video and audio cards we've discussed do. The key attribute of any remote for an HTPC is that the accompanying software can control all your applications — MP3 jukebox, DVD player software, and so on. (All these remotes come with software that makes the PC recognize them.)

We're focusing on the Windows operating system here, but Apple Macintosh computers can also make great HTPCs, with the right accessories and software. See the section, "Putting a Mac in your home theater," for more information about Mac-based HTPCs. That's really all there is to say (at our high-level view) about HTPCs. In Chapter 17, we discuss what you need to do to get this beautiful, high-tech monster hooked into your home theater.

Getting a TV tuner in your PC

While many HTPC video cards include a built-in TV tuner, you can also add a TV tuner to your HTPC separately. In fact, even if your video card has a tuner, you may want to add an additional TV tuner to your PC so that you can record one program while watching another (or record two at once). Some folks even go beyond two and put three or more tuners in their HTPCs.

You can add tuners in two ways: You can install an internal card that fits into one of your PC's PCI card slots, or you can add an external tuner card that plugs in to a USB 2.0 or FireWire port on your PC. If you're making a laptop PC into an HTPC, you'll probably need to use an external tuner card because most laptops don't have a PCI slot for internal cards.

Understanding Viiv

If you're looking for a home theater PC, Intel's got your back. It's created a system called Viiv that is based on its latest Core Duo chips and includes a range of hardware, software, and even *service* components (meaning that various entertainment providers are creating music, video, and other entertainment services that work specifically with Viiv-based equipment). Viiv-equipped PCs (and consumer electronics devices) include extra hardware and software features on the motherboard that provide support for 1080p video, 7.1-channel audio, enhanced networking, and storage features to help you get content onto your PC and store it safely. For more information on Viiv as well as a list of Viiv-enabled PCs, check out `www.intel.com/products/viiv/ index.htm`.

Getting an HTPC the Easy Way

What if you don't want to go through all this computer building? Well, your friends at Microsoft (really, they're your friends) got together with a handful of their closest PC hardware partners and came up with their own version of the HTPC called the Media Center Edition (`www.microsoft.com/windows/ products/winfamily/mediacenter/default.mspx`).

Media Center (we're just going to shorten the name to that) is available on both the soon-to-be-discontinued Windows XP and the new Vista operating systems. With Vista (which is standard on most new PCs, though a few manufacturers are sticking with XP until Microsoft makes them stop), Media Center is part of Vista Home Premium and Vista Ultimate editions (these are two of the six versions of Vista available.

With Windows XP, you could get Media Center only by buying a new PC with Windows XP Media Center Edition preinstalled — along with specific hardware (such as a TV tuner and a remote control) included in the package. With the advent of Vista, Microsoft will let you buy and install Media Center without buying it on a new PC. An online tool (Windows Upgrade Advisor) at the site just listed lets you scope out your PC's capabilities — this will let you see whether your PC can handle Windows Home Premium *before* you spend money on the upgrade.

If you buy a new PC with Media Center, what do you get out of that Media Center PC? Well, the details (such as the exact model of graphics card) depend on the vendor, but the basic features of a Media Center PC follow:

✔ **A remote control:** All Media Center PCs come with an infrared remote control that lets you control the various A/V functions from across the room (including other devices, such as cable boxes).

✔ **An "advanced" graphics card:** We put *advanced* in quotes because that's Microsoft's official term for describing it. These "advanced" cards almost always include a TV tuner function and a TV output for connecting to your display.

Many Media Center PCs include ATI's ATI TV Wonder HDTV tuner (`http://ati.amd.com/products/tvwonderdigital/index.html`). This isn't *inside* the PC (as part of the graphics card system), but is instead an external HDTV tuner that plugs in to your PC's USB port. The cool thing about the TV Wonder HDTV tuner (beyond the fact that it brings HDTV to your PC) is that it's the only solution we know of that uses the CableCARD system (see Chapter 7) for decoding encrypted digital cable services. If you're on digital cable and want to get those encrypted premium channels into your PC, this is your *only* choice.

✔ **A hardware encoder:** This turns video from your TV source (such as a cable TV) into MPEG digital video and turns your Media Center PC into a PVR.

✔ **A digital audio output:** As we discuss in the preceding section, this lets you connect your PC to your A/V receiver for surround-sound purposes.

✔ **Software that makes it all work:** This is the cool part (well, the whole thing is cool, but this makes it even cooler). Software to play your MP3s, CDs, and DVDs, and to run your PVR is included and well integrated. So you don't have to bend over backwards to make it all work.

A Media Center PC acts just like a regular PC most of the time. You use it for e-mail, Web surfing, writing books, and whatever. But when you click the remote, the PC shifts over to Media Center mode, and your normal PC desktop is replaced by a simplified interface (designed to be read from across the room on either a PC display or a home theater display). You can perform all the HTPC functions we discuss earlier in the section, "Sizing up a home theater PC," and also play games, manage and display digital photographs, and more.

There are dozens of Media Center PC vendors as we write, and more hit the market every month. Our favorite model so far is the Alienware Hangar 18 (`www.alienware.com`). Check it out; this baby can support up to *four* TV tuners (so you can record three shows and watch a fourth at the same time!) and can pack in as many as *two terabytes* of storage, allowing you to put hundreds of hours of video on its internal hard drives. Plus, it looks just like a piece of home theater gear and not like a bland beige PC.

Leave the PC on the sidelines: Media servers

You can certainly use a PC as a wonderful source for home theater content — audio, video, television, and so on. But not everyone wants to dedicate a PC for this purpose — or even use a PC part time for this purpose. An alternative is to install a *media server* in your home network that can be used as a whole-home storage device for your digital media. In simple terms, a media server is a big hard drive with a network connection and specialized software that lets it *stream* media data from the hard drive over the network to PCs, media adapters, and other devices. In Chapter 10 we talk in detail about some of the leading home server systems and tell you how to integrate them into your home theater.

Other HTPC Software Packages

Windows Media Center is the most popular (and easiest) way to get a Media Center PC, but it's not the only such package out there. You can add HTPC software and hardware to a Windows PC, or even build an HTPC using a Macintosh or a Linux-powered PC.

Building a Windows HTPC

You can build a home theater PC by using one of the following solutions (and these aren't the only ones out there, only the most popular!):

- **BeyondTV** (www.snapstream.com): BeyondTV is SnapStream's media center/DVR software system. It offers a free onscreen program guide, customized to your area, and support for multiple TV tuners (for recording more than one program at a time). BeyondTV supports HDTV viewing and recording. One neat feature of BeyondTV is its remote recording feature that lets you log in and set up recordings from any Web browser, including those found on many mobile phones! An optional component, BeyondMedia, allows you to control all the media on your PC via SnapStream's interface and your remote control. The price ranges from $69.99 for the basic BeyondTV application up to $199.99 for the full bundle, which includes the BeyondMedia software and a TV tuner card.

- **SageTV** (www.sagetv.com): SageTV is a cool media center application that can control your TV, DVR, music, video, and photos. One feature that we like about SageTV is its ability to work across a home network — so you can easily access media located on any PC attached to your home's wired or wireless network. You can even access and control the TV tuners located on other networked computers, creating, in effect, a whole-home DVR system that spans all your TV tuner–equipped PCs.

✔ **Pinnacle TV Center Pro** (www.pinnaclesys.com): Pinnacle sells both hardware and software — TV tuners and DVR/media center software. Its top-of-the-line software system, Pinnacle TV Center Pro, is included with its PCTV HD Pro Stick and PCTV Ultimate Stick — these are both external (USB) HDTV tuners. The PCTV HD Pro Stick can pick up both analog and digital (ATSC) TV broadcasts — the PCTV Ultimate Stick adds unencrypted digital cable (QAM) broadcasts. The TV Center Pro software turns your computer into a PVR. The HD Pro Stick is $99; the Ultimate Stick is $129.

Putting a Mac in your home theater

Apple has launched its own answer to the Windows XP Media Center Edition. Called Front Row, it's a media center (in the generic sense) application built right into the Macintosh OS X (10.4 Tiger and 10.5 Leopard) operating system. Front Row is a combination of software (the Front Row software) and hardware (in particular, Apple's elegant new remote control) that works with the inherent media capabilities of Apple's hardware and software to present audio, pictures, downloaded and/or home video, and DVDs on your Mac's display or an attached TV.

What Front Row doesn't include is functionality for watching or recording TV. For that, you need to add hardware (a TV tuner) and software, such as Elgato's EyeTV Hybrid ($149, www.elgato.com) or Elgato's EyeTV 250 Plus ($199). These systems include an external TV tuner and decoder hardware (which connect to your Mac's USB or FireWire ports) and DVR software (called EyeTV 3) that turn your Mac into a full-fledged DVR.

The Front Row software (everything minus the DVR, in other words) is available only from Apple — it's standard on several Mac models, including (as we write) the iMac, the Intel-powered MacBook Pro, and the Intel-powered Mac Mini. There's no additional charge for Front Row; it comes as a standard feature of these models. We expect Apple will add Front Row to more models over time, and we wouldn't be surprised to see Mac hardware that uses Front Row and adds the DVR and TV capabilities that you have to add today.

Got Linux?

If you're running a PC with the Linux operating system instead of Windows, you don't have to give up on creating an HTPC. In fact, some of the most popular HTPC media center software packages are available only for the Linux operating system.

It ain't no Myth

If you're a do-it-yourselfer (as many Linux enthusiasts are), check out MythTV (www.mythtv.org) to see whether MythTV will work on your particular Linux distribution and hardware.

Like most Linux software, MythTV comes with a great price — it's free! And also like many Linux programs, it's updated constantly. While the basic MythTV software is designed solely for DVR TV control functionality, the open-source nature of MythTV means that other folks can develop additional functionality for the product — and they have, creating plug-ins to do other HTPC/media center functions such as photo viewing, music playback, and management.

The best place to get more info about MythTV is on the MythTV wiki, at the following URL: www.mythtv.org/wiki/index.php/Main_Page.

By the way, if you're not familiar with wikis, check out http://en.wikipedia.org/wiki/wiki. This site explains the concept and uses of the wiki, which is basically an online encyclopedia format that allows multiple users to add and edit entries — a community-maintained encyclopedia or data source. They can be handy!

Linux MCE to the rescue

An alternative to MythTV comes in the form of Linux MCE (www.linuxMCE.org), an add-on to the popular Ubuntu (www.ubuntu.org) Linux build (Ubuntu is often considered the most "regular person friendly" variant of Linux, with a pretty graphical user interface that feels like home to PC and Mac users).

Linux MCE runs on a PC, but the cool thing is that it can run on more than one PC in your home. You can install Linux MCE on one central PC (called the *core*) and then run remote instances of it on other PCs throughout the home. So you could have a core in your home office and other PCs throughout the home that connect to the core over your home network and turn into media centers whenever needed. Linux MCE provides the standard audio/video/PVR functionality you'd expect of any home theater PC but expands beyond that to include features such as home automation and control, home server functionality — heck it can even act as a phone system.

You can find out all about Linux MCE on its Wiki, located at http://wiki.linuxmce.org/index.php/Main_Page.

Ooh, ooh, ooh, I'm on Fiire

If you're not feeling like too much of a do-it-yourselfer but are looking for an alternative to Windows Vista and Windows Media Center, consider Fiire. Fiire (www.fiire.com) is a company that builds turnkey (as in, bring it home and turn the key, it's ready to go) media center devices based on the Linux MCE system.

Fiire offers a number of systems. The core of the system (the core in Linux MCE terms) is a honking big PC called the FiireEngine. This system is packed with storage (up to 12 terabytes of hard drive space!) and supports audio, video, PVR and more. The FiireEngine starts at $1899, and the price goes up as you add more storage and features.

If you want one HTPC in your home, you need one FiireEngine. If you want to make a whole-home network of the system, you can buy FiireStations (starting at $549). These connect back to the FiireEngine and can be connected directly to TVs, home theater audio systems, and the like throughout the home.

Finally, Fiire offers a motion-controlled remote control (like the Nintendo Wii remote) called the FiireChief. This remote is based on Gyration's technology (www.gyration.com) and lets you point in free space (like a computer mouse in the air) to operate your FiireEngine and FiireStations.

Gyration also sells similar motion-controlled remote controls for Windows Media Center, so if you're not Linux inclined, you can still get Wii-like control of your HTPC.

Chapter 10

Accessing Digital Content at Home and Over the Internet

. . . .

In This Chapter

▶ Understanding Internet-based audio and video content

▶ Figuring out home broadband network requirements

▶ Finding content around the house

▶ Using a Media Center PC to display content

▶ Using a media adapter to display content

. . . .

*U*ntil recently, most of the content destined for your home theater came in the form of DVDs, camcorder tapes, VHS videos, burned MP3s, CDs, audio tapes, and other such content in and around the home. Not much of it came directly and in real time from Internet sources (except to those of you who figured out Napster before it was shut down!).

Soon the Internet will be the main way you get content into your home theater. Believe us — we do this for a living. You are just seeing the earliest movements toward the flood of Internet content — buying music and TV shows from Apple's iTunes, searching for home videos at YouTube.com, accessing streaming video of your local high school basketball team being filmed live by students. Video (and other content) will come from everywhere, and the vast majority of it will be delivered to your home theater over the Internet.

High-speed Internet connectivity — which again we argue is a baseline requirement for any home theater — will enable you to download a lot of content for viewing whenever you like. This will put lots of pricing and product pressure on cable, satellite, and telephone company TV offerings, and that doesn't bother us a bit!

A large number of diverse players are trying to make Internet-based content as easy for you to adopt as finding a sports score or weather forecast on any portal site. Yahoo!, MSN, Google, and others will be trying to convince you to search, view, and even buy content through their portals.

Having an Internet-based home theater is step one. After you are plugged in, the Web is open to you. You'll have digital content around your house from all over the world to keep you busy at night! Whew, and you thought you were going to get some sleep!

Understanding Digital Content for Your Home Theater

Grabbing music and video off the Internet is likely not a new topic for you. Companies such as Napster and Kazaa started the trend years ago, and online music and video stores such as Apple's iTunes Store are an often-mentioned item in almost any magazine or newspaper.

But when you get right down to it, a few high-level constructs would be good to introduce, so you know what all the fuss is about. Whether it's on a computer hard drive down the hall or on a server in Outer Mongolia, the concepts surrounding content are the same. So here's a quick hit of the key concepts we want you to know about electronic content:

- **File encoding:** Digital music and video files are _encoded_ (converted to digital formats) using specific encoding formats. For audio, MP3 is most common, but many others are out there, including Windows Media Audio (WMA), Advanced Audio Code (AAC), and even weirdly named ones such as Ogg Vorbis. We discuss these audio formats in detail in Chapter 3. Similarly, there are a number of video formats (such as WMV and MPEG), discussed in Chapter 4.

  The key thing you must keep in mind about the encoding format used for your audio or video is that your home theater equipment (be it a PC, a media player, or something else entirely) must support the format you're downloading. If it doesn't, well you're out of luck. For example, if your digital media adapter doesn't support Apple's encrypted AAC format, you won't be able to play music from the iTunes Music Store on your home theater system. We should note here that Apple is trying to get the content owners (the music labels) to let them sell music without digital copy protection included in the encrypted version of AAC — the less of this _DRM_ (digital rights management) copy protection we're all required to deal with, the better!

- **Streaming versus downloading:** Not all audio or video is delivered in the same fashion. In fact, there are two predominant ways of sending the content: streaming and downloading. *Streaming video* means that there is no local copy of the video on your device. It plays while it is delivered over your home network, or the Internet, or both. Many Internet connections aren't fast enough to play really high-quality streaming video, so you find that many Internet movies are downloaded to your machine instead. *Downloaded video* is delivered as a file to be stored inside your set-top box, Media Center PC, or other device, and then played back from that local storage. So while downloaded video can deliver a TV-like quality viewing experience, complete with the ability to fast forward, pause, rewind, and so on, you have to wait a while — usually up to an hour or more — for full-length movies to download.

✔ **Internet radio:** *Internet radio* is exactly what it sounds like — radio stations broadcasting in a streaming fashion over the Internet. So if you are a college student and you miss your favorite radio station back home, you can still listen to it via streaming audio over the Internet. We discuss Internet radio later in this chapter and briefly in Chapter 5.

✔ **Podcasts:** *Podcasts* are the equivalent of downloaded Internet radio. These files contain audio (and, more and more, video) that often is packaged like daily newscasts or commentary. Podcasts are so-named because they initially were targeted toward easy dissemination of content to iPod users.

✔ **Video search:** *Video search* is catching on fast. Video search engines scour the Web and find content based on keywords and file formats and then make this available through an onscreen interface. Google has perhaps the best-known search interface at `http://video.google.com`, but there are others, such as Yahoo! (`http://video.search.yahoo.com`) and AltaVista (`www.altavista.com/video/default`). These search engines marry the best of non-X-rated amateur videos from the Web with the ability to buy videos of TV show series and movies.

Most video search mechanisms today rely on *metadata* about the video — data collected by a person that describes what's in the video, such as subject, actors, directors, file formats, and length. A lot of smart folks are looking at ways to have machines do even more classification of video content. Eventually these systems will feed into video search mechanisms and assist the human-fed metadata search elements (which are often incomplete or unreliable). We can't wait!

✔ **File sharing:** *File-sharing* networks are networks set up for, not surprisingly, sharing files. In a very "free love" approach to content, early file-sharing networks adopted a "What's mine is yours, and vice versa" approach toward exchanging content. Basically, you were encouraged to make your music available to anyone who wanted it, and they would do the same with you. Napster, Grokster, and other early leaders in this space were taken to court by the music industry, proven to be in violation of Federal copyright laws in the United States, and shut down. Most of the large, worldwide music-sharing services used *peer-to-peer* technologies, described next.

✔ **Peer-to-peer:** *Peer-to-peer* (P2P) is a concept often associated with music file sharing because it is the way most of the illegal music download services worked. Peer-to-peer simply means that you directly connect to other people's computers to download files, instead of going to a central file server. See, not only are central file servers expensive and require a lot of costly broadband bandwidth to support music and video downloading, they're also easy to find and shut down.

Peer-to-peer networks operate without such central control and allow multiple users to share files at the same time — you'll often be downloading and uploading different "chunks" of a file to and from numerous folks at the same time. Peer-to-peer is not just used for file sharing — you also probably use it for some instant messaging services, too.

✔ **Digital rights management (DRM):** No initials in your Home Theater Glossary (you keep it under your pillow, don't you?) are more accursed than *DRM* — digital rights management. If you download a lot of iTunes songs, you've run into DRM restrictions when trying to load your songs to other devices. (Most portable music players — besides the iPod — can't play back iTunes Music Store downloads.) If you've ever tried to copy a DVD, you've encountered DRM. DRM is everywhere you don't want it to be.

To be fair, DRM exists for a reason — to protect the copyright interests of the music, movie, and other content owners. Managing who has rights to do what with which digital assets is a key function of any DRM system.

DRM is often in the news, but you may not hear it referenced as such. Back in 2006, when you saw all the hubbub over Sony putting DRM software on their CDs to protect against unauthorized copying — software that was resident in a PC's *rootkit* — that was a DRM issue. (Though the issue itself wasn't the activity of the DRM system, but rather the "secret" software that the CD installed onto people's hard drives.)

The rules for sharing content are defined both technically and legally. You can do a lot of stuff technically — that does not make it legal. You can safely assume that the law says you can't copy anything unless you are told you explicitly can. You also can pretty much assume you cannot rebroadcast or retransmit the content in any way. Indeed, some analysts question whether the Slingbox, mentioned later in this chapter (it's a device that sends your home theater TV signals across the Internet to your laptop or mobile phone), violates copyright rules by retransmitting the signals received by your set-top box.

But we did say that *part* of sharing content is defined technically. This is true. In many instances, you cannot record or copy content because special coding in the content itself prevents you from doing this.

Some of the music services explicitly allow you to make one copy, or play the songs on up to five machines, or some such limitation. This will be part of your subscription contract and should be obvious. For instance, if you download content from iTunes, you can house that content on up to five computers (and an unlimited number of iPods). Look for this when trying to decide which service to use.

We specifically talk about DRM issues throughout this book as we encounter DRM problems. For the sake of this chapter, know that much of the Internet content you download will have strong limits on where you can put it, and you will most likely be able to view or listen to the content only on the machine to which you download the content.

Over the past few years, DRM restrictions have loosened up on music, to some small degree. For example, as we mentioned earlier in the chapter, Apple has been able to offer some of its music without any DRM (this music is called *iTunes Plus*), and the company has publicly stated that it wishes to do the same with *all* the music in the iTunes store. Emusic.com, another popular online music store, has always been DRM-free (though it doesn't offer as much mainstream music as does Apple). Amazon.com has launched its own MP3 music store, also DRM-free. So the DRM situation is getting a bit better in the music world.

In the video world, no such luck. Except for the mainly amateur short clips offered on sites such as YouTube.com, you'll find that essentially all video content available online is heavily DRM-protected. What this means to you is that you can *watch* content (free or paid subscription content) on your PC or in your home theater, but can't do much else with it. In most cases, you can't save it (if it's streaming content), burn it onto a DVD, or share it. The DRM implementation of the video content provides a specific list of ways in which the content can be used, and (for the most part) there are few ways of getting around those restrictions. Our advice is to read the fine print — if the content you want to watch is, for example, restricted to streaming using only Microsoft's DRM system, you'll need a PC or other device in your home theater that can handle that.

Right now, no single device can handle *all* online audio and video content available to you and your home theater. A PC probably comes closest, as discussed in Chapter 9, but that approach is expensive and a bit of work to get into your home theater. And even with a PC you won't be able to access *everything* that's available online. Our recommendation is to look at the content sources online that best fit your needs and then look at devices that support that content.

Gauging Your Network Requirements

Figuring out digital content's impact on your computing and network requirements is a lot like trying to figure out how much space you need in your living room for books. There are big books, small books, fat books, thin books. Music, videos, and even pictures, are a little more predictable than book sizes because of the following:

- You can usually decide the quality of the content recording you are obtaining or making.

- You can determine how long you want to have the content.

- You can determine when you want to have it.

It goes without saying that if you want to download the biggest movie at the best quality *and* you want to keep it stored on your hard drive (you just love those high-definition mini-series don't ya!) *and* you want it *now,* you're going to need a lot more capacity than someone who merely wants to stream a movie to his or her small TV set in average-quality mode and be done with it.

Figuring out the basics

You'll hear companies talk about the number of songs or movies you can store on their MP3 players and other digital content media. To make these statements, the manufacturers have to make an assumption about your encoding format, and they will generally assume a lower-quality format to boost the number of songs they can brag can fit on their devices!

- For music, 384 Kbps encoding is very high quality to most people, and that implies that you can fit about 6,600 songs onto an 80GB hard drive.

- Many folks encode their songs at lower bit rates, such as 192 Kbps or even 128 Kbps, allowing even more songs to fit on the drive. You'll have to make your own judgment about quality versus space. We think 384 Kbps is a good balance between audio quality and storage space; you may be happier with a higher or lower bit rate.

- For video, near-DVD quality is about 1.5 Mbps bit rate and full DVD quality is about 4 Mbps. At these bit rates, you can fit about 130 or so near-DVD-quality movies on a 250GB hard drive, or about 50 full-DVD-quality movies on the same size drive.

- For photos, a high-resolution photo is about 2.5MB. You can fit about 30,000 pictures onto an 80GB hard drive.

✔ If you're going to be streaming a lot of content from the Internet, we think you should have at least a 4 Mbps download speed from your broadband access service — though you can get by with less if you're going to forgo trying to stream high-definition content.

Broadband access *into* your home is typically asymmetrical, meaning that your download speeds are different — and almost always higher — than your upload speeds. The nature of the Internet has been that you ask for something, be it a Web page or anything else, and you get it. The size of your question uploaded to the Internet (a few bytes worth of "Show me www.dummies.com") and the size of the file downloaded in response (all the files that constitute the whole Web page) are drastically different, and the broadband network technologies were skewed toward larger download speeds for this reason.

While truly high-speed Internet connections (such as the fiber-optic connections offered by Verizon's FiOS service) can theoretically support streaming of full bit rate (approximately 20 Mbps) high-definition programming, you won't typically find *any* online sources of streaming video that use this much bandwidth. Most streaming providers use significant amounts of video compression to make their programming fit onto standard broadband connections with download speeds of 10 Mbps or less. Download video sources similarly will compress their files to lessen the amount of time it takes to download a movie or show.

Checking your in-home capabilities

In addition to the capabilities of your PC and of your Internet connection, you need to concern yourself with the capabilities of your *in-home* network connections — the wired or wireless networks that carry content between your broadband modem, your computers, and your home theater and networked source devices in the home theater.

The size of the network *within* your home is not as asymmetrical, and files are flying all over the place between computers, your modems, printers, scanners, cameras, and so on. So your home's computer network is considered symmetrical and is designed out of the box as such. Thus, you see home networking measured in terms of overall bidirectional capacity at any one time, such as 10 Mbps. We discuss home networking for your home theater in detail in Chapter 18.

Making Your Content Digital

Although you can obtain a lot of cool digital content for your home theater from the Internet and online services and stores, you'll probably find that a good deal of things you'd like to display in your home theater comes from sources *inside* your home. You probably already have collections of movies, songs, and photographs that are not digital, but that you'd like to display in your theater. There's nothing wrong with using analog source devices (such as VCRs, cassette decks, and turntables) to get this content into your home theater, but many folks like to go all digital.

Why is this the case? Well, first, digital media is typically more durable than analog media. LP records scratch and tapes break and wear out, but digital files can be played over and over without any degradation. Second, digital media is *physically* space efficient — you can cram a lot of video, music, and photos onto a small computer hard drive and then put the bulky tapes, records, and cassettes away in the attic. Finally, digital media is more convenient — instead of pulling out a tape (for example), you can simply browse for that video on a computer interface and instantly start playing it (and pause, rewind, and skip around more easily, too!).

If your content is not yet digitized — for instance, it's still on VHS tapes, paper photographs, photo negatives, cassette tapes, and so on — you might want to digitize it.

There's an art and a process to getting your content digitized and putting it on your network — much more than we can cover in this one book. But in a nutshell, here are some options to consider:

- ✔ **Photos:** Although you can use any scanner to scan your photos into an electronic file, we recommend that you use a scanner designed to scan old photos and negatives. Most of the experts we know in this area point to Nikon's CoolScan family of slide and film scanners (http://nikonimaging.com/global/products/scanner/index.htm, $500–$2,000). You feed your negatives and slides into the scanner, and the system converts them into digital files. You will have to spend time reviewing the output, but with Nikon's raved-about software, the fixes made for dust and scratches are amazing. You can get cheaper scanners, but you get what you pay for. We advise you to spend the money and get the best you can get — there's a reason you are scanning all these pictures to begin with, so do it right.

    If you've moved on from film to digital cameras, you may not have a long-term justification for getting a film scanner — your new pictures will already be digital. In this case, it makes sense to consider using one of the myriad of film-scanning services. These services will charge you a fee to scan all your pictures. Many will have you physically mail them your film, and they then scan it and present it online for your review.

You choose only the pictures that you want (typically there will be a minimum — for example, you have to buy 50 percent or more of the scans) so you don't end up paying for scans of those pictures where you had your thumb over the lens.

✔ **Movies:** If you have shelves of VHS home movies you need to convert to DVD, doing so is a straightforward and simple process. Unless you want to pay a lot of money for an all-in-one conversion device, you can get by with a PC, a VCR, a device that converts the VCR's analog signals into digital, and some editing software to make sure everything is just right. Pinnacle Systems (www.pinnaclesys.com, $50–$130) offers an easy-to-use range of products just for transferring tapes. Its top-of-the-line Digital Video Creator 150 ($130) comes with the hardware and software to do the conversion. (The cable has RCA jacks on one end for connecting to your VCR and a USB 2.0 jack on other for connecting to your PC.) If you don't have a DVD burner in your home theater, you can get an add-on burner that will connect to your PC starting around $75 at any PC store.

Mac users might consider El Gato's EyeTV system, which does most of the same things that Digital Video Creator 150 does, only on the Apple Mac OS. Check it out at www.elgato.com.

✔ **Music:** If you have shoeboxes full of old cassettes and peach crates full of vinyl LPs, these too can be converted to digital. You don't need any special hardware — just your old turntable or tape player. Grab a cable with two RCA plugs at one end and a mini ⅛-inch stereo plug at the other, which you can get at RadioShack. Connect the RCA plugs to the Tape Out jacks on your preamplifier or receiver and connect the other end to the Line In jack on your PC sound card. Then you load equalization/sound processing software, such as Nero 7 Ultra Edition (www.nero.com, $80), turn on your source player, and the software will clean up your vinyl and cassette recordings, lifting out any annoying scratches and pops along the way. If you want, it will break the long taped recording into smaller music files so you can have each song isolated on the CD. When it's ready, it will help you burn the results to CD. If you have a LightScribe burner, it will even help you label the CD. (See the "Burning labels onto your discs in your PC!" sidebar.). An option for folks with milk crates full of old LPs (and no tapes) is to invest in the ION TTUSB (www.ion-audio.com, $149). This is an actual turntable (with all of the equalization/processing software built in) that plugs in to your PCs USB port and converts vinyl to MP3.

If your content is already digital — on mini-DV tapes in a FireWire-accessible camcorder, in a Wi-Fi outfitted digital camera, on secure digital (SD) storage cards from your cell phone camera, digital camera, or video camera, or something similar — getting it into your home theater merely involves a simple file transfer.

If you don't have an SD (or other digital card) reader in your home theater, get a universal or all-in-one card reader device that can access a wide range of memory cards and process them into your home theater gear. Transferring files directly off your digital devices really eats into the battery charge, which in turn, over time, reduces the life of the battery unnecessarily. Just pop out the card and stick it in these readers, and your files automatically transfer to the reader's parent device. If you get devices with a USB connection, make sure it supports the faster USB 2.0 high-speed version. Dazzle's Cameramate 10-in-1 Memory Card Reader/Writer (widely available online for under $20) is a great example: It reads the ten most popular memory cards from one device. That should cover all your memory card–outfitted digital devices in your home.

When it comes to getting camcorder movies into your home theater, check out Microsoft's Movie Maker software, which resides on most Windows XP and Vista PCs. (If by chance your PC lacks a copy, you can download it for free from the Microsoft site at www.microsoft.com/windowsxp/using/moviemaker/default.mspx.) This will help you get your movie onto your PC, where you can add music, move scenes around, and add onscreen text. A bit too techie for you? Then consider Muvee's Reveal software (www.muvee.com, $99). With Reveal, you select your video file, plus the music you like and style of movie you want to create, and press a button — Reveal will create the movie for you. It selects the scenes with the most apparent action and best shots and dubs in the music, resulting in a more concise view of your hours of home film footage. Your neighbors and friends will thank you. If you have a Mac running OS X, you can use Apple's iMovie software. It's standard on most new Macs, or you can buy it as part of the Apple iLife software bundle (www.apple.com/ilife). It's considered by many to be the easiest-to-use movie-making software system, but this ease of use doesn't come at the expense of capabilities. (It has all the features most nonprofessional movie makers need, and works well with Apple's iDVD software to create DVD movies you can bring with you.)

Burning labels onto your discs in your PC!

You might encounter a cool new technology when shopping for a CD or DVD burner. *LightScribe Direct Disc Labeling* enables you to burn professional, silkscreen-quality labels directly on your CDs and DVDs — if you have a LightScribe-enabled optical disc drive and LightScribe-compatible media. With LightScribe, you create or download the label of your choice. Then, after you burn your data, music, or video onto a CD or DVD, simply flip the disc over, put it back into the drive, and burn your newly created label design directly onto the disc. It looks professional and way cool. Look for LightScribe when buying a burner.

You can save a few bucks (and get results almost as good as LightScribe) by combining "printable" CDs and DVDs (look on the label when you buy) with a printer such as Epson's $99 R280 — this combination lets you pop the disc right into a slot on the printer to create high-quality labels using the inkjet printer.

Finding Sources of Content Online

Finding online digital content can be hard if you don't know where to look. Thousands of radio stations broadcast over the Internet, for instance. Most mainstream FM stations also simulcast over the Internet. On the video side, CNN, MSNBC, Yahoo!, and others offer lots of Internet video content; Google's video search capability gives surfers access to amateur video as well as Hollywood fare. Content is simply all over the place.

Lucky for you, lots of industry players have stepped up to the challenge of organizing all of this content for you through *content portals*.

When it comes to buying or accessing online content, there are three main forms of content services:

- ✔ **Download:** You download a file, and it's yours to use forever. Music downloads tend to be in this category. Downloads may be free or not.

- ✔ **Rental:** You download a file, and it's yours to use for a limited time. Many movie rentals allow you a certain number of days to view the movie before it expires and is no longer viewable. Rentals are usually paid for, but can be free on promotion.

  Most video rentals have *two* time restrictions. The first, as we just mentioned, is how long you can keep the file on your hard drive before it is disabled — this usually a week or two. The second clock starts when you begin watching the video — you typically have 24 hours (on the clock) from starting the video for the first time before it expires.

- ✔ **Subscription:** You subscribe to a service that gives you access to unlimited use of the content as it is presented on the portal, such as subscribing to 120 channels of streaming audio for a monthly fee.

In this section, we'll look at a few of these portals offering downloads, rentals, and subscriptions for audio and video content.

Audio content

Audio preceded video in terms of portals on the Internet, largely because audio could be listened to via dial-up Internet connections because of the much smaller file sizes relative to video. Video had to wait for mass broadband deployment to really take off. Some of the most popular online audio content providers (with Web addresses conveniently appended) follow:

- ✔ Apple's iTunes Music Store (www.apple.com/itunes)
- ✔ Rhapsody (www.rhapsody.com)
- ✔ eMusic (www.emusic.com)

✔ Amazon.com (www.amazon.com/mp3)

✔ Napster (www.napster.com)

The pricing and options for these services change rapidly, and we'd be doing both you and us a disservice if we tried to describe all these services in detail. Instead, we'll give you advice about how to find the best service to match your needs:

✔ **Number of songs:** The bigger services offer more choices — it's as simple as that. If you are concerned about the variety and depth of content, you should be aware that there is a big variance in the number of songs — and the number of songs from high-profile artists — each service makes available. Big services such as iTunes, Rhapsody, and Amazon.com's MP3 store have many millions of titles. In general, the wider your tastes, the more you want to go with the larger services. But smaller services such as eMusic (which isn't exactly tiny, with more than 3.5 million tracks available) have a lot of interesting music too — and may offer independently produced content that the big guys don't have.

✔ **Flexibility in use:** If you want to own all your own tracks and movies and have no problem limiting your player choice to iPod models, iTunes is a great option for you. It's simple, has an extensive catalog, is leading the pack with video purchase options, and allows things such as sharing over your LAN and on multiple PCs. The downside of iTunes is that you are married for life to the proprietary Apple world, and that world, as of the time of this writing, is very closed. You simply can't play your iTunes-purchased music or video on alternate players, set-top boxes, and so on — only Apple's own Airport Express will play iTunes Music Store–purchased songs remotely. On the other hand, if you go with the more widely accessible Microsoft Windows Media Audio–based systems, you open up your entire home to a range of players, set-top boxes, and other platforms to access your digital content. The most flexible, for music at least, are Amazon.com and eMusic, which do not use any sort of DRM (discussed earlier in the chapter) system, so you can use them on anything that plays the MP3 format.

✔ **Quality desired:** Digital content has a range of quality as well, mostly based on the encoding sampling rate used. None of the online digital content services store content in a lossless fashion, so all of them end up compromising the original recordings to some extent. You can truly notice a difference between tracks encoded at 128 Kbps, 160 Kbps, and 192 Kbps, for instance. (The higher the number, the better the quality, for those keeping track.) You do trade off the amount of music you can store on your player, though, because the file sizes are larger for higher sampling rates. But we think going for the higher sampling rate — 192 Kbps — is the appropriate trade-off.

✔ **Try before you buy:** If you like to try out lots of new bands and watch all the new indie movies, you should look at subscription services because you can listen and watch to your heart's content and buy what you like. If you go the download route, you'll buy a lot of content you end up not liking — and that's simply a waste of money. (You could buy more of our books with all that wasted money.) Of the subscription services, we like Rhapsody the most because of its user interface.

✔ **"On the go" services:** If you are constantly downloading your content and then hitting the road, you need to look at the available to-go services, such as Napster To Go and Rhapsody To Go, which take their subscription services and package them for road warriors. For about the cost of a CD each month, you can grab your music player, download anything in their full catalog, and hit the road. That's well worth it in our book. Only specific music and video players are supported, so check their sites.

We're not so sure you can make much of a decision based on sheer numbers — if you care about certain types of music or specific artists, avail yourself of the free trials and check them out.

Some services limit access to downloaded content to a specific number of computers, often called *authorized computers*. Be sure to understand where you can play your downloaded content because there usually are lots of restrictions.

If you like audio books, check out `www.audible.com` for audio content you can download to your portable music player to hear your latest book on tape. Also, if you like Internet radio, be sure to check out the following Internet radio hosting or search sites for cool stations:

✔ **SHOUTcast:** `www.shoutcast.com`

✔ **Live365:** `www.live365.com`

✔ **Radio-Locator:** `www.radio-locator.com`

Pat's favorite Internet-only radio station is Radio Paradise (`www.radioparadise.com`). You should check it out!

Video content

Many audio portals and services are getting into the movie act as well. Danny downloaded the first eight episodes of the second season of *Lost* from iTunes to catch up on what he'd missed. Some of the most popular online video sources (again, with handy Web addresses appended) follow:

✔ Movielink (www.movielink.com)

✔ CinemaNow (www.cinemanow.com)

✔ Vongo (www.vongo.com)

✔ Hulu (www.hulu.com)

✔ Netflix (www.netflix.com) — yup, the folks who mail red envelopes containing DVDs also have online movie viewing options.

✔ Apple iTunes Music Store (www.apple.com/itunes) — yes, it has video, too!

The video search engines we discussed earlier in the chapter (such as Google's and Yahoo!'s) can also be great sources of downloadable or streaming video content.

Video services change quickly as well. When looking at video services, you come up against some of the same issues you see with audio services:

✔ **Content:** Not all video services have the same content. As we write, iTunes has some TV shows and movie sales and rentals. CinemaNow and MovieLink focus on Hollywood movie fare. Over time, all of these players will move toward offering the same lineup of video content, with probably some exclusive showings here and there. But if you want to catch up on old TV shows (Danny *really* wants to watch the *Rome* series he missed), look specifically for such offers.

✔ **Subscriptions versus downloads:** For the most part, Internet-based video is offered as pay-as-you-go downloads. But some services, such as iTunes, have subscription-based services for certain types of content (such as a season of a TV series). And Netflix lets you stream an unlimited number of movies — right to your TV — with its new Netflix Player by Roku, discussed later in the chapter.

✔ **Terms of use:** Some video download services let you watch a show once. Some let you start and stop it as often as you want, but you have to finish within three days. Some let you keep it forever. The models are all over the place. Be sure to check out what you are buying. The price might be the same, but the terms could be very different.

Video content is a developing market, and lots of the involved players are trying to figure it out. Video is starting to take up more and more traffic on the networks, and at some point, there will be internal pressures on cable and telephone companies to put limits on their unlimited broadband Internet access subscribers — in other words, they'll probably figure out a way to charge more to users downloading a lot of content from the Internet. Watch for announcements along these lines if you are a big video downloader.

Using an MCE PC to Access Content

In Chapter 8, we discuss home theater PCs (HTPCs) and Microsoft's XP or Vista Media Center software for your home theater. In this section, we discuss how you might use such a PC as a source device in your home theater — specifically, how you'd use it to access Internet content.

HTPCs are good as an alternative to other home theater source devices — for example, as a high-quality way to play back DVDs. But for most folks, they're not worth the trouble just for that purpose. What really makes an HTPC useful is its ability to provide a *portal* to all sorts of great Internet-based content. Now, if you're a real PC aficionado, you might build an HTPC just for fun. But if you're like us, you're going to go down this road only if there's something in it for you. There is!

Most HTPCs and Microsoft's Media Center systems enable users to seek out and find all digital content in the home's network. So it will scan all attached computers for songs, videos, photos, and other content and then make it available to you in a consolidated portal interface, where you can view photo slideshows, watch home movies, or play music from your library.

Microsoft's Media Center Edition software has a special section for accessing Internet content — Internet TV and Online Services sections (in the XP version of Media Center this was called Online Spotlight). This area displays products and services from Microsoft's content partners. Some of the partners are ones mentioned earlier in the chapter — CinemaNow, MovieLink, and Napster, to name a few — and others are just more products to help with digital content, such as Ofoto's photo-sharing service or ABC's Enhanced TV for interactive entertainment from that network. Selecting any Spotlight partner is as simple as clicking its icon in Media Center and working in its Media Center–compatible portal.

While it doesn't specifically include an exact equivalent, Apple's Front Row software (found on most new Macs including the iMac, the Mac Mini, and the latest PowerBooks) will let Mac users gain access to downloaded Internet content in their home theater from the Apple iTunes store. And El Gato's EyeHome software/hardware combo (discussed in Chapter 8) provides full access to a Web browser on your home theater's display, meaning you can access just about any Internet content through a networked Mac. For more details on HTPCs, check out Chapter 9.

Using a Media Server or Adapter to Access Content Online

You don't have to own a home theater PC to access Internet content — some companies make it easy for you to download Internet content to your TV via a special unit that you connect to your TV set.

There are two main types of devices on the market:

- **Media adapters/servers:** Media adapters communicate with a PC and facilitate the flow of content from and through your Internet-connected PC to your home theater.

- **Standalone devices:** Standalone devices connect directly to the Internet and do not require an intermediary PC. While they usually can catalogue and access PC-stored content, it's not the main focus of these devices — so you don't need an actively running PC to gain access to Internet content with standalone devices.

Media adapters and servers

Many leading consumer electronics manufacturers offer media adapters, and capabilities and quality can vary substantially among these products. Media adapters "adapt" the PC content to the home theater environment, offering content to common stereo interfaces such as RCA and digital audio jacks, instead of the more computer-oriented USB and Ethernet jacks.

The typical media adapter is wireless, supports 802.11g or n, has video interfaces such as HDMI and a remote control, and has an onscreen or LCD interface for selecting the content choices on your linked PC.

The list of media adapter players is long. The following gives you a flavor for what's out there:

- **Roku Labs SoundBridge:** Roku Labs (www.rokulabs.com, $199) make some of the sexiest products on the market. Its SoundBridge M1001 elegantly links your home theater to a remote PC via 802.11g wireless. It supports Apple's Bonjour technology (formerly known as Rendezvous) and iTunes, as well as Windows Media Connect, Windows Media Player 10, and Windows Media DRM 10 — it's the most compatible music player around.

Remember, Apple does not allow streaming of its purchased music yet (except through its own Airport Express device), so any songs bought through iTunes cannot be played through the SoundBridge. But SoundBridge does support the AAC format, so that when Apple opens this up, Roku will support it — the SoundBridge *does* support any music that you've imported (ripped) into iTunes on your own.

✔ **Squeezebox:** Mama's got a Squeezebox, and it's made by Logitech's Slim Devices division (www.slimdevices.com, $249). The Squeezebox Classic has standard analog as well as digital optical and coax outputs, so you can link this to your stereo directly with high-quality inputs if you like. The Squeezebox has "always-on" Internet Radio, powered by its own SqueezeNetwork, that lets you tune in to Internet radio streams even when the home PC is switched off. It features Ethernet and 802.11g connections. Overall, very nice. Roku also offers a new whole-home audio player called the Squeezebox Duet ($399) that can bring music to multiple rooms and includes an LCD screen–equipped remote control that shows your entire music library right on the remote.

✔ **Apple AirPort Express:** Aside from being one of only two devices we know of that can stream Apple songs purchased in the iTunes Music Store (the other is Apple's AppleTV), the AirPort Express (www.apple.com, $99) is a small, funky little device that serves multiple roles: media adapter, travel router, print server, Wi-Fi repeater, and more. You don't get a remote control, LCD, or onscreen display. For that, you'll want to upgrade to the $229 Apple TV discussed in the "Standalone media devices" section.

✔ **Other media adapters:** Media adapters are all over the place and include the following

- D-Link's MediaLounge products (www.dlink.com, $150–$229), including the DSM-520 Wireless HD Media Player and the DSM-120 Wireless Music Player

- Netgear's Wireless Digital Media Players (www.netgear.com, $199–$349), including the high-definition capable EVA8000 Digital Entertainer HD

- Linksys's wireless entertainment products (www.linksys.com, $89 and up), including the WMB54G Wireless-G Music Bridge and a pair of Windows Media Center extenders (discussed in the "Extend your Media Center PC" sidebar.)

Extend your Media Center PC

If you have a Media Center PC (using Microsoft's Windows Media Center software on XP or Vista), you don't have to put it right next to your home theater. Go ahead, leave the PC in your home office and use a *Media Center extender.* A media extender is a specialized media adapter that replicates the Media Center interface on your TV without requiring the PC to be locally connected to your home theater. You can get a Media Center Extender in your home theater in two ways:

✔ Get an Xbox 360: Microsoft's latest gaming console includes Media Center extender functionality built right in. You don't need to add hardware or software — just connect the Xbox 360 to your home network and you can access any content (including recorded TV) on your Media Center–equipped PC(s). That's simple. (We talk about the Xbox 360 in Chapter 8.)

✔ Buy a standalone Media Center Extender: Major manufacturers such as Linksys, HP, and D-Link sell these devices (prices range from about $250 to $350). Media Center Extenders include networking capabilities (Ethernet or Wi-Fi), video connections (including HDMI, in most cases), and audio connections (including digital audio outputs).

But wait — there's more (we can never resist a Ginsu knife commercial reference). HP (www.hp.com) sells a line of high-definition LCD TVs (HP MediaSmart LCD HDTVs) with the Media Center extender built into the television. Nothing to add — just make a network connection to your PC and you're all set. Pretty neat stuff. You can find out a lot more about Media Center extenders (including a list of current products — more are coming out all the time) at www.extenderforwindowsmedia center.com.

Standalone media devices

Whereas media adapters were first out of the gate with lots of units, standalone media devices are growing rapidly. Here's a sampling of what's on the market:

✔ **TiVo:** While TiVo (www.tivo.com, starts at $149, $299 for the HD version) is known for its personal video recording (PVR) functionality, it is moving well beyond that space with deals with Yahoo!, Live365, Netflix, and others that in aggregate will open up the TiVo box to the whole Internet. Under the Netflix deal, for instance, you would not have to wait a day to get your disc — it would be downloaded in an hour to your unit. With your Live365 subscription, you can access thousands of radio stations on Live365's network through your home theater setup without even needing a PC.

✔ **Roku Netflix Player:** The folks at Roku have branched out beyond their audio-only Soundbridge players and into the home theater video world with the Roku Netflix Player (www.roku.com, $99), shown in Figure 10-1. This inexpensive player is designed for use with the Netflix video rental service (which starts off at about $5 a month). About 10 percent of the hundreds of thousands of DVDs available in Netflix's catalog are available also for streaming. If you're a Netflix customer, you can go to Netflix.com now and start streaming movies to your Windows PC. With any plan above $9/month, you're allowed *unlimited* streaming. With the Netflix Player, you can move this capability right into your home theater. The Netflix Player includes Ethernet and 802.11g capabilities (for connecting to your home network and the Internet), and has component and HDMI outputs for making a video connection to your HDTV (as well as analog and optical digital audio inputs for connecting to your home theater receiver).

Figure 10-1:
Netflix Player is a cheap and easy way of getting Internet-based movies into your theater.

The Netflix Player can access any streaming videos stored in your Netflix Queue and displays them on your TV screen almost instantly. As we write there are no high-definition movies available through this service, but the box *is* capable of high-definition. You use your PC only to select the movies that go in your queue — otherwise the Netflix Player is independent of your PC. For $99, it's a neat way of getting movies into your home theater.

- **VUDU:** VUDU (www.vudu.com, starting at $299) is a relatively new (but up and coming) player in the standalone video player market. Like the Netflix Player, it is tied to a specific service (in this case, VUDU's own service) and is a standalone device that doesn't need to work with your PC. A couple of big differences between the Netflix Player and the $299 VUDU Box (the primary VUDU product — there's also a $999 VUDU XL model for custom installations with systems such as Control4 and Crestron): First, VUDU uses a download model rather than streaming (VUDU has the first five minutes of about 5000 movies downloaded on your hard drive; when you select a movie the remainder is downloaded), and second, VUDU offers full 1080p HDTV content (something that we'll eventually see from Netflix).

  The VUDU Box has a 250GB hard drive, HDMI and component video outputs, and digital audio outputs (both optical and coaxial). These attributes combine to give you storage space for about 50 high-definition full-length movies and full connectivity to your HDTV and home theater receiver.

  VUDU works on a rental model, with more than 6000 high-definition movies available from the major studios. You pay for each movie individually, and once you rent a movie it is stored on your hard drive for 30 days — once you start watching, you have 24 hours to complete the movie.

- **AppleTV:** Like the Apple iTunes store? Want it in your home theater? Check out the AppleTV (www.apple.com/appletv, starting at $229), which looks a lot like a shrunken down Mac Mini PC. The AppleTV comes with a built-in hard disk drive and Ethernet and 802.11n Wi-Fi connectivity. It connects to your HDTV with an HDMI connection and to your home theater receiver with an optical audio connection. The AppleTV can support 720p high-definition video, and the Apple iTunes store provides both purchases and rentals (with similar rental terms to those offered by VUDU) of Hollywood movies and TV shows. Of course, you can also access iTunes music, podcasts, and other content, as well as your photo library and YouTube videos. If you're a Mac fan, we recommend that you check out the AppleTV.

Taking Your Video with You

Getting Internet and computer-based content *into* your home theater is a neat trick (and one that we highly recommend you explore). But what's even neater is being able to access your home theater content *away* from your home theater. Imagine watching a show that you've recorded on your DVR and having to hop on the train to work before it's over. Well, with the right hardware and software, you can take that content with you and watch it on a laptop or handheld device wherever you are (as long as you have Internet connectivity).

This is a new area in home theater, and one that still has some bugs to work out, both technical and legal — DRM raises its ugly head *again!* But it's something that you can do today and will become even more common in the future. Following are the first few fruits of this new category of home entertainment gear:

- ✔ **TiVo Desktop:** If you have a Series 2 or 3 TiVo DVR, you can use the TiVo's Desktop software built into the product to take your recorded shows on the road with you. This isn't an Internet-based product (such as the Slingbox, which we discuss next). Instead, it uses your home network to transfer recordings from your TiVo to a Windows 2000, XP, or Vista laptop, or to an iPod or other PMP (portable media player) *before you leave home.* When the transfer is done, you can use TiVo's software (a free download from TiVo's Web site) on that device to watch your recorded programs whenever and wherever you like. Check out www.tivo.com for more info. TiVo Desktop also works with Mac PCs if you have Roxio's Titanium Toast software ($79, http://partner.roxio.com/enu/oem/tivotoast/default.html). You can find out more about TiVo Desktop at www.tivo.com/whatistivo/tivois/anywhereyougo/index.html.

- ✔ **Slingbox:** The Slingbox AV ($149 list price) is perhaps the coolest thing to come along the home theater and Internet pike in many years. It's a funky-looking box that you connect to your home theater and to your home network/Internet connection. Slingbox hooks into your TV source devices (such as a cable or satellite set-top box, a DVD player, or a DVR) and allows you to *remotely* control, record, and watch video content. You can use a Slingbox to tune in to live TV (for example, catch the local baseball game while you're on the road in your broadband-equipped hotel room) or to access recorded content on your DVR or DVD player. The companion to Slingbox is SlingPlayer software, which resides on a Windows 2000 or XP computer and controls the Slingbox and let's you view content across an Internet connection. SlingPlayer optimizes the content you're viewing to the speed of your connection, so if you're on a broadband connection, you can get a high-quality picture. SlingPlayer Mobile is also becoming available (from Sling's Web site for $29.99), and it will allow this capability to work on any Windows Mobile device as well. Check it out at www.slingbox.com).

- ✔ **Sony LocationFree:** Sony's $249 answer to the Slingbox, the LocationFree player performs similar tasks, sending live TV and content from various DVRs across an Internet connection to remote PCs. Like the Slingbox, LocationFree let's you access your home TV programming — both live broadcasts and shows you've recorded on your DVR — from any remote location with a broadband Internet connection (such as a hotel or your office). The biggest difference between the two is that Sony's system supports playing back content on the PSP handheld gaming device (which can connect to Wi-Fi wireless networks). As we write, there's no mobile device capability here (beyond the PSP, that is), but we wouldn't be surprised to see that added over time. You can find out more at http://products.sel.sony.com/locationfreetv/.

Part III

Watching and Listening: Display and Control Devices

The 5th Wave   By Rich Tennant

"Can't I just give you riches or something?"

In this part . . .

Your journey through Home Theater Land continues with a look at the heart of your system — the receiver and controller devices. We start this part by looking at what's important about these systems in terms of interfaces, power levels, multizone capabilities, and so on. We also help you decide whether you want an integrated box (a receiver) or separate components. We even talk some about power amplifiers, which is a topic of conversation that makes lots of guys — yes, 99 percent of guys, sorry — very excited.

Then we walk you though a discussion of everything you've ever wanted to know about speakers, building off the surround-sound knowledge from Part I.

The next chapter delves into your TV display options. Your home theater's display often overwhelms the home theater with its presence — not to mention that, with displays that can go to 120 inches and higher, the options can get overwhelming. You can go in lots of directions, and we talk about choosing an HDTV and making the all-important choice between LCD and plasma. (Hint: there's no right answer, both are great!)

Then we get to the projectors. We talk about all the latest technologies and devices — including all-in-one projectors — and the pros and cons for each. LCD, DLP, LCoS — we have all the hot acronyms here.

And then finally we help you make your way through the myriad of options for remotely controlling your system. Find out about the best solutions on the market today.

Chapter 11

The Heart of Your Home Theater: The A/V Receiver

*T*he A/V receiver is the hub of your home theater. It's the device that has both the brains and the brawn to control and drive your home theater experience. A growing home theater market, intense competition, and computer industry–like efficiencies at making electronic components have all benefited the A/V receiver. It's no longer a rarefied, esoteric piece of equipment. In fact, you can get a good one for a reasonable price. Understanding the lingo and marketing speak and choosing a good one can still be difficult, but that's why you bought this book!

In this chapter, we describe the features and specifications that are important to keep in mind as you evaluate A/V receivers. We also talk about a different approach to controlling your system — using separate A/V controllers and power amplifier systems.

Digging In to the A/V Receiver

Think of the A/V receiver as the digital and electronic hub of your home theater. An A/V receiver does a bunch of things, all in one nice and relatively compact package. (It's sort of the Swiss army knife of the home theater, except you can't fit one in your pocket.) Among the tasks assigned to the A/V receiver are the following:

- ✔ **Connects and switches your audio sources:** Every audio source in your home theater should connect to your A/V receiver. The preamplifier section of the receiver allows you to easily switch to (or select) the audio source that you want to listen to.

- ✔ **Connects and switches your video sources:** With a few exceptions (which we discuss later), all your video source devices are also connected directly to the A/V receiver, which is connected in turn to your display device. This setup greatly simplifies the selection of video sources when you want to play a DVD, a show recorded on a PVR (such as a TiVo), or anything else. In most cases, you select what you want to watch on the receiver's remote and don't have to adjust anything on the display.

Some folks feel that they can get the highest video quality by *not* connecting video sources through the receiver. With the advent of high-quality component video and even HDMI (High-Definition Multimedia Interface) switching (see Chapter 16 for more on these connections), we feel that there's a lot to be gained by switching your video through the receiver, and little, if any, degradation in the quality of your video picture.

- ✔ **Tunes in radio programming:** Part of the definition of a receiver is that it includes a radio tuner so you can tune in PBS or Lil' Wayne (or whatever floats your boat between those two extremes).

A number of A/V receivers include satellite radio receivers for XM or Sirius radio (see Chapter 5 for more on this). So if you want to get Howard Stern, sports programming, or other satellite-exclusive content, you might want to consider getting this capability built in to your A/V receiver. However, you'll have to pay extra for the subscription. If you don't want to pay more but are still interested in "digital" radio, you might also look for a receiver that can pick up the new (and free) *HD Radio* format, also discussed in Chapter 5.

- ✔ **Decodes surround-sound formats:** The ability to decode analog and digital surround-sound formats (we talk about these in Chapter 3) is one of two features that distinguish an A/V receiver from a more traditional stereo receiver (the plain old stereo you've had around for years).

A few receivers now have the ability to decode the Dolby TrueHD and DTS Master Audio formats found on some Blu-ray discs.

- ✔ **Amplifies audio signals to drive multiple speakers:** Another distinguishing characteristic of an A/V receiver is the fact that it contains at least five channels of amplification to *drive* (or provide power to) your surround-sound speaker system.

✔ **Provides the user interface for your home theater:** The interface includes the receiver's remote control (or your own favorite remote, as we discuss in Chapter 15), the displays on the receiver's face, and (in many cases) an onscreen display on your television. All these elements enable you, the human (or your dog, if he's very talented), to command all the electronic components in your home theater.

In the following sections, we discuss each of these A/V receiver responsibilities in more detail.

Counting Inputs

Most people like to *ooh* and *ahh* at the bells and whistles — pretty design, big macho power ratings, and the like. When evaluating any A/V receiver, however, we think a good place to begin is by counting the inputs that let you connect source devices to the receiver. After all, if you have a Blu-ray disc player, a cassette deck, a satellite receiver, an Apple TV media player, a turntable, a PVR (personal video recorder), an Xbox 360, and a VCR, you want to hook all these devices into your home theater.

To use all your components, you'd better have enough inputs on the back of your receiver. A receiver may have enough power to wake up people across town and a design so beautiful that your home theater skeptic spouse *begs* you to buy it, but that beauty won't do you much good if you have to climb behind it and switch wires every time you want to switch sources. So before you buy anything, think about the components you have and what you'll soon be getting and make sure the receiver has enough inputs.

Most A/V receivers have enough inputs for most people. We don't want to scare you. In fact, most have enough jacks on the back to make your head swim. But many inexpensive receivers don't have enough of the *right kind* of jacks for some folks. This is particularly true for digital audio and video jacks but can also be true for analog audio inputs if you've decided to go down the SACD or DVD-Audio path, which we cover in Chapter 5, and for many Blu-ray disc players, which can use analog outputs for their higher-resolution surround-sound formats.

Deciphering digital audio inputs

Digital audio inputs (we show examples of these in Chapter 16) on an A/V receiver let you connect the audio outputs of DVD players, CD players, game consoles, HDTV tuners, Media Center PCs (Chapter 9), digital audio players for MP3 and other computer audio (Chapter 10), and many newer digital cable set-top boxes or DSS satellite receivers. Connecting these audio sources by using digital inputs (instead of the traditional analog inputs) is always a good idea because the digital signals are much less prone to electrical interference than analog signals. A more important consideration is that digital inputs are *required* to get digital surround-sound formats, such as Dolby Digital and DTS, into your receiver. (The two-channel analog outputs on DVD players and other devices move you down to the lesser Dolby Pro Logic surround-sound system. You can't get digital surround sound from these connections.)

An exception to this rule involves devices (mainly DVD players) that have a built-in Dolby Digital or DTS surround-sound decoder. You *can* connect these to your receiver using analog audio connections, but this may not be the optimal solution for the following reasons:

✔ You need to use six cables instead of one.

✔ You may lose some signal quality due to interference in the analog signal.

✔ You need a receiver that has the necessary six analog inputs on the back — and even if you have these, they may be "taken up" by the six channel outputs of a DVD-Audio or SACD player.

There are two types of digital audio connections (which we discuss in more detail in Chapter 16): coaxial and optical. Some high-end audio folks believe that coaxial sounds better; it may have a slight sonic benefit, but not so much that regular people can tell. Just make sure that you don't buy a receiver with three optical connections and one coaxial connection and then find you have three source devices with coaxial connections only. Oops. (If you don't know what these look like, again look in Chapter 16.)

One set of digital audio signals won't be carried over the coaxial or optical digital audio inputs we just discussed. These are the newest (and highest quality) surround-sound signals found on many Blu-ray discs — Dolby's TrueHD and DTS-HD Master Audio. These *lossless* systems use much more data to digitally encode the surround-sound audio — which makes them sound better but uses more data bandwidth than these coaxial or optical cables can carry. To get these signals into your home theater receiver, you'll need to use either analog cables (as we just discussed — you'll need as many as eight cables for a 7.1-surround signal) or an HDMI connection to your receiver.

That's right, a third type of digital connection can carry digital audio signals: the HDMI connection, which is increasingly used for HDTV tuners/satellite receivers and set-top boxes and which is also common in other devices such as DVD players (both regular DVD players and Blu-ray disc players, which we discuss in Chapter 6) and even in the newest game consoles such as the Xbox 360 and PlayStation 3. If you use HDMI to connect these devices to your home theater receiver, you don't need to use a separate digital audio connection — the audio and video are both carried over the HDMI connection.

You can still find a number of current model A/V receivers without support for HDMI. So if you want to use HDMI to connect your video to your HDTV, you'll run an HDMI cable from your source device directly to the TV, not to the receiver. In cases like this, you'll want to use a coaxial or optical digital audio connection to handle the surround-sound connection to your receiver. We discuss this in more detail in Chapter 17.

The key measurement here is the total number of connections — as long as the types of connections match up with your other equipment, which is usually not a problem because most source devices have both kinds of connectors on the back. Look again at the devices with digital connections mentioned at the beginning of this section. Count how many of those devices with digital outputs you have. Do the math. Many inexpensive receivers have only three digital inputs (some even fewer). If all you have is a DVD player, you'll be fine. After a few years of home theatering, however, we bet you'll have multiple devices with digital outputs, so plan ahead.

It's not just the *number* of digital inputs but also the *type* of inputs. Most A/V devices offer both a coaxial and an optical audio output, but some offer only one or the other. When you are counting up your digital input requirements, make sure that you account for the number of coaxial and optical inputs you need and choose a receiver accordingly.

Analyzing analog audio inputs

Now that we spent all that time telling you that digital inputs are so much better than analog inputs, why are we emphasizing analog inputs' importance? Well, first of all, they're not really that awful. We think digital connections are the way to go when they're available, but analog is just fine when it's all you can get. Devices that use analog audio connections include the following:

- Older CD players (without a digital output)
- External radio tuners
- Analog VCRs
- Cable set-top and DSS receivers without digital outputs
- Cassette recorders
- Older game consoles (such as Nintendo 64 and the original PlayStation)
- The newest digital audio sources, SACD and DVD-A, which we discuss in Chapter 5

Just about any device that uses a digital audio connection into your receiver — discussed in the previous section — can also use analog audio connections. We recommend using digital connections to your receiver when they're available, but if they're not, don't forget the fact that you *can* go analog. It may just get that piece of gear connected and save the day!

All the devices we mention in this list — except for SACD and DVD-Audio — use a simple pair of analog audio connections, one for the left channel and one for the right. It's not hard to figure these out. Just count up your inputs on the receiver and count up your devices. The inputs on the receiver are labeled, and these labels correspond to the buttons on the front of the console and on your remote control. It's always nice if the names on the receiver's inputs match input names on the device to which you're connecting the receiver, but it's not essential. It may not even be possible if you have some funky device that no one ever thought of when your receiver was designed.

The one exception to this flexibility in making connections are the inputs on your receiver marked *phono*. These are for your record player (phonograph) and are not standard inputs. If you have a record player, use these inputs for it. If you don't have a record player, don't use these inputs for anything else. If you do use them, it won't blow anything up, but it will sound amazingly awful, and your dog will hide under the bed until you turn it off.

For DVD-Audio and SACD players, you need a special set of analog inputs with six connectors. These formats can support multichannel audio (five channels plus a subwoofer for bass) and therefore need the extra inputs. Many newer receivers have a six-input section (called a *5.1 analog input*), so you can use an SACD or DVD-A player.

Some receivers also have a section on the back with six (or more!) inputs for an *external decoder*. These allow you to hook up a newer decoder in the future. The idea is that the future decoder will handle surround-sound formats that weren't even thought of when the receiver was designed — a nice bit of futureproofing.

The 5.1-channel input for DVD-A/SACD and the input for an external decoder are functionally identical. Some receivers will have one set of 5.1 inputs labeled for DVD-A/SACD and another labeled for an external decoder. Others have only one set. In the majority of cases, you can use these inputs for either purpose.

Some receivers also have a set of six similar-looking *outputs*. These allow you to bypass the internal amplifiers in the receiver and use a set of separate, more powerful amplifiers to drive your speakers. Again, this is a nice feature to look for if you think you might need more power some time in the future.

Verifying video inputs

When hooking up a home theater, some folks try to connect all their video devices directly to the TV or display, but they usually don't succeed because most displays have a rather limited set of inputs on the back (though some have a ton). We prefer to connect all our video devices directly to the receiver and let the receiver *switch* (that is, select) which video source goes to the display. It's just easier, neater, and simpler that way.

We're talking about the video signal coming out of these devices here. They all have an audio signal as well (for the soundtrack), and that should also be connected to the receiver using one of the two methods described in the previous sections. You won't get any surround sound if you don't perform that basic step.

Analog video connections

As we discuss in Chapter 16, there are five common types of video connections (in order of worst to best): coaxial (also called baseband — rarely found in a receiver), composite, S-video, component, and the digital HDMI system. Virtually every A/V receiver has yellow color-coded composite video inputs on the back. (They're usually right next to the audio inputs for a source device, so they're labeled *DVD, VCR,* and so on.) Coaxial is the pits, so the less said about it the better. Composite video basically stinks (relative to S-video and component), so use it only for low-resolution video sources, such as low-end VCRs; otherwise, just leave those composite plugs unused.

What you want to look for in a receiver are both S-video connections and component video connections for your analog video sources. The picture quality you get when using these connections is almost always better than what you get with a composite video connection. S-video connections can be found on better VCRs (the S-VHS models), most DVD players, DSS receivers, digital cable set-top boxes, PVRs, and older gaming consoles (Xbox, PlayStation 2, and Nintendo GameCube, for example). Component video connections can be found on DVD players, HDTV tuners, gaming consoles such as the PS3, Xbox 360, and Nintendo Wii, and on many PVRs (such as TiVo and those built-in to high-definition set-top boxes for cable and satellite TV).

HDTV signals need a special kind of component video connection called a *wideband component video* connection. Some receivers have component video connections but can't handle the higher frequencies of HDTV. If a specification is given, look for something higher than 25 MHz.

Until recently, component video inputs were a rarity on inexpensive and even moderately priced receivers. Because the popularity of DVD and other sources that can use component video (particularly HDTV) has risen, however, component video has moved into the mainstream. Even the cheapest receivers typically have two or three sets of component video inputs these days. If you run a bit short on component video inputs, you can use S-video for nonprogressive or non-HDTV sources (such as a PlayStation 2) and reserve the component inputs for your progressive-scan DVD and your HDTV tuner.

Many otherwise excellent displays have only a single-component video input, and few displays have enough S-video inputs for everything you might want to connect to them. This is a strong argument for finding a receiver that has a sufficient number of inputs. Like the audio inputs discussed earlier, this is a pretty simple thing to figure out while you are shopping. Count up what you have that uses S-video or component video and start eliminating A/V receivers that don't have what you need from your shopping list.

HDMI hits the receiver

Digital HDMI audio/video connections are used for both audio and video — all over a single cable. We talk about HDMI in more detail in Chapter 16, but here's an overview of how HDMI fits into the receiver world.

First, HDMI is still a relatively new technology in the receiver market — it's become pretty much the "go to" video connection technology for HDTVs and for high-definition sources feeding into those TVs (such as DVD, Blu-ray disc, and set-top boxes). But receiver manufacturers are still slowly incorporating the technology into their receivers. Most receivers that cost $500 or more have at least a few built-in HDMI inputs (and one HDMI output). Many under that price have just component video inputs and no HDMI. Over time, you'll find that HDMI will become standard on just about all receivers, but today you'll probably have to pay more for it.

Because HDMI has become the primary means of connecting high-definition source devices, you'll want to have as many HDMI inputs on your receiver as you can. Even expensive receivers often top out at three HDMI inputs (which would allow, for example, a Blu-ray disc player, a high-definition gaming console, and a TV set-top box to connect through your receiver). It's rare to find any more than that at any price today, though we suspect that receiver manufacturers will follow the lead of TV manufacturers (who routinely offer four HDMI inputs on their TVs) in the near future.

If you don't have enough HDMI inputs on your receiver, you can use HDMI cables to connect some of your sources directly to the TV, and then connect the audio outputs of those sources to your receiver using digital audio connections. If you have a Blu-ray disc player in your home theater arsenal, make sure you connect it directly to the receiver using HDMI, to ensure that you'll be able to get the highest quality surround-sound audio using DTS-HD Master Audio or Dolby True HD.

There's one small gotcha to keep in mind about HDMI (and we discuss this in detail in Chapter 16). HDMI comes in two versions: HDMI and HDMI High

Speed (what folks often call HDMI 1.3). The High Speed version lets you send a 1080p video signal over the HDMI connection; the regular version tops out at 1080i. This isn't an issue if you don't have a 1080p HDTV (see Chapter 13), but if you do have 1080p, you'll want to make sure that anything connected via HDMI supports High Speed — if your receiver doesn't support this, you might want to connect any 1080p HDMI sources directly to the TV.

Switching sources

With all these inputs, an A/V receiver can do all the source switching for your home theater system. Plug all your source devices in to the receiver, connect your speakers and display to the receiver's outputs, and let the receiver do the work of sending audio and video to these devices — rather than having a bunch of individual cables running to your display. As we mentioned earlier, most displays simply don't have enough inputs (particularly on the video side) to allow you to connect the myriad video sources you have (or will soon have) directly into them. Allowing the A/V receiver to concentrate and switch between all these sources just plain makes sense.

As you audition receivers, check out the quality of their video switching. We can't give you a quantitative piece of advice here, but we can tell you to do some research. Read the reviews. Most good reviewers comment on the video-switching capabilities. If you can, do your own quick test. Watch a bit of video on a DVD player hooked up through the receiver and then try watching the same video using the same type of connection plugged directly in to the display. If the picture is softer or less detailed when running through the receiver, it might not the receiver you want.

Another factor to keep in mind regarding video switching is how the A/V receiver itself connects to the display. You'll likely have a mixture of composite, S-video, and component video connections running into the receiver from your source devices. Some more capable receivers convert signals from lower-quality to higher-quality connections. For example, a receiver may convert all composite and S-video incoming connections to component video. This doesn't make the picture any better, but it does enable you to use a single output connection from the receiver to the display. It also enables you to set the display on its component input and then just leave it there and forget it, which is handy.

Many receivers use the home theater display to provide onscreen system controls. If your system converts composite or S-video to a higher-quality connection, make sure it also sends the onscreen display over that connection. Switching the display back to the composite video input just to tweak a control is a real pain in the tonsils (as Pat's mom says — though he's not sure what that means).

Understanding upconversion

A feature that has hit the market by storm recently (and that we think can be handy) is video *upconversion*. Essentially, a receiver with upconversion takes lower-resolution video input (such as composite or S-video) and converts it to a higher-resolution format, such as component video or even HDMI.

The two primary reasons to consider video upconversion in a receiver are

  ✔ Fewer cables
  ✔ Improved picture quality

You'll see two types of upconversion when you're shopping for receivers:

  ✔ Component upconversion
  ✔ HDMI upconversion

Uh oh, too few inputs on your receiver?

Sometimes, you do your homework and buy a receiver with enough inputs, and then some new video source plops into your life unannounced, leaving you an input or two short. (Or maybe you just plain fell in love with a receiver that didn't have enough inputs. We forgive you.) What to do?

Well, first check your display for extra inputs on the back (or front). Using these isn't quite as neat and integrated as using the receiver, but doing so won't hurt the image quality.

If you're still running short, look into an external video switcher. You can get your hands on a cheap one at any electronics or home theater store. You usually switch this device manually (meaning you walk up to it and push a button). Switchers accept several video inputs and send them to your receiver over a single output connection. Many switchers include an autoswitching capability (so that the *active*

source is sent to your TV, without any action from you), which is a very nice feature. At a minimum, you'll want a switcher that can be controlled by a remote control — it's no fun to have to get up and push a button to change sources — yes, we've all been spoiled rotten by the remote control.

Most folks these days run out of HDMI inputs on their receivers before any other type (as more and more sources move to HDMI). A good example of an HDMI switcher is Oppo Digital's HM-31 (http://oppodigital.com/hm31/), which can switch three HDMI inputs into one HDMI output cable. For only $99 you get HDMI High Speed, capable of supporting 1080p video and just about anything that HDMI is capable of carrying. You don't get autoswitching, but the cost is about one-fourth the price of most competing solutions.

Assessing Your Amplifier

Another essential job for any A/V receiver involves amplifying outgoing audio signals so that your speakers can do their thing. We discuss in greater detail how speakers work in the following chapter, but for now let's just say that they are based on electromagnetic systems that need a lot of electricity. The electrical signals coming out of audio source devices, however, are relatively low-powered. The amplifier does what its name says; it increases this power level.

Unscrambling power ratings

The first thing most folks look at when they see a shiny new receiver is the power rating. The rating is measured in watts per channel (usually measured as RMS, or root mean square, instead of peak, which means that it is a measure of sustained power, not the highest possible instantaneous peak). The problem is that you can't take these ratings at face value because manufacturers play a lot of interesting tricks when they give these watt ratings. The result is that a receiver can be more or less powerful than another receiver with the same rating. To get a feel for a receiver's power, examine the following four things closely:

- **Distortion:** Power is measured at a certain number of watts at a certain level of *distortion* (noise created by the amplifier). You want low distortion (of course). The tricky part comes in when you examine how the amplifier's power output is measured — specifically at what distortion level it's measured. An amp that is measured, for example, at 100 watts per channel at 0.02 percent THD (*total harmonic distortion,* the standard measurement) is quieter and is probably more powerful than one that is measured at 100 watts per channel at 0.2 percent THD. You can do a direct comparison only if both are measured at the same THD percentage. Another way of looking at this issue is this fact: If manufacturers measure power at a higher distortion rating, they can squeeze more "on paper" power out of the receiver.

- **Impedance:** Almost all amplifiers are rated at 8 ohms impedance (a measure of electrical resistance, discussed in Chapter 12), so you can compare ratings this way, but a few are also measured at 6 or even 4 ohms. These lower resistances can give an artificially high power rating — be suspicious.

Not all amplifiers built into receivers (or even in separate power amplifiers) can power 4-ohm speakers without overheating, popping a circuit breaker, or just plain breaking down. Check to see whether a receiver can support these lower impedances if you choose speakers that require it. This is rare unless you are buying high-end gear — most home theater speaker systems are rated at 8 ohms of impedance (though the actual number varies as the speakers reproduce different frequencies).

✔ **Frequency range:** Lower frequencies (the bass frequencies) require more amplifier power than higher frequencies. Because of this, some receiver manufacturers test their systems not at the full 20 to 20,000 Hz range (which is what we call *full range*), but with a limited range (such as 40 to 20,000 Hz). This can also create an artificially high power rating. Receivers that are measured at full range are often called *full bandwidth rated*.

✔ **Number of channels driven:** Home theater receivers should be capable of driving at least five speakers (some have amplifiers for six, seven, or more speakers for extra surround channels). Power ratings should state how many speakers are being driven when the system is tested. Preferably, all channels are driven simultaneously at the stated power. Some systems give power ratings in *stereo* mode (with only the front left and right speakers driven), which means that the power with all speakers being driven is less than the stated amount.

Determining how much receiver power you need

How much power do you need in your receiver? Well, we're going to weasel out by saying, "It depends." Which speakers you choose plays a key role here. Different speakers have different *sensitivities*, a measure of how loud they are, given a certain amount of power. The standard measure for this is how many decibels they produce with 1 watt of power at 1 meter's distance from the speaker. A more sensitive speaker requires less amplification to reach the same volume level.

You also need to consider the size of your home theater and how loudly you plan on playing your movies and music. If you want to create permanent hearing loss or have a room the size of the Taj Mahal, you might need a receiver that can pump out 150 watts per channel. If you have relatively sensitive speakers and a moderately sized home theater, and you don't plan on testing the thickness of your window glass with really loud music, a receiver with 70 watts per channel (or less) might do the trick. We think that receivers with about 100 watts per channel (honestly measured) are more than powerful enough in just about any home theater.

Amplifiers (whether separate or in a receiver) make their power by using transistors. In the old days, amplifiers used vacuum tubes, and some really expensive high-end amps still use tubes because some audio enthusiasts prefer their sound. Inexpensive receivers use an IC (integrated circuit), which provides the power-generating transistors for several audio channels on a single chip. Better receivers have *discrete* amplifier output transistors — separate transistors for each channel. Typically, you get more power and better sound from a discrete design.

Zoning Out to the Rest of the House

Many home theater receivers — particularly those $1,000 or higher — include a *multizone* functionality. This lets your receiver not only control your home theater but also provide music to other rooms in your house. A multizone receiver is a good way to get started down the whole-home theater path.

The simplest multizone receivers have a pair of stereo audio outputs (not speaker connectors or amplifier channels, just outputs). These outputs enable you to run an audio cable to another room and connect to a separate amplifier and speakers in that room (or to a pair of *active* speakers that have a built-in amplifier). The key feature to look for here is that this second zone is truly a second zone. That is to say, the receiver lets you send a *different* audio source to the second room, not just the one you are playing in the home theater. So the kids can listen to Barney the dinosaur sing "I love you" in the den, while you watch *Memento* in the home theater.

As you get into more sophisticated systems, you can find receivers with extra built-in amplifiers (so you don't need an amp in the extra room) and with extra zones (so you can send different audio sources to a third or fourth room). You may even find multizone A/V receivers that send out a composite video signal. With this signal, you can watch the video from a home theater video source elsewhere in the home.

In Chapter 18, we get into more detail about sharing home theater sources throughout the home. If you want to get really sophisticated with a true "every room in the house" system, you might need some more gear (which we discuss in that chapter).

Having Fun with DSPs and Decoders

Another key responsibility of the A/V receiver is to decode surround-sound formats in your audio and video programming so that sound can be sent to those six or more speakers in your theater. Two kinds of chips in the receiver handle all this digital magic: the DSP and the DAC.

Digital Signal Processors

The DSP (Digital Signal Processor) is the brains of the decoding process. This chip handles all the *steering* of surround sound, sending musical signals to the correct channels. The DSP also can provide its own sound field enhancements — essentially electronic changes in tone and timing (echoes) — though some people hate them and wouldn't use the term *enhancement* to describe them! These enhancements are called *DSP Modes,* which are modifications to the signal to create delays in the sound. The delays can make your home theater sound like something else — for example, a cathedral or a smoky jazzy club (you have to provide your own smoke).

One feature that DSPs enable (and that we love!) is the ability to *dynamically compress* music and, more importantly, movie soundtracks. Dynamic compression makes the louds less loud and also makes the quiet parts not quite so quiet. When someone is sleeping two rooms over while you watch a movie at night, you don't necessarily want that *Top Gun* F-14 flying overhead at full roar. (Pat was in the Navy and spent too much time in the Persian Gulf with jets taking off about 15 feet over his head and doesn't ever want to hear that again, but that's a different story.) This feature, often called *nighttime mode,* is great for family harmony.

Many receiver manufacturers make a big deal about which DSP they use. It does make a difference, and some aficionados have their own preferences. The key is that the DSP can support the decoding of the surround-sound formats you want and need in your home theater. At a minimum, you should pick a receiver that can decode Dolby Digital and DTS (the plain-Jane 5.1 versions of these standards) and Dolby Pro Logic II (for VHS and other nondigital sources). We like receivers that can also decode Dolby Pro Logic IIx, which does a much better job on VHS and regular TV — luckily Pro Logic IIx is becoming pretty much standard these days.

If you're getting a six- or seven-channel system, you want a receiver that can support DTS-ES or Dolby Digital EX (or THX Surround EX). We don't think that's necessary for an entry-level home theater, but if you're getting fancy, why not?

Make your receiver automatic

A cool feature that's increasingly being built into home theater receivers is an autocalibration system. If you read Chapter 19, you'll see our discussion of receiver calibration, which is essentially adjusting the volume and time delay of signals sent to each of the speakers in your surround-sound system so that your system sounds right for *your room* and speaker placement. This is a painstaking and somewhat inaccurate process if you do it manually. Luckily, many manufacturers now incorporate an automated system that lets you plug a microphone in to your receiver, press a button, and essentially walk away while your receiver calibrates itself.

The biggest manufacturer of such software systems is Audyssey (www.audyssey.com). You can find a description of its MultEQ system, along with a list of receivers into which it has been incorporated, at the company's Web site.

The Blu-ray disc player has brought Dolby's TrueHD and Digital Plus as well as DTS's DTS-HD Master Audio formats, all discussed in Chapter 3, to the home theater. For the most part you'll find the decoders for these formats *inside the Blu-ray disc player* and not in the receiver, but a number of fancier receivers are beginning to include decoders inside the receiver itself. To recap what we said in Chapter 6 (where we discuss Blu-ray disc players), you can get these high-quality surround-sound formats into your receiver in three ways:

- ✔ If you have HDMI *and* a decoder for these formats in your receiver, *and* your Blu-ray player supports it, you can send the TrueHD or Master Audio *bitstream* over HDMI to your receiver, and let the receiver's internal decoder handle the surround-sound decoding. This is great, if you can do it, but not very common as we write this.

- ✔ If you have HDMI in your receiver *and* a decoder in your *Blu-ray disc player* (not in your receiver), you can send the surround sound as *PCM audio* over your HDMI cable. This is just about as good, soundwise, as decoding inside the receiver and is much more common.

- ✔ Finally, if your receiver has no HDMI connection *and* your Blu-ray disc player has a built-in decoder, you can use analog connections for your audio. This is less convenient (eight cables for audio *plus* a video cable to your TV), but the quality is also quite good. This is also common.

Digital Analog Converters

DACs (or Digital Analog Converters) take the digitally encoded musical signals (from a Dolby Digital or DTS DVD soundtrack or the PCM — short for Pulse Code Modulation, a standard way of storing digital audio — from a digitally connected compact disc) and convert these digital signals into analog signals that the receiver's amplifier and the speakers can understand. Receiver vendors seem to be going through some kind of a race with DACs these days. Each vendor is coming out with models that have new DACs with even higher capacities.

DACs are rated by the frequency of digital signal and the number of bits they can decode (for example, 96 kHz and 24 bits). We've seen receivers with *multiple* DACs (up to 16 in a single receiver) rated at 192 kHz and 24 bits. You should choose a receiver with at least 96 kHz/24-bit DACs. If digital connections for systems such as SACD or DVD-Audio ever become common, those higher-capacity DACs will become a minimum recommendation. (Today, they are not, in our minds.)

Sometimes, you don't want to mess with all that digital stuff. Analog signals coming into the receiver are typically converted to digital signals (using ADCs — the opposite of DACs). The digital signals run through the DSP and are then converted back to analog signals with the DACs. Many audio purists feel that all this conversion can create minor (but to them, not insignificant) distortions in the audio. If your receiver has *analog bypass,* you can stay in straight, old-fashioned, pure analog all the way to the amplifier section. We recommend analog bypass for the analog inputs from an SACD or a DVD-Audio player, as well as for turntable inputs. Some receivers automatically bypass the digital stuff for these inputs whereas others have a switch on the remote. Some don't bypass it at all; so if you want this feature, check to see if your receiver will give it to you.

Dealing with Bass

Connecting a subwoofer (or more than one if you love the bass) to your home theater is an essential part of providing the sound for your movies and TV. The majority of subwoofers are *active* (they have their own built-in amplifiers). You need an output on your A/V receiver to connect a standard analog audio cable to the subwoofer. On most receivers, this output is labeled the *LFE* (Low Frequency Effects) channel and is indicated by the ".1" part of 5.1-, 6.1-, and 7.1-channel surround-sound formats. We highly recommend you get a receiver with this output; most receivers have one — it's pretty much assured if you buy a Dolby Digital– or DTS-equipped receiver.

The other subwoofer-related thing to look for is an *adjustable crossover* that lets you select which audio frequencies go to the subwoofer and which go to the main front speakers. Different speaker systems sound better with the crossover set at different frequencies. If you have small bookshelf speakers in the front, you might set the crossover to a higher frequency. If you have a set of huge tower speakers with giant woofers (bass speakers) of their own, you might set the crossover to a lower frequency and let the subwoofer concentrate on only the really deep sounds.

We discuss speakers in more detail in Chapter 12.

Interfacing with Your Receiver

A/V receivers control a lot of things in your system, such as selection of audio and video sources, volume, surround-sound formats, relative volume levels for surround speakers, and more. You interface with the receiver through the buttons and knobs on the front and, more importantly, through the remote control.

The receiver gives you feedback on your control actions through one or both of two means: lights and displays on the face of the receiver and an onscreen display on your television set. We like onscreen displays (they're easier to read), and we'd be willing to bet you will, too. However, you're not going to find this feature on most inexpensive receivers.

Whether or not you have an onscreen display, we think that checking out how the receiver's interface works is important. For example, most receivers use menu-driven controls (like the menus in a computer program). In some cases, you need to push a lot of buttons and navigate through several menus to get to important controls. That's okay for things you set once and forget about (such as your initial setup), but such controls are a real pain for procedures you do over and over again (such as selecting a video or audio source). We like systems that have easy-to-understand menus and *direct access* to key functions (meaning you have to press only one button to get to them).

When evaluating a receiver's interface, you also want to check out the remote control. These days, most A/V receivers can control other devices (such as DVD players). Many remotes are *learning* or *programmable* ones that can control devices from other manufacturers. Cheaper programmable remotes work only with equipment from the same manufacturer. When you start getting fancy, you find remotes that are backlit (so you can see them in the dark) or even *touch-screen* remotes (with a touch-sensitive LCD panel instead of a million tiny little buttons). We talk about remotes in much more detail in Chapter 15.

Making the Separates Decision

As you start moving up the price scale, you begin to reach a decision point: Do you want to stick with a (very, very good) all-in-one high-end A/V receiver, or do you want to move into separates? *Separates* break down the functions of the receiver into three (you guessed it) separate components: a radio tuner, a power amplifier (or power amplifiers), and an A/V controller. You can probably guess what the tuner and amplifiers do; the controller performs the switching and *preamplification* tasks (basically adjusting the levels of audio signals to control your volume) and includes the DSPs and DACs that do surround-sound decoding and conversion of digital audio into analog audio.

You might go with separates for a couple of reasons:

✔ **More flexibility:** A separates system lets you choose exactly which components you want. Like the amplifiers from Brand X but the controller functions from Brand Y? Mix and match! Separates give you a more flexible upgrade path, too. If you buy a Dolby Digital and DTS 5.1 decoder but someday want to move up to Dolby Digital Plus (or some future surround-sound format), you need to upgrade only the decoder, not the whole system. Keep in mind that you might have to buy extra amplifiers for extra surround-sound channels, but that's easy to do.

✔ **Better performance:** A/V receivers can offer excellent sound quality, but for that last bit of sonic realism, separates can offer the ultimate in sound. Putting all the electronics for your A/V components in separate chassis can reduce the possibility of these electronic gizmos interfering with each other and causing distortions in your sound. For example, many folks going the separates route buy fancy *mono* power amplifiers — a separate amplifier (with its own power supply and other internal components) for each channel. Most people don't have the space, budget, or (to be realistic) the need for such a setup. But it's a nice possibility to consider.

We talk about separate components in more detail in Chapter 21, where we describe moving up to the high end of home theater. If you can afford the additional expense, you might want to consider using separates. If you don't want to spend any more than you have to and prefer the simplicity (and space savings) of an all-in-one solution, stick with an A/V receiver.

Chapter 12

Speaker of the House

Although your video display often hogs all the attention in your home theater, the speaker system is what really makes your theater sing — literally.

Speaker systems don't get the attention they deserve. Many people actually see the speaker system as almost an afterthought — something bundled with the receiver or other equipment. Speakers have a double curse: They lack oodles of fancy features and display screens, and the features they *do* have are tied up with technical descriptions that most people can't decipher.

Not paying enough attention to your speaker system is a huge mistake. People notice bad audio a lot faster than they notice bad video. In this chapter, we explain how to evaluate your speakers, and we discuss issues to think about when buying speakers for your home theater. In Chapters 17 and 19, we talk about how to install your speakers and tweak them to perfection.

Understanding How Speakers Work

Unlike other components in your system, speakers are differentiated (more than anything else) by somewhat obscure technical characteristics. So an understanding of how speakers work may be just what you need to stay un-glassy-eyed when we go on and on about making sure your speakers are *in phase* and things like that.

Drivers

Speakers are actually relatively simple devices. Basically, you have an enclosure (typically a box) into which speaker drivers are attached. The *drivers* are the round elements that many people call the speakers (they're not). The drivers look like cones or horns (or even ribbons or domes), and in fact, the large surface area of the drivers is called the *cone* or *diaphragm*. These surfaces move back and forth to make the sound. If you have ever pulled the front screen off your speakers or have seen speakers without their front grille on, you've seen speaker drivers *au naturelle*.

Driver sizes

Drivers come in different sizes and modes, but generally speaking, you'll find three types, based on the frequencies they handle:

- **Tweeter driver:** These handle the high-frequency treble range (above 2000 Hz).

- **Midrange driver:** These, not surprisingly, handle midrange frequencies (200 Hz to 2000 Hz).

- **Woofer driver:** These handle the low-frequency bass range (below 200 Hz).

No single driver is well suited to handle all sounds from 20 Hz to 20,000 Hz; multiple drivers are commonly used to be able to span the full spectrum. A speaker that handles the full frequency is called, not surprisingly, a *full-range* speaker.

How drivers work

Speaker driver cones are typically made from paper, plastic, or metal. This material moves back and forth and creates changes in the air pressure (sound waves) that ultimately arrive at your eardrum and cause it to move back and forth in a corresponding fashion. This causes you to hear the sound. The cone is moved by an electromagnetic process that's caused by a coil of wire, called the *voice coil,* at the base of the cone. The electrical impulses coming from the amplifier (or the amplifiers built into your receiver) drive the voice coil, and the voice coil interacts with a permanent magnet attached to the speaker's cone or dome or whatever shape it may take. (If you want a great explanation of how speakers work in more detail, check out www.howstuffworks.com/speaker.htm.)

Drivers come in all sorts of different sizes, but (again) generally speaking, the larger the driver, the lower the frequencies it was designed for. Because higher frequencies require sound waves that have high and low pressure points close together, the cone must be smaller to be able to move back and forth fast enough to keep up. Lower frequencies have to move back and forth more slowly, and smaller drivers have a hard time with these. So you find that drivers are designed for specific audio frequency ranges.

Most speakers that have multiple drivers in their speaker enclosure have electronic circuits known as *crossovers,* which divide up inbound speaker signals and distribute them to the appropriate driver.

Drivers in speaker-market lingo

You'll most often run into two types of speakers on the market:

- **Two-way:** These have a woofer and a tweeter in one speaker enclosure.
- **Three-way:** These have a woofer, a tweeter, and a midrange driver in the same enclosure.

You'll also find speakers with multiple tweeters or midrange drivers, and occasionally *four-way* speakers with two of the frequencies divided among four different drivers (or four different sets of drivers — for example, two tweeters and two pairs of different-sized midrange drivers). You can even find some speakers (typically smaller *satellite* speakers designed for wall mounting) with only *one* driver to handle both the bass and the treble. A huge amount of variety is out there.

More drivers doesn't always mean better sound, but often speakers with multiple drivers sound better because each of the individual woofer, midrange, and tweeter drivers can be optimized to reproduce a specific range of frequencies. Keep in mind that it's hard for a driver to reproduce the whole range of audio frequencies equally well.

The use of the cone-shaped diaphragm and electromagnetic-powered movement is specific to *dynamic speakers,* the class of speakers we've been discussing so far in this chapter. Generally, these are the speakers we recommend for home theater. We should tell you, though, that you may run across other speakers when touring your local audio showroom or electronics superstore — speakers that are more expensive and are used for specific purposes. In most cases, we don't recommend the following speakers for home theater use:

- **Electrostatic speakers:** These are used primarily for stereo audio listening and are rare in home theater systems. They can't handle bass and are rather limited in where and how you position them.
- **Planar-magnetic speakers:** For similar reasons, these are not likely to be useful for your home theater application because they are best used for the higher frequencies only.

We mention electrostatic and planar-magnetic speakers in case someone tries to sell you some. Unless you really know what you're doing with these types of speakers, you're better off spending your money on quality dynamic speakers.

The pole position

You'll also run into speakers with more than one set of speaker drivers, facing in different directions:

- ✔ **Monopole:** These speakers have all the drivers on one face of the enclosure and are known as *direct radiating* speakers. These can be used anywhere in your home theater.

- ✔ **Bipole:** These speakers have drivers on two faces, opposite each other. They are designed for side/rear surround speaker applications.

- ✔ **Dipole:** These speakers have drivers on two faces, opposite each other. They are designed for side/rear surround speaker applications.

    Bipole and dipole speakers sound pretty much the same, huh? Well, physically they are quite alike, but we'll discuss in the following section how the differ *functionally*.

- ✔ **Omnipole:** These speakers radiate their sound in all directions, in a 360-degree fashion, and are popular for outdoor applications. We won't talk much about these here. We just wanted you to know they exist.

To understand the difference between bipole and dipole speakers, we have to get technical for a minute, but it's an important tangent discussion.

Harken back to your science class days when you studied topics of *phase*, specifically being *in phase* and *out of phase*. In a general sense, something is in phase when it acts in the same pattern and time session as something else, and out of phase when it doesn't. Because controlling the way sound waves interact with each other is a key component of home theater, you have to deal with the concept of phase.

Bipole and dipole speakers are designed to help contribute to your surround-sound field. All you need to know for now, however, are some basics about how they work. Bipole speakers fire their cones to the front and rear (remember, they have drivers on two planes) at the same time and in phase. In other words, the cones go out or in together, in the same direction (both out or both in) and at the same time. Dipole speakers are out of phase with each other. When one side's drivers are pushing out, the other side's drivers are pulling in. See the section, "Surround speakers," later in this chapter, for an explanation of how these speakers help create surround sound.

Although the electrical phase in bipoles and dipoles is different, the basic construction of bipoles and dipoles is very similar. You can find speakers on the market that can be both bipoles and dipoles. Most of these speakers have a switch that lets you switch the mode they operate in. Some people prefer music played back through bipoles and movies through dipoles, and these speakers let you make that choice on-the-fly.

Bipoles and dipoles (and omnipole speakers for that matter) all provide a more *diffuse* surround-sound experience. There's nothing wrong with this, and in some cases it can enhance your experience, but today's surround-sound soundtracks are recorded and *mastered* (the final mixing, volume leveling, and so on) using direct radiating speakers and the *discrete* surround-sound channels with Dolby Digital or DTS (or their new higher-resolution counterparts such as Dolby TrueHD and DTS-HD Master Audio). You'll get the best and most precise surround-sound performance when all of your speakers (front, center, and surround) are direct radiators. If you find a set of nondirect radiating speakers that you love, go for it, but if you're looking for the most precise surround sound, go with direct radiators.

Enclosed for your convenience

Your speaker enclosure, it turns out, is critical. You see, with all the shaking your drivers do, if you have a flimsy speaker encasement, it's going to make a lot of noise, fall apart, or both. Your enclosure should be able to handle the vibrations with ease and should add little sound interference to the sound emanating from the drivers.

The two major types of enclosures are sealed (also known as *acoustic suspension*) enclosures and ported (also known as *bass reflex*) enclosures. A *sealed enclosure* is what it sounds like; it's an airtight case. As your driver moves back and forth, the air pressure in the speaker constantly changes. This puts extra pressure from behind on the diaphragm as it moves in and out, and that takes extra power to overcome. On the positive side, that extra pressure makes the cone snap back and forth faster and with more precision, giving you a crisper, more accurate sound.

A more efficient speaker design is the *ported enclosure.* In the front of this enclosure is a hole (port) that equalizes pressure between the inside and outside of the speaker. When the diaphragm moves back into the speaker, it increases the internal pressure, which is funneled out through the front port of the speaker. This augments the sound waves traveling from the speaker, and increases the efficiency tremendously. The downside is that you may get less accurate results from a reproductive sound perspective. That's because a ported enclosure doesn't have the benefit of the extra pressure influencing the reverberating diaphragm. So the speaker sound might reproduce bass notes less precisely — substituting a louder boominess for a more realistic reproduction of the low notes. (Less realistic reproduction here means that your low notes don't have as much house-shaking "oomph" as they should.)

Ported enclosures can dramatically decrease your power requirements because they increase the bass output of a speaker by around 3 dB compared to a sealed enclosure. To match a 3 dB output boost through amplification, the power applied to the speaker needs to be doubled. So if a bass reflex enclosure speaker was powered with a 150-watt amplifier, a sealed enclosure speaker would require a 300-watt amplifier to produce the same output. That's a pretty awesome improvement.

In the end, you can be happy with either sealed or ported designs. Just keep in mind that these units handle bass differently and that good design and construction can minimize problems associated with either speaker design.

Inside, outside, upside down?

As if all this were not enough, you'll probably run into four generic shape and size categories of speakers for your home entertainment system:

- **Floor-standing:** These speakers can be as tall as you are, can handle the full range of frequencies, and may or may not be used to produce the low-bass frequencies often taken over by the subwoofer.

- **Bookshelf:** These aptly named speakers are designed for smaller footprints (the amount of space they take up). You often find them on a bookshelf or discreetly mounted on the wall. Sometimes, you see them on speaker stands to bring them up to ear level (which is the best way to install these types of speakers, in our opinion). They are usually designed to handle the midrange and high-end frequencies and are typically mated to a subwoofer in your installation. You may hear bookshelf speakers described as *satellite speakers*.

Many manufacturers have designed special bookshelf-style speakers with mounting brackets and a sleek (and *thin*) enclosure designed for wall mounting next to a flat-panel plasma or LCD display. These speakers are usually referred to as *wall mounts*.

- **Subwoofer:** These speakers are larger and heavier than the bookshelf models and are usually kept on the floor due to their size and weight. These contain the large drivers for low-frequency use.

- **In-wall:** In-wall speakers share most of their characteristics with bookshelf models; these are smaller speakers designed more for the midrange and high-end frequencies. Although some have enclosures that are mounted into the wall, the majority of these systems use the wall's own enclosed nature as its enclosure. The drivers and other pieces and parts (like the crossovers) are mounted in a frame that is fitted flush with the wall or ceiling.

In general, in-wall speakers are more for whole-home background music and to contribute to the surround-sound of a home theater. For the most part, the benefit of these speakers is their ability to be installed in places that have more aesthetic than acoustic appeal. They stay tucked away in corners or low on walls. Also, depending on the construction of the walls themselves, in-wall speakers that lack their own enclosure may spread sound along the wall rather than direct sound forward. If you find yourself planning in-wall speakers, take some extra time to study the best ways to optimize their location and performance. This is not to say that there aren't good-sounding in-wall speakers — there are, and many high-end manufacturers make in-wall speakers these days. But good in-walls are typically more expensive than otherwise comparable bookshelf or floor-standing speakers.

Active and passive speakers

Finally, all speakers, regardless of the number of drivers, pole type, enclosure type, or whatever, fall into one of two categories: active or passive. How they're classified depends on their relationship to the amplifier driving them.

The vast majority of speakers are passive. A *passive* speaker doesn't have a built-in amplifier; it needs to be connected to your amplifier through normal speaker wire. This speaker-level signal has been amplified enough to drive the speakers sufficiently.

Active speakers, on the other hand, have a built-in amplifier and are fed by a low-level (line-level) signal passed along an interconnect cable originating at your preamplifier or controller. Because the amplifier is an active electronic device, it needs power, and so you have to put any active speakers near power outlets.

For most home theaters, the subwoofer is probably going to be your only active speaker (though you can also find passive subwoofers; some high-end home theater systems use these). There's no practical reason for any of your other speakers to be active. Active speakers limit your ability to choose amplifiers tailored to your home theater and are generally more expensive than what we've been talking about. They are also much harder to find. Most active speakers are in either the low price/low-end category (designed for hooking into PCs or portable CD/MP3 players) or the really high end (where the speakers cost $5000 to $10,000 *each*).

Setting Up Surround Sound

Whew. You still with us? Well, if you are, the worst is behind you. Now you can apply all this newfound knowledge to a discussion of your surround-sound system. In this section, we talk about the different speakers found in any home theater system — the center channel speaker, the left and right front speakers, the surround channel speakers, and the subwoofer. (To see what a surround sound setup looks like, see Figure 12-1.

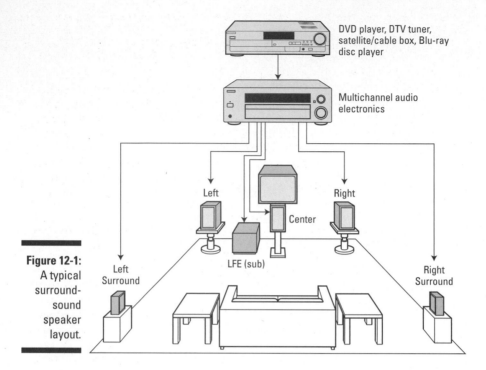

DVD player, DTV tuner, satellite/cable box, Blu-ray disc player

Multichannel audio electronics

Left

Right

Center

Figure 12-1: A typical surround-sound speaker layout.

Left Surround

LFE (sub)

Right Surround

Center speakers

We start with the center speaker. On the one hand, the center speaker is probably the most important speaker in your system; on the other hand, it's (supposedly) optional. How can that be, you ask?

Stereostone Age

If you decide to extend your home theater outside the boundaries of your home theater room, you may consider outdoor speakers for your gardens, pool area, or soon-to-be-outdoor theater greens. The discussion in this speaker section is pertinent also to shopping for outdoor speakers. One of the leading vendors is Stereostone (www.stereostone.com), which makes speakers in all sorts of simulated rock forms and colors, such as brown sandstone and black lava. There are omnidirectional speakers, subwoofers, and even stereo fountains. You can get them with or without visible grills in the layers of the rock, and with volume controls for individual speaker control. All this in weatherproof enclosures that start as low as $150 and go up to $1000 for the most sophisticated models. Other manufacturers, such as Klipsch, have begun offering their own outdoor "rock" speakers.

Connections are everything

When connecting your receiver or amplifier to your speakers, you're pretty much going to find two types of connectors: spring clips and five-way binding posts. Spring clips are considered the lower end of the two, and most audiophiles tend to put them down. You see, spring clips have more exposed wiring, less surface contact, and greater likelihood of signal degradation over time due to this exposed wiring. Five-way binding posts, on the other hand, have a much more flexible connection structure. Not surprisingly, you can connect at least five ways. There are pin-form connectors, spade lugs, banana plugs, and a large washer-like area at the base that allows for more extensive contact with bare wire. There's too much to try to put into words here; we recommend that you get someone at a stereo store to show you a five-way binding post. Just know that the five-way binding posts are the way to go if you have a choice.

Well, many people say the center speaker is optional because the left and right speakers can handle the sound that comes from the center speaker. However, we think that you miss out on a lot, and we don't recommend this setup at all. The front center speaker, we feel, is critical and not at all optional, but some budget crunchers will try to convince you that it is.

Now, why is it critical? Ah, our favorite subject. The center speaker anchors your onscreen dialog and serves as a seamless connection between your left and right speakers. As that boat zooms by from left to right, you don't want to have a gap in the middle of your sound field (a concern as screens get larger and larger). Center speakers are usually located behind the screen or above or below displays so that you can localize the onscreen sound as much as possible.

To achieve this seamless harmony with the left and right front speakers, your choice of center speaker is important. Don't skimp on the center speaker in favor of your other front speakers. Each speaker (left, center, and right) is equally important and should be of similar size, similar capability, and preferably come from the same manufacturer. In fact, if you can use an identical model speaker for the center, left, and right speakers (we talk about them in just a second), do it. Many folks can't do this because they've chosen tower speakers for their left and right speakers, and can't possibly install a tower speaker on top of their display as a center channel speaker. (And if you're not using dipole or bipole speakers for your surround channels, you should consider using another identical pair of speakers for your surrounds as well.)

Make sure any speakers that will be close to a cathode ray tube (direct-view) video display are *video shielded* — especially the center speaker. If not, the speakers will cause video distortion on your screen. This is most important for your center speaker (which may rest directly on top of your display), but can also be an issue for your left and right speakers if they are close to the display as well.

Left and right speakers

We've cheated somewhat by talking a lot about the front left and right speakers already in this chapter. If possible, these speakers should be

> ✔ **Full-range speakers:** Yes, even if you plan on using a subwoofer.
>
> ✔ **Ear level:** We'd recommend this level even for your bookshelf-style speakers. If the speakers are large, try to arrange it so that the tweeters are at ear level.
>
> ✔ **Of similar performance capability as the center speaker:** We'd even say they should come from the same manufacturer.

We talk in Chapter 2 about whether you can use your existing speakers with your home theater, and the bottom line is that if you do, try to buy a center speaker from the same manufacturer and class for the best results.

In an ideal world, you use exactly the same model of speaker for your center, left, and right speakers — all your front speakers. This isn't always practical, but we highly recommend you buy all three of these speakers from the same manufacturer and make sure that the manufacturer has designed them to be *timbre matched* — in other words, that they sound alike. This ensures that you get a more seamless listening experience.

Surround speakers

No matter what the setup of your speakers for surround sound — whether you have two, three, four, or more side and back speakers — your surround speakers play a role in your home theater that's just as significant as that played by the speakers up front. Specifically, the surround speakers add a third dimension to your audio programming — bringing a front and back dimension to the left and right dimension provided by the front speakers.

This brings us back to the bipole/dipole speakers we discuss earlier in the chapter. Recall that the purpose of the center speaker is to provide highly localized speaker information; it's coming from the center of the screen. There's a high correlation between what you see on the screen and where the sound comes from.

And likewise, the left and right speakers provide more lateral, but still highly localized and directed, sound. Together, the three represent the frontal face of your home theater sound experience. When there is a specific sound — the clash of swords, the shout of the main character, the click of a trigger being pulled back — the sound comes predominantly from these speakers.

When it comes to surround speakers, you will find some differing philosophies about how precise the location information provided by the speakers should be. Traditionally, before the discrete surround-sound systems such as Dolby Digital and DTS were so common, many people preferred the more *diffuse* sound (one that can't be easily localized to a specific point) provided by bipoles and dipoles. When the surround sounds are more ambient — for example, the sound of rain splashing on the ground — a diffuse sound pattern can be preferable. Similarly with nondiscrete surround-sound sources, such as Dolby Pro Logic, with its monophonic surround channel with a limited range of frequencies supported, a diffuse surround experience can also be a better choice.

On the other hand, with Dolby Digital and DTS (with their discrete surround-sound channels), the folks who master the audio soundtracks do so using direct radiating speakers, and they develop the soundtracks with the thought that you too will be using such speakers. So the surround track of your favorite movies and TV shows will be designed to provide audio cues that *are* supposed to be located in precise places in the sound field. To take full advantage of this, you should use direct radiating speakers for your surround speakers.

As we said earlier in the chapter, if you find some bipole, dipole, or omnipole speakers that you *love,* by all means get them. If, however, you primarily watch DVD, Blu-ray, or Dolby Digital–encoded HDTV programming in your home theater and you want the most accurate surround sound, we recommend that you choose surrounds that are direct radiators. These are easy to find (most surround speakers these days are direct radiators) — you can safely assume that if the speaker is not labeled as bipole, dipole, or omnipole, it is a direct radiating speaker.

Going virtual

In a perfect world, we'd all have room in our home theaters for eight separate speakers (including the subwoofer), and we'd have all our speaker cables neatly hidden inside the walls. In other words, we'd have a butt-kicking but aesthetically 7.1-channel surround-sound system.

Sometimes, however, reality intrudes upon our perfect home theater world. Some folks just don't have the room for a full surround-sound setup, or they have issues with the layout or construction of their room that keeps them from installing the full complement of surround speakers.

Many folks in this predicament are forced to stick with two-channel (stereo) audio and thus forgo surround sound. However, there is an alternative: Several manufacturers produce virtual surround-sound speaker systems that incorporate multiple speaker drivers and some fancy electronics in a single speaker unit, which you place in the front of the room (usually right above or below your display).

These virtual systems use a combination of physical "aiming" and electronic trickery to introduce timing delays in the sound coming out of the speakers' drivers, which makes the sound "bounce" off your walls in a coordinated fashion. The result — while typically not as immersive as a full set of surround speakers — can come a lot closer to real surround sound than a pair of stereo speakers.

The technology that drives many of these systems comes from the folks at Dolby Labs (who we've talked about a lot throughout this book, because they're at the heart of many home theater technologies). Dolby Virtual Speaker (www.dolby.com/consumer/technology/virtual_speaker. html) is Dolby's system for providing a 5.1-channel experience from two or three speakers.

A great example of a speaker system using Dolby Virtual Speaker is the Klipsch (www.klipsch.com) CS-500 2.1 Home Theater with DVD ($999). This system includes a 2.1-channel speaker system (two satellites mounted in the front of your room plus a subwoofer (discussed in the next section), along with a main unit that acts as a home theater receiver (see Chapter 11) and a DVD player (see Chapter 6). Figure 12-2 shows the CS-500 in all its compact glory.

Figure 12-2:
The CS-500 provides surround sound with two speakers and a subwoofer.

You can also find speakers known as *soundbars*. These are wide (but short), wall-mounted speakers designed to be mounted underneath a flat-panel TV. Soundbars (such as Yamaha's YSP-1100 digital sound projector, $1299) have multiple speaker drivers built into a single cabinet (the Yamaha we mention has *forty-two drivers!*) and typically include built-in amplification (that is, they are active speakers). A soundbar isn't always the cheapest option, but it is an elegant one if you want to minimize your installation work.

We've heard some great sounds out of virtual surround systems, but if your budget allows it and your room supports the installation of five to seven speakers plus a subwoofer, we recommend that you install a full surround-sound speaker system. If you can't install all those speakers (maybe you rent or have a tiny room), you'll most likely be happy with a virtual system.

Subwoofers in the mix

Most subwoofers have floor-based enclosures with active speaker systems (that is, with built-in amplifiers) for driving the low bass frequency ranges. Your biggest decision comes in *bass management*. That is, how do you want the bass signals in your system to be handled? You have a couple of options:

- ✔ The subwoofer can complement your full-range front speakers, providing an even fuller bass signal.
- ✔ The subwoofer can handle all the bass, giving your front speakers the ability to focus on the mid- and high-range frequencies.

Most home theater experts will advise you to move all bass to the subwoofer. This results in more power and attention to the mid- and high-frequency drivers and less strain on the amplifier and speaker systems. This setup also gives you a more dynamic range, because the bass can go lower than most full-range speaker woofers can themselves (hence the term *sub*woofer).

If you have a modern A/V receiver, you use a standard line-level audio inter-connect cable to connect your subwoofer to the receiver. (We talk about these cables in Chapter 16.) If you're using an older receiver as a stopgap until you purchase that nice new Dolby Digital A/V receiver, look for a subwoofer that also accepts *speaker-level* connections. These connections enable you to run the speaker wires from your receiver to the subwoofer and then on to your front right and left speakers. In this case, there's no direct connection between your receiver and your front speakers — the front speaker *outputs* on the receiver are connected directly into the subwoofer, which is then con-nected with another set of speaker cables to the front speakers themselves. This type of connection isn't as good as a line-level one, but it works.

Getting heady(phones) at home

You will see advertisements for surround-sound headphones. We hope you've understood enough in this chapter to say, "How can you cram five speakers and a subwoofer into a set of two-speaker headphones?" Hey, good question!

It's simple. No matter how many speakers you use in your system, you are still listening with two ears. These "surround-sound" headphones basically try to reproduce what is arriving at your ears by using digital signal processors (DSPs). Dolby has gone one step further with a Dolby

Headphone encoder (www.dolby.com/dolbyheadphone) that simulates Dolby Digital 5.1 over the two headphone channels and can be built right into a receiver. With Dolby Headphone, you don't use special headphones — any old pair of high-quality headphones will do the trick. Pretty cool, if you ask us.

If you plan on using headphones a lot (perhaps because your spouse does not like the movies you watch, eh, Pat?), check whether your receiver supports Dolby Headphone.

Many subwoofers come with an auto on/off function that turns the active subwoofer's amplifier on and off with the presence of a signal. So the amplifier turns itself on when you're playing music or a movie soundtrack and then off again a few minutes after you're done. Pretty handy.

Recall that the subwoofer is usually powered by its own amplifier. As such, it has a volume control and a phase adjustment switch. You adjust the volume when fine-tuning your system and pretty much leave it at that setting. Your phase adjustment switch is sometimes a +/–180 degree switch and sometimes a continuously variable switch from 0 to +/–180 degrees (preferable). Phase adjustment comes into play when trying to fine-tune your system vis-à-vis your front left and right speakers. You adjust the phase of the subwoofer so that the sound coming from each is relatively in alignment, despite the fact that the subwoofer and front speakers may be located at different distances from the listeners. By adjusting the phase, you can move the timing of the sound coming from the subwoofer.

In Chapter 21, we explain how to link your bass with *transducers* to provide a truly ground-shaking, home theater experience.

Chapter 13

Understanding Your Display Options

*W*e spend a lot of time in this part of the book talking about the audio systems that envelop you in surround sound and aurally immerse you in a movie. But let's face facts — we call it *watching* a movie because that's what we do. The audio creates the ambience, but the display is what you focus on. So choosing a high-quality video system that can properly display the content you want to watch — whether that content comes from traditional broadcast/cable/satellite TV, from DVD or Blu-ray disc, or even from Internet sources — is essential.

In this chapter, we talk about the lingo of the TV world as our way of helping you make sense of all the terms and jargon you hear when you're shopping for a new display. We also talk about what it means for a display to be considered an *HDTV* (or high-definition TV), which, by the way, we feel has become a *mandatory* choice for your home theater. Finally, we discuss the different types of displays you can run into in a home theater and give you the lowdown on each type.

In Chapter 14, we talk in-depth about each of the major categories of home theater displays, discussing the pros and cons of each type. So, if you already have a good feeling for what 1080p is, for example, as well as the difference between an HDTV and an HDTV monitor, you probably don't need to linger here. Go ahead and skip right to Chapter 14 to get to the nitty-gritty — our recommendations on what type of TV to buy.

Learning the Lingo

If you're shopping for a TV for your home theater, you're probably going to run into salespeople, Web sites, and brochures full of acronyms and unfamiliar terms. Unfortunately, the technology industry tends to market its products with a list of features that are designed to bludgeon you upside the head and leave you with glassy eyes and a maxed-out credit card.

We're here to help. The following sections cover some of the most significant features and performance stats that you'll hear as you shop.

Screen size

We won't insult your intelligence by telling you what *screen size* means, but we will tell you how it's measured. With a single exception (screens for front-projector systems), displays are measured diagonally. This is important to keep in mind because 16:9 and 4:3 screen sizes can't be directly compared diagonally — it's an apples and oranges thing. For example, a 16:9 32-inch screen is about 28 inches wide and a bit less than 16 inches high, while a 4:3 32-inch screen is 25.6 inches wide and a hair over 19 inches high.

So if you're moving from a 32-inch non-widescreen TV to an HDTV, don't think that a 32" HDTV will be exactly the same size — it will be wider, but the screen height will be smaller. In general, screen height is what people perceive as the "size" of a TV — it dictates how big Yao Min looks while you're watching that basketball game (well, he always looks big), or how big the talking heads on Sunday morning news shows are (RIP Tim Russert!). What we're getting at here is that if you're coming out of the old analog TV world and moving into your first widescreen HDTV, you're going to need to recalibrate your thoughts on how big a certain sized TV actually is. A good site that makes these comparisons in more detail than we can get into in print is www.screenmath.com/.

Before you buy any television, you need to consider the size of your room and your expected seating distance from the display. As a gut reaction, most people think bigger is better when it comes to TV, but that's not the case. Just as a TV can be obviously too small for a room (try sitting 15 feet back from a 27-inch TV), the opposite can be true. (Yes, Virginia, a TV can in fact be too darn big for a room.) And we're not just talking about being physically too big to fit in the room (or to look acceptable to your spouse, décor-wise), but also being visually too big.

Every video display has some sort of line structure (or, more accurately, in the case of digital HDTV displays, pixel structure). The picture you see on your screen is made up of a series of individual points of light. Generally speaking, the bigger the screen, the bigger these individual points. When you sit back a reasonable distance, your eyes can't discern these individual items, but if you get too close, they can. (Don't believe us? Turn on any TV in your house and walk right up to it. Take a look. See?)

Because line or pixel size depends on the size of the screen, the distance at which you can make out this structure varies by screen size. (The number of lines or pixels being displayed plays a part, too, which makes this effect slightly less noticeable on HDTVs that fit 720 or even 1080 vertically measured lines on the screen, instead of 480.)

Generally, we recommend that you sit $1^1/_2$ to $2^1/_2$ screen-size measurements from an HDTV and three screen sizes from a non-HDTV. So for a typical 50-inch HDTV, you can have an optimal picture if your seating is between 6 feet, 3 inches and 10 feet, 5 inches. This isn't a hard-and-fast rule — you can certainly get a little bit closer, or go a couple feet away without wanting to throw a shoe at the TV. Note that we said you can sit *closer* to an HDTV than you can to a traditional TV simply because the screen has more lines and pixels (which makes them smaller and harder to see individually). The real goal of these measurements is to make sure that, for any particular viewing distance, your screen is close enough to give you a truly immersive big-screen experience without being so big that you can make out the individual elements that make up the picture.

Lots of folks just want a gigantic TV. Nothing wrong with that in our minds, but do pay a little attention to these formulas so you don't end up with a screen so big that you can make out the individual pixels and lines — it makes the picture much less realistic, and it can be annoying. Certain types of displays, such as LCD (liquid crystal display) flat panels and LCD projection TVs, have pixels with physical characteristics that make them even more noticeable when you're close up — keep this in mind when you're choosing a display.

You can turn this equation around (ah, the wonders of math, huh?). If you have a good idea of how big your home theater room will be (we bet that you do) and also how far your primary seating area will be from the screen, you can use these guidelines to determine how big a display you need. If you're going for a widescreen HDTV, measure the distance to your seating area, divide by 1.5 to 2.5, and then multiply this number by 12 (assuming you measured in feet) to determine your optimal screen size in inches (measured diagonally). Substitute a 3 for the 2.5 if you're going with an old-fashioned non-HDTV set. But you really shouldn't be doing that — and frankly, you'll have a hard time even buying a big screen that's not an HDTV these days.

Many of the newest high-definition TVs, which are fully capable of 1080p display resolutions, can be comfortably viewed at even closer distances than the older and cheaper 720p HDTVs. If you're going to sit *relatively* close to a TV (again, relative to its screen size and that minimum 1.5 times screen size recommendation), you're better off considering a *1080p* HDTV, which has smaller (and therefore less discernable) pixels. With a 1080p HDTV you're much less likely to see the individual picture elements with these displays, even if you're considerably closer than 1.5 times the screen size.

Table 13-1 is a rough guideline for screen size versus distance from the screen. Keep in mind that you don't have to be *exact* here — these are guidelines. If you want to go up or down a screen size from these recommendations, feel free — it shouldn't cause you any real viewing issues.

Table 13-1	Screen Size and Viewing Distance
HDTV Size	*HDTV Viewing Distance*
30 inch	3 feet, 9 inches to 6 feet, 3 inches
34 inch	4 feet, 3 inches to 7 feet, 1 inch
42 inch	5 feet, 3 inches to 8 feet, 9 inches
50 inch	6 feet, 3 inches to 10 feet, 5 inches
55 inch	6 feet, 10.5 inches to 11 feet, 5.5 inches
60 inch	7 feet, 6 inches to 12 feet, 6 inches
65 inch	8 feet, 1½ inches to 13 feet, 6.5 inches

Aspect ratio

We already let the cat out of the bag on the subject of aspect ratio (several times in the book), but let's repeat it because it's important — displays can be shaped for widescreen material (16:9) or for traditional TV viewing (4:3).

Although you can still find some 4:3 displays on the market, for home theater purposes, we think you need to go with a widescreen (16:9) display — that's the right aspect ratio for DVDs, high-definition TV programming, and even many video games. If you're buying a cheap tube TV for the kitchen or guest bedroom, you might choose to go with 4:3, but for theater viewing, you need to go widescreen.

Picture adjustability

Any display allows you to adjust the specific settings for your picture (and this is something we highly recommend). To do so, you typically use an onscreen display and your remote control.

Most people think of these settings as something to do once and never change. In fact, different environments might call for different settings. You might have one setting for the darkened-room home theater environment and another setting that deals better with ambient light for the brightly lit Super Bowl party.

Some systems let you save these settings as presets so that you can quickly access a certain group of settings without having to manually readjust every setting each time you want to re-create your settings. It's nice to be able to press a few buttons and get things back to the optimal movie watching settings without readjusting your picture manually.

We recommend that you choose a display that lets you set the picture separately for each input or source device. That way, you can customize your settings individually — one setting for the HDTV cable box on your HDMI input, for example, and another for the DVD player and other devices coming into one of your display's component video inputs from your A/V receiver. We talk more about these settings in Chapter 20.

Connections on the back

When you get down to the business of connecting your A/V gear to your display, you need to make sure that your display has the right inputs to connect the source devices that will feed video into your home theater. Keep in mind that most video source devices have multiple types of video outputs, and that you can get the best picture quality if you use the right connection methods. So when you evaluate displays, remember that it's not just the *number* of inputs that's important, but rather the *type*. In fact, we'd argue in most cases that type is more important than the number of inputs.

We recommend that you connect most or all source devices directly to your A/V receiver, not your display, to simplify both hookup and operation. So it's typically not all that important to have, for example, four different S-video inputs on the back of your TV. You'll connect all S-video sources directly to your receiver and will need only a single S-video cable connecting the receiver to your TV.

You should make sure that your display has at least one of each of the following types of inputs (check out Figure 13-1; we discuss these inputs in detail in Chapter 16):

- Composite video
- S-video (Just like in the comic books, *S* here stands for *Super,* as in Super-video)
- Component video
- HDMI (High-Definition Multimedia Interface)

You should also expect to have a pair of analog audio inputs for each of these inputs (except for HDMI, which carries the audio on the same cable as it carries the video, which is very handy!).

You may also find the following inputs on your display, though they are much less common:

✔ DVI (Digital Video Interface), which can be used for PC connections

✔ VGA (Video Graphics Array), the old standby, used, like DVI, for connections to a PC

✔ FireWire; not common, but found on a few brands of HDTVs, mainly older models

Composite video

VGA PC   S-video

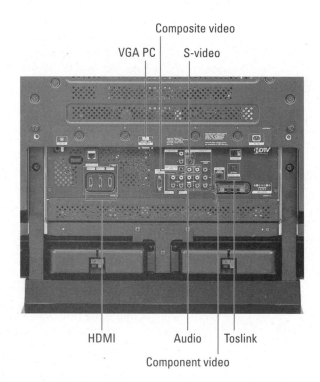

Figure 13-1:
That's a lot
of inputs!

HDMI   Audio   Toslink

Component video

While we find that having multiple numbers of each of these connection types can be overkill if you're connecting your sources through the receiver (as we recommend), in some situations you'll be very happy to have multiples of certain types of inputs:

> ✔ **Component video:** If your A/V receiver can't handle high-definition sig-
> nals through its component video inputs (almost all new home theater
> receivers can, but many older models can handle only DVD and not
> HDTV), you'll want to have at least two sets of component video inputs
> on your display.
>
> ✔ **HDMI:** HDMI, as we discuss in Chapter 16, is rapidly becoming *the*
> method for connecting source components to high-definition TVs. Many
> A/V receivers don't have HDMI video-switching capabilities (see Chapter
> 11 to find out more about video switching), and many that do can accept
> only a couple of HDMI inputs.

We highly recommend that if you're buying a new display, you choose one
that has three HDMI inputs, to increase your options and give you some more
flexibility when you add new components such as a Blu-ray disc player or a
high-definition gaming console to your home theater.

If you don't have enough HDMI inputs on your TV, you can always add an
external HDMI video switch, as we discuss in Chapter 11.

Connections on the front

If you own a camcorder or some other portable video source device (such
as a laptop computer that you may want to occasionally connect to your
home theater display), you may want to choose a display with a set of A/V
connectors on the front of the unit. It's a lot easier to make quick, temporary
connections this way than it is to try to climb behind your display and hook
things up.

Look for a display that has at least one set of analog audio and video (preferably both composite and S-video) connections on the front, Increasingly
you'll find component video or even HDMI front inputs on your HDTV, which
we highly recommend if you have a gaming console or high-definition camcorder that you want to move between TVs. Note that many flat-panel TVs,
as well as the thinner, microdisplay rear-projection models, hide these inputs
on the side or even bottom (for wall-mounted displays) of the TV.

Monitor versus television

When a display comes with a built-in TV tuner (so you can plug in an antenna
or a cable connection and immediately watch TV), we call it a *television*. Some
displays — for example, many projectors and plasma displays — come without
any built-in TV tuning capabilities; we call these displays *monitors* or *HD-ready*

displays. In fact, some monitors don't have a built-in audio speaker, so they don't offer even a minimal audio capacity. (We don't think this is a huge deal because any home theater worth its salt already has a good audio system, but for casual viewing, such as watching the news, you may not want to fire up your audio system.)

The vast majority of HDTVs sold today are truly HDTVs, with built-in tuners for picking up broadcast and (in most cases) unscrambled cable TV signals. The only HDTVs that typically do *not* have a built-in TV tuner these days are front-projection systems and some plasma TVs that are sold as *commercial* models (such as the ones you see used as digital signs or kiosks in stores, hotels, and airports).

Contrast ratio

If you look at TVs on a showroom floor, you might not ever realize this (because the displays have their brightness cranked up), but displays should be capable of showing both dark and light scenes. For example, you want to be able to see the flash of the artillery in *Saving Private Ryan* as well as the soldiers seeking cover in the shadows.

There's a measurement for how well a display can show both bright brights and nuanced darks: *contrast ratio.* You'll see this as a numeric ratio, something like 1000:1, representing the whitest white compared to the blackest black. Typically, direct-view (tube) displays and projector systems that use CRTs have the highest contrast ratios, whereas systems that use plasma or LCD technologies have the lowest. When it comes to contrast ratio, a higher ratio is better.

There isn't a standardized, approved way of measuring contrast ratios, so one manufacturer's 800:1 may not be the same as another's. You need to rely on magazine and online reviews and use your own eyes in a thorough test drive at a dealer's showroom. We like reviews that include a professional calibration of the display because that shows the display's true ultimate capabilities. When you do a test drive, use some of your own DVDs that you know well.

Comb filter

Many video sources (such as broadcast NTSC television or composite video connections from other source devices) send both the color (chrominance) and brightness (luminance) parts of the video signal as a single combined signal. (The signal carried over a composite video cable is combined in this way.) Inside the TV, a *notch filter* or a *comb filter* separates these signals into their component parts. If signals aren't properly separated, you see moving dots of color around the edges of images, a phenomenon called *dot crawl.*

Notch filters are the least effective at this process, whereas the various kinds of comb filters do a better job. You'll find three kinds of comb filters in direct-view displays:

- ✔ **2-D comb filter:** This is the least effective (and least expensive) kind of comb filter, though it's better than a notch filter.

- ✔ **3-D comb filter:** We're talking middle ground here — better than 2-D but not as good as the digital comb filter.

- ✔ **Digital comb filter (sometimes called 3-D Y/C):** Found in more expensive direct-view sets, the digital comb filter uses more sophisticated (and digital!) signal processing to separate chrominance and luminance. This is the king of the hill when it comes to comb filters.

When you connect sources to your display with S-video, component video, or HDMI cables (discussed in Chapter 16), chrominance and luminance are separated in the source device, not in your TV. The same is true for HDTV signals coming into your TV over the air or on a cable system (without a set-top box). In these cases, your display's built-in comb filter is bypassed. In other words, the comb filter is important only for nondigital TV broadcasts (which will be turned off in the United States in February 2009) and for older source components such as VCRs.

Resolution

As we discuss in Chapter 4, *display resolution* is a measure of a picture's precision and sharpness. For standard-definition programming — such as NTSC television and, to a degree, DVD — this isn't a huge deal. (Any display can handle the 480 vertical lines of resolution of these formats — which is not to say they'll all look the same!) As you start getting into HDTV sources (and even widescreen anamorphic DVDs), resolution becomes a really big deal.

Generally, display vendors spend most of their time talking about the *vertical* resolution of their sets, which corresponds to the most commonly discussed resolutions of HDTV: 720 and 1080. Some displays (particularly those that have a fixed-pixel system, such as LCD or plasma) give resolution in terms of both horizontal and vertical numbers (similar to the way resolutions are discussed in the computer display world). So you might see, for example, a plasma display with a resolution of 1280 x 720p (which corresponds to 720p). In this case, the 1280 refers to the horizontal resolution (the number of pixels, or individual points, across the screen) and 720 refers to the vertical number (like the scan lines on a conventional TV).

As we mention in Chapter 4, displays are also classified by the *input resolutions* that they can handle. These input resolutions are simply the resolutions that the display can accept from source devices. The circuitry inside the display itself converts these signals (if necessary) to the display's native display resolution. Read the fine print closely — some displays can accept high-definition resolutions such as 720p but display it at a lower (not high-definition) resolution.

When you get into high-definition digital displays, you'll find out that your display holds some circuitry that handles this conversion from *input resolution* to *display resolution*. This circuitry is known as the *scaler* because it scales the image from one size to another. When you're reading reviews of different displays that you are considering, pay close attention to the capabilities of this scaler; it will manipulate most of the video signals you send into your TV. (There aren't necessarily going to be any hard, cold, objective numbers to describe scaler performance; instead, the reviews will talk about the absence of jagged lines and other visible picture distortions for scaled images.) All else being equal, a display with a better scaler will have a better picture, especially when it displays video sources that aren't created in the display's native display resolution.

Interlaced and progressive scan

In Chapter 4 (it's a chapter you shouldn't skip!), we talk about the two *scanning* methods that video displays use — interlaced and progressive. Traditional TV systems (such as NTSC, the standard TV system in the United States) use an *interlaced* scan, where half the picture appears on the screen at a time. The other half follows an instant later ($1/60$th of a second, to be precise). The interlaced system relies on the fact that your eyes can't detect this procedure in action — at least not explicitly. In a progressive-scan system, the entire picture is painted at once, which greatly reduces the flickering that people notice when watching TV. Progressive scan is available throughout the range of TV types we're about to discuss. We highly recommend progressive scan if it fits into your budget because the picture appears much smoother and more like a film. (You can get direct-view progressive-scan TVs for under $500 these days.)

All HDTVs are progressive-scan displays — so even if the signal being sent to the HDTV is interlaced, the HDTV will convert it to progressive scan for display on the screen.

Defining HDTVs

In the next section, we talk about the physical differences between the various categories of displays (differences such as flat panel or projection). But before we do that, we want to cover one even higher-level distinction. That distinction is the following: Is the display capable of playing back HDTV at full resolution?

We talk a lot about what HDTV *is* in Chapter 4, including the fact that the next-generation digital TV (also called ATSC) has a bunch of different formats. Two of those formats, 1080i and 720p, qualify as high-definition television, or HDTV, as does the 1080p format found on Blu-ray discs.

In previous editions of *Home Theater For Dummies* we spent a fair amount of time talking about the choice between standard and high-definition TVs. At this point (we're writing this in mid 2008), there is no longer a choice to make — if you're buying a new TV for your home theater, you should buy an HDTV. In fact you probably won't even be able to find a TV that's bigger than about 20 inches and *not* an HDTV. And the good news is that moving up to HDTV capabilities won't be much of a price jump.

You can buy an HDTV for well under $500 these days, so unless your budget is tight, we really think you should make an HDTV-capable display the center-piece of your home theater. With HDTV broadcast programming becoming commonplace (see Chapter 7), and HDTV Blu-ray discs also hitting the market (see Chapter 6), there's plenty of great HDTV content to watch on your big screen. So if you can swing it, we urge you to go the HDTV route!

We talk about HDTV back in Chapter 4. Here, we want to talk about the characteristics of TVs and displays that can play back HDTV programming. The first layer of the HDTV onion that we should peel back is the concept of an *HDTV* versus an *HDTV-ready* system. An HDTV has the following key characteristics:

- ✔ **Resolution:** Can display true high-definition signals with at least 720 lines of horizontal resolution (in other words, 720 lines of picture data stacked on top of each other vertically on the screen).

  The latest and greatest HDTVs can display the full 1920 x 1080 pixels of 1080i and 1080p HDTV signals. Such HDTVs are often called *1080p HDTVs*.

- ✔ **Aspect ratio:** Has a widescreen aspect ratio of 16:9.

- ✔ **Tuner:** Has a built-in TV tuner, which is capable of decoding any over-the-air broadcast format within the ATSC digital television standard. (HDTVs that get their HDTV programming from an internal DSS receiver are also called HDTVs, even though they don't strictly fit this definition.)

An HDTV-ready set, often called an *HDTV monitor,* must meet only the first two requirements — in other words, there's no TV tuner in a monitor. All four types of displays we discuss in this book — direct-view, flat-panel, front-projection, and rear-projection systems — can be built as an HDTV or HDTV-ready system. And just like non-HDTV versions of these displays, a huge range of sizes and shapes is on the market. You can buy a 27-inch LCD (liquid crystal display — which we talk about in-depth in Chapter 14) HDTV for a bedroom or kitchen, or you can buy a $30,000 HDTV-ready projector that requires professional mounting and calibration and gives you an HDTV picture the size of some movie theater screens.

Any TV that meets the three criteria we just listed can be called an HDTV. But that doesn't make all HDTVs the same. Beyond the physical type of TV (which we discuss in the next section) and the actual picture quality of the TV (which varies TV by TV based on the type of TV and specific engineering and design decisions made by the manufacturer), you should consider some specific features and specifications when looking at HDTVs.

The following features and characteristics apply across the different types of TVs (LCD, plasma, and so on) unless we specifically say otherwise:

- **HDTV versus *Full HD* HDTV:** All HDTVs have a *display resolution* of at least 720p (1280 x 720 pixels). Those TVs which have a resolution of 1920 x 1080 — those with 1080p display resolution, in other words — are often described as *Full HD* HDTVs. Eventually (we suspect) all HDTVs will be capable of displaying all the pixels in a 1080p signal, but today many do not. Should you care? Well if you absolutely have to have the latest and greatest thing, you should definitely get a Full HD 1080p set. Or if you're going to have a particularly large HDTV for your home the-ater room (a TV so big that you'll be sitting less than 1.5 times the TV's diagonal size away from the screen), you should definitely get a Full HD 1080p HDTV.

  For everyone else, we think 1080p is a good-to-have but far from manda-tory feature. Most people with average or even good eyesight sitting a typ-ical distance from a typical HDTV (say 8 to 10 feet from a 50-inch HDTV) will *not* be able to see a difference between a 720p and a 1080p set (all other things being equal). If you want Full HD, we encourage you to get it. But if you find a TV that looks great to you, fits your budget, and is only 720p, please don't let the lack of Full HD keep you from buying it.

- **Supported input resolutions:** Just as HDTVs have a display resolution (the number of pixels on the screen), they also have supported *input resolutions* — these are the resolutions of incoming TV signals that the TV can accept and convert to the display resolution. Many HDTVs (even those with a display resolution of 1080p) can't accept a 1080p, for exam-ple. This issue mainly crops up (these days at least) with Blu-ray disc players, which are the only source for 1080p HDTV today. If you have a 1080p display and have (or plan on getting) a Blu-ray disc player, you're going to want an HDTV that can accept 1080p inputs. In the past, matching input resolutions on your TV with the output resolutions of your source components was often a source of frustration for home theater builders, but today it's not often a problem (beyond the 1080p support issue).

  For Blu-ray discs, you should consider an HDTV that has Full HD capa-bilities, supports 1080p input resolutions, *and* can support 1080p24. 1080p24 (the 24 refers the frame rate) is a special mode in Blu-ray discs that matches the frame rate of the video to the frame rate used to record movies on film. 1080p24 provides the smoothest picture because your TV doesn't need to perform 3:2 pulldown (see Chapter 4 for more on this).

✔ **Deep color support:** Most high-definition TV sources have a *color depth* (the number of digital bits used to store the color information of a particular video) of 8 bits per color (or 24 bits for red, green, and blue combined). A few new high-end HDTVs support a new system called *deep color* (or, in tech terms, *xvYCC*). Deep color takes the color depth to 10, 12, or more bits — meaning that video is then capable of supporting millions of colors (more than your eye can discern). The only source capable of deep color today is our old friend, the Blu-ray disc, and not many Blu-ray discs include this yet. But if you're futureproofing your HDTV investment, you might want to consider deep color support for the day when deep color becomes more common.

✔ **120 Hz refresh:** As you may recall from Chapter 4, common video sources (including HDTV) have frame rates between 24 and 60 frames per second. A number of LCD TVs are designed to play *all* signals coming into the TV at 120 frames per second (they do this by using some high-powered chips and some sophisticated math to *interpolate* what the picture would look like if it was recorded at 120 Hz (120 times per second). This faster refresh rate is designed to overcome a limitation of LCD TVs — namely that they have a slower *response time* to moving images on the screen (such as the ball moving across the screen in a ball game) than other TVs. The faster refresh rate is designed to improve this LCD issue (which is being improved by a range of other design and engineering tweaks as well) simply by updating the image on the screen more frequently.

No source material for your HDTV is recorded at 120 Hz, so your TV is taking something that is not 120 Hz and doing some manipulation of the video to make it an approximation of what 120 Hz video would look like. This is similar to the *scaling* of video inside an HDTV, where the differing input resolutions are converted to the TV's native display resolution. Some day we may see 120 Hz video on Blu-ray discs or other sources (perhaps on Internet-sourced video as we discuss in Chapter 10), but for now all the 120 Hz action is happening solely inside your TV.

Choosing a TV

As you shop for a display, you'll find that, beyond all the brand and size choices, you need to make some high-level decisions about what kind of display you want. For many people, a display (or TV) means the traditional tube television that's been around for decades. But new technologies have made flat-panel screens, which have no tube and are only a few inches deep, into a viable choice as well. And projection TVs, which shoot the picture onto a screen, have never been better, cheaper, and bigger. In this section, we give you an overview of the primary technologies that underlie different types of TVs. (In Chapter 14, we talk about each of these TV types in-depth, so you can understand the pros and cons of each.)

The first distinction to be made in the world of home theater displays revolves around how the picture gets to your eyeballs:

- With some displays, you are directly viewing the image created by the imaging hardware within the TV. In other words, the image is created on the screen you are watching. These displays are known as *direct view*. The most common type of direct-view display is the old-fashioned tube TV, but flat-panel (hang-on-the-wall) plasma and LCD TVs can also be considered direct-view displays.

- Other displays create the image in one place and then *project* it onto a screen elsewhere. These *projector* displays work much like a movie projector in a theater (and better than that noisy one in your third-grade social studies class) and can offer the biggest image size of any type of display. There are two types of projectors:

    - Rear-projection systems, which display an image on the *back* of the screen, which you then view from the front.

    - Front-projection systems, which display an image on the *front* of a screen (the same side you view the image on).

Beyond this initial categorization, displays are also categorized by the underlying technology that creates the image. There are a few dominant technologies here. Note that most of these technologies can be used for either direct-view or projection displays, depending on how they are implemented:

- **CRT:** CRT, or cathode ray tube, is the traditional technology behind TVs and home theater displays (for a long time, CRT was the *only* technology, but that has changed a lot in the past ten years). CRTs can be used in both direct-view and projector applications.

- **Plasma:** Plasma (sometimes called PDP, or *plasma display panel*) displays use a grid of electrical circuits sandwiched between two plates of glass to electrically excite a gas and cause it to put out light. Plasma displays are the thin TVs (often less than 4 inches thick) that everyone's dying to hang on their walls.

- **LCD:** LCDs do exactly what their name implies — they have liquid crystal particles within them that can be aligned in different ways to create different colors. When a bright light shines through these crystals, you get a video picture. LCDs can be flat-panel TVs (like a plasma display), or they can be used in projection TVs (see the bullet on microdisplays coming up). If you've seen a laptop computer (or a desktop PC with a flat-panel display), you've seen an LCD.

✔ **OLED:** The newest flat panel technology is known as *Organic Light Emitting Diode*, or OLED. OLED displays are built of an organic material that is printed onto the display, and like plasma, OLED creates its own light (so there's no backlight). OLED displays are even thinner than plasma or LCD displays and use less electricity than either. They also have extremely high contrast ratios and extraordinary color reproduction. Sounds great huh? Well it is, but unfortunately, OLED technology is still in its infancy and is mainly used in very small displays for cell phones and similar devices. As we write, only one manufacturer — Sony — makes an OLED HDTV. It has a stunning picture, is 3 millimeters thick, costs about $2500, and . . . is 11 inches diagonally. To put that in perspective, as we write, that's the same price as a top-of-the-line 50-inch 1080p plasma HDTV. Clearly OLED is a ways from being mainstream, but trust us on this, you can't wait. It's that good!

✔ **Microdisplays:** Traditionally, projection systems used CRT tubes to create the projected image. Most current projection systems use a microdisplay technology to do so instead. A microdisplay is exactly what the name says it is — basically a tiny display that uses some sort of miniaturized display technology to create an image that is then enlarged when it is beamed onto the projection screen. Several different technologies are within the microdisplay family:

  • **LCD:** The same LCD technology used for flat-panel screens can be shrunken down and used in a projector.

  • **DLP:** A DLP, or *digital light processor,* uses a special video chip from Texas Instruments that includes millions of microscopic mirrors that are moved by computer command (sort of like the robot in *Lost in Space,* only smaller!) to create an image.

  • **LCoS:** *Liquid Crystal on Silicon* microdisplays use a special variant of LCD technology that's shrunken down to the chip level.

As we mentioned, some of these technologies can be used in either direct-view or projection applications (CRT and LCD in particular), which can make things a bit confusing for the casual shopper. If you're shopping online (or just comparing prices), and you don't actually see the TV in front of you, make sure you read *all* the details. We'd hate for you to think you were getting an LCD flat panel to hang on the wall when you were actually pricing out an LCD front-projection system that goes on the ceiling and needs a separate screen!

Chapter 14

Comparing Display Technologies

Choosing the right display for *your* home theater is one of the most important tasks you'll face when you begin building your home theater. Your display is the most visible (no pun intended) part of your home theater, and a great high-definition widescreen picture can really knock folks' socks off. So choose the right display for your particular home theater, and you'll be that much closer to the "being there" experience that you get at the movies.

In Chapter 13, we talk about all the things you should understand about displays in general, including the features and capabilities to look for when shopping for a new TV or display. Those discussions apply across all sorts of display types — for example, you'll want HDMI inputs whether you are buying a plasma or a DLP rear-projection unit.

In this chapter, we take the discussion to the next level by examining each of the common types of displays you might choose for a home theater — plasma and LCD flat panels, and the whole array of front- and rear-projection TVs — and give you some insight into the pros and cons of each type. Combine this with the knowledge you gain by reading Chapter 13, and you'll be ready to start shopping!

What about Tube TVs?

Admit it. You say it, too: "What's on the tube?" C'mon, we all say it, and for good reason — for the past sixty-plus years, the vast majority of TVs have been *direct-view CRT* (or cathode ray *tube*) models. You know what they look like — kind of big and bulky, with a big (and relatively heavy) glass tube inside.

CRTs are now the senior citizens of the TV world, and the world of consumer electronics is ruthless when it comes to the next big thing. Most manufacturers have dropped their CRT television model lines in favor of flat-panel and projection TVs (discussed throughout the rest of the chapter).

Those manufacturers who remain in the CRT television business typically do *not* still make the larger sizes that work best in a home theater environment (32 inches and above), but instead manufacture only small (24 inches and below) CRTs that are more suited to use in a bedroom or kitchen, not for a home theater.

A flat-panel tube?

As the era of the tube draws to a close, a new and somewhat similar technology called SED *(surface-conduction electron-emitter display)* has begun to trickle out of the labs. Toshiba and Canon were the two big proponents of this technology, which is in many ways a hybrid of the CRT and the plasma display. (In 2007, Toshiba decided SED was taking too long to develop and abandoned the technology, leaving Canon alone carrying the SED torch.)

SED displays (none are in production as we write, but we've seen demonstrations of some hand-built prototypes) are designed to be thin and flat, like a plasma TV, but at the same time provide the bright picture and the deep, deep blacks of a CRT. Essentially, an SED display takes the electron gun of a CRT and turns it into a big, flat panel that sends the electrons across a small vacuum to the phosphors on another flat panel of glass. It looks like a plasma display (because it's thin and flat), but because it uses electrons hitting a phosphor layer, it has all the picture benefits of a CRT. (Plasma also uses electrons, but the process involves exciting a gas with an electrical charge, causing the gas to emit electrons, rather than just shooting them out of an electron gun.) And the great thing is that an SED can be high resolution (easily meeting the 1920 x 1080 resolution of the highest HDTV standards) while using less than half the power of a plasma or LCD flat panel.

We've been blown away by demos we've seen of SED year after year at the Consumer Electronics show. But that's all we (or anyone) has seen to date — demos of prototypes. Canon continues to promise that we'll see production SED TVs soon. If Canon can truly deliver on the promise of SED, plasma and LCD may very well have to move out of the way as leaders of the flat-panel pack.

And if that's not enough to anticipate, another technology (discussed in Chapter 13) called OLED (Organic LED), originally thought up by the folks at Kodak, is now hitting the market. This technology is similar to LCD but uses an organic material that can generate its own light — LCDs require a backlight to shine through the LCD — and will be thinner, and brighter than LCD. You can now buy Sony's OLED 11-inch HDTV for about $2500. The picture will make your jaw drop almost as much as the dollars per inch of screen does.

Right now, OLED has been proven to be a "real" technology, and if manufacturers can find a way to build OLED sets in sizes we need in a home theater at a reasonable price, today's flat-panel displays may well go the way of the CRT. SED must still prove itself, but like OLED, it's worth keeping an eye on.

Even more importantly, no manufacturer (that we know of, at least) still offers a high-definition CRT TV. In the early 2000s, all major TV manufacturers offered widescreen high-def CRTs — today they're all gone. In some ways that's a shame, because nothing else (except maybe the still nascent OLED TVs just hitting the market) offers a picture with the amazing contrast ratios and deep true blacks of the CRT. But CRTs were bulky (without being big in terms of screen size, they were heavy) and couldn't approach the display resolution offered by today's 1080p digital displays.

What's our point here? Well if you have a CRT HDTV and you love it, by all means keep it in your home theater — at least until the urge for something bigger and sleeker overcomes you. But if you're just starting to shop for your home theater's display, don't spend any time looking for a CRT TV to fill the role, because you just won't find one, no matter how hard you look.

Thin Is In — Flat-Panel TVs

The coolest development in the TV world in years and years (and the source of billions of dollars in revenue for TV manufacturers) has been the advent of the flat-panel (notice we didn't say *flat-screen*) display. These are TVs that you can hang on the wall. Flat-panel TVs use technologies such as LCD and plasma to create a TV that is barely bigger than the screen itself. These displays have a small frame around the edges of the screen and are about three or four inches deep. There are some tradeoffs to flat-panel displays, but if you can live with them, you can definitely find a place in your home theater for a flat-panel — literally!

Demystifying LCD

If you have a laptop computer, a digital watch, a handheld computer, or just about anything electronic, you've probably seen, touched, felt, and used a liquid crystal display, or LCD. We first saw LCDs on digital watches back when we were kids (we thought they were cool) and never imagined the size they'd grow to. We certainly never thought LCDs would one day display high-resolution images with millions of gradations of color. But that's exactly what they are doing, in an increasing number of homes and home theaters (see Figure 14-1).

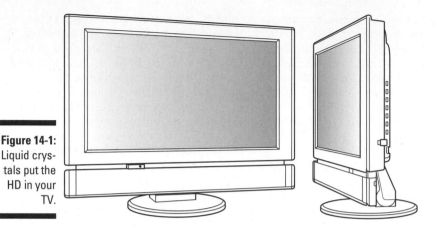

Figure 14-1:
Liquid crys-
tals put the
HD in your
TV.

You may be wondering how LCD displays work. Well here's the short answer. (Armies of lab-coated PhDs working at the manufacturers of these things can give you the long answer!) An LCD display consists of a large number of pixels, or picture elements, consisting of liquid crystal molecules held between two sets of transparent electrodes. These liquid crystals react in predictable ways when the electrical charge running between those electrodes is changed — meaning they twist and move in ways that let different amounts (and colors) of light through the crystals. The LCD has a control system that translates your video signals into the proper charges for each electrode. A light source (usually a fluorescent bulb, though LED bulbs are starting to hit the market) shines *through* the LCD panel (it's built into your display and is typically there for the life of the display) and creates your picture.

Because the light shines through the liquid crystals, rather than reflecting off them or being created *by* them, an LCD is what is known as a *transmissive* display. Generally speaking, transmissive displays are slightly less bright — you lose some of the bulb's brightness going through the crystals — but LCD makers can make up for this by using a really bright bulb for the backlight.

When compared to the *other* type of flat-panel display (plasma), LCDs tend to be found on the smaller end of the spectrum. You'll rarely find a plasma TV smaller than 42 inches, but you can find LCDs at sizes as small as 13 inches. Similarly, on the larger end of the scale, most manufacturers tend to top out at about 57 inches on their LCD displays but go all the way up to 65 inches for plasmas. We should note here that you can find limited production versions of both LCD and plasma TVs in sizes up to and exceeding 100 inches, with prices in the many tens of thousands of dollars.

More importantly for the home theater buyer's budget, LCD displays tend to be slightly more expensive for a given screen size than a plasma TV. Historically there was a significant difference, with LCDs costing 30 percent more than similar plasmas, but today any price difference is usually less than 10 percent.

It's hard to do a direct apples-to-apples price comparison between LCD and plasma TVs because the standard sizes of the two technologies are different. LCD HDTVs typically are offered in 37-, 40-, 47-, and 52-inch sizes (as well as smaller sizes), while plasmas are typically offered in 42-, 50-, 56-, and 65-inch sizes. (Note that not all manufacturers follow these conventions.)

If you do the math on a price-per-inch basis, however, a plasma will usually be slightly cheaper than an LCD, particularly in the larger sizes. But LCDs are more widely produced (think of all the LCD screens in laptop computers, PC monitors, navigation systems, and the like), so the downward price trends for LCDs may very well make them cheaper across the board by the time you read this.

We're talking about direct-view LCDs here (where you look directly at the LCD, just as you look directly at the picture tube with direct-view tube TV). LCDs can also be used in projector TVs (both front and rear), and we talk about them later in this chapter in the "Getting Into Projection TVs" section.

A few companies make mega-big LCD displays. As we write (mid 2008), we've seen prototypes for LCD displays as big as 102 inches diagonally. And new technologies, such as OLED, promise LCD-like displays in even bigger sizes in the future. We've even seen prototype systems that seamlessly combine three smaller (and easier-to-build) LCD panels into a larger single panel — making a cheaper big LCD.

The vast majority of LCD television monitors are high-definition TVs and are built in the widescreen 16:9 aspect ratio, although you can still find 4:3 versions in smaller sizes (under, say, 20 inches). We prefer the widescreen versions of LCDs because 16:9 LCDs, unlike direct-view CRTs, don't tend to wear out unevenly when used to display 4:3 video programming.

LCD displays have a few particular strong points when it comes to playing video:

- **Extremely high resolutions:** LCDs can easily reach HDTV resolutions (in fact, most LCD displays do). You can easily find a 1080p-capable LCD display in all but the smallest sizes — while many plasma displays are still 720p.

- **Excellent color:** LCDs offer exceptional reproduction of colors, with the potential for beautifully re-created colors across the spectrum. This differs from other flat-panel displays (such as plasma systems), which often tend to display certain colors inaccurately.

- **Great picture:** The newest and most expensive LCDs use an LED (light emitting diode) instead of a traditional bulb for their light source. These LEDs produce a higher-quality picture because the LED itself emits a more natural (closer to daylight) light than does a bulb (which tends to be yellowish, not true white).

✔ **Energy efficiency:** LCD HDTVs are perhaps the *greenest* HDTVs. Compared to plasmas, LCD HDTVs use less electricity to run. It's hard to generalize an actual number (since there are great variations from model to model), but you can probably expect to use about 30 percent less power for an LCD than for a similar-sized plasma. Many TV manufacturers are making power consumption a big emphasis as we head into 2009, so expect this to improve on both sides of the aisle.

✔ **PC monitor–capable:** Most LCD television displays can also do double-duty as a PC monitor, plugging directly into any PC with a standard PC video cable.

✔ **No burn-in:** If you play a lot of video games, watch the stock ticker on MSNBC, or do other things with your display that involve a lot of *static* content (images that don't change or move around) on a CRT display, you can end up with those images permanently burned into the phosphors on your screen. When these images become permanently etched into the phosphor, you see them even when you're watching something else. Because LCDs use a separate backlight instead of creating their own light with phosphors, they are immune to this problem (plasmas are not, by the way).

You can get a *stuck pixel* on an LCD screen, where a single pixel always emits a color (often red). This is a rare occurrence, but it can happen. Most people don't even notice it, but if you're sharp-eyed, it might drive you crazy.

Check your TV's warranty for its policy on stuck pixels. Some manufacturers will repair or replace a TV with only a few stuck pixels, while others will make you wait until you have dozens of them — which could leave you in the lurch with enough stuck pixels to annoy you, but not enough to warrant repair (at least not in the manufacturer's mind) before the warranty period is over.

✔ **Inherently progressive:** Unlike direct-view systems, LCDs don't display their picture using electron guns scanning lines across a screen. Instead, LCDs use millions of tiny transistors that can be individually controlled by the "brains" inside the display. This means that LCDs can easily handle progressive-scan sources, such as progressive-scan DVD and HDTV — unlike some direct-view systems that simply can't scan fast enough to display progressive video.

Besides the size limitation we discuss earlier in this section, consider a few other problem areas before you buy an LCD system as your primary display in a home theater:

✔ **Slightly more expensive for their size:** Inch for viewing inch, LCDs tend to be a bit more expensive than the plasma flat-panels we discuss next and much more expensive than CRT displays. As we write in mid 2008, you can expect to pay about $1000 to $1200 for a 40-inch LCD display. For the same price, you could buy a 42-inch plasma set — in other words, get a bigger monitor for the same price.

✔ **Poor reproduction of blacks:** Compared with direct-view tube displays, LCDs do a poor job of reproducing black images. Darker screen images never show up as true black, but rather as various shades of gray, and actions happening in these darker areas are difficult to discern.

✔ **Poor response time:** Some LCD displays suffer from a poor *response time* — meaning it takes a while for the pixels to change colors in response to a rapidly changing scene in your video program. This can bug the living daylights out of some people, particularly when you're watching sports (you might see a trail of a moving ball on the screen, for example).

Most new LCD TVs have this problem licked — but look for a response time of less than 8 milliseconds.

✔ **Limited viewing angle:** Although they are getting better due to some intensive efforts by manufacturers, LCDs typically have a poor viewing angle. If you are not sitting almost directly in front of the screen, you don't get a good picture.

✔ **Limited brightness:** Because LCDs use a backlight shining through the liquid crystal, most of the light is absorbed. As a result, the LCD displays have lower contrast and are harder to view in a brightly lit room (the picture appears washed out), compared with plasma TVs. LCD TVs with LED backlights do better in this regard.

Staying on the cutting edge with plasma

Perhaps the coolest thing to come down the home theater pike in quite some time (maybe ever!) is the larger, flat-screen monitor that uses plasma technology. A plasma TV (often called a *PDP,* or plasma display panel) contains millions of gas-filled cells, or pixels, wedged between two pieces of glass. An electrical grid zaps these pixels and causes the gases to ionize (the ionized gas is plasma — hence the name). The ionized gases, in turn, cause a layer of phosphor on the outside layer of glass to light up (just like the electron gun in a CRT causes the phosphor to light up on the front of the tube).

Plasma displays have captured the attention of the home theater industry and home theater consumers because of the sheer size and quality of the picture they can produce. They're also known for their compact size. Plasma displays are available in 42-, 50-, 56-, and even 65-inch sizes — and they can get even bigger. (Panasonic shows off a greater-than-100-inch plasma every year at the Consumer Electronics show — don't even ask about the price!) Even at the larger sizes, the display itself is usually no more than 5 or 6 inches deep — and suitable for wall hanging! All the plasma displays in these sizes (which are by far the most common, at least in the U.S. market) have a 16:9 aspect ratio.

Other benefits of plasma displays include the following:

- **Excellent brightness:** Because plasma displays use the direct lighting of phosphors (instead of a backlighting system in LCDs), they can have an extremely bright and crisp picture, just like a direct-view CRT TV. In fact, because each pixel is controlled directly by the electrical grid behind the plasma cells, the brightness tends to be extremely even across the screen. In a CRT, the electron guns shoot at the phosphors from differing angles depending on which part of the screen the gun is creating, which can cause uneven brightness in badly designed CRTs.

- **High resolution:** Some early plasmas were not HD-capable, but every plasma we know of these days is at least 720p capable. The year 2008 has brought a flood of 1080p-capable plasmas as well — in the past, LCD HDTVs were much more likely to be capable of this resolution than were plasmas. Just about all plasma displays on the market are 16:9 aspect ratio sets, which is also essential for HDTV viewing.

- **PC monitor–capable:** Like LCD screens, most plasma displays can be plugged directly into any PC (not just home theater PCs with special TV video cards) to act as a gigantic PC monitor.

- **No geometric distortion:** In a CRT display, the electron guns that shoot their beams on the phosphor screen are in a fixed location (the center/back of the tube). The angle at which these beams hit the phosphor varies; in the middle of the screen, the angle is perpendicular, but the angle is quite different at the corners of the screen. This changing angle can cause geometric distortions in the picture. In a plasma display, each gas pocket is at an identical angle (and distance) to the phosphor it lights up, so you don't get distortions around the edge of the picture. This benefit is also found in LCD flat panels.

- **Progressive by nature:** Like LCDs, plasma systems don't use a scanning electron beam to create a picture. Instead, all the pixels on the screen are lit up simultaneously. So progressive video sources display progressively on any plasma system; you don't need to buy a special progressive set like you do with CRT displays.

- **A wide viewing angle:** Unlike LCDs, plasma displays have a good picture even when you are sitting "off axis" (not perpendicular to the screen surface). In a smaller room, where some of the seating might be at an acute angle from the screen, the wide viewing angle can be a big plus.

Of course, the plasma equation has a few downsides (besides the fact that a lot of us can't afford the $3000 it costs for an HDTV plasma):

✔ **Susceptible to burn-in:** Any system that uses a phosphor screen to display video can fall victim to the phosphor burn-in mentioned earlier in this chapter. If you do a lot of video gaming or stock or news ticker viewing, you need to be aware of this fact. Although burn-in can also be an issue with a CRT set, it's an even bigger issue with a plasma, considering the price. Manufacturers of plasma TVs have made great strides in reducing the possibility of burn-in, and many plasma TVs have burn-in fix-it programs that generate a series of images onscreen designed to remove any minor burn-in from your screen.

You can minimize burn-in on any display by calibrating the set properly and by reducing the brightness from its factory setting, which is usually too high. We talk about this in Chapter 19.

✔ **Shorter life span:** Another phenomenon of any phosphor-based display system is that eventually the phosphors "wear out" or lose their brightness. Like burn-in, this degradation also happens to CRT-based direct-view displays, but it often happens faster with plasma displays. Given the considerably higher cost of a plasma, your cost per hour of viewing is much higher. Before you buy, check the manufacturer's specifications on *hours to half brightness,* which is the point at which the display is only half as bright as it was when new. For example, if this specification is 20,000 hours, and you watch the set for 6 hours a day, it will be effectively worn out in about 9 years. If you have kids, keep in mind that 6 hours a day is *not* an excessive estimate for how long the television may be turned on every day. Also keep in mind that while LCDs may not expire quite as quickly as a plasma TV will, they do have backlight systems that can burn out or dim over time.

✔ **Not as high resolution as LCD:** Even though 1080p plasmas are becoming more and more common, the majority of mainstream plasma TVs offer "only" 720p resolution. We suspect that within a year or two, just about all plasmas, at least those 50 inches and larger, will be 1080p, but today that's just not the case.

Unless you have exceptional eyesight, watch a lot of 1080p content (on Blu-ray discs), and sit close to your flat-panel TV (less than 1.5 times the screen size), the 720p versus 1080p thing isn't as much of a big deal as many make it out to be. Remember, all things being equal, 1080p is better than 720p. But all things are never equal, and most folks simply can not see the difference from a typical viewing distance.

✔ **Poor reproduction of black:** Although plasma displays are an equal to good old-fashioned CRT sets in terms of absolute brightness, they fall short in the contrast ratio comparison, though they are typically better in this regard than LCDs. Like LCDs, plasma displays have a hard time reproducing black, so black scenes end up being reproduced as shades of gray.

We think that these shortcomings are far from fatal. We love plasma displays, but we realize that they aren't for everyone. In many home theaters, perhaps the biggest factor supporting the plasma display (besides the undeniable wow factor every time you look at one in action) is their amazing compactness relative to screen size.

An acronym in the industry, SAF (spousal acceptance factor), absolutely applies to the plasma display. (Actually, the term is WAF, but we're being politically correct here.) If your spouse isn't into the concept of a home theater and hates the idea of a huge TV cluttering the family or living room, a plasma may be your home theater salvation. You don't even have to tell him or her you wanted one anyway because of the awesome picture. Grumble a little and get some brownie points out of your purchase!

Getting Into Projection TVs

When you go to the movies, the images you see are projected onto that big screen in front of you. If size matters to you (and if you have the room in your home theater — and seats far enough away from the screen), you too should consider a projector for your home theater's display system. Even if size isn't a huge deal to you, you may decide to go with a front-projection system because it can offer the ultimate in home theater image quality.

In this section, we talk about the two types of projectors available for home theater: all-in-one rear-projection systems and movie projector–like front-projection systems. We also talk about the different kinds of projector systems found in both front and rear projectors. And, finally, we get into the choices you'll find for separate screens (needed if you buy a front-projection system).

For many home theater enthusiasts, a theater isn't really a theater unless you have a projector. Until the advent of the plasma and LCD flat panel (discussed in the preceding section), projectors were the only choice for big screens (bigger than the approximately 40-inch limit of CRT direct-view TVs, at least). And while 65-inch plasmas are now on the market, you still need a projector system to get a *really* big picture. (Front-projection screens can be as big as 10 feet or more *across!*)

But projection systems don't need to break the bank either. Rear-projection systems (RPTVs) are perhaps the best value in home theater, at least in terms of bang for the buck (or inches per dollar). For about $2500, you can get a Full HD 1080p rear-projection system that's somewhere between 67 inches and 73 inches. By way of comparison, a 65-inch plasma HDTV costs more than $5000.

You can't hang one of these units on the wall, but visually the picture is at least as good as (and often better than) plasma, for thousands less. In particular, RPTVs are much better than most plasma displays at reproducing blacks onscreen, which means you get superior reproduction of darker scenes when you're watching movies or television.

When you want a *really big* HDTV (like the 68- or 73-inch models we discuss a few paragraphs back), a rear-projection system is a great bargain. In the more typical 50-inch range, the price benefit of rear-projection TVs over plasma or LCD flat panels has pretty much evaporated as manufacturers have increased their production of flat-panel systems. You may find the picture quality of a rear-projection TV superior in some ways to that of a plasma or LCD, but the convenience and sexiness factor of a flat panel outweighs this for most buyers. For this reason, many manufacturers have begun to limit their rear-projection HDTV production to only the biggest models or end it entirely in favor of flat-panel TVs. For example, Sony discontinued all rear-projection TVs in 2008 in favor of LCD flat panels. Over time we suspect that rear-projection TVs will go the way of the tube TV (in other words, rear-projection TVs will be produced in small numbers by niche manufacturers only), and we'll see a choice between flat panels for small to big displays and front-projection systems for really big displays. For now, however, a rear-projection system can still be a good choice if you're looking for the biggest picture at an affordable price.

Going all-in-one

Typically, front-projection displays are the high end of the market. Folks considering one of these in their theater will often spend $2000 or more for the combination of the projector and screen. As a result, many people who want to spend $1000 or so for a big-screen system will choose a rear-projection TV (something we recommend). But a new category of projection systems on the market turns this formula on its head — front-projection displays in an inexpensive form that anyone can afford. These all-in-one front-projection systems are the display equivalent of the home-theater-in-a-box solutions for audio that we discuss in Chapter 2. Essentially, they include a DLP-powered front projector, a DVD player, and even (in most cases) a pair of speakers. They're no substitute for a full home theater system, but they are an easy way to get up and running. We think the best use for these devices is as a home theater solution for the kids' playroom, your vacation home, or anywhere besides your true home theater. They're also great for gamers — plug in an Xbox 360 or PlayStation 3, shine the projector on the wall, and you're ready for some truly big-screen Halo or Gran Turismo action! They're also a wonderfully convenient solution for an outdoor drive-in theater in your back yard.

None of these all-in-one systems supports HDTV resolutions (though we expect that newer versions will), but you get a lot for your money (typically just a shade more than $1000). Check out Optoma's DV-11 ($899 list price) for a good example of this type of system.

Choosing between front and rear projection

The first big decision to make when evaluating projection systems is a big one: should you choose an all-in-one rear-projection TV or a two-part front projector and screen system? This used to be an easy decision — rear-projection systems were cheaper and easier to set up. But that's changing as the price of high-definition projectors drops precipitously (you can get a good-quality 720p projector for under $1000 and a 1080p projector for about $2000) and as front projectors have become easier to set up.

Although a rear-projection system remains *easier* and more convenient, we urge you to at least consider a front-projection system if you want a truly big-screen home theater. For the price of a 56-inch plasma TV or a 72-inch rear-projection TV, you could get a front-projection system capable of pictures measured in the *hundreds* of inches!

Having said that, let's define the difference between these systems. It's simple, really:

- **Front projection:** A front projector is very similar to a movie projector (except it doesn't use film). It includes a projector unit (which is usually mounted on your ceiling but can also be on a lift, on a floor mount, or in the rear wall) and a separate screen. Video sources (such as DVDs, cable, and satellite TV) are routed into the projector, which then turns these signals into light. Then, the light is (ding ding ding, you guessed it) *projected* onto a separate screen that's mounted on a wall at the front of your home theater. Figure 14-2 shows a front-projection system.

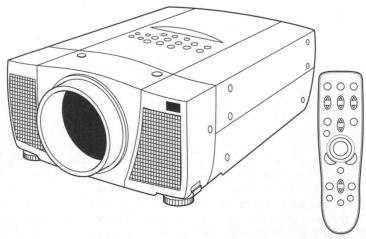

Figure 14-2:
A front-projection system.

✔ **Rear projection:** These are the traditional big-screen TVs that have been sold for years and years. If your Uncle Vinnie got a big screen back in 1987 for Superbowl XXI, this is what he has. Now some people, having seen the lousy, washed-out picture on Uncle Vinnie's TV, think that rear projectors trade picture quality for size. Nothing can be further from the truth. A good-quality, well-set-up rear projector can offer an awesome picture. A rear-projection TV (or RPTV) has both parts of the front projector (the projector and the screen) in a single, all-in-one box, and the projector illuminates the *back* of the screen instead of the front. Figure 14-3 shows a rear-projection system.

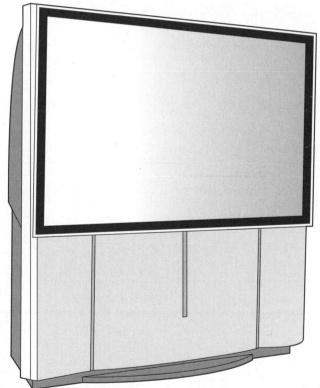

Figure 14-3: The all-in-one rear-projection system.

RPTVs are great. But they do have two limitations: a restricted viewing angle and size. Because of the way video is internally reflected toward the screen in these sets, you need to be perpendicular (or near-perpendicular) to the display to see a good picture. Keep that limitation in mind as you consider an RPTV. If your home theater room is set up with widely dispersed seating, an RPTV may not be your best choice. Also, rear-projection TVs can be very deep and overwhelm a room with their size. For some, this is a limitation.

If you have a really big room and can keep it dark enough to use a front-projection system, front projection is the way to get that truly movie theater–sized picture. But the dark room is a major *must* to get the most out of a front-projection system. Don't think you can set up a front projector in your family room (you know, the room with the picture window on one wall and the sliding glass door on the other — oh yeah, and the skylight too!) and get a good picture. You can, but only if you spend a lot of time and effort blocking out the light. You *need* a dark room to get the most out of front projection — that's why we recommend rear-projection systems for the average home theater builder who doesn't have a dedicated room and who wants to be able to watch TV in broad daylight.

It may sound obvious, but don't forget that you'll need an unimpeded path between the projector and the screen in a front-projection system. Unless you're just a huge fan of MST3k (www.mst3kinfo.org) and want to see a person's head silhouetted on the screen, you'll need to be able to keep the air between your projector and screen clear of all objects.

As we mentioned, the lower cost and easier setup make rear projectors more consumer-friendly. (You don't have to spend nearly as much time getting the projector properly aligned and aimed at the screen with a rear projector.) But with the advent of new, computer-based technologies such as DLP (Digital Light Processor) chips, front projectors have begun to drop in price from the stratospheric ($20,000 to $60,000) to the reasonable (under $1000), and the setup of these new systems is easier, too (which we explain in a minute). Rather than take up your valuable reading time with a long-winded description of the relative benefits and shortcomings of these two types of projectors, we've created the handy-dandy Table 14-1 to enlighten, educate, and energize the home theater portion of your brain.

Table 14-1	Comparing Front and Rear Projectors	
Characteristic	*Front Projector*	*Rear Projector*
Screen size	Gigantic	Merely huge
Price	Moderate to astronomical	Low
Aspect ratio (4:3 or 16:9)	Fixed or flexible, depending on the technology	Fixed
Picture quality	Great to astonishing	Great to astonishing
Setup	Moderate to complicated	Easy to moderate
Installation	Moderate to complicated	Easy

Another place where the CRT has disappeared

Less than a decade ago, almost all front- and rear-projection TVs used cathode ray tubes (CRTs) just as most TVs were tube-based. In the case of a projection system, three separate tubes (red, green and blue) were installed inside the projector and aimed at the screen (on the wall or, using a mirror, on the front of a rear-projection system) in such a way that the image from each tube *aligned* to perfectly overlap each other.

CRT projection systems were capable of extraordinary image quality (particularly the front-projection systems), but they had a few drawbacks:

✔ They were finicky. Keeping those three tubes aligned required a lot of work, often from service professionals. If you ever saw a projection TV with green, red, or blue "shadows" around images on the screen, you saw a misaligned CRT projector.

✔ They didn't put out a lot of light. To get the best picture from a CRT projector (particularly front projectors) you needed a very

dark room. Today's digital projectors don't rely on the light being emitted by a phosphor panel, but instead have a very powerful lamp that can put out several times as much light as a set of CRTs.

✔ They were expensive to build well. High-quality, CRT front-projection systems routinely cost $20,000 (or more!).

✔ They were big and bulky. Even though the tubes were small (compared to the tube in a direct-view CRT TV) they were gigantic compared to the chips used in today's digital projection systems. Remember that gigantic projection TV that took up half of Uncle Ernie's family room? Yep, it was a CRT.

Today, we don't know of *any* manufacturers who still make CRT projection systems. If you dig around, you can still find someone somewhere making one, but all mainstream TV manufacturers have dropped CRT in favor of digital projection systems.

Selecting a projection method

As you move past the rear- versus front-projection decision, you'll find that you really haven't decided anything at all. Three main *digital projection* technologies currently on the market do the work of converting electrical video source signals into light that can be projected onto the screen. Each of these technologies can be found in either front-projection or rear-projection units. Keep in mind, however, that new variants of these technologies, as well as entirely new ways of projecting video, are being invented all the time.

Projecting with LCDs

LCD technologies have been used for years and years for relatively low-quality projectors — the kind you might have in the conference room at work for projecting those ubiquitous PowerPoint slides on the white board during mind-numbingly boring meetings. (Of course, we feel obliged to say that none of *our* clients ever show us mind-numbingly boring PowerPoints, nor are the PowerPoints we show our clients mind-numbingly boring!)

Well, the LCD has come of age in the era of home theater, and now you can buy front-projection systems based on the LCD that provide a high-quality (often HDTV) picture at a price that is typically lower than that of CRT front-projection systems. (Note that LCD RPTVs aren't much cheaper than CRT RPTVs and may even cost more, simply because the small tubes used in RPTVs are dirt cheap.)

LCD projectors typically use three small LCD panels (a couple of inches across at most) — one each for red, green, and blue picture information. Behind these panel is a strong lamp that provides the light. Like plasma and LCD flat panels, LCDs (and the DLP and LCoS projectors we discuss next) are *fixed-pixel* displays, meaning that they display video at a certain resolution. You can find high-definition LCD-projection TVs with both 720p and 1080p resolutions. An internal device called an *image scaler* converts the incoming signal (such as 480p from progressive-scan DVDs or 1080i from an HDTV broadcast) to the 1366 x 768 resolution for display. LCD projectors are inherently progressive, so even standard-definition broadcasts are converted to a progressive-scan mode for display.

Some of the cheapest projectors *are not* high definition, with resolutions below 720p. (These are mainly front-projection systems; all rear projection-LCD TVs we know of are HD-capable.) These are fine for certain uses (see the sidebar titled "Going all-in-one" for a discussion of some of these projectors and where we think they make perfect sense), but with high-quality 720p projectors from major manufacturers such as Sony and Panasonic going for less than $1000, we see no reason not to choose HD when you're buying an LCD projector. And in the case of front-projection systems, where you're going to be looking at a 100-inch or bigger screen, we strongly recommend that you go for a Full HD 1080p projector if your budget can stretch the extra thousand dollars or so.

The quality of the image scaler — how well it converts other signals to the fixed-pixel resolution *native* to the LCD — is a key factor in a projector's picture quality. In Chapter 21, we talk about external image scalers that can improve the picture quality of a projection system.

Because you never know who'll come up with a better system the month after this book is printed, we generally avoid dropping brand name recommendations. However, we find that scalers from Faroudja (now owned by Genesis Microchip — www.gnss.com) are always excellent. You can find many different brands of projectors (and HDTVs in general) that use Faroudja chips (notably the *DCDI* chip) to scale, or *upconvert*, images.

LCD projector systems have several big advantages, when compared with other projectors:

- ✔ **Lower-cost front projectors:** You can buy a quality 720p LCD front projector for less than $1000.

- ✔ **More compact RPTVs:** Because the LCD panels and the lamp are small, LCD RPTVs can be much thinner than CRT RPTVs. Although many CRT systems can be 36 inches or more deep, LCD systems can be less than 15 inches deep. That helps a lot both in small rooms and with the SAF (spousal acceptance factor).

- ✔ **Bright pictures:** The separate lamp used in LCD projectors puts out a ton of light. (You wouldn't want to have someone shine one in your eyes close up!) The result is a brighter picture that can tolerate more ambient light in your home theater.

  For the best brightness and color reproduction, look for LCD projectors (typically only RPTVs) that use LED backlights instead of traditional bulbs.

- ✔ **No need for convergence:** Despite the fact that an LCD projector contains three LCD panels, it has only one light source. So you don't need to converge the picture like you had to do with the older CRT projector technology. This makes the setup much easier for mere mortals.

- ✔ **No worries about burn-in:** Plug in that Xbox or PlayStation and play all the games you want. Because LCD systems don't use phosphors, they can't get permanent burn-in like CRTs (or flat-panel plasma systems) can.

Of course, there's got to be a downside, right? LCD projectors don't do a few things well:

- ✔ **Relatively poor black performance:** LCD projectors, like LCD direct-view sets, can't display true black tints well. Dark scenes end up being gray instead. So when the Orcs are sneaking up on Frodo from the mouth of that dark cave, you can't see them all that well.

- ✔ **Short lamp life:** Nothing lasts forever, and the high-output lamps on LCD projectors tend to wear out after a few thousand hours of use. This life span is much less than the life span of a plasma TV, but LCD projector lamps cost a lot less to replace (hundreds instead of thousands of dollars).

- ✔ **"Stuck pixels" problem:** If you own a laptop computer (or a desktop computer with an LCD display), you may be familiar with the issue of *stuck pixels*. These are usually minor manufacturing defects that cause individual pixels to not light up when the display tells them to. Because the relative size of pixels in a projection system is large, you may notice a dead pixel on your screen (and be annoyed by it). Many manufacturers think that having a few stuck pixels is just part of doing business, and they will not replace your LCD panels except in extreme cases. As a result, it is a good idea to find out the manufacturer's dead pixel policy before you buy.

✔ **"Screen door":** When LCD images are projected onto big screens (like the ones you find in a front-projector system), you can begin to see the pixel structure of the LCD itself. By this we mean the physical structure of the LCD that separates the individual pixels. Because of the way LCDs are constructed, you can look closely at a large projected image and see dots of lighter and darker areas — like you're looking at the world through a metal screen door. We should emphasize that this isn't a huge issue. This "screen door" effect is typically noticeable only if you're too close to a big image.

For more information on LCD projection displays, a listing of current models, and more good old-fashioned marketing talk than you can shake a stick at, check out 3LCD.com, a consortium of manufacturers of LCD projection systems.

Deciding on a DLP

Texas Instruments has developed (over the course of many years) a completely new way of projecting video called the DLP, or *Digital Light Processor*. DLP has created a new category of inexpensive projector systems and has also led to a digital revolution in those old-fashioned movie theaters you used to go to before you got a home theater. In fact, if your movie theater talks about its "digital projection," you've already seen DLP (a super-high-end, expensive version) in action.

The DLP is an entirely digital process that utilizes a semiconductor generically called the *DMD* (*digital micromirror device*). The DMD contains over a million incredibly tiny, hinged mirrors. Each of these mirrors represents a single pixel on your video image. The DLP chip's electronic logic controls the hinges on the mirrors, turning them so that they either reflect light (onto your screen) or block it (creating a dark spot on the screen). When the DLP's "brains" turn these mirrors on and off, the mirrors create different levels of light between black and white that result in a *grayscale* version of your image. A device called a *color wheel* filters light from a lamp (like the lamps found in LCD projectors), reflects this off the mirrors on the DLP chip, and provides the color in your image. This is a Mach III fly-by of the details of DLP; if you want to know the nitty-gritty, check out the Texas Instruments site at www. dlp.com.

The DLP system we just described, with the color wheel, is called a *single-chip* DLP solution and is by far the most common in consumer DLP projectors. Movie theater projectors (and a few ultra-expensive home theater models) dispense with the color wheel and use three DLP chips (one for red, one for green, and one for blue). These three-chip projectors can produce more gradations of color than a single-chip system but cost a heck of a lot more.

Weebles wobble

Texas Instruments got together with computer/technology behemoth Hewlett Packard and incorporated one of HP's technologies into some of its DLP chips. Called *wobbulation,* this technology allows each of the individual mirrors within a DLP chip to address (or beam its reflected light at) two different pixels. What this does is allow a chip with a resolution of 960 x 1080 to effectively have a resolution of 1920 x 1080 (the full resolution of 1080i/p high definition). TI calls this technology *smooth picture.*

Many 1080p-capable DLP TVs use this technology to achieve their full resolution. Nothing wrong with that, but testing has found that some displays using wobbulation don't quite achieve the full resolution in the real world. The latest DLP displays (announced as we write, but not yet on the market) will offer true 1080p resolution without this wobbulation technique — which promises to provide a better picture.

When looking at DLP projectors, the most important factor to consider is the capabilities of the DLP chip, which is the heart of the system. Like LCDs, DLPs are fixed-pixel displays, and Texas Instruments has a few chips on the market with different aspect ratios and different resolutions. Early DLP chips were designed for 4:3 video reproduction (with a lower-resolution 16:9 mode), but current models are designed for 16:9 aspect ratios.

Most DLP systems for home theater solutions (for both front- and rear-projection TVs) offer a Full HD 16:9 aspect ratio and a 1920 x 1080 pixel resolution, but there are still some DLP projectors with lower, non-HD resolutions. These chips are typically used in business projectors (those ubiquitous PowerPoints at the boring meeting again) and not for home theater.

As is the case with LCD projection systems (and with LCoS, which we discuss in the next section), we strongly recommend that you consider a 1080p-capable system if you're using a front projector with a large screen.

DLP projectors share many of the advantages of LCD models: low price, compact size (with particularly thin RPTVs possible), and immunity from image burn-in. They also share what many find to be the biggest of the same drawbacks: less-than-perfect reproduction of blacks (but better than most LCD projectors). However, DLPs don't have the "screen door" issue we mentioned earlier and, additionally, have one big advantage over the other types of projectors we've discussed so far: They are brighter and therefore better in rooms that aren't too dark. In a DLP chip, light from the lamp is reflected off the mirrors, but in an LCD, light is transmitted through the liquid crystals, which causes a decrease in brightness.

One issue that some folks have with DLP projectors is something called the *rainbow effect*. During a highly contrasted scene (such as white on a black background), some folks can see a shimmery colored image (like a rainbow, naturally!) in their peripheral vision. Not everyone can see this, but some small percentage of the population sees it and is annoyed (to the point of headaches or even dizziness). You can minimize the rainbow effect by choosing a three-chip DLP set with individual DLP chips for red, green, and blue — many folks believe that the color wheel in single-chip projectors causes the effect.

The newest trend in DLP is to use a single chip but to replace the color wheel and single light source with three LED light sources (red, blue, and green). This helps get rid of the rainbow effect and has the additional benefit of improving the color reproduction of the DLP projector. LEDs are cool — we think you'll start seeing them more and more in home theater displays (as well as in everyday objects such as flashlights, car headlights, and other lighting systems). They have the advantage, when compared with incandescent lighting, of truer colors, lower energy consumption, and greatly increased life spans.

We love the future of DLP projectors (both front and rear). They have great pictures, are relatively inexpensive, and are a snap to set up. As the technology matures, we think this may end up being the predominant projection system of the future — already more than 75 manufacturers use the technology in their projector systems. Given the nature of the microprocessor business, we think that DLP chips will get much cheaper and much more capable faster than you can bat an eye. You can already buy a good-quality HDTV-ready front-projection DLP system for less than $1000.

Looking at LCoS

Another "projector-on-a-chip" system that has hit the market in recent years is the LCoS (Liquid Crystal on Silicon) system. Several manufacturers are making LCoS systems, but the most prominent to date have been JVC, with a system called D-ILA (Digital Direct Drive Image Light Amplifier) — we're puzzled by the acronym, but we guess DDDILA is too hard to remember — and Sony, with its SXRD (Silicon Crystal X-tal — for acronym purposes — Reflective Display) projection TVs.

LCoS systems are basically a new variant of LCDs. LCoS systems still use liquid crystals, but instead of transmitting light through the liquid crystal like an LCD does, LCoS reflects the light like a DLP, resulting in a significantly brighter image.

There are only a few manufacturers of LCoS-projection systems, but those that are available — that is to say, JVC's D-ILA models, Sony's SXRD models, and a few others — have perhaps the finest picture quality of any projection displays available.

LCoS systems offer true 1080p resolution (with no tricks like the *wobbulation* we discuss in the "Weebles wobble" sidebar) and an incredibly smooth, film-like image. LCoS beats out LCD-projection systems in the brightness game, while avoiding the rainbow effects found in DLPs.

LCoS is also known for exceptional black reproduction that rivals, if not quite matches, the blacks displayed by the super-expensive CRT projection systems that used to be the high end of the market.

What's the catch? Well, LCoS projectors are more expensive than LCD or DLP projectors — there simply isn't the kind of volume production of the LCoS microdisplay components to bring the prices down to those levels yet. You can expect to pay about 25 percent more for a 1080p LCoS display than you would for an identically-sized DLP display.

The good news here is that the prices are coming down rapidly. For example, Sony's first generation of SXRD RPTVs cost about twice what similar-sized DLP projectors cost at the time. The models shipping as we write (less than a year into the technology's life span) are only about $500 more than a similar DLP and offer a better picture. So keep your eye on LCoS, because it may very well give DLP a run for its (and your) money!

Keeping other features in mind

Regardless of technology, keep in mind a few other things when evaluating projection systems:

- ✓ **Fixed versus variable focal length (front projectors only):** Some front-projection systems (including many fancy CRT models) have what's known as a *fixed focal length.* This means that, for a given screen size, the projector must be placed a fixed and predetermined distance away. This can limit your placement in the room. If a heating duct on the ceiling is right where the projector needs to be, that's too bad. Projectors with variable focal length can be placed in different spots to fit your room's layout and then adjusted to focus on the screen properly.

- ✓ **Light output (front-projection only):** We've already discussed the various projector types with regards to their relative brightness. But within these categories, projectors vary from model to model in their overall brightness. This is measured in *ANSI lumens* and is a good indicator of how well a system will work in a bright room. Brighter, high-end projectors are often rated at 1,000 or more lumens, whereas cheaper ones are often below 500. We don't recommend that you use any projector in a brightly lit room, but if you simply can't make the room dark, go for a brighter unit.

Just because you can crank your amp up to 11 doesn't mean that you should. (Please excuse the shameless, pop culture, *Spinal Tap* reference.) The brightest setting your projector supports may cut through the daylight streaming in your windows, but it won't give you the best picture you can get. In Chapter 19, we talk about how to set your brightness settings (and a bunch of other settings) on your display.

✔ **Aspect ratio:** In the RPTV world, systems have a fixed aspect ratio. They're either 4:3 (standard squarish TV) or 16:9 (widescreen). We recommend that you get the widescreen version unless *all* you watch is *Leave It to Beaver* reruns. Some front projectors also have a fixed native aspect ratio, but many systems can be adjusted to work at either aspect ratio. If you don't have a choice, go with the widescreen, and if you pick a system with an adjustable aspect ratio, enjoy it!

✔ **Projector noise:** Many front-projection TVs employ a cooling fan — particularly LCD and DLP systems, which need bright (and hot!) lamps to create the picture. DLP systems may also make an audible noise when the color wheel spins. In a small room, you may hear these noises, which can be annoying. Try to audition your projector in your dealer's showroom and pay attention to the noise it makes. You have to live with it after you buy it!

✔ **Everything we discuss in Chapter 13:** This is our convenient catchall category. In Chapter 13, we list a ton of things to consider when evaluating a display system, such as the number of inputs and the adjustability of the system. We don't feel like repeating ourselves, and we don't like typing that much (or even cutting and pasting!) either. So go read Chapter 13 because it all applies here, too.

Selecting your silver screen

As they say in the ginsu knife ads, "But wait, there's more!" We've talked about the projectors themselves, but in the case of front-projection systems, we've talked about only half the equation. You gotta shine that nice, high-def image onto something, and we definitely don't recommend an old bedsheet or the wall. You need a real screen — just like a movie theater.

Screens come in several different forms:

✔ **Portable screens that sit on a tripod:** You can fold these up and put them away when you're done (but who's ever done with a home theater?). These are less than optimal (if you take them down, you need to get them back in *exactly* the same spot or refocus the projector — if it can even be focused!). We don't recommend these at all.

✔ **Retractable screens:** These can be manually or electrically powered. Although nothing is cooler than pressing a button on the remote and having the screen come down, this setup will cost you more than the manual version. You also need to make sure that these systems are properly installed so that they are flat (otherwise the image can be distorted), and periodically check to make sure they haven't become misaligned with use.

✔ **Fixed wall- and ceiling-mounted screens:** If you have a dedicated home theater and you'll never want to hide the screen, these are probably the best way to go.

Even more important than the form are the technical characteristics of the screen. The big four are the following:

✔ **Gain:** Gain is a measure of how reflective the screen is — how much of the projector's light gets bounced back to your eyeballs. There's a standard industry reference for gain, and systems that have exactly as much gain as that reference are rated at a gain of 1. More-reflective (high-gain) screens are rated greater than 1 (say 1.2), while less-reflective (low-gain) screens are rated below 1 (many are rated at 0.8). Generally speaking, match CRT projectors with high-gain screens (between 1 and 1.3, though you can go higher if needed). Brighter, fixed-pixel systems such as LCD or DLP can use a low-gain screen (0.8 or lower).

✔ **Viewing angle:** Most display systems have a limited angle (from perpendicular) in which they look best. Sit outside that angle, and the picture becomes dim. For front-projector screens, this viewing angle is inversely proportional to gain. In other words, the higher the gain, the smaller the angle in which viewers will get a good picture. For this reason, you are best off choosing the lowest gain screen that works with your projector in your room. This is why low-gain screens are recommended for fixed-pixel projectors; LCD, DLP, and LCoS projectors have light to spare, so why not trade some of it for a wider viewing angle? Viewing angles are usually listed in a number of degrees (such as 90). Your viewing angle is half this amount (45, in this case) on either side of perpendicular.

✔ **Hotspotting:** One reason you shouldn't use a screen with too high a gain for your projector is the *hotspotting* phenomenon. When this occurs, one part of the screen is brighter than the other parts. Typically, the center of the screen gets too bright relative to the edges, which makes the picture on the edges appear washed out.

✔ **Aspect ratio:** Screens are available in either the 16:9 widescreen or 4:3 aspect ratio. You should choose the same aspect ratio as that of your projector. You can buy (or make your own, if you're crafty) *masks* to cover the unlit portions of the screen when you're watching material of a different aspect ratio, so you can cover the sides of the screen with a mask when you're watching a 4:3 TV show (more *Leave It to Beaver*?) on your 16:9 screen.

Choosing a screen is not something for the faint of heart. Find out what screens your projector manufacturer recommends, ask your dealer what he or she recommends, and if at all possible, look at your projector (or the identical model) on the screen before you buy.

The three major manufacturers of screens for front-projection displays are Da-Lite (www.da-lite.com), Draper (www.draperinc.com), and Stewart Filmscreen (www.stewartfilmscreen.com).

Chapter 15

Remote Controlling Your Home Theater

Remote controls have come a long way since the first clunky universal remote controls let you manipulate multiple devices from one gadget. Today, you have all sorts of options: tiny, large, color, touch-sensitive, voice-controlled, time-controlled, and on and on. You can spend $19 on a great remote or $5000 on a "gold-plated" touch-screen, whole-home remote control that not only controls all the devices in your home theater but also runs all the electronics in your home. Decisions, decisions.

Sifting through Remote Control Options

The remote control is nothing more than a means to tell your system what to do. The term *remote* just means you don't control your home theater equipment manually (by getting up and pushing buttons). Just to show that we all can be as high-tech as the next guy, let's treat the remote control as an *interface,* and say that you can interface with your system in multiple ways.

Types of remotes

Hundreds upon hundreds of remotes are out there. Generically, they fall into the following categories, which are presented in increasing order of functionality and desirability:

✔ **Standard/dedicated remotes:** These are the device-specific remotes that come with your system. If you stopped here, you might have ten or so remotes on your coffee table!

✔ **Brand-based remotes that come with a component:** Brand-based remotes work with all sorts of devices from the same manufacturer. For instance, the Panasonic remote you get with a Panasonic home theater receiver usually has buttons for your Panasonic, Blu-ray disc player and your Panasonic plasma TV. There are buttons for each supported device.

A number of branded remotes that come with devices can be programmed (by inputting codes) just like the universal remotes discussed next. You'll also find universal remotes included with devices such as cable set-top boxes that you rent or buy from your television provider.

✔ **Third-party universal remote controls:** Many leading electronics brands sell so-called *universal remote controls.* These remotes supposedly work with any electronics device by way of onboard code databases. These remotes generally come with manuals that walk you through setting up your remote for your specific components. This environment is ever-changing, however, and we've found that you get what you pay for. We've never been happy with cheap universal remotes (like the $20 do-everything universal remotes you see at the megasize electronics stores). Some capability is always missing. We prefer the slightly more expensive *learning remotes.*

Typical universal remotes come with a booklet full of codes. To get the remote to work with your specific gear, you usually need to look in this book, find the *type* of component (say, DVD player), and then the brand. When you find the brand name, you'll see a number of codes (usually 4-digit numbers) — follow the directions with your remote to enter these codes. You usually have to press a button to put the remote in programming mode. You enter the first code on the list — if it works, you're done; if not, you need to go through each of the codes listed until the remote starts to interact with your chosen device. Tedious, but doable.

✔ **Learning remotes:** Learning remotes can learn codes from your existing remote controls. You simply point your remotes at each other, go through a listing of commands, and the remote codes are transferred from one to the other. These remotes have a higher success rate than universal remotes because you are essentially using the same codes as your present remote — not codes that a database says *should* work. Some learning remotes have an onboard, preprogrammed database against which they try to match the codes being learned; others are completely learning-based. The downside of a completely learning-based remote is that, if you lose your original remote, it's almost impossible to train this one.

✔ **Programmable remotes:** Programmable remotes allow you to create *macros,* which are sequential code combinations that do a lot of things at once. So say you want to watch a movie on a DVD. You could program a macro to turn on your TV, receiver, and DVD player; set the receiver to the appropriate source and output modes; and start the DVD in the tray — all from one button. Now, if it could only pop the popcorn, too.

✔ **Proprietary systems:** A number of closed-system control devices enable you to integrate control of all your home theater devices on a single control system. Companies such as Control4 (www.nilesaudio.com) and Crestron (www.control4.com) are renowned for their control systems.

Remote control features

As simple as a remote control seems to be, the world of remotes is insanely complex. This section discusses some ways in which remotes have become more complex lately.

Radio frequency (RF) versus infrared (IR)

It used to be that all remotes were infrared-based. Now, many are touting RF connectivity, which is in many ways better than IR. First, RF signals tend to travel farther than IR. Second, you don't need to point the remote at the TV set; RF can go in all directions, even through walls and cabinet doors. The biggest downside of RF remotes is that you can't easily integrate them into one remote (such as a learning remote) — at least not yet. Still, we prefer RF to IR if we can get it.

The only real downside of RF remotes is the possibility that you could unintentionally control devices in other rooms. In the vast majority of cases, you won't run into this issue, because those other devices won't be using the same remote codes as the ones in your home theater room.

Most home theater equipment uses an IR remote control system, so if you use an RF system, you need some equipment to convert the RF signals to IR to control these IR-only devices. We talk about how to do this in Chapter 18.

Touch-screen displays

Color and grayscale displays are replacing hard buttons on remotes, enabling them to be far more programmable and customizable for your system. It's not unusual that your remote would connect to your PC to customize the "soft buttons" on your remote's screen. We are finding that standalone touch screens are even replacing remotes.

New control options

A lot of new stuff is coming down the pike, but we think two-way operation and voice control are innovations that will grow in popularity. With two-way operation, higher-end remotes can interact with the controlled unit to determine its *state*. So, for instance, if a unit is already on, your programmed macro won't turn it off at the start of its session. And with two-way operation, you can check your actions to make sure they were carried out.

Nice, but not earth-shaking enough in its newness for you? Then try voice control, which lets you bark orders to your remote control (and even to other microphones in your home theater). Want the volume turned up? No problem: "Higher volume please." (Have we reached a new threshold when a couch potato doesn't even have to lift a thumb?) Voice-control functionality is making its way into a lot of devices, including standalone Web tablets, making voice control a key future item in your home theater.

Another interesting innovation is the docking cradle. A cradle might enable your remote to charge, to access the Internet for revised programming schedules, or to update its internal code databases. (We think docking cradles are really a covert plot to make sure you always know where your remote is located.)

IR (infrared) emitters/blasters

When one IR device wants to control another device, it often sends signals to the other device's IR port through an *IR blaster* — a small device that sits some distance from (or in the instance of very small versions called *emitters*, is taped to) the IR port. Many PC applications interface with your home theater system through an IR blaster, to do things such as change the channel on your satellite receiver to start recording a program. You might find you have several IR blasters for different devices in your system. No one feels that this is the best long-term approach because newer devices allow for direct data interface via Ethernet, low-speed data connections, or even RF. But for now, IR blasters are the only option for many older systems.

Within specific brands of A/V gear, you will find IR ports for interconnecting and sharing IR data directly into the motherboard — bypassing the IR port. This is one of the benefits of using a single manufacturer for your gear. Examples include systems such as Sony's S-Link, which uses a special cable to connect Sony devices to each other.

For the rest of this chapter, we focus on some of the highlights of this section — the things that we think you'll likely run into or want to have.

Remotes for the rest of the family

Got kids? Try the weemote from Fobis ($24.95, www.weemote.com). This is a remote designed for three- to eight-year-olds, so you can limit the channels they watch and make them responsible for their own remotes (in other words, keep their paws off yours). A typical setup with a cable-ready TV takes about five minutes. Fobis also has a cheaper weemote (the weemote dV, $19.95) that's especially made for letting kids navigate interactive components of DVDs or digital TV services. There's even a Senior weemote (the weemote SR, $24.95) that's designed for older folks who might not have great eyesight or manual dexterity and therefore can't handle the 97 or so buttons on the typical universal or learning remote.

Going Universal

Universal remotes are constantly changing and vary in price from about $20 on up. They can have backlit buttons, touch screens, color screens, voice commands, and so on. A lot of it depends on what you want out of a remote control. The more you spend on your entertainment system, the more you'll probably spend on your remote control.

Here are examples of some of the neater remotes you can get:

✔ **Universal RF-10** ($59, www.universalremotes.com): This remote includes both IR *and* RF technologies in a single inexpensive universal and programmable remote. While it lacks some of the fancy features (such as elaborate macros and PC or Mac programming) of more expensive remotes, it's about the cheapest remote you can buy that can support RF. To get the RF working, you need to spend another $59 on Universal's MRF-100B PowerBlaster RF Base Station, which provides RF-to-IR capability supporting up to six devices with included IR emitters.

You don't need to utilize the RF to get the most out of the RF-10, but it's a good bit of futureproofing in case you'd ever like to move your home theater around and need an RF remote.

✔ **One For All Universal Remotes** ($various prices, www.oneforall-na.com): The One for All remote line is so vast we couldn't choose just one remote, but suffice it to say that this is a brand with a remote for everyone, ranging from inexpensive remotes for simple systems (code-based universal remotes such as the $20 8-DEVICE Learning Universal Remote) up to the still inexpensive $50 URC-9960 Kamelon remote, which uses special backlighting to show only the keys you need for the task you're doing at the time.

✔ **Monster Home Theater Controller 100** ($299, www.monstercable. com): The folks who bring you the famous (and expensive) Monster Cable audio cables have a lineup of very fancy (and very nice) universal programmable remote controls. The entry-level model in this lineup, the Home Theater Controller 100, has a beautiful color screen, easy computer-based programming, and the ability to control *everything* in your home theater. Like many remotes in this price range, it includes lithium ion rechargeable batteries and a cradle to hold and recharge your remote. For another $200, the Home Theater Controller 300 includes RF capabilities *and* Omnilink (Monster's brand name for Z-Wave wireless home lighting and automation controls). With that remote you can control anything in your home theater and just about anything electrical in your entire house.

✔ **Philips Prestigo line of remotes** ($179 to more than $1000, www. pronto.philips.com): Philips has a solid line of remote controls that have defined the leading edge of home theater remotes in a lot of ways. The $179 fully programmable and learning Prestigo SRU-8015 is the entry level to the Prestigo range, but it has a lot of features, including a big (but not color) touch screen, 4MB of memory, a scroll wheel, and the ability to program your remote using your PC. It even has a library of over 400 TV channel icons, so you can see on the remote exactly what channel you're tuned in to.

Many more remotes are available. A great site to check out remote control options is Remote Central (www.remotecentral.com). It has great reviews and tracks the newest remotes on the market.

You can go universal with your remote in another sense: You can control your home theater from anywhere in the home! We talk more about these capabilities in Chapter 18.

Programming on Your Remote

We mentioned earlier that remotes are becoming learning-friendly and programmable. Nothing exemplifies this more than the $249 Logitech Harmony One Remote Control (www.logitech.com) shown in Figure 15-1. Harmony One, like all Logitech Harmony remotes (and many of those offered by Monster Cable, Philips, and others) helps you do more than control different devices; it helps you control different actions. Harmony's remote has an LCD touch screen and links to your PC or Mac via a USB connection to program the remote to tie together multiple actions at once, in order. The touch screen is a big deal at this price — most touch-screen remotes on the market cost many times more than Harmony One (but they do have bigger screens for that price).

Figure 15-1:
Harmony
One is
one of our
favorites for
automating
our home
theater.

Say you want to listen to a CD on your AudioReQuest CD server. You have to turn on the TV, set it to video mode, turn on receiver one, set it to CD, turn on receiver two, set it to CD, scroll down to your desired playlist, and press Play. Harmony reduces this to a simple one-click task. It makes schedules and listings available on your remote's screen, and when you click it, all the requisite actions on your CD player, receivers, TV set, and so on are done in one quick series of signals from the remote to the devices. So Harmony is designed to help you perform activities such as watch TV, play a CD, and play a DVD. That's what we call click and play!

Getting super fancy

A number of manufacturers build touchpad controllers that are not just simple remote controls but rather whole-home control systems, which let you tap into lighting, HVAC (heating, ventilation, and air conditioning), drapery controls, alarm systems, automation systems, and more. An example is Crestron (www.crestron.com), a company that develops incredibly cool (and

incredibly expensive) home automation, control, and entertainment systems. This is the stuff of *MTV Cribs* that can be found in those $20-million dream homes that we all wish to buy when we win the lottery. Crestron rules the upper end of touch-screen options, as discussed in detail in Chapter 23. Crestron's color touchpad systems are to die for, or at least second mortgage for.

The really cool feature is Logitech's online configuration tools. Simply plug Harmony One into your Mac or PC with the supplied USB cable and go to Logitech's Harmony Web site. As you answer a series of questions onscreen about which equipment you are trying to control and how it's all hooked together, the "logic" of your remote's macros is automatically built for you. So you don't have to laboriously (okay, it's not labor, but it *is* a time waster), manually program a macro to, for example, "select receiver, select menu, down arrow twice, select enter, up arrow once, select enter again," or whatever arcane combination of keystrokes will make your equipment do what you want it to do. The Logitech database already "knows" all this and simply downloads the right instructions to your remote over the Internet. So you just press the "DVD" command, for example, and your remote will tell your DVD player, your receiver, your TV, your . . . well, whatever . . . what to do. We like it when technology works for us, rather than the other way around.

Harmony is also a learning remote and has, in addition to the touch screen, a number of dedicated feature buttons, a docking and recharging station, and more. Trés cool. For the price and simplicity, every home theater owner should check out these Harmony remotes.

If you want a really big touch screen, Harmony 1000 ($500) offers a big 3.5-inch touch screen and moves almost all the controls from dedicated keys to the touch interface. Again, this is a lot less money than the high-end systems we discuss in Chapter 23.

Part IV
Putting It All Together

The 5th Wave
By Rich Tennant

"Wait a minute...This is a movie, not a game?! I thought I was the one making Keanu Reeves jump kick in slow motion."

In this part . . .

So you know what stuff you need to buy to set up a home theater, and you may have even bought it. Well, if you're like us, buying stuff is a reflexive act. We could do it in our sleep. The hard part is figuring out how to hook it all up. Fear not — Part IV to the rescue.

First, we talk about the cables and connectors you can use to connect the components of your home theater. This is an important section to read because in many cases you have a choice of cable types, and some cables are simply much better than others in terms of creating a home theater that looks and sounds like it should.

Next, we talk you through the "insert tab A into slot A" aspect of connecting a home theater. Now, remember that this advice is generic. Home theater equipment vendors are always coming up with their own little "modifications," making it hard for us to give concrete advice that applies in every situation. But we get you 99 percent of the way there.

We also talk about how to do some nontraditional things with your home theater. First, we discuss how to connect your home theater components into a whole-home net-work that lets you view, listen to, and control expensive home theater gear anywhere in your home. We also give you some details about how to hook up the home theater PCs we talk about in Part II, so that you can bring the power of the PC (and the Internet) to your home theater!

Chapter 16

Home Theater Cable Basics

*O*ne of the most puzzling, infuriating, blood-pressure-raising tasks in assembling a home theater is finding the right kind, size, shape, and length of cables. Someday in the not-so-distant future, if the stars align just right, there may be a single type of digital cable that can connect every-thing — this is the holy grail of the consumer electronics industry. All that's needed is some widespread agreement among *all* parties to make this happen.

There's hope here — a cable system called *HDMI,* capable of carrying both audio and video, is becoming popular. (Those in the know know that HDMI stands for High-Definition Multimedia Interface.) It won't solve the problem for your older gear, but it's becoming almost standard on new equipment, even on networked devices that bring Internet content to your home theater. We discuss HDMI in the section titled "Employing digital video connections."

We may soon see an even better solution to the cabling problem: no cabling at all. The day is coming when inexpensive yet high-performance wireless systems will let you connect your components together without worrying about which plug goes where — or which throw rug to buy to hide that tangle of speaker wire.

We can dream of the day when complex cabling is no longer necessary, but although it's getting closer, it hasn't arrived yet. In this chapter, we discuss the different kinds of cables required to hook up the common components in a home theater as well as those needed to share your theater with the rest of the house. When there's more than one way to hook one component to another, we tell you which cable is best.

Working with Short Run Cables

Most of the connections you make in a home theater are *short runs* — that is, connections between components that are sitting just a few feet from each other (or are at least in the same room). The cables you use for these connections are typically called *interconnects*. Later in this chapter, we talk about the long-run cables that make up the infrastructure of a whole-home audio and video network.

Choosing quality cables

We should take a moment here to talk about cable quality — right up front, in the beginning of the chapter. You can get audio cable (or most any kind of cable) for free in the box when you buy new equipment. Or you can pay literally $1000 a foot for the double-secret-mojo, cold-fusion-reactor-type cables. In case you think we're kidding, we're not. (Well, we are about the cold-fusion part.) Some people pay thousands of dollars for each cable in their system. Our take on the matter is this: Don't use the free *el cheapo* cables that came in the box — because you *do* get what you pay for — but don't pay $1000+ per cable either unless you are both rich and absolutely convinced that you can hear an improvement in your sound or see an improvement in your video. There's a happy medium. Bottom line: Yes, there is a difference in cables, but no, you don't have to pay a ton for good cables.

 Look for cables that use oxygen-free copper (OFC) conductors and have gold-plated surfaces on the jacks. Oxygen-free copper is a purer form of copper, and the gold-plated surfaces resist corrosion. Use the shortest run of cable possible because the longer that audio signal travels over the cable, the more likely the signal will be audibly degraded by interference or *attenuation* (the weakening of the signal as it travels over any cable).

Dozens of companies make high-quality cables at a wide range of prices. Right off the bat, we can name Blue Jeans Cable (www.bluejeanscable.com), Kimber Kable (www.kimber.com), and AudioQuest (www.audioquest.com). By the way, there are so many good cables out on the market, please don't feel like our short list is anywhere near exhaustive. We could have filled a page with company names.

Joining the RCA mania

The most common type of connector in any home theater is the standard analog *audio interconnect*. Traditionally, these cables came in pairs for two-channel (stereo) audio connections, but in the realm of the home theater, with its multiple surround-sound channels, cables don't always work in neat pairs. You may find yourself using these cables individually (like the cable that connects a subwoofer to the receiver or controller), in big bunches (like the six cables that connect an SACD [Super Audio CD] or DVD-Audio player to the receiver, or in even bigger bunches (the eight cables for connecting a Blu-ray disc player's audio output).

Audio interconnects use a standardized jack known as an _RCA jack,_ which is nice because any audio interconnect with RCA jacks will plug in to any corresponding RCA plug on a piece of A/V equipment. Figure 16-1 shows an RCA plug on a stereo (dual) pair of audio interconnects.

Figure 16-1:
The ubiquitous RCA jack and plug.

If you go shopping for audio interconnects, you'll find a huge array of different cable constructions. The typical audio interconnect is a _coaxial_ cable, which means that it has two electrical conductors surrounded by a shielded jacket within the cable. This jacket is called _shielded_ because it is designed to keep stray electromagnetic energy from getting into the conductors and causing interference with the audio signal. But you'll find a lot of variation out there, and some cables are unshielded but twisted. (Twisting has a similar effect to shielding — due to the black art of physics, twisted cables can _cancel out_ interferences.)

Connecting your speakers

Another cable that you'll find in every home theater (except for those that use active loudspeaker systems, which we discuss in Chapter 12) is the speaker cable. Speaker cables connect the outputs of the power amplifier or the amplifier section of the receiver to the speaker. These cables carry the high-powered electrical currents required to move the internal components of the speaker (the magnets that move the drivers, as described in Chapter 12). You need one pair of speaker cables for each speaker in your system (except for the subwoofer if it's an active system — which most are — and which uses an analog audio interconnect cable instead).

Some expensive speaker systems can use two pairs of speaker wires per speaker. These systems are either biwired or biamped:

- ✔ **Biwired:** Two sets of speaker wire connect to the same output on the receiver or power amplifier, and you plug them into two sets of terminals on the speaker itself.

- ✔ **Biamped:** The speaker uses two separate amplifiers — one for the low-frequency drivers and one for the high-frequency drivers.

Biwiring is one of those audiophile tricks that most people don't really hear. If it works for you, and you have speakers with such a setup, by all means use it. But for us, it's just not worth the expense of the extra set of speaker cables.

Because they typically go for longer distances (especially in the case of surround speakers) and carry more electrical current than interconnects, speaker cables are considerably beefier and thicker than interconnects. The thickness of speaker cables (or the conductors within, to be precise) is referred to as *gauge* (using the standard AWG, or American Wire Gauge, system). The lower the gauge, the thicker the conductors.

Thicker conductors have less electrical *resistance* to the current flowing through them. Too much resistance is a bad thing (it can alter the audio signal), and the longer the cable, the greater the resistance the signal faces while traveling over the cable. We recommend cables of no higher than 16-gauge thickness, and prefer 14-gauge cables. For longer runs of 40 feet or more, such as runs to surround-sound speakers in a large room, we recommend moving down (in gauge number, up in size) to 12-gauge cables if they fit your budget.

If you want to hide your speaker cables in the wall or are running speaker cables through the wall for a multizone audio system, you need to get cables that are specially designed for this purpose and that meet electrical code requirements. You should choose cables that have been certified for this purpose by Underwriters Laboratories (UL-certified) and that meet the *CL3* specification (which relates to the insulation on the wires and helps prevent fires).

Unlike audio interconnects, which share the common RCA connector, you have a ton of connector choices when it comes to speaker cables (these connectors are sometimes called *terminations*). The most bare-bones approach is to just use the bare wire itself (stripped of any insulation), but many folks prefer some sort of a terminating device on the ends of the cable, mainly for aesthetics, but you may also find that the connectors on your speakers or receiver work better with a wire that's been terminated with one of the connectors we discuss shortly. (Often choosing a cable connector is just a matter of *fit*, especially if you're using a set of big, fat, 12-gauge speaker wires.)

You'll see three main types of connectors (besides the bare wire) on the market:

- ✔ **Pin connectors:** These look like they sound — a straight or angled pin at the end of the wire (though it's not sharp, so you won't put your eye out). These work best with the spring-loaded clip type of speaker connectors, which you find on less expensive receivers and speakers. Pin connectors also work with the preferred five-way binding posts found on better models. (We talk about five-way binding posts in Chapter 12.)

- ✔ **Spade lugs:** These U-shaped connectors fit behind the screws on a five-way binding post. You slide the open part of the U over the post and then screw down the plastic nut. Spade lugs can provide the tightest, most reliable connection because of that screwing down. Some spade lugs go beyond the U shape and are shaped like three-quarters of a circle, to hook around your binding post. These "hooked" connectors tend to be even more secure.

- ✔ **Banana plugs:** If you squint really hard, these plugs may actually look like bananas, but they really look more like pin connectors that are fat in the middle. By bowing out in the middle, they provide a tight fit into the binding post. Banana plugs come in single and dual configurations. The dual variety is just two banana plugs (one for each wire in the pair of speaker wires) stuck together in the same housing.

Figure 16-2 shows the pin, spade lug, and banana plug, and Figure 16-3 shows a five-way binding post.

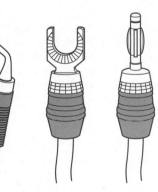

Figure 16-2:
From left to right, a pin connector, a spade lug, and a banana plug.

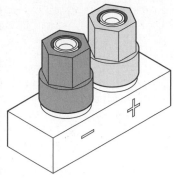

Figure 16-3:
The five-way binding post is your versatile friend.

Although the spade lug provides the ultimate in speaker wire connections, we think the banana plug provides a connection that's very close in quality. The banana plug is also much easier to use because the banana just slides into the binding post (nothing to tighten or adjust). Banana plugs are also handy because the back of a multichannel surround-sound receiver is a crowded place with the speaker terminals often *quite* close together. Banana plugs give you the ability to connect the wires by just sticking them straight into a hole on the binding post (perpendicular to the back of the receiver). We can tell you from experience how much easier this is than trying to jam fat wires through seven pairs of speaker terminals located about a half-inch apart.

Your choice of speaker cable connectors is largely driven by the receiver and speaker choices you make. While ideally manufacturers would create gear that could accept any of these connectors, the real world of designing and manufacturing A/V gear often makes that difficult. When you look at the sheer number of speaker connections that sprout on the back of a 7.1-channel receiver (at least fourteen individual connectors just for the speakers — not to mention all the audio and video interconnects), there's often just not enough room to accept many of the larger connectors (such as spade lugs). When you're purchasing speaker cables, try to be sure that the connectors will fit — and make sure you can return the cables if they simply won't fit on your gear.

Using digital audio interconnects

With the advent of computer-chip-laden receivers and DVD players, home theater has moved home A/V gear into the digital age. True, CD players have been digital for years, but for the majority of people, all the digital stuff happened *inside* the CD. The connections between the CD player and the receiver were all analog. Surround sound (specifically digital surround-sound systems, such as Dolby Digital and DTS) has made the digital interconnect commonplace.

As we mention throughout the book, digital audio interconnects (to connect DVD players, HDTV tuners, video game consoles, and more to the A/V receiver or controller) are divided into two main types: coaxial and optical (or Toslink).

The HDMI connection (discussed later in this chapter, in the section called "Employing digital video connections") is primarily used as a method for making digital video connections, but HDMI can also carry up to eight channels of digital audio. As A/V receivers begin to include HDMI connections (and a growing number are), you'll be able to use a single cable to connect a source device such as a Blu-ray disc or DVD player or set-top box to your receiver, and also a single cable to connect the receiver to your display. Home theater cable nirvana is within sight (at least for new equipment that includes HDMI)!

Coaxial digital interconnects

The *coaxial interconnect* looks an awful lot like a single (mono) audio interconnect. It has standard RCA jacks on both ends and a coaxial cable between them. Put the analog audio and coaxial interconnects side-by-side on a table (unlabeled of course), and you really can't tell them apart. But the conductors inside coaxial cables are of a different construction that's designed to handle the higher frequencies of digital signals. You shouldn't use standard audio interconnects in place of a coaxial digital cable. It's tough to explain the difference in sound you may experience if you use the wrong kind of cable here, but if your digital audio just doesn't sound *right,* check to see whether you have the correct digital interconnect hooked up.

Coaxial digital interconnects are not the only example of cables that use RCA plugs and look like audio interconnects but are not. Both the composite and the component video cables we discuss shortly also appear to be identical to audio interconnects, but in fact use different internal conductors and designs.

Also keep in mind that the term *coax* is typically used to describe the cables for connecting antennas, cable TV feeds, and satellite dishes to your home theater. That type of coax (using the F connector) is a *completely* different kettle of fish from a coaxial digital audio cable.

Optical digital interconnects

The Toslink optical connector uses fiber optics instead of copper cabling and carries the digital signal as pulses of light instead of as an electrical signal. The connector on a Toslink interconnect, viewed head-on, looks like a nice little house in suburbia — except most houses don't have a laser flashing out of the side of them. (Well at least ours don't — we won't presume to speak for you.) Figure 16-4 shows the Toslink cable connector.

The *female* Toslink connector (on your receiver or DVD player or wherever you're plugging a Toslink into) is usually covered by a little removable dust cap. If you don't take off this cap, you're going to curse like a sailor trying to plug in that cable.

Figure 16-4:
Fiber optics in your house! The Toslink optical interconnect.

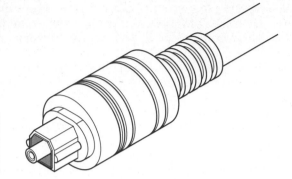

Some folks argue strongly either for Toslink or for coaxial digital audio connectors — we don't have any qualms recommending them both. Our basic advice is to use whichever is available to you — if they're both available, they're both equally good, assuming you don't use cables that fell off the back of a speeding van in your neighborhood.

Using analog video connections

The majority of video connections in a home theater are still made using analog connections (though an increasing number of devices can use the newer digital video interconnects we discuss in the following section). You'll find three types of *short-run* analog video connections in a home theater.

To truly understand the differences between the types of connections, you need to first understand what kinds of signals these cables carry. There are two components to a video signal: the *luminance* and the *chrominance.* The luminance provides the video display with the brightness information that determines which parts of the screen are darker or lighter. The chrominance adds information about what color each segment of the screen should be.

A definite hierarchy exists among video connections. One is visibly worse (in terms of picture quality) than the other two, and of the two superior methods, one is better (though not as significantly) than the other. In ascending order (worst to best), these connection types are as follows:

- ✔ **Composite video:** Both luminance and chrominance are combined into a single signal. The *comb filter* inside the display (discussed in Chapter 13) separates these two components and sends them to the appropriate internal circuitry.

- ✔ **S-video:** In S-video, luminance and chrominance are separated onto two separate signal paths, so the signal can bypass the comb filter in the TV. This usually results in a much clearer picture, with more defined colors and images.

- ✔ **Component video:** Component video separates the signal even further, providing one path for luminance information and two separate paths for chrominance information. Component video connections can be further enhanced in a *wideband* component video connection, which allows the higher frequencies needed for HDTV to travel from the source (such as an HDTV tuner) to the HDTV monitor.

So the big difference between composite (the lower-quality video signal), S-video, and component video connections is the fact that the better connections carry luminance and chrominance information separately. Why is this a big deal? After all, the display *does* have a comb filter to take care of that problem. Well, here's a dirty little secret: Comb filters do an imperfect job of separating these two signals and can leave visible *artifacts* in your picture. You want the sharpest, most colorful picture you can get, don't you?

In some cases, you might not choose the highest-quality connection available to you. We talk about such cases in Chapter 17, when we discuss hooking up your home theater.

Both component and composite cables use standard RCA connectors and bear a striking resemblance to the analog audio interconnect (and the digital coaxial interconnect, for that matter). Composite video cables are loners (you need just one), and component video cables travel in small packs of three, often labeled Y, Pr, and Pb.

Composite video cables are usually color-coded yellow (that is to say, the connector usually has a yellow ring around it, or the rubber boot around the connector is yellow). Component video cables are also typically color-coded with red, green, and blue connectors.

S-video is an unmistakable beast, with its own special connector (the S-video connector of course). This connector has four small pins that correspond to four small holes on the S-video plug on your gear. Figure 16-5 shows an S-video connector.

Figure 16-5:
Separate that chrominance and luminance with S-video.

S-video connectors can be a real pain in the butt to line up and connect. One set of pins is slightly more widely spaced than the other (the bottom ones are farther apart). If you're really killing yourself, check to see that you aren't pushing this cable in upside down. A little plastic doohickey keeps you from really messing things up, but bent pins are far from unknown to first-time S-video users. Most of the time, they're not so bent that you can't use your fingertip to get them straightened back out.

Employing digital video connections

The consumer electronics industry (in association with content providers) has been working overtime to develop some digital video interconnection systems that satisfy the following requirements:

- **Preserve the digital signal:** The video connection systems we discuss in the previous section are all analog systems. They carry analog video signals, not digital ones. Nothing is inherently wrong with analog connections, but they are more susceptible to interferences and other losses of signal quality when compared to digital connections. And in the case of digital signals (such as HDTV and other ATSC digital television broadcasts), there's no reason to convert to analog until the very last minute (inside the display itself). As Dick Vitale might say, "Keep it digital, baby!"

- **Minimize cables:** Some of these analog connections (particularly component video) also require multiple cables per connection. So if you want to connect the component video output of your HDTV tuner to your receiver and then to your display, you need six cables (three for each link). Add a DVD player using component video into the mix, and you have six more cables. Pretty soon, you have spaghetti. And this doesn't even include the cables required for audio!

- **Provide copy protection:** These analog connections don't have inherent copy protection systems. If there's one thing that content providers (movie and television studios) want to prevent, it's people copying their content. They don't even really want to let you make copies for personal use, such as copying *CSI* when you're out of town on business so that you can watch it after you come home.

We discuss the most common digital video connection options in the following sections.

FireWire

One of the first systems for digital video crossed over from the computer industry. *FireWire,* which is also called IEEE 1394 or i.LINK, depending on who's talking, was originally developed by Apple Computer for connecting peripheral devices to Macintosh computers. Companies such as Sony picked up on the technology and began incorporating FireWire into its camcorders and PCs, and FireWire grew from there. (The FireWire in camcorders is often called *DV.*)

For several years, some HDTV devices (such as JVC's D-VHS) used FireWire connections, but as we write, FireWire appears to have all but gone away as a means of connecting HDTV devices.

So why do we mention it? Well, for starters, you can still find a few HDTV systems that use FireWire. Additionally, FireWire is beginning to become more common in the *audio* side of the home theater. The DVD Forum (a coalition of companies that helps develop the DVD standard) has recently approved FireWire as a connection method for the audio output of DVD-Audio players. When these players (and compatible receivers or controllers) hit the market, you'll be able to replace those six analog audio interconnects with a single cable. That will be nice!

Although HDMI, FireWire's biggest competitors in the digital video connection world, appear to have won the war of digital video interconnects, battles are still being fought, and FireWire may still have a little life left in it. A group called HANA (High-definition Audio-Video Networking Alliance, www.hana alliance.org) was formed to create yet another set of standards for connecting your A/V gear, and FireWire is a big part of that system. So we can't count FireWire out completely yet.

Digital Visual Interface

One reason that FireWire never took off in the world of home theater was the success of a competitor called DVI (Digital Visual Interface). DVI is another technology adopted from the computer world, where it was developed as a means of connecting computers to digital LCD screens and projectors. Along the way, DVI picked up a strong copy protection system called HDCP (discussed in Chapter 13) and became a favorite of the HDTV industry.

HDCP makes DVI a relatively *dumb* connection — all it does is send video in one direction (for example, from the tuner to the display), and HDCP can limit your ability to make a digital copy of what you're watching. Figure 16-6 shows a DVI connector.

Not all devices with a DVI connector incorporate HDCP. For example, LCD computer monitors may use DVI without HDCP. If you connect an HDCP-enabled HDTV tuner to a non-HDCP display using a DVI cable, you can't get a full HDTV signal. Instead, the signal is converted to a lower resolution.

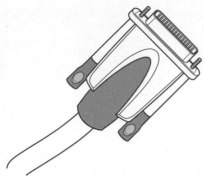

Figure 16-6:
A DVI con-
nector for
yummy,
digital video
quality.

DVI provides a great video connection but it doesn't carry audio like its successor, HDMI does. For the most part, in new equipment such as TVs and Blu-ray disc and DVD players, DVI has been phased out in favor of HDMI. If you have a piece of gear in your home theater that uses DVI but needs to be connected to a newer piece of HDMI-only gear, you can buy a cheap (usually under $20) adapter to connect the two. There will be no audio over that DVI-to-HDMI connection, but the video will work just fine.

The state of the art in digital video connections: HDMI

The latest and greatest in digital video (and audio) connections is the HDMI cable. HDMI stands for High-Definition Multimedia Interface, and you can find out more about the technology at the HDMI Web site at www.hdmi.org.

HDMI is being included in a variety of devices these days, including HDTVs, DVD players (both the current generation of DVD players and the high-definition Blu-ray disc player), cable and satellite set-top boxes, Media Center Edition PCs, gaming consoles such as the Sony PlayStation 3 and Microsoft Xbox 360, and even in digital media adapter devices such as the Apple TV or Roku's Netflix player (discussed in Chapter 10).

Why you will love HDMI!

What's so great about HDMI? Well, a few things:

- **It's all-digital.** Like DVI and FireWire, HDMI provides an all-digital path for your standard and high-definition video signals.

- **It's high-bandwidth.** HDMI can support data signals as fast as 4.9GB per second — with the newest High Speed variant supporting 10.2GB per second. That means it can handle HDTV with plenty of room to spare. (In fact, many HDTV signals uses less than half this bandwidth, so the HDTV signals don't have to be compressed.) FireWire, by comparison, tops out at 400MB per second (there is an 800MB per second variant, but it's not common) — less than half the bandwidth.

✔ **It can support all variants of HDTV.** 720p, 1080i, even 1080p can run over an HDMI cable.

✔ **It can carry up to eight channels of digital audio.** So a single HDMI cable can carry your HDTV *and* your 7.1-channel surround sound. Nothing like reducing the tangle of cables behind your system, huh?

As you shop for HDMI cables, you might consider consulting a cardiologist simply because the big-name HDMI cables in your average electronics store are incredibly expensive and may cause your heart to palpitate. Don't fear — HDMI cables don't have to be super-expensive. In fact, certified HDMI cables can be relatively cheap, and there are many good online sources for them. For example, Pat recently installed some HDMI cables in his wall that were about one-fifth the price of those at his local retail store, and they work *great!* We highly recommend that you spend a few moments perusing some of the other sources of information we discuss in Chapter 23 (such as the AVS Forum) and see what the home theater enthusiasts are using and where they're getting it online. You'll probably get a great bargain.

As long as your HDMI cable runs are less than 10 meters, you can buy one of these inexpensive cables and expect excellent results. When you get past ten meters (that's more than thirty feet — a long way!), we recommend that you consult a specialist because you might need some special active components to boost the signal level. But we're confident that most folks won't need to go more than thirty feet!

We think HDMI is the way to go. If you're shopping for a new TV, a new receiver, or a new DVD player, or choosing an HDTV set-top box or satellite receiver, go with HDMI if you can. HDMI can provide the highest-quality video signal and throws your multichannel surround-sound audio in on the same cable. You really can't go wrong here!

HDMI is fully *backward compatible* with DVI. What that means is that you can interconnect HDMI and DVI devices. So you can connect, for example, a DVI connector on your HDTV cable set-top box to an HDMI input on your new plasma TV (or vice versa). Keep in mind that such connections will carry only video signals — DVI doesn't support audio. If you're buying all new gear, it's best to choose HDMI all around, but if you're upgrading, the good news is that HDMI won't strand your investment in DVI-equipped gear. All you need is an inexpensive adapter (about $20) or HDMI-to-DVI cables, which have an HDMI connector on one end and a DVI connector on the other. We love it when something new doesn't make us have to throw away our old gear — don't you?

Understanding the latest developments in HDMI

If you read about Blu-ray disc players in Chapter 6 (go ahead, read it, Blu-ray disc players are *really* cool), you might recall the confusion that Blu-ray *profiles* have caused a lot of otherwise smart people. Well HDMI has been facing a similar problem over the past couple of years as the technology has matured and new capabilities have been added to HDMI.

In fact, the problem that HDMI buyers have been facing is exactly the same one that Blu-ray buyer's have faced: confusion and uncertainty based on some technical terms that really should never have been part of the public discussion of the technology. In Blu-ray's case, profiles made people wonder "Well, is this thing going to be obsolete in six months?" In HDMI's case it was versions of the technical standard for HDMI as the folks developing HDMI chips moved from version 1 to version 1.1 to version 1.2 and now to version 1.3. How the heck are we supposed to keep up with all of that?

Well the short answer is, we're not, and the smart folks at HDMI licensing (who oversee the development of HDMI) are working to give us all some new commonsense plain English terms that describe the different types of HDMI. By the time you read this chapter, HDMI cables will be classified into two groups:

- **HDMI:** These cables have been tested to support up to 1080i HDTV signals. They may very well support 1080p (and in almost all cases will do so at shorter distances — 2 or 3 meters or less), but they've not been tested and certified to do so.

- **HDMI High Speed:** These cables have been tested up to the very highest speeds available in HDMI (10.2GB per second), and will support 1080p as well as other special video enhancements such as deep color and faster refresh rates (120 Hz, for example) as they become available in high-definition source devices and TVs. (We talk about deep color and higher refresh rates in Chapter 13.)

Having said all that, we (and the HDMI licensing folks) know that the horse is out of the barn, and that you're going to hear about HDMI 1.whatever when you're shopping for equipment. Here's a quick rundown on the different versions of HDMI.

These descriptions discuss all the features that a particular HDMI implementation may include. Manufacturers are not required to offer all the features incorporated in a particular version of HDMI. So a manufacturer could offer a system (such as a DVD player) with an HDMI 1.3 chip (and advertise it as HDMI 1.3 equipped) and not provide every feature we're about to mention. It is always important to look beyond the HDMI number and review the actual features included with the equipment. For example, if it's important to you that your HDMI-equipped Blu-ray disc player and receiver can carry Dolby TrueHD bitstreams over the HDMI cable, it's not enough to just see the HDMI 1.3 check box filled in on the spec sheet — you need to make sure that this specific feature is included on *both* devices.

- **HDMI 1:** This is the first version of HDMI, supporting up to eight channels of audio and 1080p video.

- **HDMI 1.1:** This version added support for the audio from DVD-Audio players over the HDMI connection.

✔ **HDMI 1.2:** This version includes support for SACD audio players, and additionally incorporates a control system called HDMI CEC (discussed in the sidebar titled "HMDI CEC gives you control").

✔ **HDMI 1.3:** This is the latest version of HDMI and includes some of the biggest changes yet in the standard. The really big news here is the increased bandwidth it allows (the 10.2GB per second we mentioned earlier in the section), which allows HDMI 1.3 to support 1080p video *plus* the bitstreams of the highest resolution surround-sound codecs such as Dolby TrueHD and DTS-HD Master Audio, plus additional features such as deeper color depths. In fact, so much bandwidth is available on an HDMI 1.3 connection that a manufacturer could make a 3D TV that was fed *two* 1080p connections at the same time. That's a lot of bandwidth.

All HDMI systems are *backward compatible* so any HDMI-equipped system can be connected to any other HDMI-equipped system and work just fine. Some features (such as 1080p or Dolby TrueHD bitstreams) may not be enabled, but you'll be able to make the connection and get a fine high-definition picture and surround-sound audio without worries. Additionally, all versions of HDMI use the same cable connectors, so you won't need to swap out cables in most cases.

HMDI CEC gives you control

When the 1.2 version of HDMI came out a few years ago, it included a new HDMI feature that manufacturers are starting to incorporate in their home theater gear today: *HDMI CEC* (CEC stands for *Consumer Electronics Control*). HDMI CEC is a two-way control system that allows different components in your home theater to "talk" to each other to send control signals and to understand the current state of each component. In an HDMI CEC–equipped home theater, one button press on the remote can turn on a number of components — so if you wanted to watch a movie on a Blu-ray disc, one button press would turn on the TV, the Blu-ray disc player, and the home theater receiver.

In essence, HDMI CEC is a built-in version of the *macros* we discuss in Chapter 15 when we talk about remote controls. But instead of the remote sending out separate IR (infrared) commands to each component, HDMI CEC uses the HDMI connections between components to send out commands.

We're still in the early days of HDMI CEC, with only a small number of components having the feature. The best implementations of CEC, as we write, are *within* a specific vendor's product line (such as Sony's BRAVIA theater sync system). HDMI CEC *does* work across and amongst vendors (so your Panasonic TV could "talk" with your Sony Blu-ray disc player), but you'll find that a vendor's own implementation will have more features and more commands.

We're excited about HDMI CEC and expect to see it become a standard part of new home theater gear as time passes.

Working with Long-Run Cables

When you start thinking about connecting your home theater to the rest of your home (perhaps to share a video source device with TVs in other rooms), you'll run into a new set of cables. These *long-run* cables are designed to minimize signal loss and get your audio and video to any spot in the house. Although you can distribute audio and video around the home in many ways, the three most common ways are the following:

- ✔ **RG6 coaxial cabling for video:** This cable (which we describe later in this chapter) carries video signals (and the associated audio tracks) from antennas, satellite dishes, and cable TV feeds from the street. With devices called *modulators,* you can actually create in-house TV channels and use this cable to share your own video sources with other TVs in the house.

- ✔ **Speaker cabling for whole-home audio:** We discuss speaker wires (appropriately rated for in-wall use) in the "Connecting your speakers" section, earlier in this chapter. You can use this same speaker wire to connect a multizone receiver (or a separate whole-home audio system) to speakers throughout the house.

- ✔ **Category 5e (CAT-5e) or Category 6 (CAT-6) network cabling:** This is the cable used for computer networks — the stuff you put in your walls if you are creating a whole-home network. With the appropriate gear on the ends of these cables (we discuss this in Chapter 18), you can use this cable to carry audio and video signals.

Going with RG6

Coaxial cable (usually just called *coax*) is a metallic cable most often used for transmitting radio frequency (RF) signals, such as broadband television video and radio signals. Coaxial cable contains two conductors, or *axes,* to carry data. A layer of dielectric insulating material surrounds a single center conductor. The other conductor is a metal shield, usually made of a braided metallic wiring, that goes around the dielectric (insulating) layer. The outer-most layer of coax cable is an insulating jacket. The connectors on an RG6 cable are known as *F connectors.*

You may encounter coaxial cables labeled RG6QS or RG6 Quad Shield, which means that the cable has additional shielding beneath the cable jacket — four layers, as the *quad* implies. These layers provide additional protection against interference from external sources. Because of this extra shielding, we recommend you use Quad Shield coax. It doesn't cost a lot more, and it's worth the investment.

CAT-5e/CAT-6 cabling systems

If you've ever spent any time building, designing, or just using a computer network, you've encountered CAT-5e or CAT-6 cabling — often generically called *Ethernet cables.* (These are two similar types of data cables — CAT-5e is the most common, so we refer to it here, but both will work just fine.) CAT-5e is a type of UTP (unshielded twisted pair) copper cabling and can be used for phones, computer networks, home automation networks, and audio/video distribution systems. CAT-5e cables typically consist of four pairs of wire (eight total conductors) wrapped in a single jacket. The ends of CAT-5e cables are terminated in connectors known as *RJ-45 jacks,* which look exactly like the common RJ-11 phone jack, only wider.

CAT-5e cabling can be used to connect your home theater to your computer LAN (local area network) and through this LAN to the Internet. For example, CAT-5e connectors are commonly found on MP3 servers, PVRs, and increasingly on audio source devices that are designed to play back Internet radio stations or MP3 files located on a computer in your house. CAT-5e cabling may be used also to connect the A/V source components in your home theater to other rooms in the house. (We discuss systems that do this in Chapter 19.)

There is actually a range of category-rated UTP cables (for example, CAT-3 cabling is often used for telephone wiring). CAT-6 is the current top-of-the-line UTP cabling, suitable for very fast computer networks, but CAT-5e cable is the most common for home use and is more than adequate for your home's wiring.

Each piece of a CAT-5e system (the cables themselves, the RJ-45 jacks, and so on) is subject to the CAT-5e rating system. If you use CAT-5e, make sure *all* the pieces and parts are rated CAT-5e. The "weakest link in the chain" rule applies here. Any piece that's rated below CAT-5e brings the whole system down to that lower rating. Many A/V-over-UTP systems require CAT-5e and don't work well on identical-looking but lower-rated cables. All CAT-5e cables and connectors will be clearly marked with a label of some sort, so just read the fine print (on the cable itself) to be sure.

Identifying Other Cable Odds and Ends

We end this chapter with a hodgepodge listing of other cables and connectors that may show up in your home theater. These connection systems are less common than the ones discussed in preceding sections, but none of them is a complete stranger to the world of home theater. This is particularly true if you are hooking your home theater into a whole-home network or connecting PCs and other computer-like devices (such as PVRs and MP3 servers) into your home theater.

Wireless connections

Wireless networking technologies have made a huge splash in the computer networking world — everyone, it seems, has gone crazy for a system called *802.11* or *Wi-Fi* (a type of wireless computer LAN). (Read our books *Smart Homes For Dummies* and *Wireless Home Networking For Dummies,* both published by Wiley Publishing, Inc., for a ton of information about this technology — and you Mac folks might want to check out *Airport and Mac Wireless Networking For Dummies,* by Michael Cohen, as well.)

As more people begin to use PCs and the Internet in their home theaters, this technology is increasingly moving from the computer world to the consumer electronics world. Many manufacturers, such as NETGEAR (`www.netgear.com`) and D-Link (`www.dlink.com`), are creating devices called *Wi-Fi Ethernet bridges* specifically for home entertainment/home theater gear. These bridges make it easy to connect Internet-capable home theater gear to your home's Wi-Fi network with the help of an Ethernet port. (Ethernet is the common computer network that uses CAT-5e cabling and RJ-45 jacks.) For about $100, you can buy one of these bridges and use a short length of CAT-5e cabling to connect it to your PVR (personal video recorder), MP3 server, home theater PC, or even your gaming console (such as Xbox or PlayStation 3). The bridge then connects wirelessly (using radio waves) to your DSL or cable modem through a device called an *access point*.

In Chapter 10, we discuss a number of Wi-Fi–enabled systems that let you get content into your home theater.

RS-232

If you've ever connected a modem to an older PC, you've probably used an RS-232 connector and not even known it. RS-232 is a standard computer communications system that's more commonly known as a *serial* connection. Until the advent of the USB system (discussed in the following section), RS-232 was the standard connection for modems, handheld computer cradles, and many other PC peripheral devices.

In the home theater world, RS-232 is *not* used for carrying audio and video. It is, however, often used for connecting A/V components to automation and control systems (such as the Crestron systems we discuss in Chapter 15). You can also find RS-232 ports on the back of many advanced A/V receivers, where they can be used to connect the receiver to a PC for upgrading the software system within the receiver.

USB

USB (or Universal Serial Bus) has pretty much replaced RS-232 in the PC world. These days, most printers, external modems, handheld computers, portable MP3 players, and other PC peripheral devices connect to PCs via USB. In the home theater world, USB can be found on the back of many computer-like source devices (such as MP3 servers and PVRs). USB has not yet replaced RS-232 for connections to automation and control systems, but probably will eventually.

The most common use for USB in a home theater is with a Wi-Fi system. You can outfit source devices that can connect to the Internet with a USB Wi-Fi network adapter. This adapter enables you to connect back to the access point and out to the Internet. USB is used also for remote control connections for PCs. The remote control receiver for the PC connects to the PC via a USB cable.

Multiple types of USB devices are out there. (With more than 1 billion USB-enabled devices in use around the world, that's probably no surprise.) The latest and greatest variant of USB is *USB 2.0 High-speed,* which supports data transfers at speeds of up to 480 Mbits per second. The older and slower USB 1.1 standard doesn't cut it for home theater use, because it can barely handle audio signals and just plain can't do high-quality video.

You can also find a few A/V receivers (such as JVC's RX-D201S — www.jvc.com) that have a USB connection that lets you connect to a nearby PC to feed digital audio signals (such as MP3 files) from the PC to the receiver without using one of the media adapter devices we discuss in Chapter 10.

IR connections

In Chapter 18, we talk about ways that you can connect your home theater to speakers and displays in other parts of your home by using a whole-home entertainment network. As we discuss earlier in this chapter, you use RG6 coaxial cable, speaker wire, CAT-5e cabling, or any combination of the three to carry your audio and video around the house. There's one other piece to this whole-home puzzle, however. You need some sort of system for controlling remote devices when you are watching them (or listening to them) in a different part of the house. If the phone rings, you want to be able to turn down the music or pause the movie.

Most A/V systems use IR (infrared) systems for their remote controls. IR is a great system, but because it uses a beam of light to carry control signals, it can't penetrate walls (unless you have a glass house, we suppose). So you need some sort of wired system that can carry IR signals from remote locations back to your home theater. (You can also find wireless alternatives from companies such as X10 — www.x10.com.) You can set up an infrared system in four ways:

- ✔ **IR cabling:** Many home networking vendors sell cables designed for carrying IR signals from remote locations back to the home theater.

- ✔ **CAT-5e cabling:** If you're using CAT-5e cabling for audio and video distribution (using some of the systems we discuss in Chapter 19), you'll find that these systems have a built-in capability to carry IR signals for remote controls. If you're not using one of these systems but have put CAT-5e cabling in your walls when building your home, you can use extra (unused) CAT-5e cables in place of the IR cabling we just mentioned.

- ✔ **RG6 coaxial cabling:** Using special devices called *IR injectors* (available from vendors such as ChannelPlus, www.channelplus.com), you can carry IR signals over the RG6 coax that you use for distributing cable or broadcast antenna TV signals.

  You can't use an IR injector on the RG6 cables used to connect a DSS dish to DSS receivers.

- ✔ **Proprietary systems:** If you opt to install a high-end automation system, such as those from Crestron (www.crestron.com), you need to use special proprietary cables from the manufacturer. For example, Crestron uses its own special cable called CrestNet.

Chapter 17

Hooking Up Your A/V System

· ·

· ·

*Y*ou've picked a room, collected all your A/V gear, opened the boxes, and *oohed* and *aahed* at your shiny new stuff. Now it's time to get down to the work of hooking up your home theater. At first glance, this can seem like a daunting task. You have a lot of cables and connectors to deal with, and even experienced home theater folks may find the back of an A/V receiver confusing at first. The key is to take a methodical approach. With a few key concepts in mind, hooking up an A/V system can be easy and even fun!

In this chapter, we talk about where the various pieces and parts of an A/V system should go in your home theater and how they should be connected to each other. However, the advice we give in this chapter is *generic*. Although the majority of home theater components connect in a similar fashion with identical cables and connectors, there are always a few differences among different brands and models. For example, what we call CD Audio In might be labeled CD Line In or even Aux In on your receiver. For the exact terms and procedures that apply to your system, you need to read your manual.

Many home theater receivers have *assignable inputs* — inputs that can be used for different components and that let you customize which audio input and which video input work together (for example, letting your receiver play Component video 3 and Coaxial digital audio 2 when you watch your DVD player). This feature is great because it adds a lot of flexibility. It also adds a level of complexity because you'll need to program those inputs (using the receiver's onscreen display). If you are using a receiver with programmable inputs, we highly (highly!) recommend you spend a few minutes with your user manual, familiarizing yourself with the process. While we could probably program your receiver if you invited us over (and gave us a nice cup of coffee and maybe some donuts), it's just about impossible to give you the precise steps you'll need to take here.

Planning the Room Layout

After you've read those oh-so-fun manuals, you might think it's time to start plugging away. The temptation is to get things hooked up and working. You want to watch a movie *right now,* admit it . . . so would we. But by devoting a few minutes to planning your next steps, you can make the process easier and get better results when the time comes to watch and listen to your system.

At a minimum, your home theater has six speakers (including the subwoofer). Each of these speakers plays a role in creating the illusion of being "in the action" when you watch movies or shows (or listen to multichannel audio on DVD-A or SACD). So you have to get the speakers in the right spots relative to your listening position. Incorrectly positioning your speakers creates gaps in the sound field that surrounds you. These gaps can be distracting or downright annoying and can also cause room interactions that reduce the fidelity of the audio you are re-creating.

No matter what you do, your speakers are going to interact with your room, creating echoes and reflections that have some impact on the sound. The key is to reduce the negative effects of these interactions and, instead, use them to your advantage.

Getting the front speakers in place

The front speakers — left, right, and center — provide the bulk of the sound you listen to while watching a movie. One of the key jobs of these front speakers is to provide a realistic reproduction of dialogue — you want people in the middle of the display to sound like they're right in front of you, and those on the left and right to sound like that's where they are. Proper placement of these three front speakers is essential in creating this effect and minimizing any gaps in the speakers' coverage (so when dialogue moves from side to side, it does so seamlessly). Keep the following points in mind when setting up your front speakers:

✔ **Set up your center channel speaker first.** The placement of the left and right speakers depends on the position of your center speaker.

✔ **Make sure the front surface of the center channel speaker is flush with the display.** Most center channel speakers are designed to be placed directly on top of the display. Keep the front surfaces of both flush with each other to minimize reflections. If your equipment physically permits, you might try to get the front of the speaker (the baffle) *in front of* the surface of the screen. (This is hard to pull off in the real world, which is why we recommend just making them flush.)

If you have a wall-mounted display (like a flat-panel plasma or LCD TV), you might have a hard time getting your center channel speaker flush with the display (unless you're using wall-mounted speakers especially designed for such applications — which are becoming popular these days). Don't sweat it; just try to keep the front of your center channel relatively close to the same vertical plane as the front of your display — don't stick it too far out in front if you can avoid it.

✔ **Keep the right and left channel speakers the same distance from your listening position as the front speaker.** Some people place the three front speakers in a straight line across the front of the room. This actually makes the center speaker closer to you than the others, meaning that sounds from the center speaker reach you sooner than sounds from the others. Instead of a line, the front speakers should form an *arc* in front of you, in which each speaker is the same distance from your primary viewing position (or the middle of the viewing position, such as the center of a couch or the middle of a group of seats).

If you're using wall-mount speakers with a wall-mounted flat panel, you're not going to be able to do this. Again, don't sweat it; it's not a huge deal as long as you take the time to "teach" your receiver where your speakers are when you configure it. Because these speakers will be a bit farther away from you than the center channel when you're sitting directly in front of the display, you'll simply have the receiver introduce a bit of *delay* in the signals sent to these speakers, so the sound arrives at your ears at the right time.

✔ *Toe-in* **the left and right speakers.** The front panels of the left and right speakers should be placed so that they are aimed directly at (or immediately behind) your seating position. Many wall mounts allow you to angle the speakers this way.

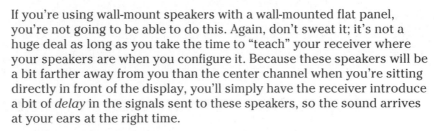

Some speakers are designed such that their front panels are already toed-in when the speakers are placed parallel to the wall. Check the manual that comes with your speakers to see if there are any recommendations on toe-in.

✔ **Place the left and right speakers at a 45- to 60-degree angle from the listening position.** Start off with the speakers at the wider angle. Place each speaker 30 degrees to the right or left of the center speaker from your viewing position. If you find, while listening to movie soundtracks, that sounds seem unnatural and too widely spaced, you can move the right and left speakers closer to the screen. Conversely, if it's hard to distinguish right from left from most seating positions, spread the speakers a bit farther apart. When you do so, maintain the arc we mentioned.

✔ **Place the speakers' tweeters at or near the viewers' ear level.** Keep in mind the seated height of your viewers in the seating you've selected and adjust your speakers accordingly when selecting stands or wall mounting. Even if you have floor-standing speakers, you can buy small stands to raise the height, if necessary. If your center speaker is above you (maybe you put it on top of a gigantic RPTV), you can at least aim it down toward your listening position. Our first technical editor (who's a genius at this stuff) likes to use rubber wedge-shaped doorstops under the backside of the center speaker to do this aiming.

Dealing with surrounds

Many people think of their surround-sound speakers as their rear speakers. Indeed, many receivers label the surround outputs as Rear, so people imagine that these speakers need to be along the back wall, behind the listening position. This isn't always the case — particularly with the bipole or dipole surround speakers, which are the most common kinds (we prefer dipoles).

5.1-channel surround sound

For 5.1-channel surround sound, we recommend that you place bipole or dipole surround speakers along the side walls (preferably mounted on the side wall). Position them even to or slightly behind your home theater seating, and about two feet above the listeners' seated ear level. If you are using direct-radiating speakers for your surrounds, the best placement is behind the listeners, aimed so that they radiate (face, in other words) toward the *back wall*. That might sound a bit counterintuitive, but if you face them directly toward the listening position, you don't get the diffuse surround sound that you're looking for.

If your room layout supports it, you should place your surround speakers on either side of your primary viewing/listening position so that they are each within a 90- to 110-degree angle from your head — where straight ahead (looking at the screen) is 0 degrees.

Other types of surround sound

If you're using Dolby Digital EX or DTS ES, you have an extra speaker (or two) to deal with. These systems have side surrounds (which are placed like 5.1-channel side surrounds) and *center-surround* channel speakers (one or two, depending on whether you're using a 6.1- or 7.1-channel setup).

These center surround speakers should be placed behind the listener. In a 6.1-channel setup, they go directly behind the listening position. In a 7.1-channel system, the two center surround speakers should be placed along the rear wall, on either side of the seating position.

In a 7.1 system, you should put each of the rear surrounds at an angle of 130 to 150 degrees from your main listening position — again relative to your display being 0 degrees.

Placing the subwoofer for optimal bass

You'll often hear people talk about low-frequency sounds being *nondirectional,* which is a fancy way of saying that you can't really locate where they are coming from by ear. Proponents of this concept will tell you that your subwoofer can be hidden well out of the way — under the proverbial end table, far away from the action. Subwoofers are nondirectional, to a degree, but putting your subwoofer too far away from the rest of your speakers (and from your listening position) can lead to situations in which you do hear where the bass is coming from. Indeed, if you move your subwoofer too far to the left or right, the bass isn't well integrated with the sound coming from the other speakers. In most cases, it's actually better to not hide the subwoofer. Treat it like any other speaker — show it off!

Many vendors recommend that you place your subwoofer in a corner. This placement reinforces the bass significantly, and we think this is a good place to start. However, in some rooms, you can get too much reinforcement of your bass in the corner, and you end up with boomy bass. What we mean by *boomy* is that the bass notes become indistinct; you just hear a low-frequency sound and can't distinguish between the different frequencies. So if you're listening to a recording of someone playing a Bach fugue on a pipe organ, you don't hear the distinct notes in the lower register. If this happens to you, try moving the subwoofer out from the corner a bit.

One good (if slightly unscientific) way of finding a place for your subwoofer (after you have it hooked up, of course) is to swap places with it. Put the subwoofer right up where you sit and turn on some bass-heavy music (or a bass-heavy movie soundtrack). Walk around the room until you find the place where the bass sounds best. Now, swap back by putting the subwoofer in the spot where the bass sounded best.

Figure 17-1 shows a typical 5.1-channel, surround-sound speaker configuration. As we discuss in the previous sections, the center and front left and right speakers are equidistant from the viewing position, with the left and right speakers 45 to 60 degrees apart (or 22 to 30 degrees on either side of the display from your main viewing position). The surrounds are beside or slightly behind the comfy home theater seats, and the subwoofer is placed along the front wall of the room.

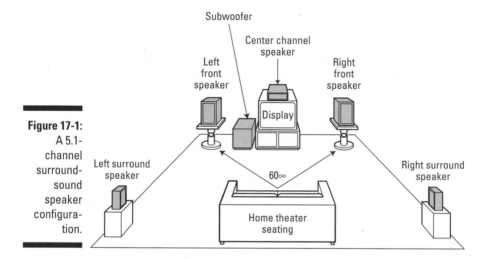

Figure 17-1:
A 5.1-channel surround-sound speaker configuration.

In a typical 7.1-channel configuration, the center, front, and surround speakers are in the same location as they are in a 5.1 layout, but you've added two additional rear surrounds located farther behind the main listening position.

Hiding Unsightly Cables

One drawback of a surround-sound audio system is that having those speakers alongside or behind your seating position makes hiding the speaker cables difficult. Now, some people out there love the look of fancy speaker wires. (Pat has a set of Kimber speaker cables that he just loves to stare at, though his two-year-old likes them for entirely unsafe play purposes.) But for most people, speaker cables are an unsightly reminder of all the work they've put into building their home theaters, and hiding these wires is a good thing.

The best way to hide cables, if you can pull it off, is to put them inside the wall. If you have a basement or attic under or over, respectively, your home theater room, using in-wall speaker cabling is pretty easy. Just make sure that you have the proper kind of speaker cable (UL-rated CL3 or higher) and that you use a thicker cable (lower gauge), such as 14- or even 12-gauge. See Chapter 16 for details about cables.

What about going wireless?

The ideal way to avoid dealing with hard-to-run and hard-to-hide speaker wires for the surround speakers in your 5-, 6-, or 7.1-channel surround-sound system would be to dispense with the wires entirely, right? Heck, yeah it would be — if only it were that simple. Wireless speakers have been a bit of a holy grail for home theater manufacturers for some time, and a number of manufacturers are now shipping home theater speaker systems (or *home-theater-in-a-box* — *HTIB* — systems that included the speakers, receiver, and DVD player all in one package) with wireless surround speakers.

Wireless systems use a variety of *RF* (radio frequency) systems to transmit the sound output from your receiver to the surrounds: Many use the Bluetooth technology in mobile phones, for example, others uses variations of *Wi-Fi* (the wireless networking built into your laptop or desktop PC), and still others use proprietary wireless systems (that work only within the closed environment of that manufacturer's equipment).

Although the wireless connection may be built into the receiver and speakers, more often systems are sold as *wireless ready,* which means you buy an extra module or two (the wireless transmitter and receiver) and plug them into your receiver (the transmitter) and speakers (the receiver). A good example of this is Sony's DAV-HDX279W BRAVIA Home Theater System. This HTIB system comes with a combined receiver/DVD player unit, five speakers, and a powered subwoofer (all for only $399). It's wireless ready, and with Sony's optional WAHT-SA1 S-AIR wireless surround-sound speaker kit

($179), you can cut those cords to the back of the room. Manufacturers such as Samsung and Panasonic offer similar kits.

Our experience with these systems is that they work just fine, but keep in mind that if you're looking for a truly high-fidelity surround-sound experience, wires are always going to be better.

Another thing to keep in mind is that even though you won't need speaker wires running to the back of the room with wireless surrounds, but you *will* need power — both to run the wireless receiver and also to provide amplification to the surround speakers (there's usually an amplifier built into the wireless receiver module or into the wireless surround speakers themselves (in which case they'd be *active loudspeakers* as discussed in Chapter 12). So you're not going to be truly wireless, just front-of-the-room-to-back-of-the-room wireless.

If that particular pathway is your big problem (hey, we understand that *all too well*), you should definitely look into wireless systems. If you think you're going to get away with just one plug in the front of the room and no other wires, well we hate to disappoint your, but you're not!

Wireless is getting a *lot* of attention from home theater engineers and designers, and wireless technologies themselves are advancing pretty darned rapidly (who here ran out to get a 3G iPhone the day they came out? C'mon, fess up!). Over time wireless will be a natural part of many home theaters. Today it's a niche product for people with specific needs and requirements.

Sometimes, you just can't get your cables in the wall. For example, Pat's house (like many in southern California) doesn't have a basement, and the ceiling over his home theater is raised to the roof (no attic access). In these cases, you can try to hide your cables under carpets or rugs. If that doesn't work, you might consider installing a *raceway* along the baseboards of your room that can contain the wires (the raceway can even be the baseboard itself, as long as there's room for cables behind it) or using thin (but wide) flat cables. For example, Monster Cable (www.monstercable.com) sells flat speaker cables in its "Invisible out of wall" series. Taperwire (www.taperwire.com) also offers flattened versions of most wiring you find in the house — including speaker cables. These flat cables are hard to see when placed along your baseboards and can even be painted to match your wall colors.

Attaching Components to the A/V Receiver

Getting your speaker cables and speakers mounted in place is a good first step. Hooking up the rest of your A/V gear is the next step. (Keep in mind that you might have to go back to the speakers and tweak the placement of at least some of them after everything is up and running.)

Spaghetti isn't just what's for dinner. It's also what you get when you pull out all the cables you bought for your home theater components. There sure is a lot of wire behind the scenes in today's home theater. (We hope that this will decrease over time as digital connections, such as HDMI, become more popular.) Luckily, any home theater worth its salt has a device — the A/V receiver or controller — that provides a central connection point for all these wires. Also, if you have a rack for your gear, the rack should have a good cable management system to help you out. We talk about racks in Chapter 20.

At the highest level, connecting components into your home theater is as simple as using the right cables to connect them to the back of your A/V receiver (or controller). With very few exceptions, you don't connect other components directly to each other. Let your A/V receiver do its job!

Some folks believe that you get the highest-quality video signal by connecting your components' video cables directly to the inputs on the back of the display itself, bypassing the video source switching functionality of the receiver. (Video switching is when you run all video into the back of the receiver and then let the receiver send the signal you want to view to your display.) For most folks, we think this isn't worth the inconvenience — today's receivers typically have very high-quality video switching circuitry, and most displays simply don't have enough inputs anyway. We particularly believe that you should take advantage of your receiver's HDMI switching and *upconversion* facilities if you have these features on your receiver. (Upconversion takes standard-definition signals and coverts them to a higher resolution for display on a high-definition TV.)

If your DVD player, set-top box, or satellite receiver (or other video source component) offers a digital video connection such as HDMI, and your display accepts these connections but your receiver doesn't offer HDMI switching (your receiver probably doesn't if it was built before 2008 — even many current models don't), we recommend that you ignore our previous advice and make those video connections directly, bypassing the receiver. In many cases, the quality of an HDMI signal is worth ignoring the convenience of receiver video switching.

Hooking up your speakers

The next step is to connect your speaker wires to the appropriate speaker outlets on your A/V receiver. This is a simple process, but there are a few things to keep in mind:

- **Keep your speakers in phase.** Each speaker wire consists of two conductors, a positive and a negative. If you connect these out of phase (that is, the positive on the receiver to the negative on the speaker, and vice versa), you'll hear a definite effect on your sound. Specifically, your speakers can't create the appropriate *soundstage,* so sounds that are supposed to clearly come from the right or the left won't. (By the way, *right* in this context means to the listener's right when facing the display or the front of the room.) Most speaker cables are color-coded red and black to make this job easier (or you may have a white stripe on the jacket of one of the conductors in the speaker wire).

- **Make sure you have a tight connection.** For the best sound quality and for a connection that won't stop working over time, make sure your speaker connections are solid. We like banana plugs or spade lugs on five-way binding posts because you can get these suckers nice and tight, but a bare wire can be just fine, and many smaller surround speakers don't have enough physical space to fit larger connectors. Make a good connection the first time, and you won't need to touch it again for years. We discuss these different connections in more detail in Chapter 16.

- **Don't forget to connect the subwoofer.** Most subwoofers are *active* speakers (they have their own built-in amplifiers), so you don't use speaker wires to connect them. You need a long analog audio interconnect cable, which runs between the Subwoofer Out or LFE output on the back of your receiver and the input on the subwoofer itself. Make sure you get a cable that's long enough to let you move the subwoofer around because you may need to reposition your subwoofer as you discover how it interacts with your home theater's room.

Connecting to the A/V receiver

Take a look at the back of any typical A/V receiver, like the one shown in Figure 17-2. Wow, that's a lot of jacks, huh? Well, they're not all back there for show or to make the designer happy. They're there to give you a flexible, home theater system that can do what you need it to do.

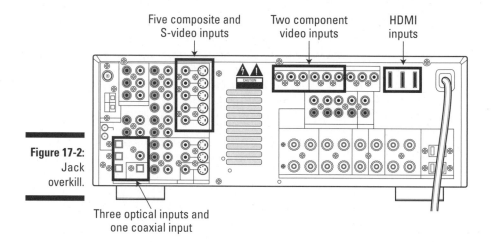

Five composite and S-video inputs

Two component video inputs

HDMI inputs

Figure 17-2:
Jack overkill.

Three optical inputs and one coaxial input

Each component in your A/V system has a set of audio connections or video connections or both to your A/V receiver. The receiver itself connects to your speakers and to your display (with another set of audio and video cables).

First, you connect audio interconnects and video cables to each source device. Remember the following:

✓ **Keep your right and left in mind with audio cables.** Any device that connects with analog audio cables has two connections (the cables themselves usually, but not always, come in attached stereo pairs). One jack (the right) is usually colored red, and the other is colored white. Make sure that you connect the left output on the source device to the corresponding left input on the back of your receiver.

✓ **Use digital audio connections whenever possible.** Use coaxial or optical digital audio cables to connect DVD players, game consoles, DSS receivers, or any source that has a digital audio output. If you want to use Dolby Digital or DTS with any of these sources, you *must* use the digital audio connection. The great thing about digital audio connections is that there's just one — no getting left and right confused.

Some folks feel that optical (Toslink) digital audio connections sound better than coaxial ones. We're not convinced of this and recommend that you don't get too wrapped around the axle on this — use what you have. If both types of connections are available on the device and the receiver and you have a preference, go with it. Otherwise, don't sweat this too much.

✔ **Keep track of which connections you use on your receiver.** One nice thing about the standardized connections used in home theaters is the fact that you don't have to "color inside the lines." It's fine to plug sources into jacks on your receiver with labels that differ from the device you're plugging in. For example, if you have a video game console (but no corresponding Game inputs on your receiver), you can plug the game console into those Laser Disc Player inputs — assuming, of course, that you don't have a laser disc player in your system. This is where keeping track of your connections comes in handy. To send the audio and video from the game console to your speakers and display, you have to select the laser disc input on your receiver. You might even want to make a little cheat sheet to keep near your system (with all your little home theater quirks written down), so the rest of your family can run the system.

As we mentioned at the beginning of the chapter, fancy A/V receivers and controllers often have *assignable* inputs that let you select the names that correspond with each set of inputs on the back of the receiver or controller. In many cases, you can even "type" custom input names into your receiver's display by using your remote so that you can see the right input name on the front of your receiver or on your onscreen display. This is a handy feature to have, especially when someone unfamiliar with the system is using it.

✔ **Use an extra set of audio and video cables to connect your recording systems.** Your receiver has an extra set of A/V output connectors that correspond with its VCR inputs (usually labeled VCR1, VCR2, and so on). When you connect your VCR or PVR (personal video recorder) to these inputs, use an extra set of cables to connect the receiver back to the inputs on these sources (labeled Audio In and Video In on the back of the source). This lets you route audio and video through the receiver for recording purposes. (You may not be able to record DVDs this way because of DVD's Macrovision copy protection system, which we discuss in Chapter 6.)

✔ **Use the highest-quality video connections available to you.** If you can use digital video connections (HDMI or DVI), do! Otherwise, use component video if your sources have these connections. If you must, use S-video for sources that don't have component video connections, such as DSS receivers. Some sources (such as many VCRs) have only composite video connections.

After you've connected all your sources to the receiver, you can connect the receiver to your display unit by using one or more video cables (we discuss this shortly) and a set of analog audio interconnects.

Using this set of audio cables between the receiver and the display may seem to be a bit of cabling overkill. After all, you already have a surround-sound audio system connected to the receiver. We find that, sometimes, we just want to use the built-in speakers in our display, like when we flip on ESPN to catch the college basketball scores, and then turn the TV back off. If you don't think you'll ever do something like this, you can skip this step.

If you're using an HDMI connection between your receiver and display, you might be able to skip the step of adding an analog audio connection to the display. HDMI cables can also carry digital audio, so there's no need for separate audio connections. You can skip the analog connection, however, only if your receiver is connected only to HDMI sources (not common, but becoming more likely if you're going all HD) *or* if the receiver has an *upconversion* feature that takes non-HDMI sources and sends them to the display over the HDMI connection.

A step you won't want to skip is connecting the receiver to your display with video cables. This can be a somewhat tricky proposition — the first step you need to take here is to understand whether your receiver has any *upconversion* or *conversion* capabilities (see the sidebar called "Upconversion and conversion, what gives?"). Many receivers these days will upconvert composite and S-video sources (such as non-HDTV cable boxes and VCRs) so that their signals can be sent to your display over component video cables. A growing number of receivers will even upconvert composite, S-video, and component video signals to HDMI, which is a really cool feature!

We refer to conversion and upconversion generically as *upconversion* in this chapter (it's more common to see receivers that do upconversion than just plain format conversion). But in terms of plugging your home theater together, it makes no difference.

If your receiver *can* upconvert, you can simply connect the receiver's video outputs to the inputs on your display by using component video or HDMI cables (depending, of course, on which kind of upconversion — component or HDMI — your receiver offers).

If your receiver doesn't handle upconversion, you need to have one set of video cables for *each kind* of input you make into the receiver. So, for example, if you have a VCR connected via composite video, a game console connected via S-video, and a DVD player connected via component video, you need to have one of each of these types of connections running *out* from your receiver to the display.

Upconversion and conversion, what gives?

We talk about *upconversion* a lot in *Home Theater For Dummies*. In short, upconversion (which can occur in a DVD or Blu-ray disc player, inside a home theater, or inside an HDTV itself) is simply a scaling of one resolution of video to another higher resolution. Every HDTV does this itself — if you send a 480i or 480p standard definition video (from broadcast TV or a DVD) to your TV, the TV will use *scaler* circuitry to change (raise) the resolution of the video it receives to the native resolution of the TV (usually 720p or 1080p).

Inside a receiver, a little more is going on. First, a receiver may do a *format conversion*, where it takes a video signal entering the receiver on one type of connection (for example, an S-video signal from a VHS or older gaming console) and change that signal to an HDMI or component

video signal *at the same resolution*. (This is usually called *analog-to-HDMI conversion* or *component video conversion*.) If the receiver also changes the resolution of the video signal when it does that, well then it's doing analog-to-HDMI *up*conversion (or component video upconversion).

You see both systems on the market, and they're both incredibly handy when you are assembling and connecting your home theater. Since your HDTV will already upconvert incoming signals, there's no *need* to do upconversion in the receiver, but many folks prefer this if they're buying a fancy receiver, simply because they feel the upconversion (scaling) circuitry in their receiver does a better job of upconversion than does their TV.

If you connect a source to your receiver with an S-video or composite video cable but use only a component video cable to connect the receiver to your display, you'll find that you get sound but no picture when you try to play that source. In the HDTV world, this is something you'd probably never do (you'd be using component video or HDMI), but we've seen it happen, so we wanted to warn you.

You don't need multiples of these video connections between the receiver and the display — just one connection for each type of connection you have *coming into* your receiver. So if you have three component video sources running into the back of your receiver, you need only one set of component video cables running to your display.

Getting television signals

TV comes into your system from a cable TV service, a DSS satellite dish, or an antenna for broadcast TV (or in some cases, from a combination of these devices). Regardless of the system, an RG6 coaxial cable connects these TV sources into your system.

If you use an antenna for non-HDTV over-the-air broadcast TV (or for non-digital cable without a converter box), this connection is usually simple. Just connect the coaxial cable coming out of your wall outlet to the Antenna/Cable In input on the back of your display. (**Note:** Your cable company may have installed a similar RG59 cable instead of an RG6 cable; if you're running your own cable, we recommend you use RG6.) If you have a PVR or VCR, run the cable coming out of the wall to it first, and then to the inputs on the back of your TV.

If you have digital cable, an analog cable with a converter, or a DSS dish, or if you're picking up over-the-air broadcast HDTV signals, you need to run the RG6 cable to the appropriate set-top box, DSS receiver, or HDTV tuner. These devices are connected through your A/V receiver, just like any other source device. You can use the receiver to send the video from these sources to your VCR for recording (if it's allowed).

If you're using broadcast HDTV and you have a true HDTV (with an integrated tuner), you can connect the coaxial cable running from this antenna directly to the back of your display.

Similarly, if your display is *digital cable–ready* (or DCR) and can use a CableCARD, you can connect the coaxial cable from your cable TV feed directly into your TV and forgo the cable set-top box. As we discuss in Chapter 7, this is convenient but means that you won't be able to access some digital cable features, such as video-on-demand (VoD) or the onscreen program guide.

If you have digital cable, you may want to route your cable signal through the PVR or VCR before you connect it to your set-top box. Many digital cable systems transmit a number of standard analog channels that your PVR or VCR can tune in to. Routing this cable through the PVR/VCR lets you record those analog channels while your set-top box is tuned to a different channel (analog or digital) for simultaneous viewing.

Adding your gaming console or Home Theater PC

Very few A/V receivers have made provisions for connections from game consoles or Home Theater PCs (HTPCs). Although these devices are too new to have been incorporated into most receiver designs, that's no reason to give up hope. You can still get these devices hooked into your surround-sound system and display.

The key thing to keep in mind is that HTPCs and game consoles are no different from any other source device. They have analog and digital audio connections. They have composite, S-video, and (in many cases) component video outputs. Your receiver doesn't care whether these signals come from a DVD player or an HTPC. Neither does your display.

So connect these devices just as you connect any of the other source devices we mentioned earlier in this chapter. Keep the same rules in mind: Use digital audio connections, if you can, and use the highest-quality video connection system that the device supports.

As we hinted at earlier in this chapter, you probably won't find any inputs on the back of your receiver marked HTPC or Xbox. So find an unused set of inputs and use them.

 If you have one of those fancy touch-screen remote controls that we discuss in Chapter 15, you may be able to program the remote to use the name of the device you're using. So even if the HTPC is connected to the VCR2 input on your receiver, you can make the remote button say "HTPC." With this setup, the babysitter can easily use your home theater. (We're not sure whether or not that's a good thing.) If your receiver has *assignable* inputs, you may also be able to change the labels that show up on the front panel of the receiver and the TV's onscreen display — customizing them to match what you've plugged in to a specific input.

Powering the Network

After you've made all the connections, the temptation to plug everything into the wall and get going is strong. Hold off for one more step: making the power connections safely. We're not talking about your personal safety here, but the safety of your equipment. You probably forgot about power cables, but you should have some plans for these, too. There are lots of them, and they certainly get in the way.

You'll have to confront two big issues: the number of connections and the quality of the connections (or, put another way, where to plug your home theater gear in and how to keep that gear from getting fried).

You will simply have way more power cables than you think. The great thing about power management is that you can add connections as you need more with few issues. So if you need more outlets, no problem — just add some more outlets in the form of power strips. The overall power usage of your home theater is relatively light compared with, say, a dishwasher, so in general, connecting several home theater devices into one outlet is not a huge problem.

Some home theater components — high-powered receivers or power amplifiers and large displays — do draw a lot of current. It's always best to plug these items directly into your surge protector (which we discuss next). Other items, such as DVD players or CD players, can safely be plugged into either the surge protector or into one of the auxiliary outlets on the back of another piece of equipment (many receivers have such outlets).

Two kinds of outlets are used on the back of receivers: *switched* and *unswitched.* Switched outlets turn on and off with the receiver, while unswitched outlets are always on. Keep that distinction in mind if you have something plugged into your receiver's power outlets that you want to use even when the receiver is turned off.

The bigger issue is surge protection. Electrical currents are like water currents; they flow up and down, and if they get too high (a surge), it's a problem. (If they get too low [a brown-out], that's a problem, too.) You need to consider professional-class surge protection (*not* what you buy at Wal-Mart). One good lightning strike can toast your home theater (and not in a good way). Leviton (www.leviton.com), for example, has a Home Theater Surge Protector that has nine outlets plus a neat expandable modular outlet that can handle surge protection for telephones, modems, faxes, DSL modems, cable modems, computer LANs, and satellite and cable TV systems.

If you are building from scratch or have the luxury of adding some outlets, put in electrical lines that are dedicated to your home theater and that go straight to your electrical panel so that no intermediate devices can cause in-home surges on your lines.

In general, we also advocate whole-home power protectors that can help groom the power coming from the street. That's where some of the big surges can come from, and these surges can hit not only your home theater but everything else in your home. We consider these $300 to $800 "first line of defense" units a must for any home. They sit between all the electrical lines coming in and your electrical panel, truly stopping any problems before they get to your house. You can find models that also protect your satellite and cable connections at the home level, too. You can get these from Leviton and other electrical suppliers.

We talk more in Chapter 21 about power conditioning, which is the next step up after surge protection. Power conditioners use various techniques to restore your A/C power to a true 60 Hz, 120-volt signal and can offer better audio and video performance.

Chapter 18

Plugging In to a Whole-Home Entertainment Network

We strongly believe that you should spend time thinking about how to exploit your investment in your home theater by taking it whole home. In many instances, you've already done the hard part by deciding that a home theater is worth the big investment. Now, telling you to take it to the limit (oops, Eagles pop culture reference) by going whole home — expanding your home theater's audio and video capabilities to other parts of your house — shouldn't be tough.

The point of this chapter is to expose you to some of the varied ways you can accomplish whole-home networking of your audio and video gear. If you're serious about this (and you know what's coming here — shameless self-promotion time!), we absolutely insist you think about getting our *Smart Homes For Dummies* book (Wiley) because it goes into all the requisite details for you to do this by yourself.

In this chapter, we talk in detail about some whole-home wiring systems that we recommend you install when you build or remodel your house. For most folks, the installation of whole-home wiring is *not* a casual project. If you don't have a whole-home wiring system in place and can't put one in, don't freak out! We also talk about some solutions that use wireless networks or existing wires in your wall to expand the reach of your home theater components.

Introducing Whole-Home Entertainment

Let's talk about what it means to go whole home. If you read Chapter 2, you may recall that you need to plan around two major concentrations of equipment:

- ✔ **Wiring hub:** This is generally the place where nearly everything comes into the house from the outside. The electrical panel is likely there, along with your incoming telephone lines, your cable or satellite service connections, and maybe your cable or DSL modem if you were smart and planned ahead. Ideally, most of your in-home communications and information services are connected together in this area, with *home run* wires running throughout the house in a hub-and-spoke fashion. (In a home run wiring system, each outlet has a dedicated wire running directly to it from the wiring hub.)

- ✔ **Media hub:** You can consider the main home theater to be your media hub. Most of the gear we discuss in this book resides in the media hub, either on shelves out in the open or in a configuration where you have some gear in the open and some in a nearby equipment closet or rack.

When you go whole home, equipment also resides in your media hub and in other rooms around your house. For example, Danny has a kids' computer lab where four computers are clustered so that his two sets of twins (he has always been an overachiever) cannot fight over the computers to do their homework online. (Actually, Pat knows they are secretly playing *Civilization* and *MathBlaster.*)

In most cases, you are likely to have gear spread all over the house, particularly in the master bedroom, where you might have another TV, VCR, and cable/satellite receiver (maybe even another surround-sound system) and potentially something in the kids' rooms.

So the question — and opportunity — is how can you link all your gear to minimize your costs (yes, you can *save* money by not having to buy a PVR or a satellite receiver for each room) and exploit your investment in your media hub? Well, have we got some ideas for you!

Think about what *whole home* means for you. Although you can grow your whole-home network, you can save money in the long run if you have a better idea of what you want to do up front. After you've already built the network, adding things can be more expensive. There's a world of difference between running an extra set of speakers to the bedroom or dining room for your audio and wanting to have background music in every room. If your whole-home plans are limited, you can almost always get inexpensive (under $100) devices from Radio Shack (www.radioshack.com) or SmartHome (www.smart home.com) that can meet these needs.

But if you want to have more flexibility to mix and match in any room, or to have higher-quality connections, you may want to think about looking into a whole-home *distribution panel* for your signals. These panels, also called *structured cabling systems,* can support voice, data, and video distribution in the home relatively cheaply. You can get a good panel for under $1000 and then add jacks and wiring accordingly.

Not all distribution panels are alike. Some are for one specific application (such as video), and others allow you to select whatever you want to put on any connection. For example, a CAT-5e–based system (using that standard computer-network cabling) might let you put phone, computer data, video, or audio on any line. You merely change the outlets at the terminating end according to your needs in that room.

You can find a list of structured cabling vendors on the Web site for our book, *Smart Homes For Dummies.* Check it out at www.digitaldummies.com.

At a bare minimum, a structured cabling system should provide

- ✔ **A flexible telephone network** using high-quality, unshielded twisted-pair (UTP) phone cabling and a modular, configurable termination system in the wiring closet (the central location where all of these systems are connected together)

- ✔ **A computer network** of CAT-5e (the standard for Ethernet computer network cabling) UTP cabling for data networking

- ✔ **A centrally distributed coaxial cable (usually RG6 — the standard video cabling) network** for distributing video signals

- ✔ **An all-in-one modular termination panel** to neatly terminate all this network wiring in your wiring closet

- ✔ **Customized wall outlet plates** to provide connectors for your phone, data, audio, and video outlets that can be easily changed and reconfigured

Connecting to a Whole-Home Audio System

Whole-home audio is a pretty simple baseline that a lot of people consider when moving out of the home theater and into the other parts of the house. After all, the first step can be as easy as merely stringing another set of speaker wires from your multizone-capable A/V receiver (we talk about these in Chapter 11) in your home theater to, say, remote speakers located in the dining room. Keep in mind, however, that the limitations of a whole-home audio network are based on the limitations of your A/V receiver. Most A/V receivers that have multizone capabilities can support audio in only one or two other rooms — not zones in every room in the house.

So if you want a true whole-home audio system, you probably need to consider installing additional equipment in the media hub (or nearby). With this equipment in place (and the appropriate wires in the wall), you can share the audio source devices in your home theater with any room in the house. In almost all cases, this system provides *stereo* (two-channel) audio, not surround-sound (multichannel) audio, in rooms outside your home theater. The sidebar, "The trouble with whole-home surround sound," talks about this issue a bit more.

You can get audio from your home theater to other rooms in the house in four primary ways:

- ✔ **Use your receiver:** As we mentioned earlier, many receivers (at least above the $500–$600 price range) include multizone functionality that lets you run speaker wires or a long audio RCA cable pair. You can really run these only into an adjacent room, not the entire length of the house, due to signal loss. This is the simplest way to get audio elsewhere in the home.

- ✔ **Buy a whole-home audio distribution system:** These systems come in both multizone and single-zone-versions (we explain the difference later in this chapter) and use their own amplifiers and control systems to send audio to any room in the house. You can buy whole-home audio systems that support up to eight or more rooms.

- ✔ **Use a CAT-5e audio-distribution system:** These systems can distribute line-level stereo audio signals over standard CAT-5e computer network cabling. Many of these systems are designed to carry both audio and video. Some (such as the SVC-10 from ChannelPlus, `www.channelplus.com`) can even carry the higher-quality S-video signals and digital audio signals (such as Dolby Digital) over this network cabling. Most of these systems, however, can carry only composite video and stereo audio.

- ✔ **Use a wireless audio-distribution system:** Two types of wireless audio-distribution systems are available:

  - • Remote speaker systems: Many receiver manufacturers now offer an option for wireless speakers in remote rooms. So if you want to be able to hear the TV when you walk into the kitchen, you can use a wireless remote speaker. These systems are usually similar to (or even identical to) the wireless surround speakers we discuss in Chapter 17. They're just used for a different purpose in a different room.

  - • Whole-home wireless audio-distribution systems: These systems are designed to take audio from your PC or home theater or both and distribute it to remote speaker locations throughout the home. An example of this is the Sonos Music System (`www.sonos.com`), which we'll talk about later in this chapter.

Many of the CAT-5e and wireless audio-distribution systems we are about to discuss can also carry video signals.

Some of the whole-home audio network systems that we talk about use CAT-5e cabling, and we expect (in the not so distant future) to see systems that can distribute surround-sound audio around the house digitally using this cable. Until these systems become available, however, we think it's best to stick with good, old-fashioned two-channel stereo for whole-home audio networks.

Zoning out: Single-zone versus multizone systems

After you start sending audio to a whole-home audio network, you have some decisions to make. The biggest decision is what you want to listen to in different parts of your house. No, we're not talking about what CDs you're going to play, but rather what kind of flexibility your system has to play *different* audio sources in different parts of the house simultaneously.

In a *single-zone audio system,* you have only one audio source distributed to every endpoint across the network at any given time. You can turn various sets of speakers on or off, but you don't have the ability to listen to different audio sources in different parts of your house at the same time. A *multizone audio system,* such as the one shown in Figure 18-1, allows one family member to listen to, say, a CD in the family room while another person listens to the audio channel of a DVD in his or her bedroom. Some multizone systems let you get really fancy and share source devices in multiple locations throughout the home, while others distribute audio sources from one location to multiple places in the home — in other words, some play equipment from your home theater anywhere, while others play equipment from all over the home in any room you choose.

The trouble with whole-home surround sound

The stereo audio standard, in which sound is separated into two channels (left and right), still dominates music production. With the advent of home theater, however, music can now be produced using multiple channels to drive a multitude of speakers.

For the average home (read that as a nonmillionaire home), we recommend that you don't add multichannel capabilities to your whole-home audio network — at least not right now. Although you can build an audio network that goes beyond the two-channel (stereo) limit today, the network quickly becomes extremely complicated and prohibitively expensive. We think the best way to create a second multi-channel surround system is to simply install a second, standalone surround-sound system in that other room. If you're just trying to get surround sound in a bedroom or kid's room, you might consider an inexpensive home-theater-in-a-box solution that will give you surround sound for only a few hundred dollars.

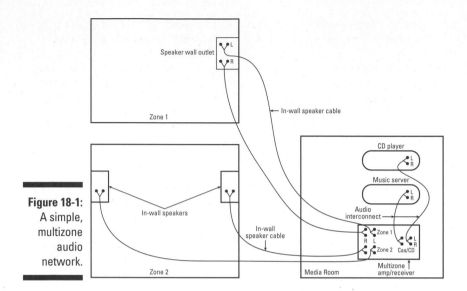

Figure 18-1:
A simple,
multizone
audio
network.

Single-zone systems are easier and cheaper to build, but obviously less flexible than multizone systems. The good news is that the basic architecture (the wires you put in your walls) is usually the same for both types of systems. So you can install an inexpensive single-zone system and then upgrade your equipment to multizone later on.

Using speaker wires to build an audio network

The traditional way to expand an audio network is to simply extend in-the-wall speaker wires from your home theater or media center to remote locations in your house (anywhere you want to have audio). Remember that you need to use UL-rated CL3 speaker wires — given the distances traversed by these wires, we recommend 14-gauge or smaller wires. Refer to Figure 18-1 for a look at a simple multizone audio system. Chapter 16 explains cables and wires in more detail.

If your A/V receiver has multiroom capability, you can connect these speaker wires directly to your receiver by using a device called an *impedance-matching system* (which we describe in more detail in the sidebar, "A word about impedance-matching systems"). This device is necessary when you are connecting more than one pair of speakers to a single pair of speaker terminals on a receiver or an amplifier — if you're just hooking up one set of speakers to that multiroom output, you can skip the impedance-matching system.

A better way to use those speaker wire connections to multiple remote rooms is to use a special-purpose, multiroom, integrated amplifier. This device contains individual pairs of amplifiers for each remote pair of speakers, so you don't need an impedance-matching system, and you get plenty of power (and volume) in remote rooms. You can get multiroom integrated amplifiers in both single-zone and multizone configurations. These integrated amplifiers are available from companies such as Niles Audio (www.nilesaudio.com).

If you want to create a relatively inexpensive two-zone audio system, look for a multizone A/V receiver that has *line-level* outputs, instead of speaker-level outputs, for the second zone. With these systems, you can simply plug the receiver into a single-zone, multiroom, integrated amplifier using a pair of standard audio interconnect cables. Your home theater is zone 1, and the rest of your house is zone 2. It's not as good as a true multizone system, but it's a lot cheaper and easier to set up.

Besides a centralized amplifier/control system and speaker wires in the wall, you need to install speakers in the remote rooms. Most folks decide to use *in-wall* speaker systems (often placing these speakers in the ceiling), but you can also install speaker terminal wall jacks and then use standard loudspeakers. You connect the loudspeakers to these wall jacks just as you might connect them to the back of a receiver.

Connecting source devices to a multiroom system

Most audio source devices (such as CD players) have only one set of audio outputs on the back, and you probably already have this set connected to your A/V receiver. So how can you also feed this audio into a separate multiroom amplifier system? There are two options (besides buying a second CD player).

The easiest (and cheapest) way to do this is to use a Y-splitter audio cable that splits a single pair of stereo audio signals into two pairs. One branch of the Y goes to your A/V receiver, and the other to your multiroom system. You can buy these cables at Radio Shack and similar retailers.

Some multiroom installations use separate amplifiers for each zone. In these systems, you need more than a simple two-for-one split from a Y-splitter. The solution here is to use a *signal distribution amplifier*. This device takes the output of a source device, splits it into multiple outputs, and then amplifies these outputs to ensure that your signal is not degraded. (If you split the signal without amplifying it, it could be too weak and would cause distortion that you would hear as a background noise or hiss.) This is the best approach if you are using separate amplifiers for each remote pair of speakers.

Controlling whole-home audio with IR

The other big challenge for a whole-home audio system is controlling your A/V components from remote rooms. Remember that most A/V components use IR (infrared) remote control systems, and that IR doesn't travel through walls and other obstacles. So you'll need a remote control system that can carry IR signals from IR sensors (that you simply aim a remote control at) or wall-mounted volume controls and keypads in your remote rooms. These whole-home IR systems typically require special three-conductor IR cabling but can also be carried over other cables, such as CAT-5e computer network cables or even over the RG6 coaxial cables that carry video signals around the house from an antenna or a cable TV service.

You need a few components to connect a whole-home IR system together:

- **IR sensors or keypads in remote rooms:** These are the end of the line for your IR network. Each run of IR cable terminates in one of these devices. IR sensors and keypads send IR control signals over the IR cabling as electrical signals.

- **An IR connecting block in your media hub:** This device connects to the other end of the IR cable runs and *concentrates* the IR signals they carry into outputs that can control your A/V components. You need a connecting block because you want only one IR input connected to each component in your system, but you have IR sensors or keypads in multiple rooms. The connecting block allows, for example, the IR signals coming from five different rooms to be sent to a single CD player.

- **IR emitters (IR blasters):** These devices run from the connecting block to the components themselves. IR emitters have only one function in life: They convert the electrical control signals back into IR (light) signals that A/V components can understand.

Building a whole-home IR distribution system is a relatively complicated process. The hardest part is programming keypads and getting the right IR signals to the right A/V components. We highly recommend that you work with a professional installer if you want to implement a whole-home IR network.

CAT-5e or wireless audio distribution systems can often carry IR control signals for you, so you won't need a separate IR network.

Plugging into CAT-5e

Aside from speaker cabling, you have other whole-home audio cabling options, such as CAT-5e. Systems from a variety of manufacturers can successfully carry line-level audio signals (the signals carried over audio interconnects) over CAT-5e cables in your walls. On the inexpensive end, you can get systems that convert the left and right line-level outputs of an audio device into a balanced signal. If high-end is your thing, go all the way with full-fledged, expensive audio-distribution (and video-distribution!) systems that provide true multizone audio over CAT-5e.

You can distribute audio signals around the home using CAT-5e in three major ways, which we discuss in the following sections.

Point to point with baluns

Baluns are deployed in pairs for point-to-point use — meaning that they send a signal from one place to a single other location (as opposed to a *point-to-multipoint* system, which can send a signal to multiple different locations). A *balun* is just a little passive device (meaning it doesn't need any external power), about the size of a deck of cards, with receptacles on both sides (an RJ-45 on one side and two or more RCA jacks on the other).

One balun is associated with the source device (such as a CD player or the Audio Out ports of a receiver). This balun connects through an RCA audio interconnect to the left and right Audio Out channels. Then, you plug the balun into the CAT-5e cable by using a CAT-5e patch cable. At the other end of the network — down another leg of your home's CAT-5e that you've dedicated to audio — the process is reversed. The second balun plugs into the RJ-45 outlet on your wall (again using a patch cable), and then plugs into the left and right Audio In jacks of the remote amplifier or receiver that you're feeding the signal to. An example of one of these products is MuxLab's Stereo Hi-Fi Balun (www.muxlab.com).

You can also find baluns that can distribute digital audio signals — such as the *bitstream* outputs of DVD players and other Dolby Digital or DTS sources — over CAT-5e cables. In many cases, these baluns can carry high-quality component video signals as well. An example of such a product is Intelix's V3AD HDTV Component Video and Digital Audio over CAT-5 Balun (www.intelix.com). These units can connect to any source device with component video and coaxial digital audio outputs and send the signal over up to 1000 feet of CAT-5e cabling.

Most folks find that this sort of balun is most useful not for sending signals to a second room but rather for use *within* a larger home theater room. For example, if you are trying to hide your source components in a closet or equipment room on one side of a large home theater room and are installing a display and speakers rather far away, you can use inexpensive CAT-5e cabling and baluns rather than running more expensive audio and video cables.

Single-zone CAT-5e audio-distribution systems

In the world of audio and CAT-5e, the next step up moves beyond the point-to-point limitation of baluns and provides a single-zone audio-distribution network to multiple locations throughout the home. These systems, from vendors such as Russound (www.russound.com) and Leviton (www.leviton.com), typically use custom faceplates (the plastic plates that cover standard wall outlets) that replace standard RJ-45 faceplates in each room. These faceplates have a pair of female RCA audio jacks that can connect to any standard audio source device or amplifier/receiver. In the room containing the source device you want to share throughout the home, you simply plug a stereo audio patch cable between the device and the faceplate.

In remote rooms, you use an audio patch cable to connect the faceplate to the inputs of a local receiver or amplifier. Connecting these remote outlets is a special CAT-5e audio hub located in your wiring closet. This hub takes the source signal and distributes it to every other CAT-5e outlet connected to the hub.

Multizone, CAT-5e audio-distribution systems

If you want the utmost in flexibility and capability in a CAT-5e-based audio-distribution system, you need a system that can carry different audio programs to different parts of the house simultaneously — a multizone, multisource system. Like the multizone speaker-level systems discussed earlier in the chapter, multizone CAT-5e systems are high-end solutions that offer the utmost in sound quality and convenience. Because sending audio over CAT-5e is still not a mainstream technology, it's not cheap. You'll probably end up paying $1000 or more for the components alone, and that doesn't include the speakers and amplifiers or receivers in each room. And that price is for the (relatively) cheap versions of these systems. Some high-end systems can cost tens of thousands of dollars. You can get systems from players such as Crestron (www.crestron.com), Russound (www.russound.com), and Niles Audio (www.nilesaudio.com).

A word about impedance-matching systems

In Chapter 11, when we talk about A/V receivers, and particularly about their amplifier sections, we mention that many receivers have trouble dealing with speakers with an impedance (a measure of electrical resistance) of 4 ohms or less. This really comes into play in whole-home audio systems. That's because when you try to drive two sets of speakers from the same stereo amplifier, the impedance of the speakers is effectively halved. That is to say, if you plug two sets of 8-ohm speakers into a *single* stereo amplifier, you end up with an effective impedance of 4 ohms. Add a third set, and you're in the danger zone for most receivers.

If you have a multizone audio-distribution system, impedance isn't an issue (each pair of speakers has its own amplifier), but in a single-zone system, many folks try to cram multiple pairs of speakers onto a single amplifier. The safe way to do this is to use an *impedance-matching* system. These systems let you hook up two, three, four, or more pairs of speakers to a single stereo amplifier without the impedance dropping to an unsafe level. Keep in mind that the amplifier power provided to these remote speakers will be reduced as you add extra sets of speakers onto the system. So the impedance-matching system will protect your amplifier, but you may not get enough power to reach the volume levels you want.

Going wireless

The most popular way of getting audio around the house without a dedicated network is with an RF (radio frequency) wireless system. These come in two main flavors:

- ✔ **Wireless speaker systems** connect to the line-level outputs of a source device or preamplifier and send the signal over a 900-MHz or 2.4-GHz channel to a pair of self-amplified stereo speakers.

- ✔ **Wireless line-level distribution systems** hook up to your source components in the same fashion but send their signals to a receiver that hooks into your own amplifier and speakers on the far end.

One major potential difficulty with many wireless systems is that they use a line-level input — something that most source devices have only one of. So you may run into trouble hooking up a CD player, for example, to both your A/V receiver (or controller) for local listening and to one of these devices for remote listening. Luckily, many of these units also accept the output of your receiver or amp's headphone jack, so you can avoid this problem if you have a headphone jack available. Alternatively, you can use one of the Y-splitter audio cables we mention in the sidebar, "Connecting source devices to a multiroom system," earlier in this chapter. Prices for these wireless systems range from about $75 to $200.

A good example of a simple point-to-point wireless audio-distribution system is the Terk LF30S system by AudioVox (www.audiovox.com). This $99 system will bring stereo audio (as well as a composite video signal) from your home theater to any other room in the home. You can even add a second receiver to bring the same audio to a second room.

The current state-of-the-art in wireless audio distribution systems involves systems that use 802.11 (Wi-Fi) wireless networking to distribute audio around the home. Our current favorite system is the Sonos Digital Music System (www.sonos.com). The baseline Sonos system (the Sonos Bundle 130) starts at $999 and supports two rooms.

This technogeek's dream system consists of a controller (the brains of the system), a "zone" player (the endpoints of the system where all the speaker and system interfaces are housed, as well as a four-port switch so that you can network other items in the vicinity — nice!) and matching speakers you can use if you want everything to match.

Most buyers of the Sonos system also buy a local NAS (Network Attached Storage) hard drive because the Sonos itself doesn't have one — a non-NAS system just plays music found elsewhere, like on your PC. You can also have more than one Sonos zone player; the players talk to each other and the controller in a "mesh" fashion (meaning the signal can hop from station to station, rather than only radiating out from the main base station), so if you have a really long house, you can still use the Sonos system. In such instances, the Sonos system synchronizes the music so that it all plays at the same time, avoiding any weird echo-type sounds around the house. Sonos uses 802.11g for its wireless protocol — but doesn't connect to your Wi-Fi access points (it creates its own "mesh" network) — hopping from Sonos to Sonos throughout your home.

Sharing Video Components throughout the Home

Sharing video in the home used to be a lot simpler a few years ago than it is today. This is largely due to the advent of all sorts of signal encryption as well as the introduction of digital transmissions into the mix. These have added their unique flies in the whole-home networking ointment.

You can share home theater video signals in your home (speaking generally here, of course) in four major ways:

- ✔ Use *modulators* to send your video over the coaxial cable carrying your antenna or cable TV signal
- ✔ Use a CAT-5e audio- and video-distribution system
- ✔ Use a wireless audio- and video-distribution system
- ✔ Use a system that carries audio and video over your existing phone wires

As the price of video source devices (such as DVD players) plummets, the economics of creating a video-distribution network in your home turns on its head. A few years ago, when DVD players cost $500 apiece, it made sense to create a system that could share the DVD player in your home theater with TVs in other rooms. Now that you can buy a good quality *upconverting* DVD player for well under $100, most folks simply choose to have an extra set of video source devices in remote locations. You may, however, run into a situation in which you'd like to share some sources in your home theater with displays in other parts of the home — in the following section, we tell you how to do so.

Using your TV cables

Most structured cabling systems (complete prepackaged home wiring products) include a centralized video-distribution system. This system differs from the standard cable company installations in one big way. Most cable installations use a *branch and tree* architecture, with the cable coming into your house from the street and then being fed into a series of *splitters* — little "one in, two out" devices that split a cable signal into two branches. A centralized video-distribution system uses a special splitter, called a *video-distribution panel,* that splits the incoming cable (or antenna) signal into multiple lines running to all your TVs — each a home run cable in a hub-and-spoke architecture.

With a central video-distribution panel, you can create your own in-house television channels using modulators over your in-home coax cables. Simply put, a *modulator* takes the composite or S-video output of a video source device (as well as the stereo analog audio outputs) and transforms it into an RF (radio frequency) signal — just like a television station does. You simply set the modulator to broadcast over an unused channel and connect it to your video-distribution panel. When you want to watch that source somewhere else in the house, you just need to tune your remote TV to that station, and voilà!

Figure 18-2 shows a modulated signal (in this case, a VCR, but it can be any video source, such as a DVD player or a DSS satellite receiver).

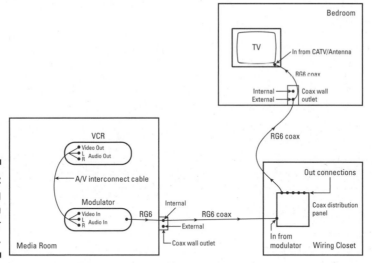

Figure 18-2:
Watching
a VCR in
another
room.

Modulator systems don't work for everybody. New digital cable systems are designed to use all or most of the available spectrum on your home's coax network, so carving out bandwidth for your piggyback data transmission is not so easy. In many instances, it's almost impossible. You are likely better off pursuing some of the nonmodulator alternatives we're about to discuss instead.

Does your home theater need a phone connection?

In the age of broadband Internet connections, most telephone line connections that people used to have into their home theaters have gone away in favor of Internet connections. For example, gaming consoles used to use dial-up Internet for gaming over the network — now they use broadband Internet connections.

There is one place where phone lines may still be required: Satellite TV systems need to be able to "phone home" to authorize your account.

If you don't have a phone outlet near your satellite receiver, you can get a wireless phone jack (such as RCA's RC926) for around $80 that uses the electrical lines in your house to transmit your telephone communications. You plug a standard telephone line into an adapter that then plugs into the electrical outlet at your home theater. Then, in a room where there *is* an available phone outlet, you do the same, only this time you run a phone cable from the electrical outlet into the phone outlet. Shazaam! One phone line. Do not use a wireless phone jack with a surge protector because this may block the frequencies over which your phone line communicates; plug the unit directly into the wall.

CAT-5e and wireless systems

Many of the CAT-5e and wireless systems we discuss earlier in the chapter can carry video signals in addition to audio signals. In the case of CAT-5e systems, we think that you can actually get a higher-quality video signal around the house than you can with a modulator system. That's because the process of modulating and then *demodulating* a video source (when it gets back into your remote TV) tends to diminish your picture quality. Some of these CAT-5e systems can even carry component signals and digital audio for high-quality video (even HDTV!) and *surround-sound* audio in remote locations. (You need an A/V receiver and surround speakers in these remote locations to take advantage of this.)

Connecting to Your Computer LAN

We talk in Chapter 2 about having a wiring closet for your Ethernet hubs and routers, in Chapter 6 about Ethernet ports on your DVRs, in Chapter 9 about gaming consoles with network interfaces, and so on. Computer networks are becoming an important part of your home theater infrastructure.

Accessing a whole-home computer network (also known as a *local area network* — LAN for short) opens up your home theater to any data point on your network. A good example is Danny's AudioReQuest CD server. It has an onboard Web server that allows access to this music from wherever he wants, in the house or over the Internet. He can synchronize his boxes in Maine and Connecticut because they are connected to the Internet. As soon as he finishes this book, he's going to extend that to synching with his car stereos, too — over wireless computer network connections. The same is true with his SnapStream PVR. He can record programs while he is away and download them from anywhere on the planet. Now he can catch up on *Weeds* from Kiev!

Although we've not heard of anyone having this problem, it is possible that your ISP (Internet service provider) may forbid this kind of "server" connection. Most ISPs have absolutely frightening terms of service agreements that forbid just about everything but checking your e-mail and surfing the Web on your connection. Most of these agreements are not strictly observed, but if you start using a lot of bandwidth, your ISP may either make you stop or make you pay for a more expensive connection.

Getting your home theater devices to communicate with your computer network is getting easier all the time thanks to newer technologies, lower costs, and equipment vendors' increased experience with the consumer market. It's getting to be almost automatic!

So, assuming this is the case, the question then becomes, "How do you interconnect with that LAN?" Well, it depends on the extent of your LAN, if it exists at all. Although we don't have space in this book to discuss all the ins and outs of computer networking, we want to offer a little guidance to help you on your way toward a whole-home computing backbone that can make use of your home theater system. Here are a few networking points to keep in mind:

- ✔ **You can carry data signals around your house in at least four major ways: CAT-5e cabling, wireless, electrical cables, and regular phone wiring and coaxial cables.** We recommend, if you can do it, that you run new CAT-5e cables through your walls to the places where you want it. If you use CAT-5e for your audio or video distribution, you are likely building a new home or renovating your current one, and running the cable shouldn't be a problem. A wired infrastructure gives you much higher data rates, more reliability, and more flexibility for the future — and it can add to the value of your home.

- ✔ **Wireless options are great.** These are quickly coming down in price, and you can build a home data network just by adding a wireless access point to your network. (A *wireless access point* is a base station of a wireless network — think of it as the equivalent of a cordless phone base station.) You then bring your devices online by adding *PC cards* (which plug into standardized PC card slots on the device) or USB-based *dongles* (or adapters) that plug into the USB ports. Most devices follow the 54 Mbps 802.11g wireless standard, and a few use the newer (and better suited for video) 802.11n standard, which provides speeds of up to 300 Mbps and can also use different frequencies (which are less crowded with cordless phones and the like).

If you have a piece of equipment that has an Ethernet connection (and no built-in Wi-Fi) and your network is wireless only, you can pick up an inexpensive *Wi-Fi to Ethernet Bridge* (often called a *Wi-Fi gaming adapter*). These devices have Wi-Fi built-in and an Ethernet port on the back, and they do exactly what their name implies — bridge between the two networks. They're exceedingly handy things to have in a home theater. A good example of a Wi-Fi Ethernet bridge is WET54G from Linksys ($89, www.linksys.com).

✔ **You can transmit signals over electrical cables, too.** The trick here is to use low-cost devices that conform to the HomePlug AV standard — a standard networking protocol for Ethernet connections using AC power lines. This standard allows speeds up to 200 Mbps, but speeds vary substantially based on where you plug in the devices and what is turned on at any particular time. A great example of a HomePlug-based system designed for moving audio and video around your home comes from the folks at Belkin (www.belkin.com). The $179 Powerline AV+ Starter Kit (not yet on the market but due out soon) can support up to three Ethernet connections by simply plugging the two adapters in the kit into your wall. Pretty cool. Want to add a room? Plug in an electrical module. Done.

Check out www.homeplug.org for more information about this new standard and for product availability.

✔ **You can also use the coaxial cables and phone lines in your house to send signals from room to room.** A few networking systems use unused higher frequencies on the cable to send the data, so you can still talk on the phone or watch video at the same time. This is based on the Home Phoneline Networking Alliance (HPNA) standards. In general, the other options we mention are preferable to HPNA at this time, but new, faster versions of HPNA have been promised. Check out www.homepna.com for information about product availability.

Some new systems use coaxial (cable TV) cables to send data around the house. MoCA (Multimedia over Coax Alliance, www.mocalliance.com), for example, can provide speeds of up to 200 Mbps over these cables. Another similar technology, TVnet by Coaxsys (www.coaxsys.com), provides speeds of up to 70 Mbps. MoCA and TVnet are not products you can just go out and buy at the store, however. Instead, they are being built into devices, such as cable set-top boxes, to allow cable companies to send TV signals between boxes in the home.

✔ **If you have a high-speed cable, DSL, or satellite Internet connection, you have your high-speed Internet modem located somewhere on your network.** It doesn't matter where you put the modem, from the home theater perspective, because there really is no specific reason why the broadband Internet connection has to be located in your theater room. In fact, most people like to put their modem either close to their computing area or in the wiring closet, out of sight.

✔ **You need a router if you want to support multiple Ethernet devices on one network and have them interface with the Internet.** Often, the DSL/cable/satellite modem is also a router. The router has a built-in hub that enables you to interconnect multiple data lines.

✔ **If you are going to be routing video or large files over your LAN, consider getting an Ethernet *switch* instead of a hub.** In this way, you can make sure you get all the bandwidth you need for a quality transmission. (Most routers include an Ethernet switch, but you may need an external switch with more ports if you have lots of devices on your network.)

Although many vendors will try to push you into one solution ("You need Wi-Fi." "No, you need HomePlug."), you might find that these various networks can complement each other. We think a wired CAT-5e network should be the basis of your computer-LAN infrastructure (and phone network, and maybe even your audio and video network). But we also think that all the data-networking technologies can be used in concert when you build a whole-home network.

Just for fun, here are a few examples:

✔ Build a wired Ethernet LAN but add a Wi-Fi access point in your living room for cordless, sofa-based Web surfing.

✔ Use Wi-Fi as the basis for your home-computer LAN, but use HomePlug or HPNA to extend your network to access points in distant locations out of reach of your primary base station (such as by the pool).

✔ Use wired Ethernet for your computers, but use a HomePlug system to connect your Xbox to the broadband Internet connection for online gaming.

We could keep this list going and going, but we think you get the picture. Think creatively and use wired and unwired technologies together to get your LAN wherever you need it to go.

Part V
Letting Your Home Theater Be All It Can Be

The 5th Wave   By Rich Tennant

WARREN ENJOYED SHOWING OFF HIS NEW 52" FLAT PANEL HDTV DINNER

In this part . . .

This part is all about what to do after everything is put together. First, we discuss how to use the controls on your video systems (your television and your video source devices) to get the best picture possible.

We also discuss how to tweak your audio system so that you can adjust it to the dynamics of *your* home theater. Our friends in the installation business are constantly amazed at how bad good audio gear can sound if it's not set up properly. Conversely, even modestly priced gear can sound great if it's properly tweaked.

We also talk about ways you can improve your home theater's environment. If you think about it, home theater is really all about creating light and sound that you can interact with. If you keep environmental lights and sounds from interfering with your theater, you can get more enjoyment out of your gear.

Finally, we talk about the high end of home theater and how to go all-out in pursuit of a home theater experience. And if you have budget limitations, you can at least get a preview of the future of home theaters.

Chapter 19

Tweaking Your A/V System

Getting your A/V system hooked up can be a bit of a challenge, but it's rewarding to have all that "on your hands and knees" plug-fest work behind you. You have to take one more step, however, before you sit back and really enjoy your home theater. You need to spend some time tweaking your system — adjusting the video display and getting your surround sound set up properly.

In this chapter, we discuss ways to calibrate your system. This may seem like overkill to some folks, but it is critical. Joel Silver, the president of the Imaging Science Foundation — these folks know a thing or two about setting up home theaters! — tells us that more than 90 percent of home theater displays are set up incorrectly. With a few tools, you can be part of the small percentage of home theater owners who are getting the most out of what they've paid for.

Calibrating Your Video

We've said it before — and we'll say it again, because it's important — most displays come from the factory improperly calibrated. The brightness and color are set at unnatural levels to make the displays stand out on the showroom floor (in a brightly lit store). At these settings, if you put them in a darkened home theater, the picture looks awful.

If you have a plasma display, you have an additional reason to calibrate your video: The overly bright settings that most of these units come with can reduce the life span of your display! Even if your display is not brand new or not all that fancy, a calibration can breathe new life into your picture quality.

On your average display, you (as a nontechnician) can make five adjustments. A few sets let you adjust more, and service techs with the proper manuals and codes to get into the service menus of the display can adjust just about anything. But an average person (like you or us) can adjust the following controls:

- **Contrast (white level):** Don't confuse this with *contrast ratio,* which we discuss earlier in the book. (It's the ratio between the brightest and darkest images a display can create, if you didn't get to that part of the book yet.) In terms of display adjustments, your contrast control adjusts the *white level,* or degree of whiteness, your screen displays. You see, in video displays, whites and blacks are measured on a scale called IRE (Institute of Radio Engineers) units, which are represented as a percentage: 0 percent is black, and 100 percent is white. You can actually drive your TV beyond 100 percent if your contrast is improperly set. If you do this, white portions of your picture tend to bleed over into the darker portions surrounding them.

- **Brightness (black level):** Now to throw in a counterintuitive statement. The brightness control on your display actually adjusts the *black level* that you see on the screen. Weird, huh? If the black level is set incorrectly, you can't discern the difference between darker images on your screen.

- **Sharpness:** The sharpness control adjusts the *fine detail* of the picture — its ability to display minute details on the screen. If the sharpness is set too low, you have a fuzzy picture; if it's set too high, your picture appears *edgy,* often with blobs around the edges of objects instead of clearly defined lines.

- **Color:** Along with tint (which we discuss next), color is one of the two controls that let you set the balance of the colors (finally, a name that says what it means!) on your display. If your color setting is too low, images begin to appear as black and white. If it's too high, images take on a reddish tinge (for example, Nicole Kidman's face will turn as red as her hair).

- **Tint (hue):** On most TVs, this control is labeled *tint,* but a few are more technically correct and call it *hue.* The tint control adjusts your display's color within a range between red and green — your job will be to find the perfect balance between them.

Almost every display we know of has an onscreen display that shows the status of each picture setting as you are changing it. Typically, you'll find a horizontal bar across your screen; a vertical hash mark shows your current setting or the entire bar moves left or right as you increase or decrease, respectively, that particular picture attribute. Some displays also have a numeric display (usually running from 0 to 100) that shows your current setting.

We like the numeric displays because writing down a number is much easier (if you want to re-create a setting in the future) than trying to remember exactly how far across the screen a particular bar was.

Using a calibration disc

The best way to adjust your video is to use a DVD *home theater calibration disc.* We consider these discs (which cost about $50) to be an absolutely essential investment in your home theater. Unless you've had a professional calibrate your system (or you've spent so much on everything else that you can't afford the disc), we think you simply must get one of these discs. (And no, no one is paying us to say that.)

The most common home theater calibration discs are the following:

✔ **Digital Video Essentials HD Basics:** The Digital Video Essentials (DVE) DVD (discussed in the next bullet) has long been considered the definitive consumer-accessible (as opposed to professional) calibration disc. The same folks have the first (and, as we write, *only*) *high-definition* calibration disc. DVE HD Basics provides a suite of audio and video calibration tools and tests in a *Blu-ray* disc format with options for both 1080p and 720p displays. DVE HD Basics can be found online at www.videoessentials.com, and costs $29.95.

You don't *need* a high-definition disc to calibrate a high-definition TV. So if you've not yet got a Blu-ray disc player, you can do a good job of calibration with one of the DVD-based systems discussed next. If you *do* have a Blu-ray disc player and you don't already own a calibration DVD (or even if you do!), you should strongly consider HD Basics as your calibration disc.

✔ **Digital Video Essentials:** This is the definitive calibration DVD. One cool thing about Digital Video Essentials is the inclusion of video footage that you can watch to see the results of your adjustments with actual video, instead of just on a test pattern. Digital Video Essentials lists for $24.99 and is widely available online.

The folks at Joe Kane Productions (who created Digital Video Essentials) also have a six-disc professional set called *Digital Video Essentials Professional,* which retails for $350 and includes some high-definition calibrations (using the Windows Media system for high-definition 720p and 1080i signals). Like the Avia PRO, this is probably overkill for most folks (you can probably have a pro calibrate your display for less money), but we wanted to let you know this was out there.

✔ **Avia II: Guide to Home Theater:** Available from Ovation Multimedia (www.ovationmultimedia.com), this disc contains a ton of great background material about home theater. It explains a lot of the same stuff we talk about here in *Home Theater For Dummies*. It also has a series of easy-to-follow onscreen test patterns and signals that let you correctly adjust all the settings we discuss in the preceding section. It also gives you test tones to help calibrate your surround-sound audio systems (which we discuss in a moment). This disc runs $49.99 directly from Ovation.

A high-definition Blu-ray disc version is due out from Ovation sometime in 2008.

We suspect most folks will find it to be overkill, but Ovation also produces a professional-quality variant of its test disc, the Avia PRO. This $250 set consists of seven DVDs and an elaborate user manual for the ultimate in calibration.

✔ **Monster/ISF HDTV Calibration Wizard DVD:** Monster Cable (makers of those famous audio and video cables) teamed up with the folks at the *Imaging Science Foundation* to jointly create their own calibration DVD. Like the other DVDs we discuss, it's loaded with audio and video test signals and programs, and uses a "follow along" wizard-style interface. Monster and ISF's disc is widely available online and at www.monster cable.com and retails for $29.95.

✔ *Sound & Vision* **Home Theater Tune-up:** This one is also produced by Ovation Software, but in conjunction with *Sound & Vision* magazine (one of our favorites). In addition to general display calibration, this disc includes tests that demonstrate aspect ratios and let you test your S-video and component video outputs on your DVD player (to see which works better in your system). You can find the disc (priced at only $21.95) at http://shop.soundandvisionmag.com.

While we think this disc is still useful, we don't believe that it's been updated in quite some time. We're not *not recommending* it, but we wouldn't be surprised if the folks at Sound & Vision either discontinued this disc or created a new high-def version.

We like all five of these discs and would be hard pressed to recommend one. As we mentioned, if you have a Blu-ray disc player, it makes sense to consider the DVE HD Basics disc. Otherwise, you'll probably get a good calibration from any of the other discs.

When you buy one of these discs, you'll notice that one or more colored filters (they look like a pair of those cardboard 3D glasses used in movie theaters) comes in the package. Don't toss your filter in the trash on the mistaken assumption that it's an especially pretty piece of packaging — you need this filter when adjusting some of the color and tint settings on your display. You look through the filter to block out certain light frequencies.

Using one of these discs is a simple process — one we don't try to re-create here step-by-step because the onscreen audio and text instructions do a better job than we can in a book. Before you adjust any of these settings, get up off your comfy home theater seating and close the blinds! Ambient lighting has an immense effect on what you see on your screen (regardless of what type of display you have). So lower the blinds, close the door, and dim the lights. You want to adjust your picture in exactly the same lighting conditions you'll have when you sit down to play movies or watch TV in your home theater. Then just follow the instructions on the DVD, step-by-step. It's easy and even kind of fun.

When you're done, you'll notice that your picture looks different. (We sure hope it does!) It's going to look darker. If you're not used to a calibrated video picture, this might be a bit disconcerting. Give yourself some time to get used to it, though, and you'll notice a more detailed picture, a picture that looks more like the movies. And isn't that what you're after in a home theater?

Some displays come from the factory either pretty well calibrated or with a picture *mode* you can select on your remote that will set your picture close to the state it would be in after you manually calibrated it. Sony displays are famous for this (Sony calls this its Movie mode), and other manufacturers such as Pioneer, Panasonic, and others have followed suit. A number of high-end manufacturers are now offering HDTVs that are *precalibrated* to Imaging Science Foundation standards — although these TVs may still be in that super-bright showroom mode when you buy them, they have a calibrated setting stored in a bit of *nonvolatile* memory (which means you can't erase the settings) that can be turned on when you buy the TV. You still may want to tweak the display a bit with a calibration disc, but it's handy to have your display be 99 percent of the way there with the push of a single button (or right out of the box).

Using an optical comparator

If you want to get really fancy with your home theater calibration process, you might consider not relying on your eyeballs and instead use a tool such as *optical comparators* or *colorimeters*. These devices are simply machines that can analyze the colors and patterns on a screen with a much higher degree of accuracy than you'll be able to do with your naked eyes. Both devices do essentially the same thing (measuring your display's light output); generally speaking colorimeters are less expensive for mere humans, while optical comparators are expensive tools typically used only by professional display calibrators.

Using an optical comparator or colorimeter can be especially useful if you are one of those folks with some degree of color blindness (which can include, depending on which study you believe, up to one in twelve men).

For the most part, these color-sensing devices are too expensive for the average home theater — you can buy a 50-inch, high-definition plasma TV for the price of many common hardware kits. For example, Ovation Multimedia's OpticONE system, a popular hardware and software solution, retails for $2,200. Consequently, many folks turn to professional system calibrators (discussed in the upcoming section, "Hiring a professional") who can amortize this investment over a number of customers.

But there *are* solutions that are in the price range of mere mortals, such as ColorVision's Datacolor Spyder3TV colorimeter ($199, www.colorvision. com). (The SpyderTV is so named because it has spiderlike suction-cup legs that stick to your display — ignoring the fact that it has three legs, not eight!)

To use the Spyder3TV you simply stick the unit's suction cups to the front of your display and then plug the USB cable running out of the Spyder3TV in to your computer (Windows 2000 or XP is required, and a laptop is a lot more convenient for this task but is not required). Then place the supplied test pattern DVD in your DVD player, and you're ready to start.

For flat-panel plasma and LCD displays, the Spyder3TV includes a special suction-cup attachment device — you're not supposed to use the suction cups built into the three legs of the Spyder3TV for these kinds of displays.

After everything is hooked up, you just need to follow the steps included in the Spyder3TV software running on your PC (it comes on a separate CD with the rest of the Spyder3TV gear). Have your display's remote handy and follow the onscreen steps to tweak your TV's display settings. This all takes 40 minutes or more, so have a little patience (that's one reason why the pros charge hundreds of dollars to do a calibration), but the end result should be a better and more lifelike picture.

Although we didn't have a big issue with this personally, some folks have complained that it's tricky to get the Spyder3TV attached to your display. You may want to consider mounting the unit on a tripod in front of your display if the suction cups don't work well for you.

Other tuning system options

If you haven't had a chance to get your hands on one of the home theater calibration discs but still want to improve your picture, you can do a couple of things.

One way to get a subset of the video tests on these discs is to play a movie DVD that contains the *THX Optimizer*. You find this somewhere in the disc's main menu (usually in the Special Features section). Like the discs we described earlier, the Optimizer walks you through a series of steps to adjust your display (and your audio system). All THX-certified DVDs released since 2000 (including Pat's daughter's favorite, *The Lion King*) include the THX Optimizer. You can find more details, including instructions on THX's Web site (`www.thx.com/home/dvd/optimizer/index.html`). Now if he could just teach her to calibrate the plasma for him. Maybe when she turns five she'll take over the task. (If it could be done on the Wii, she'd already be there!)

With this program, you still need that blue filter; if you didn't get one with the DVD itself (and you probably didn't), you can get one for free from THX by filling out the order form online. (You do have to pay a couple of bucks for shipping and handling.)

We recommend that you at least rent one of the movies on the THX Web site so you can use the Optimizer. You can adjust your video just by eyeballing it. Until you get a test disc in your system, you should, at a minimum, turn down the brightness until the level is about ⅓ across your screen, but using a test disc or the Optimizer is much, much easier and more accurate.

One way to get your display dialed in at least somewhat close to an optimal calibration is to read the posts about your particular TV or monitor on the AVS Forum Web site (`www.avsforum.com`). Many models have ongoing threads for owners, and you'll often find other people's calibration advice within these forums. Remember that not every unit is going to be exactly the same. (There are always at least minor variations in manufacturing, and over time, the settings can change a bit — for example, as a projector's light bulb gets dimmer.) But you can at least find out what works for other folks and try it out as an initial setting until you do a more formal calibration.

Hiring a professional

You may decide — either right up front or after you realize that you just can't handle that remote control very well — that you want a professional to calibrate your display. Well, that's nothing to be ashamed of. In fact, if you can afford it, we highly recommend that you consider having a professional calibrate your system. They have tools (such as light meters) that you don't have, and their calibration is more precise and ultimately better than anything you can do with a calibration DVD and your eyeballs.

If you have a CRT front-projection system (these aren't common any more — you can't buy a new one, but there are a lot of them still out there in people's homes), you really *must* have a professional set it up. You'll waste tens of thousands of dollars if you don't. In fact, if you're buying any high-end display (such as that $17,000, 61-inch, HDTV plasma display Pat has his eyes on — don't tell his wife!), go for a professional calibration. When you start getting in this price range, you should expect this kind of service from your home theater dealer. A professional calibration usually costs between $200 and $500, depending on what type of display you have.

Great DVDs to put your system through its paces

After your video system is calibrated and ready to go, it's time to start watching some movies. Why not enjoy the view with some classics and with some newer movies that can really test the limits of your system's capabilities? For some reason, most home theater enthusiasts love action movies (but hey, who doesn't?) and trot out their well-worn copies of *Terminator 2* and *The Matrix.* These are indeed fun to watch in your home theater and can be demanding discs (*The Matrix,* in particular, seemed to overpower many early DVD players), but you also might want to check out some other films that show off your home theater in subtler ways. The ISF (yep, the same guys we mentioned elsewhere in this chapter) has a list of films that it recommends to its affiliated dealers as great demo discs. You can find this list online at www. filmsondisc.com/ISF_Reference_ DVD_Program.htm. You may even be surprised to find favorites like *Muppets from Space* and *Wayne's World* — excellent!

If you go with a professional calibration, make sure you choose someone who has been certified and trained by the Imaging Science Foundation, or ISF (we mentioned them earlier in the chapter). The ISF has trained (and continues to train) thousands of home theater dealers in the art of system calibration. You can find a trained calibration professional near you by searching ISF's Web site at www.imagingscience.com.

Don't call ISF directly asking them to calibrate your system. Those folks know how to do it, but they're in the business of training others, not coming over to your house.

Adjusting Your Audio System

Just as your display needs a tune-up to look its best, your A/V receiver (or A/V controller, if you've gone with separates) needs a once-over to ensure you get the best possible sound from your home theater. You need to do the initial setup to make sure that your A/V receiver knows what kind of speakers you're using, and then you need to adjust the amplification levels for each speaker.

Get out your A/V receiver's manual before you start doing any of the stuff we recommend. Your particular receiver may have different (but similar) terminology. The manual can also help you navigate your receiver's setup menu system.

Managing bass

Your A/V receiver sends low-frequency sounds to your subwoofer through its LFE (or low-frequency effects) channel. Subwoofers are very good at one thing — reproducing bass notes — and not much good at anything else. In general, you want to send only the lowest possible frequencies to the subwoofer because you want to minimize the use of the subwoofer for relatively higher frequencies.

At the same time, you must balance this requirement with the needs of your other speakers. If you have a set of small bookshelf speakers for your center, right, left, and surround speakers, and they can't reproduce bass notes very well, you're better off letting the subwoofer handle nearly all the bass.

You need to set the speaker size for each group of speakers — center, front (or main), and surrounds. So step 1 in setting up your audio is to go to your A/V receiver's setup or configuration menu and navigate to the menu that lets you select your speaker size. You typically have a choice of Large or Small. The Small setting cuts off the low frequencies that are sent to your main speakers (the speakers other than your subwoofer) at a higher frequency than does the Large setting. In other words, the Small setting sends almost all low-frequency audio signals to the subwoofer, whereas the Large setting sends the low frequencies to *both* the subwoofer and your other speakers.

You'll probably find a setting in this menu for the subwoofer — an On or None setting that indicates the presence or absence of the subwoofer. Make sure you select On if you have a subwoofer.

You can use two criteria to select a setting for your speakers:

- ✔ **Frequency range of your speakers (best):** If you have access to the manufacturer's data about your speaker, find out the frequency range at which the manufacturer rates its speakers. (You may also find this information from a reviewer who has tested the speakers.) If the low end of the speaker's frequency response is rated below 40 Hz, set your receiver to the Large setting; otherwise, use the Small setting.

- ✔ **Woofer size (not as good):** If you don't know how low your speakers can go, you can use the size of your speaker's woofers as a rule of thumb. If the woofers are 6 inches or larger, try the Large setting; otherwise, go with the Small setting.

If you don't know either of these things (you can always take off the speaker's grill and measure the woofer), start off with the Large setting. You can always switch over to the Small setting if you notice that your main speakers aren't handling the bass very well. (In other words, they're causing audible distortions with low-frequency audio tracks.)

If you don't have a subwoofer in your system, make sure you set the front speakers to the Large setting and set the subwoofer control to Off. Even if your other speakers are small, you need to select Large here, or you'll get absolutely no bass from your system.

Setting up surrounds

After your speakers are put in the right place (see Chapter 17) and turned on and you've selected sizes, it's time to configure your surround system. You need to configure two settings, which we describe next and then expand upon in greater detail later in this section:

- **Delay:** If all your speakers are the same distance from your listening position, sounds emanating from them arrive at your ears at the same time. That's a good thing because delays in the arrival of sounds can ruin your sound field. You want sounds to have delays only when the director of the movie intends it (such as when a footfall echoes behind you). If speakers aren't equidistant from the listening position, your A/V receiver can compensate with its own delay settings.

- **Channel balance (or level):** Set the sound level of each speaker so that you hear an equal volume from each speaker during testing. If one speaker (or set of speakers) is too loud, you experience an unbalanced sound field while listening to your system. (When you play back actual movies or music, the volume coming from each speaker depends on the volumes encoded in the source material.)

A growing number of A/V receivers have a built-in calibration tool that uses either a microphone that's built into the receiver itself or (more commonly) an accessory microphone that comes with the receiver or that you buy separately. These systems let you skip all the steps that follow by simply invoking the auto-calibration command on the receiver. A computer in the receiver sends out test tones and automatically adjusts the receiver's settings. Some people think that they can do a better job manually — with an SPL meter, discussed in the next section, or with the audio portion of one of the video test discs discussed previously — but for the average person (and by that we mean anyone who's not an audio geek!), these automated calibration systems are a lifesaver.

Setting the delay

Depending on your A/V receiver, you'll find two ways to set the delay: You can enter either a distance or a delay time (in milliseconds). In either case, get a tape measure and measure the distance from your listening position to each group of speakers (center, front, and surround). You should have to measure only one speaker from each group, because the left and right speakers within a group should be equidistant from your listening position. If your receiver uses distance, simply enter the number of feet that you've just measured for each group of speakers.

If the receiver uses delay settings in milliseconds, things get a bit more complicated. Typically, the delay settings are measured in relation to the main (right and left) speakers, so you enter a delay for the center channel and for the surround channel (or channels in 6.1- or 7.1-channel systems). To do this, compare the distance of the group you are setting to the distance of the main speakers. If the speakers are *farther* away, you typically set the delay to 0 milliseconds (because the added distance will naturally add a delay — so you don't want to artificially increase this delay). If they are closer than the main speakers, you set the delay to 1 millisecond for each foot. For example, if your main speakers are 9 feet from your listening position, and your center channel is 7 feet away, set the delay for 2 milliseconds.

Adjusting the channel balance

Your A/V receiver will have a special test tone mode designed for setting your channel balance. In this mode, the receiver generates a series of tones (at an equal amplification level) to each individual speaker in your system. The tone comes out of only one speaker at a time and shifts from speaker to speaker (either automatically or when you press a button on the remote control). The goal of this test is for you to set the level of each individual speaker until you hear an equal volume from each speaker.

Even though this test tone starts off with an equal amplification level for each speaker, you probably will hear a different volume level on the first round of the test. That's because different speakers have different *sensitivities*. (We discuss sensitivity in Chapter 12; it's a measure of how loud a speaker plays with a given power input.) Even if you had five identical speakers in your home theater (with the same sensitivity), their distance from your seating position and their acoustic interactions with the room can affect the volume you hear at your listening position.

As you run through your receiver's test mode, you can adjust the volume level of each individual speaker. Most people can do a good job at this by using their ears alone. To get your channel balance really nailed down, consider purchasing an inexpensive sound-level meter (known as an SPL — sound pressure level — meter). You can get a good one for under $50 from Radio Shack (www.radioshack.com). With a meter in hand, you can get an accurate channel balance setting. An even better approach is to mount the meter on a tripod at your seating position — that's how the pros do it.

The test tones are also a good check to make sure your speaker wires are hooked up to the right speaker terminals on the back of your receiver (or power amplifier if you're using separates). The receiver's display (or onscreen display) tells you what speaker you should be hearing each tone from. If the display says left surround and you hear a tone from your right surround, you know that you've made a mistake! Don't ask us how we know this one.

Using test discs

The home theater calibration discs we discuss elsewhere in this chapter — such as the Avia II disc — are for more than just adjusting the video settings on your display. They also have relatively robust and elaborate audio setup sections that can supplement the test tones built into your receiver.

For example, in addition to test tones for setting channel balance, the Avia disc has a test that lets you verify the phase of each of your speakers.

Just follow the instructions on the screen, and you can find out if you've accidentally wired one of your speakers with the negative and positive terminals crossed. You can even do more advanced tests, such as checking for room interactions with your speakers (if you're working on tweaking your speakers' positioning in the room) and voice matching, which helps you decide whether certain speakers work well together.

Dealing with old-fashioned stereo sources

Although most movies are designed for surround-sound listening, music is generally recorded in stereo and mixed, edited, and produced for systems with two speakers. CDs, radio, cassette tapes, and LPs are all stereo recordings. In the audio-only realm, only DVD-Audio and SACD provide multichannel surround sound–ready recordings. Indeed, not all these recordings are multichannel, as many SACDs are stereo-only.

If you take a look around your home theater, you'll see that you have at least five speakers (not counting the subwoofer). What's an audiophile to do?

Well, most A/V receivers let you select whether you want to listen to stereo recordings in stereo, or *direct,* mode (through the front left and right speakers) or in a surround mode (using all your speakers). Which you use is your preference. A/V receivers can use Dolby Pro Logic II (for 5.1 channel systems), Pro Logic IIx (for 7.1 channel systems), or a custom surround mode (discussed later in this chapter) to artificially create surround effects for these stereo recordings.

We prefer playing back our CDs and other stereo sources in the stereo mode. It just seems more realistic to us. If you like the surround modes, feel free to use them. It's your theater, so use it the way that makes you happiest.

Most TV shows are broadcast in stereo, and many older movies on DVD or VHS are stereo as well. For movies and TV programming in stereo (not in Dolby Digital or DTS), we like to use Dolby Pro Logic II/IIx to create surround sound.

Playing with custom surround modes

As we discuss in Chapter 11, A/V receivers and controllers use devices called *DSPs* (Digital Signal Processors) to decode surround-sound signals. These DSPs are basically powerful computer chips that can do all sorts of neat manipulations of audio signals. They're designed to tweak signals, not crunch numbers like the computer chips in your PC.

Many receiver manufacturers — the majority of them, to be honest — have harnessed this computer horsepower to create *custom surround modes* (or DSP modes), which manipulate the audio signal and create artificial surround-sound modes. These custom surround modes use computer-generated models to adjust the volume and delay of signals coming from the surround and center channels to reproduce different "venues." For example, some receivers have a mode that tries to re-create the ambience of a cathedral by reproducing the delays and echoes you'd hear in a cathedral.

Most audiophiles despise these custom surround modes, feeling that they are artificial and just get in the way of the music. We tend to agree; but again, this is an area where we leave you to your own devices. Feel free to play around with these modes and see what you think. We won't come to your house and turn them off if you like them.

Chapter 20

Customizing Your Home Theater Environment

. . . .

In This Chapter

▶ Mounting your display

▶ Soundproofing your theater

▶ Lighting your theater just right

▶ Adding remote control capabilities

▶ Choosing your ideal theater seating

. . . .

*I*n earlier chapters, when we talk about creating an atmosphere in your home theater, the context is adding equipment to it. Building from the discussion in Chapter 2 about where to put your home theater, this chapter delves into more detail about how to craft a home theater environment that lets all your high-tech devices put their best foot forward.

If you are building a home from scratch or renovating an area for your home theater, you have a lot to think about. But even if you are just sprucing up your living room or that room over the garage, this chapter has a few tips for you, too.

We want to warn you that some of the topics in this chapter require intense construction. You need to do more research online and consult with your manufacturers and contractor, if you have one, to determine your exact course of action. We give you some manufacturers' Web addresses as we discuss different options, and we point out good resources as we go along.

Mounting Your (Expensive) Display (Carefully!)

One of the biggest advances in TV displays in recent years has been the depth of the units — displays are getting thinner and thinner. Instead of just plunking your new display on top of a tabletop, consider mounting it on the wall or ceiling (such as in the case of projectors).

Mounting a display can be easy if you plan and design well up front. As you will read, there's more than one way to mount a display. You should ask yourself some questions about how you intend to use your TV before you settle on a particular mounting approach:

✔ **Is viewing flexibility an important consideration?** If you want to be able to see the display from two locations, a swing arm mount is great — you can merely swing the display around to face the desired room. You might do this, for example, so that you can watch your plasma TV in the family room, but then swing it out so that it can be viewed from the kitchen, too. It's great for watching cooking shows!

✔ **Where do you want to put the display in the room?** Plan for your cabling. Are you mounting the display on a brick wall or in front of a window? In these instances, a ceiling mount may be better because it will be easier to run your cables invisibly.

If you are interested in a better understanding of how to prepare your home for all your digital home wiring needs, check out our *Smart Homes For Dummies* (Wiley), which deals with all types of whole-home networking.

✔ **Are you planning on mounting your display over a fireplace?** It can get hot over a fireplace that's in use, and this heat can damage your display. A lot of TVs don't have a cooling fan — they use convection for cooling and have to be 5 inches from the wall. If you are short on space and cooling is a concern, look for a TV with a fan. If a lot of heat is coming up from the fireplace, you need a mantel to deflect the heat away from your TV.

✔ **How do you want to use your display?** Will you want to view this sometimes while lying on the floor and other times on the couch? You might want a swing mount with a high degree of pitch so that you can change the angle as you desire. Do you want to press a button and have the display automatically appear? Look for pop-up and ceiling automated products for this purpose — often used in places such as apartments in the city, where you might have limited space.

If you intend to use a swing mount and have chosen to buy third-party (that is, nondisplay-driven) speakers, you will want to make sure you can purchase an add-on accessory to mount your center speaker onto the display itself, rather than bolting that particular speaker to a wall. Doing so ensures that your center speaker swings along with the TV . . . thus avoiding that embarrassing situation in which lips move in one place but the corresponding dialogue comes from another — yech!

✔ **Is this room subject to different lighting during different times of the day?** Pitch wall mounts — ones that can shift a display up and down — are good for rooms that have glare during certain times of the day.

✔ **Is this a permanent installation or something you might change as newer TV display models come out?** Many homes trade up TVs every few years and swap TV sets from room to room in a hand-me-down fashion. Automated lift mounts are pretty permanent installations in most instances.

✔ **How does this have to look?** Is decor an issue? If you need this to be really flush with the wall with all your cables well hidden, you might want to go with a swing arm (as opposed to a static) mount because a swing arm allows you to use a recessed area in the wall. You can connect the mount to the wall and then pull out the mount and connect all the cables and display. When you are done, you push the mount back against the wall and have a fashionable flush installation. You may not be able to do this with a static mount because it's harder to hide all the connected cables. Also, you can design your mounting so that you can go with artwork that slides over the display or opt for a decorative trim to the display. You can even buy a certain material to cover your display that acts like a mirror when the display is off but is transparent when the display is on. Pretty James Bond if you ask us!

✔ **Do you care about specific orientations for your display?** With some mounts, you can rotate your display to a vertical position. If you are into photography, the display can change to portrait mode, for instance, for those vertically oriented pictures. Or, you might want to view the display horizontally but store it vertically, if space is a consideration.

Understanding your mounting options

Three basic types of mounts are available:

✔ **Flat-panel mounts:** These are designed predominantly for plasma displays and LCDs. You will find versions for ceiling, wall, and pole mounts (for floor-based mounting). Flat-panel mounts can be static, pitch, and swing mounts. Static mounts don't move. Pitch mounts pivot up and down. Swing mounts articulate up and down and side-to-side.

✔ **Projector mounts:** Projector mounts are generally based around one design, but they tend to come with a lot of accessories that let you use the mount on a ceiling or wall, deal with a drop ceiling, and so on.

✔ **Automated solutions:** For super-slick installations, projector ceiling lifts and pop-up plasma lifts hide your gear when not in use. You can also automate swing arms so that, with the press of a button, your TV swings into a preprogrammed position.

If you're thinking about an automated solution, a different level of expertise is typically required to manage the environmental, electrical, and other design elements of a successful implementation. These are generally not do-it-yourself projects. If you're looking for help mounting a display, we recommend that you check with your home theater dealer, look on the mount manufacturer's Web site, or look for installers in the homeowners section on the CEDIA (Custom Electronic Design and Installation Association) Web site at `www.cedia.ne`.

What to look for in a mount

When looking for a mount, consider these attributes of a manufacturer's products:

✔ **Design/ease of installation:** Look for a mount with a lot of open space in its structure so you have a lot of room to do everything else you need to do when mounting a display. Check for a wall plate with minimal surface area so that you have more flexibility in where your cable and electrical outlets are located. There's nothing worse than finding that your electrical outlet is hidden by a big piece of unnecessary metal. Also, look for hands-free wall mount installations. The best designs allow one person to install them — for example, Chief Manufacturing's flat-panel mounts (`www.chief.com`) allow you to pound a nail in the wall and temporarily mount the whole unit on that one nail, leaving your hands free for leveling and final bolting. Some swing arms can weigh up to 50 pounds, so you'll want to be able to preinstall the top two lag bolts and then slide the mount over those bolts — leaving the remaining bolts easier to install. Less-installer-friendly units don't have such slide-on options — all the bolt holes are encircled with metal so you have to screw the bolt in while holding the mount to the wall. (As an installer, you make the mistake of installing a mount out-of-level only once.)

✔ **Ease of use:** Ease of adjustment after installation is important. You should be able to adjust the tilt of a mount with a push of your fingertip. When you move a display, it should stay there without having to tighten knobs. Truly, this is the test of a high-quality mount.

✔ **Weight capacity:** Make sure the mount is rated not only for your display but also for any speakers, decorative trim, and other accessories that can add weight.

We suggest that you look for mounts that are UL (Underwriters Laboratories) listed. These are tested at several times their rated weight capacity, so you're less likely to have a failure should your annoying in-law lean up against the mount during your annual holiday party.

✔ **Range of motion (tilt, swivel, extension, and so on):** Make sure that the mount not only fits in your space but also provides the range of motion desired when the size of the mounted display is taken into account. We've seen instances in which someone bought a mount with the expectation of a 45-degree angle, only to find that, because of the size of the display and the limited extension from the wall, the full 45 degrees could not be achieved.

✔ **Integrated cable management:** You'll want to hide your cables. Spend time understanding how your wiring will be run. This is especially true for ceiling mounts in which the cabling may go through the center of the pipe. More than one installer has been tripped up trying to thread a wide DVI or HDMI connector through a too-thin mount-extension column for a projector. If you have to run cables outside your installation, check for snap-on covers that help hide the cables.

Be careful of ceiling mounts that have a flange at the top — make sure you understand how you will route the cables out of that flange if you are, say, mounting this to concrete. There are instances in which cabling run through the center of a mount cannot "get out" of the column due to the nature of the mounting surface itself.

✔ **Quick detach/attach capability:** If you ever have to remove your display — to change the filters or lamps in a projector, for instance — you want a mount designed to maintain all the mechanical settings of the mount itself. You don't want to have to reset and reconfigure your gear each time you put it back.

✔ **Integrated lateral shift capability:** While awfully techie sounding, *lateral shift* is merely the ability to install a mount off center, when taking into account the spacing of the studs in your walls. After all, it would be just dumb luck if the spacing of the studs happened to perfectly coincide with where you wanted to center your display. A high-quality mount will allow you to displace your mount at least 4 inches to the left or right with 16-inch or 24-inch centered studs. An installed display should be able to be positioned vertically as well — quality mounts allow for at least 3 inches of vertical shift.

✔ **Aesthetics:** Look for mounts that look good to you. Check for multiple colors to choose from. Low-profile mounts are important, and details count, such as covers for lag bolts on the wall.

✔ **Quality:** While it's hard to judge quality as an amateur, obvious indications, such as being UL-approved, are a good sign that a manufacturer cares about its quality image.

✔ **Don't go cheap on your mount:** A good mount will last you many TV displays. Consider the future when making your purchase . . . nickel-and-diming here will only hurt you later.

Tips for installing your mount

So you have your mount picked out and you're ready to install. Here are some tips to make sure you have as successful an installation as possible:

✔ **Choose the right fasteners for the job.** Specific types of wood require specific anchors. We won't make you writhe through stories of homeowners who tried to mount a 50-inch plasma with drywall screws. Most mounting instructions start with the assumption of wood stud installations, but most mounts have specialty kits for concrete anchors, drywall anchors, metal studs, and so on. Don't go cheap here; your homeowner's insurance probably has a big deductible, and you don't want to have to use it. A good rule to plan around: Your anchors need to hold five times the weight of what you are putting on the mount. Most manufacturers test their products with ⁵⁄₁₆-inch lag bolts (some use ⅜-inch) — a 2½-inch-long lag bolt is generally acknowledged to be acceptable for large mounts. The main goal is to hit the center of your stud with the bolt. To be sure you do, drill pilot holes to find the width of the stud so you can determine its exact center.

✔ **Range of motion/clearance requirements.** On most mounts, the display is lowered onto the mount. This means you need to have a little more clearance above the mount to make sure you can slide the display into place. Generally, this ranges from 4 inches to ½ an inch of extra space, depending on the manufacturer. So if you have a tight space, think about this in advance. If you are installing an electric lift for a plasma display or LCD, know that these lifts are generally wide open to the elements in its hidden state — so if you lift this into an attic that has no moisture controls, the plasma will be exposed when not lowered into the house. (That's bad, in case you needed us to tell you that.) Projector lifts, on the other hand, tend to be enclosed in a box that has a plenum rating (meaning they're safe for installation in air flow areas — they have special fireproof coatings) and can go in a false ceiling.

✔ **Properly gauge your wall structure to make sure it can hold the weight.** Having a top-of-the-line mount secured to a wall studded with 2-by-2-inch wall studs won't get you far with a 60-inch display. The bigger the display, the more you may need to create a special mounting structure to support the mount — and you'll probably want to call in the cavalry (that is, a professional).

✔ **Triple-check your measurements (and then ask your spouse to recheck them for you).** Use the actual screen and mount when taking measurements, and where possible, confirm your measurements by holding the equipment in the space itself. Having good lateral and vertical shift will help, but that can cover up only the most minor of mistakes.

✔ **Consider hiring a professional installer.** This is one area you don't want to mess up. There's no honor in a broken, 42-inch LCD screen, just you out a thousand bucks. The more precise the installation needs to be, the more likely it is you'll need to hire a professional to help.

Adding that extra touch

Some available accessories for your mounted display can add to its attractiveness in your house (that is, if black matte finish doesn't turn you on as much as it does Pat). For instance, you can get old-style picture frames that make a display look more like a painting on the wall than a TV. Some manufacturers (such as Panasonic) actually sell *framed* plasma flat-panel displays that come out of the box with a fancy wooden frame instead of the standard plastic and metal.

Many home theater sites carry masking systems that will hide your screen altogether. For instance, BEI Audio/Visual Products (www.beionline.com) has something called the BEI Motorized Artwork System that is designed for raising and lowering a framed canvas artwork to conceal or reveal a plasma display. Just tap a button, and the canvas slides away, and the NCAA basketball tournament game comes on. The system offers more than 300 reproductions of works by the Great Masters — Monet, Manet, Millet . . . you have a broad selection of the most popular works of art. (Danny's

partial to Caillebotte's "Nude on a Couch" but is pretty sure his wife won't agree.) You pick from a range of more than a dozen classic wooden frames to match your decor. A BEI system will cost you around $2,500. (Curiously, BEI has the option of shipping the unit with bulletproof glass. We've heard of hating a picture, but that's a little extreme. However, if you really need to protect that plasma, this product's for you!)

Of course, no picture-framed display would be complete without digital art. If you have your PC connected to the screen (or a TV that has support built right in), check out GalleryPlayer Media Networks (www.galleryplayer.com). GalleryPlayer is a digital home gallery service that delivers museum-quality art and photography to any high-definition display, transforming it to a digital canvas. The application is free, and you can display hundreds of free images, as well as browse premium (for-pay) services containing individual pictures and collections that will turn your screen into an art gallery. Images cost less than $1 each, so check it out.

Racking up your gear

Most people spend a lot of time figuring out where and how to mount their flat-panel or projector TV, but they don't spend nearly enough time thinking about where to put the rest of their gear.

A proper equipment rack will complement your home theater much more than a simple shelving system will. You've seen equipment racks before — if you've ever seen a computer room, or high-end home theater, or Mission Control, you've probably seen a vertical bank of computers and other gear housed in an equipment rack. The boom of home entertainment has presented a growth opportunity for these vendors to enter the consumer space, and with that has come racking options for residential use.

Home equipment racks not only store your equipment but also keep it cool and manage all the wiring behind it. As the types of gear you put in your home theater become more complex, and as new wiring options come on the market, you're going to have to access the rear panels of your equipment and move wiring around (at least, until intelligent wireless patch functionality is invented!).

It used to be that you could just stack all your equipment on each other. That was fine, until the equipment starting having more energy-hogging processors and other components that collectively generate a lot of heat. If you stack your gear on top of each other nowadays, you will burn out components, particularly if you put a PC in your cabinet. If you stack your equipment and you've found that you seem to go through DVD players a lot, it's not because the players are bad — they are just susceptible to heat damage. You need to space the equipment and you need a cooling strategy for your gear. The right rack can solve these problems for you.

Any piece of gear that has a built-in fan (such as a PC) or a large number of ventilation holes (such as a receiver or a set-top box) is giving you a big clue: It gets hot and needs room to breathe. Make sure you don't stack things directly on top of gear like this.

When looking for a rack, get one that

- ✔ **Cools:** Don't buy a racking system without a built-in cooling system. Some offer the ability to daisy-chain fans in one system so it can be automatically turned on and off based on temperature.

- ✔ **Powers:** Your racking system should have a way to connect to multiple output power bars so that all your power cables can be managed nicely. The best power bars have slide-on stabilizing clips that make sure your power plugs don't come out of the power bar. *Note:* These power bars typically are not surge protectors — they are power cable management devices designed to help you keep all your cables in order. You'll still want to route these to a surge protector at some point. You can buy high-end, rack-mounted power protection (as we mention in Chapter 21) that will make sure your power levels remain constant in your entertainment center.

- ✔ **Slides:** Unless you have a special situation where you have rear access to your rack, say from a side room, changing cables in the back of your equipment is complicated. You have to pull equipment forward to reconfigure jacks, and this can disconnect your other lines at the same time. A sliding rack brings the equipment forward, out of your cabinet, so you can access the rear panels.

- ✔ **Rotates:** An added bonus is if the rack rotates after it's out of the cabinet, so you can maintain your connections. Once you've owned a rotating rack, you'll never go back!

When Danny was outfitting his home theater with a rack system, he asked a lot of people about racking because the market for residential racking systems was still new. Most mentioned Middle Atlantic Products, Inc. (www. middleatlantic.com). Danny got a Middle Atlantic ASR-HD-42 system that can hold up to 350 pounds of equipment, has adjustable shelves, and rotates 60 degrees. It has ventilated shelves, power and cooling management options, and, if you believe Danny's raves, is the best looking, best-made residential equipment rack on the market (which Pat believes, but never wants to give in so easily to Danny on such things).

Racks can be pricey — you can spend more than $1,000 on a high-end racking system. But if you go cheap here, you could lose much more than that in equipment. This is simply one area to invest in for the long haul.

Soundproofing and Improving Acoustics

No matter how good your system, if you put it in an environment that is not geared toward good sound quality, even the best audio system will sound horrible. The room's construction, furnishings, and window and wall treatments have a massive effect on the quality of sound from your home theater.

Many of the rooms chosen for home theaters are substantially less than optimal from a sound perspective. Your biggest enemy is vibration. Just about everything — the walls, the ductwork, suspended light fixtures, the drop ceiling — can vibrate. When a subwoofer produces its strong low-frequency acoustic energy, that sound wave travels through the room, hitting walls and ceiling surfaces. It's absorbed by the walls, which vibrate in reaction to this energy. This vibration then is conducted through any solid surface that it's in contact with it, including studs, joists, and flooring. From there, it travels up through the framing of the house, and you end up with a shaking house, making a special noise of its own. That's where you need sound planning (pun intended).

You want to try to control two major types of sound distortions:

✔ Intrusive sounds from outside your home theater (and, to be fair, sounds from inside the home theater that seep into the house and keep Mom and Dad awake until the end of the midnight movie)

✔ Sound reflections and refractions from the audio system itself

If you're building a new home or renovating, you have the opportunity to address this at the architectural level. You essentially want to create a room within a room so that you can isolate and control the effect of the sound system's signals on the room itself. Seek to isolate your inside walls, ceilings, and floors from the rest of the house as much as possible. The following list gives you some ideas on how best to go about this task:

✔ **Place studs appropriately, double your drywall, and insulate for sound.**
You want to avoid having the studs of two adjacent walls touching each
other. By keeping studs from touching, you cut off a primary means for
sound to travel between the room and the house (in both directions). You
can also dull vibrations by adding a second layer of drywall.

To further dampen any sounds, apply insulation inside the wall cavity.
(If this is a concrete basement, consider a vapor barrier as well to keep
moisture out of your home theater.)

✔ **Apply soundproofing between studs and drywall.** Consider adding a
layer of soundproofing material between the studs and drywall. This
serves not only to suppress sounds going back and forth but also as a
vibration trap between the drywall and the studs themselves — further
reducing unintended effects from your sound system. For instance,
Acoustiblok (www.acoustiblok.com) sells an effective sound barrier
that comes in rolls like tarpaper.

When applying soundproofing layers, keep it somewhat limp between
the studs so it can absorb the acoustic energy more efficiently. Also,
soundproofing materials are usually pretty heavy, so be sure to buy
some prime steaks and beer before you ask your neighbors to help!

✔ **Apply soundproofing to the floor.** Think about a *floating* floor, which is
a multilayered floor designed to isolate your home theater from the rest
of the house. The topmost floating layer, for example, might consist of
tongue-and-groove chipboard bonded to a layer of plasterboard. That in
turn would be laid on a spongy layer made of some sort of mineral fiber.
You could then glue the spongy layer to the existing floor or even mount
the whole thing on its own joists.

✔ **Apply a soundproofing system to the finished drywall.** Adding specialized sound control panels to the walls can help control unwanted
reflected sounds. When placed at your speakers' first reflection points
(typically, the sidewall boundaries and rear wall behind the main listening position), sound treatment panels reduce your reflected sound.
(This reflected sound could cause a blurring of the sound image and
lack of intelligibility.) Sound treatments also reduce the overall sound
volume in the room, enhancing low-level dialogue and environmental
effects delivered over today's high-quality audio systems.

A good way to find your speakers' first reflection point is to sit in your
listening position and have one of your home theater–loving buddies
move a mirror along the walls. When a speaker becomes visible in the
mirror (from your perspective in your comfy theater seating), you've
found the first reflection point.

Who you gonna call?

The following companies offer products that can be used when soundproofing your walls:

- ✔ **Kinetics Noise Control** (www.kinetics noise.com): Kinetics Noise Control offers a Home Theater Absorption Kit that contains special decorative panels. The midwall absorptive panels take care of sound reverberation, and the triangular corner panels are specifically engineered to absorb low-frequency bass sound that tends to gather in corners. This company also makes special spring mounts for suspending your ceiling (so it doesn't rattle) and other special items for dampening other sounds in your room.

- ✔ **Acoustic Sciences** (www.acoustic sciences.com): Acoustic Sciences has a neat product called the Acoustical Soffit, which is a discreet acoustic treatment that runs around the ceiling borders of your room. This architectural acoustic component is designed to control low-end bass responses while also serving as an internal raceway to hide wiring, HVAC, and lighting. Neat idea.

- ✔ **Acoustic Innovations** (www.acoustic innovations.com): When it comes to in-room soundproofing treatments, there are many different approaches, and often your taste in decoration drives your selection. For instance, Acoustic Innovations has solid hardwood frames in mahogany, cherry, walnut, and oak stains for its Maestro line of panels that can reduce unwanted sound reflections.

- ✔ **Additional resources:** Check out other offerings from companies such as Auralex (www.auralex.com) and Owens Corning (www.owenscorning.com).

Our friend Jim Millay decided to make his own acoustical treatments. He got some stiff insulation (like you'd put in your house) and wrapped it with professional-looking fabric: voila, instant inexpensive panels. We can't really compare these with the professionally manufactured ones just discussed, but if you are on a budget, consider Jim's approach. Of course, he'll want a contribution for his idea.

The cost of the materials for soundproofing a home theater fluctuates, depending on what you decide to do. You can spend a few hundred dollars or upwards of $35,000. Over time, you'll probably add at least some of these interior sound treatments to deal with the sound in the room.

Remember that your cheapest first line of sound defense is simply securing everything that is around the room and listening for things that add noise. Subwoofers can definitely shake things up; if that problem rears its ugly head, get some inexpensive isolation pads for the subwoofer's feet. Projectors can make a ton of noise, too; consider a special mounting for the projector that contains its noise, but remember not to block the fan and airflow because it puts off a lot of heat, too.

In Chapter 2, we discuss having a central wiring hub and a media hub for your electronics. People often put these all in a place where they can show them off, but with that approach comes heat and noise (from cooling fans) that you must deal with. If you can put all the power amplifiers outside the room, there is less heat and noise to dissipate, which is something to think about in your plan.

Dealing with Home Theater Lighting

Lighting plays a crucial role in setting the right atmosphere for your home theater. A bright light in the wrong place or the wrong glare from an open window can be just as annoying as someone's cell phone going off in the middle of a show.

Most home theater planners agree that the video on your display looks best when the room lights are off (or significantly dimmed), the doors are closed, and the shades are drawn. This is where the creative use of dimmers, motorized drapes, window treatments, and a lighting control system can become pivotal pieces of your home theater environs.

Wall-mounted dimmer switches allow you to control the intensity of an individual light or series of connected lights. In most instances, this is a simple and cheap way to change the ambience, and you can do it with $5 and a trip to Home Depot.

If you want to have real fun, think about moving to a complete lighting control system. For as little as $300, you can get a system designed for controlling lights in one room (your home theater). From a wall-mounted keypad, a remote control, or both, you can turn on/off, brighten, dim, or otherwise control each light fixture in the room.

If you choose a sophisticated lighting control system (we talk about a few in this section), you can program the system to do some elaborate lighting tricks. For example, you might set up a preshow mode that has lights on all over the room, maybe accentuating your bar area or couches, if you have them. Then you might have a viewing mode that would dim the sconces, cut the overhead lights, initially highlight the front of the home theater, and then fade, open the curtains in front of your home theater, and start the show. (These different lighting modes are known as *scenes.*) Way cool.

With not too much more effort, you can use remote controls, like the ones we talk about in Chapter 15, and integrate your electronics further. So in preshow mode, you can control the music, and in viewing mode, you can control the projector or display. With a good system, the macros you can set up are limitless. (*Macros* are those stored programs in your remote that let you perform multiple commands with a single button push, allowing you to create new modes for whatever mood.)

There are new construction and retrofit solutions for lighting control, depending on whether you are building from scratch or making a system fit your existing space with existing wiring. Systems can communicate via wireline signaling (using existing AC power lines) or wirelessly. You can get single-room systems from players such as Leviton (www.leviton.com), Lightolier Controls (www.lolcontrols.com), LiteTouch (www.litetouch.com), Lutron (www.lutron.com), PulseWorx (www.pulseworx.com), SmartHome (www.smarthome.com), Vantage (www.vantageinc.com), and X10 (the company — www.X10.com).

Lutron's $1,800 Home Theater Package is designed for existing rooms where rewiring isn't practical. This product includes four dimmers, a tabletop master control, and an infrared receiver so that users can control lights from their favorite universal or learning IR transmitter. Lutron also has a higher-end system that sports RadioRA, a wireless, whole-home lighting control system that uses radio frequency technology instead of AC power lines — most lighting systems use the X10 protocol and your home's power lines — for signal communication.

X10

In the not-too-distant past, if you wanted a whole-home lighting system, you had to install an expensive package from a brand-name lighting retailer. Now, many of these same retailers are adopting new industry approaches that use your home wiring and wireless technologies to provide low-cost lighting that everyone can afford.

X10 is the granddaddy protocol for controlling (turning on and off and dimming) electrical devices, such as lights and appliances, through your home's electrical lines. It has been around for years, establishing itself to such an extent that it is now an open standard — meaning that other companies are free to sell devices that use this protocol as well. All standards-compatible products display an X10-compatible logo on their packaging or on the product itself. When you see this logo, you know that the product works with other X10 products regardless of the manufacturer.

As you explore the world of X10, you'll find a bunch of tools in the X10 toolbox, but the two that ended up being most applicable to home theaters are their wall outlet modules and dimmer switches. *X10 modules* are devices that receive and translate X10 signals to control individual lights, appliances, or other electrical devices. An X10 wall module is a small, box-shaped device that's no bigger than the AC plug-in transformers that power many home appliances, such as telephones and answering machines.

Setting up an X10 module is easy. The module has a standard electrical plug on the back and a place to plug in your lamp or other device on the front or bottom. First, turn the device "on" (for example, turn on the light switch), and then the X10 module turns the device off and on and dims as appropriate. *X10 dimmer switches* replace your normal switch and are likewise controlled via the X10 signals over your electrical lines, or manually by you at the switch.

X10 doesn't require specific network architecture other than your existing electrical system to work. X10 sends its control signals from the controller over your power lines to every outlet in the house. The controller can have a remote control or a PC interface.

The successors to X10

But X10 is old, almost older than Pat and Danny (but not *that* old). It has had its share of problems, and at least three new initiatives — each backed by their share of industry powerhouse names — are vying for your previously X10-bound, home-automation budget:

- **INSTEON (**www.insteon.net**):** Backed by the founders of SmartHome. com (one of our favorite sites), INSTEON is the next generation of X10 — it's an integrated dual-mesh network that combines wireless radio frequency (RF) with the home's existing electrical wiring for communications. (By the way, in case your head just spun around, *integrated dual mesh* means that INSTEON can use both RF and powerline signaling at the same time, in an integrated way.) Homeowners with existing X10 networks can migrate to an INSTEON network without having to discard their X10 devices.

- **ZigBee (**www.zigbee.org**):** ZigBee uses only RF transmission instead of X10's powerline transmission protocols to create a home wireless network for home automation. We discuss Control4, a whole-home networking company that uses ZigBee, in Chapter 21.

- **Z-Wave (**www.z-wavealliance.org**):** Z-Wave also focuses just on RF, using a mesh network that hops from location to location in your home — making it easy to extend the network throughout a large home.

These are all different approaches to the same problem. Each offers similar modules: plug-in dimmers, plug-in on/off switches, wire-in dimmers with the standard paddle design, wire-in dimmers with a keypad, and so on.

In choosing from among the X10 successors, here are some thoughts:

- **You're smart to buy an X10 successor rather than X10 proper.** We recommend you look at these new technologies over X10 unless you've already made a commitment to X10.

✔ **Be mindful of X10 compatibility.** If you have X10 installed, look at INSTEON because it's compatible with X10.

✔ **All of these successors work.** These represent the next generation of home automation and as such provide the best performance for your money. However, each of these new approaches has its pros and cons.

✔ **All of these successors are mesh.** These wireless technologies use some form of a mesh network, meaning each device in the network can communicate with each other device and retransmit a signal if it can't confirm a signal was received.

✔ **All of these successors can be programmed and controlled through multiple access points.** How multiple are we talking here? How about computers, Web browsers, mobile phones, remotes, and wall switches, for starters?

✔ **The number of supported devices should not matter.** Z-Wave's addressing scheme allows for only 256 devices. INSTEON and ZigBee have addressing schemes that allow many thousands of devices to be added to a network. Some pundits will argue that that matters. We would be surprised if you need more than 50 addresses in your home, so we think this is not an issue.

✔ **Wireless frequencies could be a concern, but it's too early to tell.** INSTEON and Z-Wave use the 900 MHz frequency spectrum to transmit their wireless signals in the United States; ZigBee primarily uses the 2.4 GHz frequency spectrum, which is also used by Wi-Fi and other wireless technologies. If you have a lot of 802.11-based systems in your house, you could conceivably have issues with a ZigBee system. However, ZigBee uses all 16 channels in the 2.4 GHz band, and if a channel gets too noisy, the network moves to a clear channel, so it was designed to deal with this. It's not enough for us to get too worried about it in our own implementations.

In the end, it's likely to come down to the cost for you to install a particular set of capabilities in your home — price each solution and see what works best for you. Some of these will likely have a package — like a home theater lighting package — that makes it easy to accomplish what you want. Such packages are easier to install the first time, and you can expand these as your needs change.

A great resource for ideas about lighting control systems — and your home theater in general — is *Electronic House* magazine (www.electronichouse. com). It's inexpensive, available on newsstands, and has helpful hints about how to approach your projects from many angles (including lots of home theater–specific articles).

Hidden advantages of lighting control systems

Although having a lighting control system for your home theater makes sense, expanding it to other parts of your home makes even more sense. In addition to setting the mood in your home theater, a lighting control system

✔ **Saves money on electricity bills:** Want to turn off all your lights at night and enter Sleeping mode? One button can do that, no matter the condition (on/off) of the lights at that time.

✔ **Adds security:** Automatically illuminating dark halls or that creepy space by the garage at night not only adds to peace of

mind but also reduces the likelihood of problems.

✔ **Supports your lifestyle:** Whether it's making sure your kids' lights are out at 9:30 or automatically turning on your lights when you drive in the garage, a lighting control system can help support the way you use your home.

If you want to find out more about extending your lighting control system to the rest of your house, check out *Smart Homes For Dummies* (Wiley), which we also wrote.

Controlling Your Home Theater Environment Remotely

Many lighting control systems can interface with or drive whole-home automation capabilities. Although whole-home automation is beyond the scope of this book (Dare we say it? Why not? Read our *Smart Homes For Dummies* book for a whole-home approach), you can get whole-room automation with many systems.

Many of the better remote controls we discuss in Chapter 15 support home-automation commands. And some manufacturers offer complementary products that work off the same remotes. For instance, Lutron's Sivoia QED (www. lutron.com/sivoia) motorized shade and drapery system is integrated with the firm's GRAFIK Eye, RadioRA, and HomeWorks lighting and home control systems. Each new control offers Open, Close, Raise, and Lower buttons, along with three programmable, preset stop locations for shades or draperies. With this, you can control the dimming of the lights and opening of the drapes, just like in a real theater.

Closing the drapes and shades without leaving the couch

Motorized shade/drape kits are simple to install and can add a professional touch to your home theater. You can get electronic drapery kits that open and close on your command. If you have ever installed a drapery rod, a kit is basically the same thing with a motor. For instance, the Makita Motorized Drape System (www.smarthome.com) is a self-contained system for your home theater drapes. You can get a single drape system or a double drape. You screw in the tracks, mount the drapes, and plug it in. You can customize the length merely by cutting the tracking. Pretty simple.

You can also get motorized window-treatment hardware from manufacturers such as BTX (www.btxinc.com), Hunter Douglas (www.hunterdouglas.com), Lutron (www.lutron.com/sivoia), and Somfy (www.somfysystems.com).

 Check to see whether these systems can link to your home automation system as well. Most of these manufacturers have begun to offer INSTEON, ZigBee or Z-Wave controllers for their window treatments (we just love saying "window treatments," it makes us feel so sophisticated).

Starry, starry night . . .

Fiber optics can add a neat effect to any home theater. Here are some ideas, suggested by Acoustic Innovations (www.acoustic innovations.com):

✔ **Starlight fiber-optic ceilings:** To make your ceiling look like a nighttime sky, you can have fiber-optic ceiling panels applied to your existing ceiling. The panels not only make your ceiling more fun but also offer acoustical correction. However, you might find yourself spreading out a blanket on your home theater floor to watch the ceiling!

✔ **Infinite starfield panels:** What better accompaniment to your Pink Floyd *Dark Side of the Moon* midnight laser show than an infinite starfield in your home theater? These are made of multiple polycarbonate mirrors and fiber-optic lighting and create an illusion of infinite depth. (Not suggested for theater ceilings.)

✔ **Fiber-optic carpeting:** This carpet is filled with tiny points of light (50 fiber-optic points per square foot, to be precise).

✔ **Fiber-optic curtains:** These classic, velvety curtains can twinkle, too. Très chic.

All illuminators come complete with a remote locatable dimmer, speed control for twinkle, and an on/off switch. You even get to choose between a twinkle or color change wheel. Decisions, decisions.

Turning up the heat from the comfort of your recliner

Automation isn't just lights and drapes. You can monitor and control temperature settings as well. Don't forget that you need to maintain the temperature for all those electronic components per manufacturer specs — usually above 55 degrees Fahrenheit at a minimum. If your theater is located in a part of the house where you might have to warm it up or cool it off in advance, consider integrating the heating system in your home theater room with your controller system, too.

Again, without getting waist deep in detail, you can get X10-, ZigBee-, Z-Wave-, and INSTEON-controlled heating and air conditioning modules that interface with your environmental controls to

- ✔ **Make sure they stay within a specified temperature range**
- ✔ **Allow you remote control in case you want to prep your theater**

Many of the firms mentioned for lighting control systems have similar systems for heating and air cooling. These systems are usually tack-on modules to their other systems and can cost as little as $30 to $50. A decent bidirectional home automation thermostat will probably run you $200. Check out www.smarthome.com, www.automatedoutlet.com, and www.X10.com for some good options. Again, whole-home options cost considerably more because you start getting into multiple zones and probably several interface formats. But for your home theater, the ability to preset your environmental controls from remote locations won't cost much.

Getting Comfy

Finally, *getting comfortable* in your home theater means different things to different people. To Danny's wife, it probably means having about 20 large pillows from Pier One Imports lying around the floor. To Pat's wife, it would mean having theater seats wide enough for Opie the beagle to sit next to her (with some beagle-proof fabric covering them).

You have many options for home theater seating comfort: chairs, couches, and lounges; seating that's motorized or manual; some with storage and control compartments; some with speakers built-in; the list goes on.

You're probably looking at around $300 and up per seat for specialty theater seating, and seats can quickly get into the $2,000–$3,000 range if you start piling on the extras. You can really sink money into your seats.

Going Hollywood all the way

For those of you who want to go all the way with the theater theme, you can buy all sorts of add-ons to create that atmosphere:

- **Personalized home theater intro:** Open each showing with your own customized one-minute video, just like in the theaters. (Your DVD player must be able to play DVD-R for this to work.) For $160 or so for a customized DVD from www.htmarket.com, you can personalize one of five home theater intros, from an awards night theme to a classic popcorn theme. How fun is that?!

- **Specialty rugs:** You can get rugs festooned with stars, film reels, popcorn, and so on. The cost is about $50 per square yard on average (but there's a huge range). HT Market (www.htmarket.com) has these rugs.

- **Posts and ropes:** If you wanted that velour rope and stainless steel post look, you've got it. Expect to spend around $120–$300 a post and $80–$100 a rope. Maybe there is some poetic justice about making your boss wait in line at your home theater! Pat's going to buy a set of these the next time Danny is in town. Check out www.stargatecinema.com if you're interested in picking up some posts and ropes for yourself.

- **Popcorn machines:** Complete with the swing down popping bucket, these $300–$900 machines give you freshly popped popcorn and that movie-theater smell. Check out www.popcornpopper.com for some cool models.

- **Wall sconces:** You can get theater lighting that will give you that interior decorated look on a budget (about $200–$250 apiece). You don't need to go anywhere special for these — you can hit your local hardware store or go to Lowes or Home Depot.

- **Film posters:** Decorate the outside of your theater with current and past movie posters, just like you see while waiting in line to get your tickets. These run about $10 to $20 for current films, in their usual 27-x-40-inch formats. Check out www.allposters.com for new ones or find vintage posters at places like www.moviemarket.com.

- **Sound Edgelits:** Add some of these table-top back-lit signs to let your viewers know which sound systems you have in your theater. These $225 signs sport Dolby Digital, THX, DTS, and other surround-sound logos. You can find these (and more) at places such as www.hometheaterdecor.com and www.htmarket.com.

Some things to keep in mind, no matter what you buy:

- **Sound implications:** You'll set up your sound system so that no matter where you sit in your theater, you have a similar (breathtaking) aural experience. Three couches in a U-shaped configuration may sound right for you, but make sure that your speaker configuration is designed to handle it. You may need some additional speakers or ones with a different capability to support weird configurations. Seating configuration and speaker configuration simply go hand-in-hand.

✔ **Visual implications:** Although high-backed theater chairs may look good in the showroom, they can block your rear surround-sound speakers. If you want multiple rows, these high-backed seats may necessitate a tiered floor (so back-row viewers see the screen, not the back of a chair).

✔ **Food:** The "You can't take food into the living room" rule doesn't go over well with a viewing population trained to eat popcorn while they watch movies. So you need to consider how you will handle food. You may want built-in trays or drink holders or nothing. Maybe you need tables between chairs instead. All we ask is that you think about how you'll handle food when you're buying the furniture and rugs. No sense setting yourself up for yelling at the kids later.

You need to consider seating more than some other aspects of your home theater because many people are used to viewing movies in bed, on couches, on the floor, and so on. You really need to think through how you define *comfortable* and then design toward that.

Cuddlebags (www.cuddlebag.com, $499–$699) has theater beanbag-style pillows — they're comfortable, washable, and malleable, too. They come as big as 8 feet wide. Wow, that's a lot of cuddling!

Chapter 21

Moving Up to the High End

*O*ne somewhat vaguely defined concept that we talk about throughout *Home Theater For Dummies,* 3rd Edition, is the idea that you can move up to the high end when you're buying components and setting up a home theater. Everyone has his or her own definition of *high end,* but for us it means equipment that offers the ultimate reproduction of music and movies.

In this chapter, we quit talking about high end in the abstract and get concrete by introducing you to some awesome high-end systems. (Watch out for nose-bleeds here.) The systems' designers are so single-minded in their pursuit of musical and video fidelity that they've created proprietary systems that they feel do a better job than standard mix-and-match components. When we say a system is *proprietary,* we mean that it is designed to work best (or in some cases only) with other components from the same vendor. So if you buy part of your home theater from one of these vendors, you'll probably end up buying all of it from them — at least on the audio side. These systems usually work with any display. When you buy a proprietary system, you are in effect taking a bet on this company's ability to do things better than the industry in general does — and on the company's ability to stay in business and support you in the future.

Later in this chapter, we also talk about some of the *video processing* systems that let your top-of-the-line display look as good as (or better than) the movies you see in the theater.

Introducing High-End Home Theater

In the introduction to this chapter, we start to define what we think high-end theater is. Our definition of *high end* starts and ends with the philosophy of the designers and engineers who create the product (which can be speakers, a display, an A/V controller or power amplifier, or even an A/V receiver, though high-end systems usually consist of matched sets of separate components, rather than all-in-one receivers).

Anybody designing a piece of consumer electronics equipment has to balance a lot of different (and often conflicting) requirements: performance, price, size, interoperability with other gear, aesthetics, and so on. High-end gear skews this delicate balance toward the performance side of the equation, and as a result, the high-end components can be much more expensive, big, proprietary, and even ugly (although through the right set of eyes, these devices are beautiful).

A few years back, there was a bit of a geographic divide (or at least, a perceived divide) between high-end and mass-market A/V components. High-end vendors were located in the United States, Canada, and Europe, while big consumer electronics companies based in Asia were focused on high-volume, middle-market products. We're not convinced that this perception was ever correct, but we're sure that it's not true today. Although many high-end manufacturers are based in the traditional places, you can find some awesome (and expensive) gear coming from those big Asian consumer electronics companies. Just because a company sells a ton of $299 A/V receivers doesn't mean that it can't build a great $3,000 receiver. So throw any perceptions of brand bias out the door because you may be surprised by who has some fine high-end products these days.

Separating Your Amps

Within the audio realm of the home theater domain, the most common step for manufacturers moving up to higher-quality products is to transition from the all-in-one A/V receiver into separates. We talk a little about separates in Chapter 11, but in this chapter, we get a bit more detailed.

Basically, separate components take the many functions of an A/V receiver and divide them among several separate components. Doing this has two major benefits: greater flexibility and better performance.

A/V receivers are pretty darned good these days, and there is such a thing as a high-end A/V receiver. These receivers (from companies such as Denon, Yamaha, and Marantz, to name just a few) compete performance-wise with most separates systems in their price range.

The functions of an A/V receiver are usually doled out to the following components:

- **A/V controller:** This device handles all the surround-sound decoding and digital-to-analog conversions. It also switches audio and video (from source devices to the amplifiers or display) and performs the *preamplifier* functions (from adjusting the power level of audio signals going to the amplifiers, to adjust the listening volume). A few A/V controllers include a built-in radio tuner, making them essentially A/V receivers without built-in power amplifiers.

   Depending on who's talking, you might hear these devices referred to as *surround-sound processors, home theater preamps,* or something else entirely. If it decodes the surround-sound signals and switches between audio and video sources, it's an A/V controller.

- **Power amplifier:** These devices boost the power of analog audio signals coming out of the controller to drive the speakers and create sound. As we just mentioned, you don't control volume with the power amplifier (the A/V controller does that). Basically, a power amplifier is a big box with an on/off switch, speaker terminals, and one or more RCA jack audio inputs on the back for connecting to the A/V controller. Most home theater power amplifiers are *multichannel* amplifiers, meaning they have five, seven, or more built-in amplifiers for powering your surround-sound speakers. Some systems are designed around *mono* power amplifiers, in which *each* channel in the system has its own amplifier. (You can also find two- and three-channel amplifiers to mix and match into a five- or more channel system.)

- **Radio tuner:** We discuss these in Chapter 5. Just remember that the majority of A/V controllers don't have a built-in tuner, so if you want to listen to the radio, you need to buy a separate tuner. If you have digital cable or a DSS satellite dish, you might get around this requirement if you can receive radio stations through these systems (and if you like the channel lineups they offer).

Connecting a separates system is only minimally different from the process of hooking up a home theater based on an A/V receiver. Just as you do with an A/V receiver, you want to route all your source components through the A/V controller. All your analog audio, digital audio, and video connections connect directly from the source device to the A/V controller. (The only exception to this rule is this: If you don't have enough of the right kind of video inputs on your A/V controller — specifically if your controller doesn't have HDMI switching — you might connect the video cables from some of your components directly to the display.)

Your powered (active) subwoofer connects directly to the A/V controller, just as it connects to your A/V receiver. The rest of your speakers, however, are connected differently. You use an audio interconnect cable (the standard

RCA plug cables we discuss in Chapter 16) for each channel of your 5.1-, 6.1-, or 7.1-channel surround-sound system and route this signal from a set of Power Amplifier Out connections on the back of your controller to the appropriate Preamp In connections on the back of your power amplifier(s).

Moving to Integrated Systems

One method that many high-end vendors use to create a high-performance system is to come up with their own integrated way of doing home theater. Some of these systems use proprietary connection systems (their own special cables) to link components, whereas others use standard connectors and cables but have components that are specially designed to work together.

These systems are basically the steroid-enhanced siblings of the inexpensive home-theater-in-a-box systems we discuss in Chapter 2. You buy a complete system from a single manufacturer, rather than picking and choosing between components from different vendors. It's a high-end, soup-to-nuts approach; the power amplifiers, A/V controllers, DVD and CD players, and speakers — everything but the display itself, in most cases — come as one integrated package from one company.

In the sections that follow, we talk about some of the leading integrated systems. Just keep in mind that these aren't the only manufacturers who build these kinds of systems, just a sampling.

Going modular

As you've no doubt noticed while reading this book, the technologies that allow us to replicate a movie theater in our homes are not static. Over the last decade we've moved from VHS tapes to DVD discs and now on to Blu-ray (and quite possibly on to downloaded video stored on hard drives). Surround sound has gone from Dolby Surround to Dolby Digital and now on to Dolby TrueHD. Movie audio has moved from stereo to 5.1 channels and now to 7.1 (and may end up reaching 13.1 some day!). The video itself has gone from 480i to 1080p. Nothing has stood still.

Your investment in home theater may be significant, and nothing guarantees that what you spend good money on today will be capable of handling the best of tomorrow's home theater. If you're spending thousands and thousands of dollars on a high-end receiver or separates system, this thought may bother you more than a little bit.

Many manufacturers of high-end gear understand this and developed *modular* systems designed more like PCs than traditional audio gear, with replaceable cards (much like the modular cards used in PCs for graphics and networking) that can be added or swapped out over time as new developments in home theater begin to outstrip the original capabilities of your equipment.

Examples of this include NAD Electronics' (www.nadelectronics.com) T765, T775, and T785 home theater receivers and T715 preamp/processor. Each component is built around five separate circuit cards (handling HDMI video, component video, digital audio, stereo analog audio, and multichannel analog audio). This approach allows a simple circuit card upgrade/replacement when a new standard in one of these areas comes to pass. A number of manufacturers have adopted this approach, which probably won't be cheap but will cost less than buying a new component.

Another aspect of this more PC-like approach to home theater components is that many components include an Ethernet connection. Through this connection to your home network (and on to the Internet), your component can download *firmware* upgrades — upgrades to the software that controls the component's functionality. In many cases, new features and functions can be simply turned on with a firmware update (just as is the case on your PC, where operating system updates provide new features).

Meridian's DSP-based system

Meridian (www.meridian-audio.com) offers some of the coolest, highest-end A/V equipment anywhere. One Meridian feature that we think reflects the future of A/V gear is its computer-like construction. Meridian systems are incredibly modular and upgradeable. So if your current Meridian processor, for example, doesn't support a new surround-sound format, you can simply have your dealer pop in a new card. By the way, Meridian is the developer of *MLP* (Meridian Lossless Packing), the lossless audio compression technique used for Dolby's TrueHD surround-sound format.

Meridian's products are known for being some of the finest in terms of dealing with digital audio signals (no surprise given Meridian's expertise in the field). Meridian does a couple of things differently than most other A/V component vendors:

✔ **Smart Link:** Meridian has an all-digital connection called Smart Link for carrying DVD-audio signals to the controller. In Meridian's own words (and we believe what they're saying), Smart Link allows "the full resolution of multichannel audio from DVD-A recordings [to] be losslessly transferred in the digital domain from player to surround controller to loudspeaker." That's a mouthful, but it means that digital audio signals remain digital until the very final link in the audio chain — the speakers. Meridian can do this because of Smart Link, and also because of the item we discuss next.

✔ **DSP loudspeakers:** Meridian builds active loudspeaker systems designed to connect and integrate with its lineup of CD/DVD players and A/V controllers. Like all active speakers, these have built-in power amplifiers, so you don't need a separate amp. The difference comes with the digital signal processor (DSP) that gives them their name. This digital signal processor allows Meridian to send fully digital audio signals to the speakers. So the digital chain is broken only when the speakers themselves convert the signal to analog internally. You benefit from a clean, interference-resistant digital connection. Additionally, the DSP speakers do all the things that normal loudspeakers do (such as *crossovers* that send different frequencies to different drivers within the speaker) entirely in the digital domain. There's even a separate amplifier within the DSP speakers for each individual driver.

All this modularity, flexibility, and digital audio goodness doesn't come cheap. Meridian's flagship speakers, the DSP8000, cost $40,000 a *pair*. They're not for the faint of heart or the shallow-walleted. But the sound is awesome.

We understand that most folks can't afford (or won't spend the money on) $20,000-a-piece loudspeakers. (We can't either, to be honest, at least not without second mortgages.) But we're telling you about this product because these kinds of systems give you a feel for what's possible in home theater. And the technologies featured in these systems will eventually, in the words of Ronald Reagan, "trickle down" to more affordable gear. We certainly can't wait for DSP-based active loudspeakers and modular, upgradeable components to hit the Crutchfield catalog instead of super-expensive boutique audio stores.

Exploring High-End Video Systems

Audio isn't the only part of home theater that fits into the high-end category. If you've read earlier parts of the book (particularly the discussions of front-projection display systems in Chapter 14), you already know that high-end video systems (such as the $30,000, three-chip DLP projectors we keep mentioning) are on the market, waiting to be gobbled up by well-to-do home theater enthusiasts. If you want to go high-end with front projection, look for units from Faroudja (www.faroudja.com) or Runco (www.runco.com).

In this section, we talk about a group of high-end devices called *video processors* that complement these displays (particularly projection systems) in many home theaters.

Improving resolution

If you go for a front- or rear-projection system or the biggest plasma display, you get a really big picture in a home theater. The problem is, the picture is so big that you begin to see the line structure of analog NTSC television broadcasts (and other low-resolution sources, such as VHS VCR tapes). These sources don't have sufficient resolution, and you end up with a picture that looks okay on a 20-inch TV in the bedroom but like a disaster on your fancy projection TV. Simply put, the 250 horizontal lines that make up a VHS picture will be so far apart on a big-screen display that you can see them (and the black lines between them) without sticking your face up next to the screen. This is, to say the least, annoying.

To get around this problem, many high-end projectors (and other displays as well) use a device known as a *line doubler*. A line doubler, in its simplest form, takes the two fields that make up a frame in an interlaced video system and combines them. (We discuss frames and fields in Chapter 4 if you're not sure what we're talking about here.) These newly reconstructed frames are then sent to the display twice in a row, until the next pair of images comes along (¹⁄₃₀ of a second after the first). For example, with NTSC broadcast TV signals, the 480 interlaced scan lines of the broadcast come out of the line doubler (and head in to your display) as 480 progressive-scan lines. This makes for a much smoother image and helps hide those visible scan lines because twice as many are displayed at a time.

To take advantage of a line doubler, your display must be able to handle progressive-scan video. Look for displays with scan rates of 31.5 kHz or higher. (We discuss scan rates in Chapter 13.) Most HDTV-ready or progressive scan displays already have an internal line doubler built in. As you start moving to really high-end home theater installations, many experts like to bypass these by using a top-of-the-line external line doubler (or more likely, one of the devices we discuss in the next section).

Investigating top-of-the-line video processors

Video processors go beyond simple line doubling. You can find processors that *quadruple* the number of lines on your display, and increasingly you can purchase a processor that *scales* a video source to a specific (and often custom) fixed resolution suitable for displays such as plasma, LCD, and DLP, which have a specific number of pixels onscreen.

Going quad

Some video processors do more than just double the lines of resolution. For example, *line quadruplers* (as the name implies) quadruple the number of scan lines sent to the display. These systems don't wait for four fields to come in and then repeat them four times (which is what you might think they do, given how line doublers work). Instead, line quadruplers do some math and *interpolate* what might come between a pair of lines. (Because there's no actual picture data for the new extra lines, the quadrupler uses various mathematical models to guess what might be there.)

For NTSC analog video signals, a quadrupler gives an output of 960 progressive-scan lines. (In other words, it doubles the 480i output to 480p, and then doubles that again to 960p.)

Line quadruplers are rare these days simply because most folks have begun using digital displays (such as DLP projectors or plasma flat panels), which have fixed resolutions. If you want to enhance the video quality for these types of displays, you use one of the *scalers* we are about to discuss.

Scaling the video heights

The most advanced video processors available (usually called *image scalers*) can convert an incoming video signal to a customized resolution — a resolution that is most suitable for a particular projector or other display. In other words, these particular video processors don't do a simple doubling or quadrupling of a signal. For example, if you were using a 1080p DLP projection system, the scaler would convert an incoming video signal to a resolution of 1920 x 1080 pixels, with progressive scan.

Instead of a scan rate or a number of lines of resolution, fixed-pixel displays need a video signal that contains a certain number of horizontal and vertical pixels. For example, if you have a DLP-based projection system using Texas Instruments HD-2 chip (which has a resolution of 1280 x 720 pixels), you want a scaler that can output a 1280 x 720 video signal.

All fixed-pixel displays have internal scalers that can perform this image scaling. Many home theater enthusiasts (at least those who are spending $5,000 or more on a display) bypass these internal scalers and use an external image scaler that they feel does a better job of interpolating and creating video signals.

Most image scalers also contain circuitry to perform *3:2 pulldown,* the process of removing artifacts found in video when a 24-frame-per-second video is converted to a 30-frame-per-second video. (We discuss this in detail in Chapter 4.) This feature is also found in many DVD players and a number of displays, but standalone image scalers often have superior systems for this process.

The following models are a couple of the most popular image scalers:

- **Gefen Home Theater Scaler PLUS:** Gefen (www.gefen.com) is widely known throughout the home theater community for its high-performance video switching and processing solutions. In particular, Gefen is *the* go-to source for folks who need to deal with switching and distribution of HDMI sources. The folks at Gefen entered 2008 (and the annual CES trade show) with some big announcements, including a $499 video processor called the Home Theater Scaler PLUS. For considerably less money than competing products, the Scaler PLUS can accept S-video, component, and HDMI connections and scale them to resolutions up to 1080p, as well as switching those sources and their corresponding audio.

- **DVDO iScan VP30:** DVDO (a division of Anchor Bay, www.anchorbay tech.com.com) is one of the original big names in the imager scaler business, and its iScan VP30 is a neat unit that can play several roles in a home theater. For $1,999, the unit combines a high-quality scaler with an HDMI switch — accepting up to four HDMI inputs from different video source components in your home theater (a big deal because very few TVs have more than two HDMI inputs, and even fewer receivers have any HDMI switching — so the VP30 can come in useful if you're trying to connect an HDMI set-top box, a DVD player, and a PS3 all at the same time). The VP30 can scale any input resolution up to HDTV resolutions, including 1080p, and also offers a *Precision AV LipSync* function that ensures that your digital audio and video always stay synchronized (so you don't end up thinking you're watching a poorly dubbed Kung Fu movie due to audio/video timing issues).

Relating scaled images and HDTV

You may have noticed that some video processors can output video at resolutions that would qualify as HDTV resolutions (720p or higher). So the question may have entered your mind, "What's the relationship between scaled images and HDTV?" Well, to begin with, a scaled image (no matter how high the resolution and how good the system that created it) is not high definition. After a lower-resolution video signal is run through a high-quality scaler, the signal can look great — spectacular even. But no interpolation system (which is what all scalers are, in essence) can put missing information back into a video signal. Scalers can come close, but they can't match the real thing. Having said that, we hasten to add that scalers make great companions to HDTVs and HDTV-ready displays. For this reason, the majority of HDTV displays already have some sort of built-in internal scaler, which *upconverts* lower-resolution video sources to an HDTV resolution. External image scalers can often improve on these internal systems and make everything you watch on your HDTV look better.

Using High-End Controls

One of the most common things folks add to a home theater is a high-end control system for providing local and remote control of their audio and video masterpiece. You can get a complete system that provides this control, and such systems are most often focused on whole-home control.

Crestron

Crestron (www.crestron.com) is a well-known company in the realm of whole-home automation and control. Crestron doesn't make DVD players, A/V receivers, or projection displays, but their products (along with those of a company called AMX, www.amx.com, which offers a similar lineup of products) can be found in many high-end home theaters. Crestron offers a whole lot more than the remote controls we mention in Chapter 15. In a nutshell, Crestron builds whole-home control systems that use LCD touchpads to control just about any electrically operated device in a home. A Crestron system can raise and lower your drapes, dim your lights, adjust your HVAC (heating, ventilation, and air conditioning) system, *and* control all the devices in your home theater. And this list is by no means exhaustive. There's really not much you can't do with a complete Crestron system.

Specifically for home theater, Crestron makes several models of home theater control systems that incorporate wired or wireless touchpads and centralized controllers (not A/V controllers, despite the name). These touchpads and controllers interface with the IR or RS-232 ports on your A/V gear. Crestron's computer-like devices have enough intelligence that you can easily program them to perform complex *macros* (sequences of control actions). So with only a single tap of a virtual button, you can set into motion all the things you might do manually when turning on your home theater's systems and getting ready to watch a movie.

Crestron sells hundreds of components designed to control a home theater (and a home!), and we won't even try to run through them here. This isn't off-the-shelf, DIY-type stuff. You need to go through a Crestron dealer (many high-end home theater installers also install Crestron) to have a system designed for, and installed in, your home theater. All this automated goodness doesn't come cheap. The typical Crestron installation is more than $50,000, and that *doesn't* count the home theater components themselves.

Control4

A new competitor to Crestron, Control4 (www.control4.com) has made a big splash over the past few years with a range of components that do a lot of the same things that Crestron's systems do but at a significantly lower price.

Control4 offers products that fill all sorts of roles in an automated home, ranging from controllers that can dim your lights and adjust your heating or air conditioning to touchpad systems that let you send commands to your home theater gear. Control4 even offers audio distribution systems that can store digital audio and send it wirelessly throughout the home.

Control4 keeps the price down by leveraging standardized components and technologies such as Ethernet and Wi-Fi wireless networking (and their gear is significantly cheaper than Crestron's). So Control4 gear doesn't contain a bunch of custom-built electronics, but instead uses some of the same components as PCs — stuff that is built in the tens or hundreds of millions for very low prices.

Among the most interesting parts of the Control4 lineup (from a home theater perspective) are the audio distribution systems. The Media Controller ($1,495) contains an 80GB hard drive for storing digital music, a CD player for importing new music, and Ethernet and Wi-Fi outputs for distributing the music around your home. You can mix this with the company's $1,995 touch-screen controller and use its big 10.5-inch LCD screen to control your music or anything else in the home connected to one of Control4's systems.

Part VI
The Part of Tens

In this part . . .

Top-ten lists abound here! Look in this part of the book for our top-ten lists on some key home theater topics. We start with ways to accessorize your home theater with fun add-ons, such as a theater-style popcorn popper without the $6 per bag price tag!

Then, find out where to go for more information — those extra-special places where you can track down more ideas for your home theater experience.

Are you having fun yet? We are!

Chapter 22

Ten or So Accessories for Your Home Theater

Depending on where you put your home theater, you can envision adding all sorts of extras to flesh out your home operation. But in our minds, some things you just gotta have — well, stuff you might really *want* to have if you're going for the ultimate home theater. We list a lot of them here so that you have a checklist next time you're online or at that home theater store.

Wireless Headphones

Ever want to use the home theater when your spouse, significant other, or roommate is asleep, working, or performing brain surgery in the other room? Ever get told to *"Turn it down!"* in no uncertain terms? Well, maybe you need that marriage- or friendship-saving device, the wireless headphone.

You can find some cool models of headphones out there. Some cancel out ambient noise (so the kids can scream and smash things, and you won't hear a thing), others use special digital signal processing to recreate 5.1-channel Dolby Digital surround sound. Some fit in your ear canals, and some totally cover your ear with a huge "can." Whatever you like, you can find it in the headphone world.

We love wireless headphones because they enable us to get more popcorn or let the dog out without catching a long cord on something. So wireless headsets, which use radio waves to connect to a base station plugged in to the home theater receiver (like a cordless phone uses radio waves to connect to the phone base station plugged in to a phone jack), are the way to go for us.

For serious listening (what the high-end audio types call *critical listening*), you might not want to use cordless headphones, which probably don't have quite the ultimate fidelity of corded models. But for more casual use, we find that many cordless models sound great.

One of the more interesting wireless headsets we've seen comes from Sennheiser (`www.sennheiserusa.com`). The RS 130 wireless headphone, which has a list price of $179.95 (and can be found for about $20 cheaper in many places), is a good entry point into the world of wireless headsets. It even includes a switchable SRS surround-sound function so you can simulate the surround-sound effects of your home theater's speakers with just the two speakers built into the phones. (See Chapter 12 for more about headphones and surround sound.)

Dolby has a capability called Dolby Headphone (`www.dolby.com/dolby headphone`) that can take up to five channels of audio from any source, feed it to your normal two-channel headphones, and make it sound like it's coming from that many speakers in a real listening room. The difference relative to stereo headphones is amazing. Look for the Dolby Headphone logo on your receiver. If your receiver has Dolby Headphone capabilities, you don't need special surround-sound headphones. Any old headphones will give you excellent surround-sound effects.

Power Conditioner

Close your eyes and think about your electrical power lines. No, really. Imagine a current flowing (or alternating) from Homer Simpson's nuclear power plant, over the high-voltage lines of Springfield, across hill and dale, and finally ending up in a transformer on a pole outside your home. Think about all the other junk attached to that electrical power grid. Even within your home, tons of electrical devices are connected to your power lines. All this stuff adds its own little bit of degradation to the nice, clean, sine-wavy alternating current coming out of those turbogenerators at the power plant. End result: power at your home theater's outlets may be of an incorrect voltage or full of electrical noise that keeps all your A/V components from being their best.

At a bare minimum, you need (absolutely need) some surge protection in your home theater. But even with surge protection, you still may have issues. For example, if your voltage drops (not an uncommon occurrence), it may lower the output of your amplifier. You can also run into ground issues that can either cause hums in your audio or create annoying lines in your video display. So you might want to consider investing in a power conditioner that improves and stabilizes your AC power. For example, Monster Cable's Home Theater Power Centers provides surge protection, voltage stabilization, and noise filtering. The more expensive ones even have a digital voltmeter read-out on the front. Check them out at www.monstercable.com/power.

Shake It Up, Baby (with Transducers)!

If you're like us (and we feel that you are if you've read most of this book), you like to get totally into what you're watching. After all, a home theater is supposed to help suspend disbelief. You can get one giant, T. Rex–step closer to that goal with audio transducers from companies such as Clark Synthesis (www.clarksynthesis.com). You'll see these called many things — *bass shakers, tactile transducers,* or as one vendor calls them, *butt kickers.* They add an element that goes well beyond the sensation of a subwoofer, one that helps change your whole theater into a sensaround environment. (Remember *Earthquake* in the theaters?) The units are screwed onto the bottom of your furniture or into the frames of your floorboards. Transducers operate a bit like a subwoofer — vibrating in time with low-frequency sounds — but instead of moving air (and therefore creating sounds), they transmit vibrations into solid objects (such as the floor) for bass that you can *feel* as well as hear.

These transducers are friendlier to the rest of the house than cranking up massive subwoofers that can seem to shake the neighborhood. Because the low end of the sound is effectively isolated to a more specific area, namely the couch or chairs, transducers virtually eliminate any bleeding of this sound into adjoining rooms or connected housing units.

Transducers are also great for houses built on concrete slabs. Unlike wood subfloors, concrete slabs don't conduct bass particularly well.

The sky is the limit with transducers. You can get low-budget ones (such as Aura Bass Shakers for under $100, www.aurasound.com) that do a fairly good job. If you want more power and precision, check out the Clark Synthesis models, which can run from $100 to $300 depending on the model (www.clarksynthesis.com/), or the Buttkicker from The Guitammer

Company, Inc. (`www.guitammer.com`, starting at $299). The difference is astounding and noticeable. One thing to note: Some products support frequencies up to 200 Hz, and some go even higher (up to 800 Hz). We prefer keeping it low, say between 5 Hz and 200 Hz; otherwise, there is a constant background rumble that gets nauseating after a while. Keep the effect directed and precise — you'll like it better. To control the frequency sent to your transducer, consider an equalizer such as AudioSource EQ200 (`www.rodinaudio.com/audio Source/electronics.php`), which runs about $120.

Consider using more than one; try, say, three across the bottom of your couch. The middle transducer would acquire its signal from the LFE/subwoofer out of the processor-receiver, and the two side ones would derive their signals from the left and right front channels, respectively. With this setup, you can get a better sense of the action in three dimensions. If you are watching *U571,* for instance, when a depth charge goes off to the right of the submarine, you get a sensation from the right channel, and when the lower part of the compression from the bomb and water splash enters into the soundtrack, you feel the sub channel and right channel together.

If you mount transducers directly to your furniture, you can get rubberized molded mounts for your chair or couch legs that isolate the noise and vibration to your furniture.

If you install more than one of these transducers, you probably would do well to power each unit with its own amp. Read the manufacturer's recommendations closely. For some of the cheaper models, powering them with anything over a 20-watt amplifier is probably not a good idea. Some of the fancier models call for an amplifier of at least 100 watts. You can find transducers that come bundled with an amplifier (active transducers); consider getting one of these if you have questions. In any case, the amp should have its own volume control so that you can tune the effect relative to the audio level. The hi-fi quality of the amp is not critical, so you can use relatively inexpensive amplifiers.

You can get shaker units that attach to the floorboards of your house and can shake the whole room. There are pros and cons to this. On the pro side, you don't have to worry about being on a particular piece of furniture to get the effect. On the other hand, you are shaking the foundation of your house (never really a good thing), and the vibrations can bleed into other areas of your house. So before you experiment with your foundation, think about which surrounding rooms will be affected.

Motion Simulators

If moving with a movie is your thing, and you have a fairly open budget, check out the motion simulators from D-BOX (`www.d-box.com`). Unlike bass shakers, which provide only vibration, or shaking, in response to the audio track and are merely transducers that vibrate rather than move air, the D-BOX system is a sophisticated motion-simulation system that lifts seating and occupants on an X-Y-Z axis (pitch, roll, and yaw) at up to 2Gs (think F-14 at full throttle) of acceleration.

D-BOX provides dramatic motion that is precisely synchronized with onscreen action, which draws in viewers even more by allowing them to accurately experience the accelerations, turns, and jumps that they could previously only imagine. When a car rounds a corner in a 007 chase scene, turn with it. If the *Top Gun* jet fighter suddenly moves into a climb, climb with it.

Just about everyone who's tried this system loves it, but the price tag will set you back. An entry-level system runs $15,000 and up.

The D-BOX system consists of two parts:

- ✔ The controller itself: D-BOX sells three controllers, two models which integrate into a PC located in your home theater and a third standalone controller (for folks without a home theater PC). This device connects to your home network (via an Ethernet port), downloads and stores the motion codes that correspond with a particular movie title, and sends those codes as motion controls.

- ✔ The motion device (*actuator*): The actuators are pistons and motors built into D-BOX's home theater seating devices (there are also seats specifically built for gaming). The actuators receive motion commands from the controller and turn those commands into actual motion.

The experience is possible thanks to a D-BOX DVD or Blu-ray disc with controller codes that map motion to movies. You can see a listing of supported movies at www.d-box.com/en/codes/index.html. Movies not on this list don't have the controller codes and therefore cannot provide the motion simulation experience.

Turn It Up! Turn It Down! Turn It Up Again! Argh!

Sometimes, you just want everything at a quiet but intelligible level (like when everyone else is sleeping). To help you in this endeavor, many A/V receivers (and some TVs) have a *compression* circuit built into the digital signal processor that keeps the louds from being too loud and the quiets from being too quiet (this is often called *night mode*).

If you're using older equipment that doesn't have this feature, you need a *leveler* (also called a *levelizer* or a *stabilizer*). This device automatically adjusts your volume to a reasonable level (even as the source material gets louder or quieter). If the source volume increases, the leveler attenuates the signal down; if the source signal decreases, it adjusts the signal up.

To use a leveler, you generally adjust the volume to where you want it, and the leveler keeps the volume at that level. An audio leveler connects between any line-level stereo or mono audio source and an amplifier (with RCA output/input jacks) or between your TV or VCR outputs and the inputs to your stereo tuner. Levelers range in price from $70 to $300 (you can check out various units at www.smarthome.com).

No more having to constantly juggle that remote (at least not for changing the volume). Keep in mind, however, that these devices are really not for serious movie watching, when you *want* to have all the loud parts loud and the quiet parts quiet. They are instead intended for nighttime viewing, when you don't want to wake up the family *and* still want to hear the quiet parts.

Be sure to check the types of audio input/output jacks supported by the system you buy. You don't want to have digital audio connections everywhere in your system and then buy an audio leveler that takes it down to a lower common denominator with analog connections.

Docking Your iPod in the Wall

The iPod. We suspect that you know the iPod, probably have an iPod and — more importantly — probably *love* your iPod. Are you aware that you can easily integrate your iPod into your home theater as an audio source device? Back in Chapter 11 we talked about home theater receivers with iPod dock options (a number of manufacturers offer such an option these days).

Another way to get your iPod into your home theater (and indeed, into your whole-home audio system, should your build one to accompany your home theater) is to consider an in-wall iPod docking system.

A few manufacturers build these systems, which are exactly what the name implies: a small alcove built right into your wall that sends audio (and video) from your iPod while simultaneously charging it! (They're easy to install — just slightly larger than a standard light switch.)

The leader in this market is iPort (www.iportmusic.com). It offers five models of its iPort IW (in-wall) docks. To install an iPort, you need two CAT-5e cables between your home theater receiver and the iPort dock itself (one handles audio and video, the other brings power and control signals to the iPod). At the other end (behind your receiver) you install an iPort Audio or Video Wallplate, which connects to an electrical outlet and provides audio (and video, in the case of the Video Wallplate) jacks that can be plugged in to the back of your home theater receiver.

iPort also makes freestanding iPod docks (the FS series), if you don't want to get as fancy as an in-wall dock. Either way, they make getting an iPod into your home theater as easy as can be.

Putting Your Face on the TV

For more than 40 years — since AT&T (then Bell Telephone) demonstrated the first "Picture Phone" at the 1964 New York World's Fair — the telecommunications industry has been trying to get people to videoconference. Whether it's shyness from being seen on a screen to a discomfort with the quality of the picture, videoconferencing has been limited to select business populations — the mass consumer market has not caught on.

But recently, with the boom in Web cams and camcorders that connect to PCs, as well as newfangled cell phones that can stream video from an onboard camera, people are finally coming around to sending live video of themselves.

Adding videoconferencing to your TV set so the kids can conference with Grandma and Grandpa is easier than ever before. Companies such as D-Link (www.dlink.com) have launched products designed for adding videoconferencing to your TV set. D-Link has its DVC-1000 i2eye VideoPhone ($159), which is designed to allow videoconferencing without an intermediary computer. You just plug one cord of the DVC-1000 in to a standard telephone, plug another cord in to a television via RCA composite connections, connect the DVC-1000 to your broadband Internet connection using a standard Ethernet network cable, and you are ready to conduct real-time videoconferencing.

You can't use a telephone plugged in to the i2eye VideoPhone to place regular phone calls because the phone would not be connected to a standard phone line. Only VideoPhone calls over the Internet can be made with a telephone connected to the DVC-1000.

The DVC-1000 can send and receive video at up to 30 frames per second. The remote control that comes with the DVC-1000 allows you to easily answer an incoming videophone call or initiate a new one. Or, you can use the attached telephone to initiate calls if you are more comfortable with that interface.

The DVC-1000 has a port for an external microphone, too, if you'd rather talk into a headset or a mic.

D-Link also sells the DVC-2000 ($350), which includes a built-in 5-inch color LCD screen, in case you don't want to use the TV display as your screen.

Putting Fine Art on Your HDTV

What do you do with that HDTV when you're not watching TV? How about putting some fine art on the screen? With GalleryPlayer (www.gallery player.com), you can do just that. Gallery Player is an Internet-based subscription service that you can get onto your HDTV in one of two ways:

- ✔ You can buy an HDTV with GalleryPlayer built in. Panasonic, Mitsubishi, and Samsung sell HDTVs that include the ability to display GalleryPlayer content on the TV. Just download your favorite galleries to your PC, transfer them to an SD card or a USB memory stick, and you're all set.

- ✔ You can use a PC. If you have a home theater PC hooked up to your HDTV and home theater, you can subscribe to GalleryPlayer via the Internet-connected PC. This works only with Windows computers using Windows XP, XP Media Center Edition, or Windows Vista operating systems.

GalleryPlayer content ranges in price depending on what you're buying and how much of it you're buying, but typically images run about $0.99 each or $9.99 for a complete gallery.

Traditional fine art is available, as well as nature photography, action and sports photography, museum collections, content from National Geographic, history, geographic explorations, and even nudes. If it's art, it's probably covered.

It's not made any more, but if you can find Roku's HD Media Player on eBay, you'll have a cool digital media player that can play high-definition photos on your HDTV. The Roku HD Gallery Collection includes a lot of art that's similar to what's offered by Gallery Player.

Improving Your Game Console Connection

If you read Chapter 16, you had a chance to check out our discussion of interconnect cables — the short-run cables that hook together A/V components. We hope we convinced you of the importance of the hierarchy of these cables and of using the best cable you can in all situations. (In the video world, component is best, S-video is a close second, composite video lags way behind, and RF coax connections are on the bench trying to get the coach to let them in the game.)

When it comes to game consoles, however, we do find that many people just use whatever cable came in the box. As Jeremy Piven says in that movie masterpiece *PCU,* "Don't be that guy." (If you missed *PCU,* the whole line is: "You're wearing the shirt of the band you're going to see? Don't be that guy.") Most gaming consoles come with a lowest-common-denominator video and audio cable. For example, Nintendo's Wii comes with a cable system that only has composite video (the component video cable is optional); some versions of the Xbox 360 come with a component video cable (HDMI is optional). We recommend making the upgrade to the highest-quality video connection you can use with your video console — component video with the Wii, HDMI with the Xbox 360 or PS3. Get the best gaming video you can get by upgrading the cable!

Turning Down the Lights Automatically

An excellent way to improve your picture is to minimize the light that comes from anywhere but your video screen — in other words, to minimize the ambient lighting by turning off light bulbs and closing drapes. You could get up to turn off the lights and pull down the shades. A little exercise never hurt anyone. But how cool would it be to press a button and have the lights dim, the motorized drapes lower, and the A/V system power up?

Sound kinda like *The Jetsons?* It's not. Home automation isn't rocket science. For just a few hundred dollars, you can put together a simple X-10 system that dims the lights (theater-style, even) and activates the drape motors. You can find lots of packages at www.smarthome.com. Automation systems are also a task that a good dealer can help with. The superstore isn't going to do this for you, but a good home theater dealer/installer should also do automation packages.

This is too big a topic to cover in one section of one chapter. Home automation is a cool addition to your whole home. We like this stuff so much, we wrote a book about it (*Smart Homes For Dummies*); you can find out how all this automation stuff works there.

Stick This on Your DVD!

If you have a personal video recorder in your home theater — or you have a lot of MP3s, digital photos, or home videos — chances are you're going to burn these to CD or DVD at some point — possibly for Mom and Dad for their birthdays. That's great — burning CDs and DVDs is something that's easy to do.

But after you've crafted a movie from all your camcorder footage and pains-takingly matched it to your favorite musical score — and managed to get it onto a DVD for playing on any DVD player on the planet — there's something sinful about taking a marker and scribbling on the disc.

Well, lucky for you, a few companies have put together easy-to-use labeling kits that help you design and print self-adhesive labels that stick to your DVDs and CDs. (So next time you're in a bar, you can tell that good-looking person next to you, "I own my own CD label.")

Check out products from Fellowes and Avery — both come with software to help you create the label images. The kits also contain paper that you stick in your laser or inkjet printer. Figure on spending $15–$30 for a kit that comes with about 100 sheets of label sticker blanks. You can also buy spine labels and blank plastic packaging for an impressive custom DVD package.

For a few more bucks, consider upgrading to a printer that can print directly onto the discs themselves. Epson (www.epson.com), Canon (www.canon.com), and others make inkjet printers that let you feed "printable" DVDs and CDs (like TDK's *PrintOn* blank discs) right into the printer itself. We think this is the best-looking labeling system for the discs themselves — though you may still want some other labeling product described earlier for your CD/DVD storage cases, booklets, and the like.

Coming soon to a set-top box near you may be the ability to burn a disc *and* print a silkscreen-quality label on the disc, all inside the set-top box. That's right, set-top boxes from your cable, satellite, and telephone providers soon will be outfitted with the ability to not only burn a movie or other content to a DVD but also to print that movie's label by using HP's LightScribe technology (already available on some PCs). So you can not only order a movie on demand whenever you want, but also buy the movie, burn it to a DVD, and then print the label on the disc — without having to go to a video store. Now that's useful — and legal, because when you "buy" the movie, you are buying the rights to create a DVD copy of the movie.

If you're using a PC to burn DVDs for your home theater, you may already have a LightScribe-capable DVD burner. Check out the LightScribe site at www.lightscribe.com for more information.

Disc-O!

Although they're not as sexy as fish on your TV or tush-rattling transducers, some disc accessories you simply must have in your high-def cabinet.

First and foremost are disc cleaning and repair kits. You can find these for $10 at Radio Shack, Crutchfield.com, or just about any electronics store. These kits include a disc-spinning device and a solution to polish the plastic CD/DVD to get rid of scratches (we *hate* those), smudges, and other generally unwelcomed surface anomalies on your discs. Just pop your disc into the unit, give it a spin, and voilà! — clean disc. SmartHome.com sells a nice battery-powered unit for around $40.

There are disc cleaning kits and disc repair kits — cleaning kits do not necessarily repair scratches. Be sure you get a cleaning and repair kit in one.

You may also want to get a lens cleaner kit, which will clean your DVD/CD player's laser eye to make sure your discs are read as clearly as possible. Again, this is as easy as sticking the cleaning disc into your DVD or CD player and "playing" the disc. These also are inexpensive — around $15.

An optical head should not need cleaning very often, unless your room is really dusty. (In which case, you should get an air filter!) Often, merely blowing your lens area with canned compressed air is the easiest and safest way to deal with such problems. You can get compressed air at any office or computer supply store. However, many people like the simplicity of using a lens cleaner kit.

Do not attempt to use a lens cleaner kit designed for CD/DVD players on your notebook or laptop computer DVD drives. The locked spindle in most computer drives would cause the brush to push against the optical head with too much force. That could knock the head off its alignment track, damaging the drive permanently.

Finally, believe it or not, there are special cleaning solutions for your expensive displays, too. The problem with using regular window cleaning spray is that it will run down the screen and get into your display — that's not good because these displays don't like moisture. And even if you are smart enough to spray the rag and not the display before swiping, regular window spray can streak, and regular paper towels and rags can also scratch your screen.

Some displays have special antireflective coatings that can be damaged by cleaners that contain ammonia, alcohol, or some other substances. Read the manual for your display before you try cleaning it!

So leave it to the folks at high-end accessories maker Monster Cable (www.monstercable.com) to come up with the Monster ScreenClean product ($20). There's no dripping — Monster ScreenClean's drip-free cleaning solution stays where you spray it until you wipe it off. It cleans without leaving annoying streaks, and the kit sports a scratch-free microfiber cloth that polishes screens with crystal clarity and color. You can use this for your camera lenses and other glass-outfitted gear, too.

So spend the few extra dollars to really take care of all your expensive gear.

Chapter 23

Ten Great Sources for More Information

We can in no way cover the entire home theater industry in one book. So we're leaving a few nuggets for other publications to cover. It's only fair.

Here's a listing of the publications that we read regularly (and therefore recommend unabashedly) and that you should get your hands on as part of your home theater project. Most publications allow you to purchase back issues of their magazines, so you can have a library at your fingertips in about a week. You know what they say: You can never be too rich or read too much about home theater before you become too poor.

Because this is the 21st century, we include some virtual items in our home theater library — Web sites, in other words. Keep in mind that the Web sites we mention here have a *ton* of information online, but you might have to try different search keywords to find exactly what you're looking for. Topics vary substantially from site to site. All sites are free unless otherwise noted.

Home Theater Magazine

Phone: 800-264-9872 or 850-682-7644
Web site: www.hometheatermag.com

Home Theater Magazine is one of the main sources for information about home theater. It is a high-end publication and will certainly expose you to a range of systems, from budget items to those on the finer side of home theater. Don't be scared when you see $30,000 projectors reviewed, for instance, because every issue has something to offer, no matter what budget constraints you're dealing with. And you can always find out about the leading trends in the industry, which is important because there's nothing like buying yesterday's technology on sale and thinking you got a great deal. (How *about* that sale on Betamax VCRs, huh?) The accompanying Web site offers archives of prior articles. An annual subscription costs $12.97 for 12 issues — quite a deal. For the same price, you can also subscribe to a *digital edition* of the magazine for reading on your PC or Mac.

The same folks also publish a dynamite *Home Theater Buyer's Guide Annual Directory,* which lists more than 5,000 source devices, controllers, speakers, home-theater-in-a-box packages, video displays, and all sorts of accessories. The buyer's guide is divided into three sections — audio component products, video component products, and speaker products — for $3.95 a section or all three for $9.95. They are delivered in .pdf form to your e-mail address.

Ultimate AV

Web site: www.guidetohometheater.com

Ultimate AV focuses on the high-end sector of the home theater market. It used to be a nice glossy magazine called *Stereophile Guide to Home Theater* but is now a fully Web-based publication called *Ultimate AV*. The guide's cadre of industry experts is dedicated to providing in-depth gear reviews on everything from projectors to line conditioners to DVD players to HD tuners. Instructional how-to columns on fine-tuning your system, special features, and software reviews help you get the most out of your system. But it's the reviews we crave here.

Stereophile

Phone: 800-666-3746 or 850-682-7644
Web site: www.stereophile.com

Stereophile is devoted to the high end of the market, concentrating on the better audio equipment and recordings available. Again, that does not mean there is nothing for the budget-minded — it's found in the feature stories and advice columns on topics such as the placement of speakers for maximum effect. If you are going to buy some new audio gear, read the reviews here. You can also check out the AV Marketplace for what's for sale — you tend to find dealers dumping demo models for fairly decent prices. An annual subscription runs $12.97.

Playback Magazine

Web site: www.playbackmag.net

A long-time home theater enthusiasts' favorite, _The Perfect Vision_ morphed in January 2008 from a paper-based subscription magazine to a free online publication called Playback Magazine. Playback has great reviews and how-to articles (just as _The Perfect Vision_ did), but it adds a whole lot of reviews on the stuff that feeds your home theater — namely, music and movie reviews.

Playback uses an extremely user-friendly online format that makes it easy to skip between articles, search each edition, and even download, print, and share articles. If you're willing to give up your e-mail address, you can have each new edition delivered right to your e-mail inbox every month — free of charge. It's definitely worth a _lot_ more than you pay for it!

Sound & Vision

Phone: 800-876-9011 or 212-767-6000
Web site: www.soundandvisionmag.com

Another respected home theater publication that captures the essence of home theater and its various components is _Sound & Vision_. This publication regularly has helpful articles in nontechie language about how to set up your speakers, tune your system, and more. The buyer's guides are ample and feature checklists. All in all, this is a friendly publication for the beginner, with meat for the more advanced home theater enthusiast as well.

The accompanying Web site contains archived issue content, and its S&V Forums are a great place to ask questions. The editors moderate the forums, which are heavily trafficked. You can even listen to Sound & Vision Radio streamed via RadioAmerica.org. A one-year subscription to the printed publication costs $10.

Electronic House

Phone: 800-375-8015 or 508-663-1500
Web site: www.electronichouse.com

Electronic House is one of our favorite publications because you can read a lot of very easy-to-understand articles about all aspects of an electronic home, including the home theater domain. It is written for the consumer who enjoys technology.

Although only a portion of each issue deals with home theater topics, *Electronic House* provides coverage of the key issues of the systems that make up a home theater, including audio, video, remote controls, speakers, wiring, and lighting. Each issue also devotes time to neat new things on the market — most within the budget of any family — such as new remote controls, cool new consumer devices, and accessories for your entertainment system. *Electronic House* also offers an *Electronic House Planning Guide,* which walks you through all sorts of issues you're likely to encounter when upgrading your home for the 21st century.

Top online HDTV buying guide centers

Many sites are getting into the HDTV game by offering online areas devoted just to getting an HDTV. While certainly not as complete or as friendly as our *HDTV For Dummies* book (Wiley), they do help you find info fast if online researching is for you. Here's a sampling of sites focused on HDTV articles, reviews, and buying tips all in one place:

✔ **Cnet HDTV World:** www.cnet.com/hdtv-world/

✔ **ExtremeTech's HDTV Buying Guide:** www.extremetech.com/article2/0,1558,1736620,00.asp

✔ **PC Magazine's Essential HDTV Buying Guide:** www.pcmag.com/article2/0,1895,1630224,00.asp

✔ **Sound & Vision Magazine HDTV Buyer's Guide:** www.soundandvisionmag.com/custom/default.aspx?cid=14

✔ **Consumer Reports's TV Decision Guide (Subscription required):** www.consumerreports.org/cro/electronics computers/televisions/index.htm

✔ **Amazon.com's HDTV Buying Guide:** www.amazon.com/exec/obidos/tg/feature/-/372297/002-9198507-1808064

And if you want to get an idea of who has the best coverage in terms of reviews, in a "turn the table on the reviewer's" approach, Consumersearch.com reviews the most recent HDTV articles and reviews of HDTVs at www.consumersearch.com/www/electronics/hdtv/reviews.html. What a neat idea!

We think that, after you start reading this magazine, you'll want to expand your interests beyond home theater to the whole home at large. (Then you'll want to buy our _Smart Homes For Dummies_ book, too!) A one-year subscription to _Electronic House_ is $19.95.

Crutchfield

Phone: 800-955-9009 or 434-817-1000
Web site: www.crutchfield.com

This is the perennial catalog that sits by the toilet for constant perusing while in the, er, office. _Crutchfield_ offers a free catalog of all sorts of A/V and home theater gear, and it's great for just getting ideas about what's out there. Its companion Web site is laid out very simply and offers a Home Theater and A/V Info Center. For instance, you can find some great photos of the various connectors at www.crutchfield.com/S-UcwlNAzImN9/learningcenter/home/connections_gallery.html. (This URL might change, so look around for its Home A/V Connections Photo Gallery if you can't find it.) Overall, we pick up our _Crutchfield_ when we want to know, "Does anybody have something that will . . ."

CNET.com

Web site: www.cnet.com

CNET.com is a simple-to-use, free Web site where you can do apples-to-apples comparisons of home theater and electronic equipment. You can count on seeing pictures of what you are buying, videos of an editor playing with it, editor ratings of the equipment, user ratings of the gear, reviews of most devices, and a listing of the places on the Web where you can buy it all — including pricing from multiple online stores. It's a one-stop resource for evaluating your future home electronics purchases. We especially like the ability to compare different devices side-by-side, so we can see who has which features. Overall, a solid stop on your Web research trip.

Home Theater Forum

Web site: www.hometheaterforum.com

Home Theater Forum is a massive, Internet messaging site where people interested in home theater gather to discuss their issues and solutions. You can find areas for discussion of home theater basics, construction, DIY solutions, sources, displays, and so on. You really should check it out, if for no other reason than to see that lots of other people just like you are also trying to figure out what's going on in home theater.

The HT Construction, Interiors, and Automation forum is a great place to find issues that DIYers have had with putting in their home theaters, and tips and tricks for avoiding problems. When we last checked, there was a great thread about how to find old theater seats that you could renovate and put in your home theater. Fun!

AV Science

Web site: www.avsforum.com

Similar to Home Theater Forum, AV Science (or AVS) Forum is an online community of technical enthusiasts who wallow in the minutest details of a home theater installation. But think of it this way: It's a collection of the-guy-next-door-who-knows-how-to-install-A/V-gear's pearls of wisdom — a proverbial hothouse of information and opinions to help solve your problems.

The site is organized in folders according to interests. If you want information on how to fine-tune your TiVo, for instance, you'll find a whole group devoted to that. There are also places where people are selling their old gear. As the techies buy the latest gear, they sell their leading-edge stuff from a few years back — at great prices. The manufacturers themselves monitor this site for feedback from customers about what they want in their next versions. It has that much to offer.

If you're considering buying a specific piece of gear for your home theater, check the appropriate forum folder and see if there's an owner's thread. We find that these discussions (where folks who actually have that equipment discuss their experiences and the issues they've encountered) are the best part of AVS Forum. For example, when Pat was considering buying his Vizio P50HDM plasma TV, he spent a ton of time on this forum and was able to find out about some issues with the initial versions of this TV and was also able to figure out that the unit he was buying had already had the "fix" performed as a running change on the factory assembly line.

eBay

Web site: www.ebay.com

Although eBay started out as a place where people could sell everything in their attics, it has matured into a place where all sorts of equipment is bought and sold. Companies sell excess equipment here. Old home theater gear is available in the listings. Even new stuff is being sold online. You never know what you are going to find here, and it is a "let the buyer beware" environment. You indeed get what you pay for. Nonetheless, you can get a good handle for street prices for used gear here, and we've known people who have built their home theater by trading up equipment through eBay, spending a fraction of what they would have if they had bought new components in stores.

Other Sources

Almost any major retail store chain where you might purchase home theater equipment has a Web site. These sites often contain information centers about home theater and are a good stop before going to meet the geeks at the store. For instance, Circuit City has a starter section on the basics of home theater (supplied by the folks at Consumer Reports). Sears has its Buying Guides.

In addition to these information boutiques, here are some other sites for you to sample.

Magazines:

✔ *Audio Video Interiors* (www.audiovideointeriors.com)

✔ *Home Theater Builder* (www.hometheaterbuilder.com)

✔ *Widescreen Review* (www.widescreenreview.com)

Web sites:

✔ Game Spot (www.gamespot.com)

✔ PC Gamer (www.pcgamer.com)

  ✔ Remote Central (www.remotecentral.com)

  ✔ Video Help (www.videohelp.com)

Organizations:

  ✔ CEDIA (www.cedia.net)

  ✔ Consumer Electronics Association (www.ce.org)

Industry:

  ✔ Dolby (www.dolby.com)

  ✔ DTS (www.dtsonline.com)

  ✔ THX (www.thx.com)

Index

• E •

• *W* •